Date: 5/9/22

BIO GILBERT
Lee, John W. I.
The first Black archaeologist
: a life of John Wesley ...

THE FIRST BLACK
ARCHAEOLOGIST

J. W. Gilbert, A. M.

THE FIRST BLACK ARCHAEOLOGIST

A LIFE OF JOHN WESLEY GILBERT

JOHN W. I. LEE

OXFORD
UNIVERSITY PRESS

OXFORD

UNIVERSITY PRESS

Oxford University Press is a department of the University of Oxford. It furthers
the University's objective of excellence in research, scholarship, and education
by publishing worldwide. Oxford is a registered trade mark of Oxford University
Press in the UK and certain other countries.

Published in the United States of America by Oxford University Press
198 Madison Avenue, New York, NY 10016, United States of America.

© Oxford University Press 2022

Library of Congress Control Number: 2021917261
ISBN 978–0–19–757899–5

DOI: 10.1093/oso/9780197578995.001.0001

1 3 5 7 9 8 6 4 2

Printed by Sheridan Books, Inc., United States of America

The author donates all royalties from the sale of this book to support Paine College and the William Sanders Scarborough Fellowship of the American School of Classical Studies at Athens.

To learn more about Paine College, visit www.paine.edu.

To learn more about the American School, visit www.ascsa.edu.gr.

CONTENTS

CONTENTS

FIGURES

MAPS

FOREWORD

I first learned of Paine College as a boy attending Williams Institutional CME Church in Harlem, New York, in the 1950s. The church's music director, Dr. Captolia Dent Newbern, was a Paine alumna. She had a doctorate in education from Columbia University (1954) and also a master's degree in social work from Columbia. In 1980, at the age of 80, she would earn a doctorate in ministry from United Theological Seminary in Ohio. At her own expense, Dr. Newbern sent an older friend of mine, Woodie White, to Paine College. Woodie graduated in 1958. Ten years later, he was named General Secretary of the United Methodist Commission on Religion and Race, a position he held until 1984, when he was elected a bishop in the United Methodist Church. He recently retired from Emory University, where he served as bishop-in-residence. Channing Tobias, a 1902 Paine graduate and a former student of John Wesley Gilbert, was associate pastor at Williams Institutional. I needed no further convincing of the value of a Paine College education.

When I arrived at Paine College in 1960, the president was the Rev. E. Clayton Calhoun. He served from 1956 to 1970 and was Paine's last white president. President Calhoun was preparing for the fiftieth anniversary of John Wesley Gilbert's mission to the Congo with Bishop Walter Russell Lambuth, senior bishop of the Methodist Episcopal Church, South. President Calhoun greatly admired John Wesley Gilbert. One could not be at Paine in those days without hearing stories of Gilbert and Lambuth.

John Lee and I met online in 2016. I was researching the history of Paine College for a book that I am writing. John and I were connected via e-mail by President Calhoun's son, the Rev. Ashley Calhoun, a United Methodist minister. Together we began to talk about John Wesley Gilbert. In 2017, John made his first visit to Augusta and Paine College. As the college historian, I took him to see the important places and monuments of Gilbert's life. We began at the Gilbert-Lambuth Chapel, a monument to the two men who founded one of the first Methodist missions in Africa. We walked Paine's historic campus and explored the historic black neighborhoods of Augusta, looking for the addresses where Gilbert once lived. We went to Springfield Baptist Church where the Augusta Institute, which later became Morehouse College, was founded in 1869. Gilbert attended Augusta Institute as a teenager, and, at Paine, he later taught John Hope, the first black president of Morehouse College and Atlanta University. We visited the village of Hephzibah, now a suburb of Augusta, where Gilbert was born into slavery in 1863. We ended our tour in Cedar Grove Cemetery, where Gilbert is buried.

John knelt at Gilbert's grave for many minutes. He said nothing. He appeared to be in deep communion with the man he had spent so many years researching, tracing his journey from Augusta to Brown University, to London, Paris, Athens, and beyond. Now, for the first time, he had finally caught up with Gilbert, in Cedar Grove Cemetery. And for history's sake, John knew that he had to resurrect him.

In this book, John tells the story of how Gilbert earned the distinction of being "the first black archaeologist." He explains Gilbert's work at the American School of Classical Studies in Athens, Greece, and his archaeological excavations and surveys at the ancient city of Eretria. Gilbert was only the third African American to attend Brown University, and, in 1891, he became the first African American to earn an advanced degree from Brown. But, as John reminds us, John Wesley Gilbert was more than the first black archaeologist. He was Paine College's first student in 1884, its first graduate in 1886, and, in 1888, its first black faculty member. Paine College (which opened in 1884 as Paine Institute) has a unique interracial history. It is the only college started by former slaves and former slave masters. It is the only school founded by black and white Southerners as an interracial enterprise— whites working for and with blacks. It is the only college started co-operatively by a black denomination, the Colored (now Christian) Methodist Episcopal Church (CME) and a white denomination, the Methodist Episcopal Church, South (MECS).

Gilbert and Lambuth's mission to the Congo was the second interracial venture between the CME and the MECS. A CME minister, Gilbert represented the CME Church and, thus, became the first CME foreign missionary. Gilbert learned several African languages and also served as French interpreter for Bishop Lambuth when dealing with Belgian officials. He was such a polyglot that it was said that as long as he was on the faculty of Paine College, Paine had the best foreign language department in the Southeast. Gilbert later headed Paine's Theology Department and briefly served as president of Miles Memorial College in Alabama.

During his travels, Gilbert also studied people, especially the interactions between blacks and whites. CME minister J. C. Colclough, who wrote a eulogy of Gilbert in 1925, said Gilbert was the father of the interracial movement. Gilbert began teaching interracial harmony first in the Paine College chapel programs, then in his public speeches, and always in his personal interactions. He preached that the mutual understanding required for peace and goodwill between blacks and whites must come through the Church and Church schools. And he believed that the Church must generate the spirit and the schools must be the intellectual expression of that spirit of the Church. The real question before the Churches, Gilbert said, was how far they could gain and keep leadership in the new community movement, adding that the question could not be dismissed by hiding behind such expressions as "separation between church and state" or dismissing the various issues as not being within the scope of church concern. The essence of the question, he said, is whether the Church saw an opportunity for the immediate application of "the good news" of Jesus Christ, the gospel of good will in community problems. Gilbert believed, however, that what a church practices is more important than what that church advocates.

He was fond of saying, "What you do speaks so loud that I cannot hear what you say."

Remarkably, the first beneficiaries of the Gilbert program were Southern whites. For more than seventy-five years Paine's white presidents, its white faculty members, and other white supporters of the school were ostracized to varying degrees in the Augusta white community and elsewhere in the South. George Williams Walker, the school's president from 1884 to 1911, his wife Susan, and others suffered the slings and arrows of white ostracism in Augusta and other places in the South. And they all benefited from the counsel of John Wesley Gilbert, which served as a balm for their common pain. Recalling the rejection that he encountered because he was Paine's president and because of the school's interracial nature, Dr. Walker was often heard saying, "I just could not have made it by, were it not for Mr. Gilbert." Colclough said that Gilbert early understood, and early began to teach, one race ministering to the other. "By training and unction," Colclough said, Gilbert "had a special revelation of these needed facts to impart to the country, the immediate answer to which was that the white people of the South were the first to believe the message and to lead off in its understanding and good will."

Kneeling at Gilbert's grave, John no doubt sensed the awesome weight of the responsibility of his book: to bring Gilbert to life in such a way that academia and history will finally and fully appreciate the work of this magnificent, extraordinary man.

Dr. Mallory Millender
Augusta, Georgia
February 12, 2021

ACKNOWLEDGMENTS

In 2015, as a break from slogging through the vast secondary literature on another project, I set out to write what I imagined would be a brief article on John Wesley Gilbert, who in 1890–1891 was the first African American student of the American School of Classical Studies at Athens. Founded in 1881, the American School, or ASCSA as it is often called, is the United States' first overseas research institute. I had walked in Gilbert's footsteps before I knew his name, for I was an ASCSA student in 1996–1997. In Athens, I climbed the Acropolis and the Areopagus as he did. I explored Marathon and Corinth and Eretria and other ancient sites he had visited a century before. I wrote my first scholarly article in the very library room where he had written his master's thesis. After learning about Gilbert from an article by classics scholar Michele Valerie Ronnick and seeing him described on the internet as "the first black archaeologist," I became curious. I was struck by the common threads of ancient and modern Greece that joined us. Yet I knew little about the early history of the ASCSA or about the history of African Americans in Greco-Roman classical studies. Determined to find out more, I put that other project aside, and as I traced Gilbert's steps in Georgia, North Carolina, Rhode Island, Greece, and elsewhere, the brief article I initially imagined grew into the volume you hold in your hands. Though my name is on the cover, this book embodies the collective contributions of dozens of people around the world. Thank you, all of you.

Michele Valerie Ronnick, whose publications were my starting point, encouraged me to expand my research into a book during a memorable

rainy afternoon conversation in Santa Barbara. She has provided expert advice and helpful suggestions all along the way and shared with
me several of her important archival finds, including a long-lost speech
of Gilbert's that she discovered in Howard University's archives.

Providence led me to two men who have become cherished
friends: Ashley Calhoun, whose father Eugene Clayton Calhoun
served from 1956 to 1970 as president of Paine College, and Mallory
Millender, who taught French and journalism at Paine for many years
and now serves as the college's historian. Dr. Millender shared with
me his unparalleled knowledge of Paine College, guided me through
Augusta, introduced me to the local community, and helped me make
Paine connections around the country. Reverend Calhoun offered invaluable information on his father's work at Paine and on Methodist
history more generally, welcomed me on my visit to the Methodist
Study Center at Lake Junalaska, North Carolina, and applied his keen
copyeditor's eye to my chapters.

As a specialist in ancient Greece and Achaemenid Persia (550–330
BC), I had no serious experience with research in modern history before
beginning this project. My University of California, Santa Barbara,
colleague Patricia Cline Cohen offered me almost a second graduate
education, helping me navigate finding aids, archives, databases, and
other resources; teaching me how to find evidence where I thought
there was none to be found; and urging me never to stop looking.
She also read the entire manuscript and offered extensive comments
and suggestions. Chapter 1 in particular would not exist without her
guidance.

My in-person research mostly took place in and around Augusta.
Paine College archivist Alana Lewis and her staff welcomed, assisted,
and supported me in every way possible. So, too, did Joyce Law and
Corey Rogers at the Lucy Craft Laney Museum of Black History, and
Tina Rae Floyd and her colleagues at the Georgia Heritage Room of
the Augusta-Richmond County Public Library. Dr. James Carter shared
his encyclopedic knowledge of the historic neighborhoods of Augusta's
black community. Erick Montgomery of Historic Augusta offered advice on the history of the city's streets and deciphered historical property

records at the Richmond County Courthouse. Deacon Walter Wright of Springfield Baptist Church and Reverend Dan Wilson of Hephzibah United Methodist Church helped me consult their churches' historical records. Helen Bratton, Russell Brown, Lee Ann Caldwell, James Daggett, Frank Delley, Patrick Hill, Robert Jones, Lillian Wan, and Dennis Williams provided essential advice, assistance, and information.

In Greece, Natalia Vogeikoff-Brogan, archivist of the American School of Classical Studies at Athens, guided and supported my research from the outset, welcomed me to the School archives, assisted me in securing research materials, and gave feedback on many chapters. In the last days before this book went to press, she identified in the American School archives a previously unknown photograph of Gilbert in Greece. Sylvian Fachard, formerly of the American School and now Director of the Swiss School of Archaeology and of the Swiss excavations at Eretria, shared his expertise on the topography and fortifications of the ancient city and provided other key assistance. Three distinguished American School scholars from whom I have learned since my student days—John Camp, Jack Davis, and Ron Stroud—generously offered advice and suggestions. John Tsevas of the Greek Historical Evangelical Archive scoured his collections for evidence of Prof. Gilbert and the ASCSA, provided historical photographs and information, and warmly welcomed me to the First Greek Evangelical Church in Athens, the church Gilbert attended in 1890–1891.

At Brown University, I thank John Bodel, Yannis Hamilakis, Johanna Hanink, and Graham Oliver for their advice and assistance. Aliosha Bielenberg, Annaliese Fries, and Amanda Mickelson generously shared with me their undergraduate research projects and their online publications about Gilbert's life at Brown and his subsequent career.

To tell Prof. Gilbert's story required materials from dozens of archives, libraries, and collections that I could not visit in person. I am deeply grateful to the many people and institutions who furnished me with electronic files, photocopies, and other documents or information:

Rev. Jody Alderman, St. John's Methodist Church, Augusta
Elaine Benton, Augusta Richmond County Historical Society
Jennifer Betts and Gayle Lynch, Brown University
Mazie Bowen, University of Georgia
Cassie Brand, Drew University
Frank Callahan, Worcester Academy
Nan Card, Rutherford B. Hayes Presidential Library & Museums
Ashley Cataldo, American Antiquarian Society
Chad Cavanaugh, Brown University Facilities Management
Gary Cox, University of Missouri
Ioannis Demetropoulos and Stavros Kotrogiannis, Municipality of
    Eretria
Father Leonard Doolan, St. Paul's Anglican Church (Athens)
Chrystyne Douglas, Meharry Medical College
Simon Elliott and Molly Haigh, University of California, Los
    Angeles
Kara Flynn and Lillian Wan, Augusta University
Jenée Force, Boston Conservatory at Berklee College of Music
Michael Frost, Yale University
Barbara Green, Claflin University
Todd Gustavson, George Eastman Museum
Brooke Guthrie, Duke University
DeLisa Harris and Lisa Hager, Fisk University
Richard Hilton, Jr., Brown University Office of Residential Life
Frederick Horn, Westminster College (Pennsylvania)
Hayley Jackson, Luther College
Louis Jeffries, The Hill School (Pennsylvania)
Amalia Kakissis, British School at Athens
Susan Kindstedt and James Smith, Portsmouth Athenaeum
Tiffany Atwater Lee and staff, Atlanta University Center
Rev. Herman (Skip) Mason, Trinity CME Church, Augusta
Ka'mal McClarin, Frederick Douglass National Historic Site
Debra McIntosh and Jamie Wilson, Millsaps College
Peter Monteith, King's College, Cambridge

Tal Nadan, New York Public Library

Tim Noakes, Stanford University

Dale Patterson and Frances Lyons, United Methodist Church General Commission on Archives and History

Barbara Péclard, Olympic Studies Centre (Lausanne)

Maryalice Perrin-Mohr, New England Conservatory

Cristina Prochilo, Historic New England

Lisa Reilly, University of Memphis Lambuth Campus

Geoffrey Reynolds, Joint Archives of Holland, Hope College (Michigan)

Jeff Sauve, St. Olaf College

Charles Scott, State Historical Library and Archives of Iowa

Kathy Shoemaker, Emory University

Molly Silliman, South Carolina Historical Society

Rafa Siodor, University College London

Staff, Archaeological Institute of America

Staff, Cedar Grove and Magnolia Cemeteries, Augusta

Staff, Concordia College (Minnesota)

Staff, The Evergreens Cemetery (New York)

Jordon Steele, Johns Hopkins University

Gratia Strother, United Methodist Church, Tennessee Conference

Morgan Swan, Dartmouth College

Squirrel Walsh and staff, Princeton University

Kristina Warner, Norwegian American Historical Association

Nancy Watkins, United Methodist Church SEJ Study Center

This book could not have been written without the research assistance of Leda Costaki (Athens), Donna Anderson and Adam Parison (Atlanta), Margie Benton (Augusta), Stephanie Riley (Columbia, South Carolina), Ryan Hughes (Lausanne), Abby Wollam (Moorhead, Minnesota), Roland Goodbody and Christian Rhoads (Portsmouth, New Hampshire), Luther Karper (Providence, Rhode Island), and Kevin Westerfeld (San Diego). Kyriaki Katsarelia deserves special recognition for deciphering the handwritten nineteenth-century municipal records of Nea Psara and for examining and photographing segments of ancient Eretria's fortifications.

I am grateful for several wonderful telephone conversations. I was able to speak with descendants of two of Gilbert's ASCSA classmates: William Brownson, Jr. shared memories of his great-uncle Carleton Brownson, while Katherine Tenthoff spoke with me about her great-grandfather, John Pickard, and shared with me priceless documents from 1890–1891. Antoine Dimandja and Bill Lovell taught me about the history, languages, and culture of the Congo and shared stories of their lives at Wembo Nyama, the mission Gilbert helped found. Michael (Michel) Kasongo provided historical information on the Methodist Church in the Congo. Bishop Othal Lakey provided key insight on the history of the CME Church. Bishop Woodie White shared his student experiences at Paine College and offered historical context on the school's significance.

I benefited from many opportunities to present my developing research to diverse audiences. I gratefully acknowledge invitations by Helen Morales (University of California, Santa Barbara), Jerry Hardee, Cheryl Evans Jones, and Luther Felder (Paine College), Caroline Stark (Howard University), Yannis Hamilakis (Brown University), Krzysztof Janowicz (UC Santa Barbara), Natalia Vogeikoff-Brogan (ASCSA), Joyce Law and Corey Rogers (Laney Museum), Ken Howle and Nancy Watkins (Lake Junalaska), and Sheila Murnaghan (Society for Classical Studies). A portion of Chapter 5 was presented at the 2019 Association of Ancient Historians conference (Emory University).

At UC Santa Barbara, I thank my History Department chair, Erika Rappaport, and my colleagues, especially Tony Barbieri, James Brooks, Sarah Case, Mhoze Chikowero, Elizabeth Digeser, Nelson Lichtenstein, Rose MacLean, John Majewski, Patrick McCray, Stephan Miescher, Robert Morstein-Marx, Giuliana Perrone, Adam Sabra, and Paul Spickard, for their advice, assistance, and support.

For other assistance, information, and support from around the world, I thank Dickie Bridges, Cécile Bushidi, Maggie Davey, Alison Dorsey, Stephen Dyson, Mary Ann Eaverly, Frances Ellison, Harriett Fertik, Robert Fikes, Tom Gallant, Brien Garnand, David Gill, Nancy Glaser,

Anne Groton, Sandra Harper, David Herlihy, Jan Hinshaw, John Veeder Hinshaw, John Hannavy, Tim Howe, Helen Hu, Heather Hughes, Nancy Hunt, Alison Jefferson, John Kaufman-McKivigan, Mary Kershaw, Kostis Kourelis, Kevin Kruse, Claire Lyons, Rachel Mairs, Georgia Malouchou, Harold Mann, Dennis Mark, Joshua Nall, Ferdinand Pajor, Yannis Pikoulas, Rahul Prakash, Elizabeth Pryor, the Rakowski family, Christopher Richter, Kim Roberts, the people of Saint Mike's Episcopal Church in Isla Vista, Nancy Savaides, Sara Schechner, Christopher Stray, and Elizabeth Varon. My apologies if I have inadvertently omitted anyone.

Stefan Vranka of Oxford University Press saw the potential of my research at an early stage, encouraged me to develop it, and offered numerous helpful comments. He and his colleagues skillfully shepherded my manuscript into print. Several anonymous readers for the Press offered vital suggestions, corrections, and advice. Any errors or omissions in this book are, of course, my responsibility.

I completed almost a third of the writing and revising of this book after March 2020. During the darkest months of the pandemic, my wife's employer Yardi Systems Inc. and her manager Sheryl Yankovich offered crucial support and flexibility to our family. My in-laws, David and Lisa Bjerke, opened their home to us in summer 2020, enabling me to write more in six weeks than in the previous six months. My mother, Marilyn B. Lee; my siblings Kammy, Tom, and Andrew; and the rest of our 'ohana provided steadfast love and aloha. My deepest thanks are to my wife, Ali Bjerke, for her infinite love, patience, kindness, and understanding through what seemed like endless years of research and writing, and to our wonderful children Madeline, Sammy, and Marilisa, the latter two of whom were not even born when I began this book. Kids, your father is at last out of "daddy jail" and will no longer live in his office.

Goleta, California
May 21, 2021

ABBREVIATIONS

AA	*Archäologischer Anzeiger*
AΔ	*Αρχαιολογικόν Δελτίον*
AE	*Αρχαιολογική Εφημερίς*
AM	*Athenische Mitteilungen (Mitteilungen des Deutschen Archäologischen Instituts, Athenische Abteilung)*
ABHMS	American Baptist Home Mission Society
AIA	Archaeological Institute of America
AJAHFA	*American Journal of Archaeology and of the History of the Fine Arts*
AME	African Methodist Episcopal
AMEZ	African Methodist Episcopal Zion
APA	American Philological Association
ASCSA	American School of Classical Studies at Athens
BHMM	*Baptist Home Mission Monthly*
BSA	British School at Athens
CME	Colored Methodist Episcopal (after 1954, Christian Methodist Episcopal)
DAI	Deutsches Archäologisches Institut, Abteilung Athen
DBCS	Database of Classical Scholars, Rutgers University (https://dbcs.rutgers.edu)
FRUS	*Papers Relating to the Foreign Relations of the United States*
GCAH	General Commission on Archives and History, United Methodist Church
IG	*Inscriptiones Graecae*

IOC	International Olympic Committee
MECS	Methodist Episcopal Church, South
NAACP	National Association for the Advancement of Colored People
NAHA	Norwegian American Historical Association
NARA	National Archives and Records Administration
ΠΑΕ	*Πρακτικά της εν Αθήναις Αρχαιολογικής Εταιρείας*

INTRODUCTION

OUT OF THE ASHES

No one was sure how the fire started. In the pre-dawn hours of August 3, 1968, flames swept through Haygood Memorial Hall, the main building of historically black Paine College in Augusta, Georgia (Figure I.1). Hundreds gathered to watch helplessly as the blaze climbed up, engulfing Haygood's famous clock tower, which for nearly seventy years had rung out the hours loud enough to be heard across town. The structure was still smoldering at sunrise. The clock tower stood but was too damaged to save and had to be pulled down. Inside was devastation. Though fireproof cabinets protected recent student records, the offices of Paine's president and vice president were destroyed, along with a priceless collection of African artifacts. Many of the school's early catalogues, newspapers, and other records also perished. By 1978, a new building, Haygood-Holsey Hall, would rise on the spot, but the papers burned that terrible night were gone forever.[1]

The tragic loss of so much of Paine's historical record has hindered study of the school's history and especially of its first student, first graduate, first black faculty member, and perhaps most famous alumnus: John Wesley Gilbert. The destruction was all the worse because a series of floods and fires in Augusta between 1880 and 1920, which often hit black neighborhoods the hardest, had already wiped away much written evidence of his life. Anything that Gilbert's family hung on to after his death in 1923 began to disappear as his children scattered from Augusta, and he had no grandchildren to preserve heirloom papers. By 1968, Paine held the last surviving copies of many documents of Gilbert's career.[2]

FIGURE 1.1 Paine College, circa 1920, with Haygood Memorial Hall and its clock tower at center. At right is the original Paine Institute building, first occupied by the school in 1886.
Courtesy of Collins-Callaway Library, Paine College.

For much of the twentieth century, John Wesley Gilbert was best known for his 1911–1912 mission to the Belgian Congo with white bishop Walter Russell Lambuth of the Methodist Episcopal Church, South (MECS), a mission that was chronicled in MECS publications, in Lambuth's writings, and in several books. The best of these books, *Of Men Who Ventured Much and Far*, was published by Paine College president E. C. Calhoun in 1961. Gilbert also appeared briefly as a background character in 1948 and 1998 biographies of his fellow Augustan John Hope, the first black president of what is today Morehouse College. Gilbert's 1890–1891 sojourn in Greece as the first African American student of the American School of Classical Studies at Athens (ASCSA or American School), in contrast, often received passing word but never serious study. After his death, his name was soon forgotten outside Methodist circles. No reference to his pioneering contribution appeared in accounts of the development of classical archaeology or of the American School. Discussions of the history of African American archaeologists, which drew on a different set of disciplinary and institutional perspectives, also left him out. Robert Slater of *The Journal of Blacks in Higher Education*, building on the work of Brown University archivist Martha Mitchell, mentioned Gilbert in his 1994 survey of early black university graduates, but it was only with the research of Michele Valerie Ronnick starting in the late 1990s, and especially with her traveling "Black Classicists" photo exhibition, that Gilbert returned to wider notice. In 2011, the newly founded Society of Black Archaeologists recognized him as the first professionally trained African American archaeologist. Today, he is often called "the first black archaeologist." Yet his life, and especially his year in Greece, has never received the in-depth exploration it deserves.[3]

1890–1891 was no ordinary year. Gilbert was the first African American and one of the first fifty Americans of any race, ethnicity, or background to attend the American School of Classical Studies at Athens (often called the American School or ASCSA). Founded in 1881 by a consortium of American colleges and universities to foster the study of ancient Greek literature, history, art, and archaeology, the ASCSA was the United States' first overseas research institution and is today an internationally recognized research and teaching center. During his year in Greece, Gilbert was among the very first Americans to do professional archaeological work in Greece—indeed, anywhere in the Mediterranean and Near East. Gilbert's journey to Greece received national attention in the African American press. He arrived at the American School during a pivotal stage of its institutional and academic development, amid hopes that Americans would soon be digging up ancient Delphi, only to witness the French win the excavation rights. He probably met Heinrich Schliemann, the excavator of Troy, and attended Schliemann's January 1891 funeral in Athens. Gilbert was the first American scholar to write about the urban demes (neighborhoods or districts) of Athens, a topic of fundamental importance to understanding Athenian democracy. His thesis on the demes won him a master's degree from Brown University, making him among the first African Americans to receive an advanced degree in classical studies. At Eretria, he took part in the widely publicized excavation of "the tomb of Aristotle" and, more importantly, worked on one of the very first American archaeological and topographical surveys

of an ancient site. In addition, Gilbert experienced Greece at a pivotal moment in the country's modern history. He watched as premier
Charilaos Tricoupis suffered a surprise election defeat to rival politician
Theodoros Deliyannis, and he saw firsthand how European influence,
railroads, the international market for commodities such as raisins
and tobacco, and the beginnings of mass tourism were reshaping the
country's economy and society.[4]

Interest in African American engagements with Greek and Roman
classics—call it Classica Africana, black classicism, or something else—
has burgeoned over the past few decades. This interest, however, has
typically been framed in terms of black receptions of and responses
to classical literature, with much less consideration of archaeology
or art history. Meanwhile, studies of African American trans-Atlantic
travelers during the late nineteenth and early twentieth centuries have
tended to focus on western Europe rather than Greece. There have
been biographies of several of Gilbert's archaeological contemporaries,
among them Annie S. Peck, the ASCSA's first woman student (whom
Gilbert probably met while at Brown University), British classics
scholar Jane Harrison (whose books he read in Greece), and Eugénie
Sellers, first woman to attend the British School at Athens (whom he
met there), all of whom have significant archival trails. In contrast,
researchers seeking to learn more about Gilbert in Greece face an apparent absence of sources. Paine's archives today preserve some crucial
documents of the school's history, such as the trustees' minutes, that
were not in Haygood Hall in 1968, but almost nothing directly related to Greece. The ASCSA archives have more to offer, including the
records of the School's Managing Committee, but there are some notable gaps: for one thing, the notebooks from the 1891 excavations at
ancient Eretria, in which Gilbert participated, are missing.[5]

My own research began with the American School's readily avail-
able 1890–1891 annual report, which provides an overview of
Gilbert's activities but little detail. In search of more information, I de-
cided to investigate the men Gilbert knew in Greece: students Carleton
Brownson, Andrew Fossum, and John Pickard, and professors Rufus
Richardson and Charles Waldstein. All five, I discovered, left behind

invaluable evidence of the group's year together, including published articles and letters; personal reminiscences by Brownson, Fossum, and Pickard; and Waldstein's detailed diary. The official report's offhand mention of a "Miss Harris" led me to a trove of letters by Pickard's mother-in-law Caroline Gerrish and her niece Edith Harris, who spent 1890–1891 in Greece and met Gilbert repeatedly. I found letters and articles by US consul Irving Manatt, a frequent visitor to the American School; a diary by a young American traveler who met Gilbert at the School; and handwritten municipal records from the village of Nea Psara, where Gilbert lived during the archaeological campaign at ancient Eretria. Thanks to a major digitization project at the ASCSA archives, I was also able to study several sets of glass plate photographs and film negatives taken at Eretria in 1891; some of the negatives had been inaccessible before the development of new scanning technology around 2010.

Another digital development proved crucial to recovering John Gilbert's story. Over the past decade or so, thousands upon thousands of old newspapers, periodicals, catalogues, books, and other documents, in English, French, German, and modern Greek, have become easily accessible and searchable through online databases. Such databases have their pitfalls. For example, I quickly learned to search for "Gilbet" and "Filbert" as well as "Gilbert," "T. W." as well as "J. W." and "John W." and a host of other variations; and, of course, many publications remain undigitized. Even so, these databases led me to reports of Gilbert's work in Greece, some only a sentence long, which otherwise would have been impossible to track down. I also searched obsessively for accounts by other travelers who visited Greece during the late 1880s and early 1890s, finding dozens more articles, essays, letters, and other materials that together provide a vivid, multifaceted picture of the country as Gilbert saw it. Most importantly, digital searching led me to some of Gilbert's own writing from Greece, originally published in now-lost Augusta newspapers but preserved in the form of quotations or summaries in other papers. These priceless fragments let us read his Greek experience in his own words. Though some large gaps remain, the archival and digital sources together are remarkably rich and diverse. Indeed, John Wesley Gilbert's year at the ASCSA is the single best-documented year of his entire life.

Gilbert's work in Greece was the culmination of twenty years of ceaseless striving for knowledge, beginning with his first school lessons in Augusta, Georgia, around 1870 and made all the more remarkable because he was born into slavery in 1863. Using a combination of archival and digital sources, in the first part of this book I trace Gilbert's family origins, his early life, and his education in the public schools of Augusta, at the Baptist-sponsored Augusta Institute and its successor Atlanta Baptist Seminary, at Paine Institute in Augusta, and at Brown University in Rhode Island. I show how Gilbert's early interest in Greek and Latin reflects a powerful current in post–Civil War African American intellectual life, in which black leaders and educators saw the classical curriculum as "providing access to the best intellectual traditions of their era and the best means to understanding their own historical development and sociological uniqueness," and ordinary black people young and old found in Greek and Roman classics a touchstone for learning and equality. I pay special attention to Gilbert's studies at Paine Institute (renamed Paine College in 1903), a unique cooperative venture of Southern black and white Methodists, and to his relationship with Paine's white president, George Williams Walker, who would become a beloved father figure. I also focus on Gilbert's experiences at Brown, where he was the university's third African American graduate, especially on his work with Albert Harkness, professor of Greek and a founding member of the ASCSA's Managing Committee.[6]

The last part of this book follows Gilbert's career after Athens, as he earned a national reputation as scholar, teacher, community and church leader, and missionary to Africa before dying prematurely in 1923. I show how Gilbert fell out of touch with the broader classics and archaeology professions as he focused on other priorities, especially raising money to sustain Paine College. I place Gilbert into the wider context of African American history from 1890 to 1920, highlighting his educational and civil rights advocacy while also noting how he, like many contemporary Southern black leaders, accepted white paternalism and segregation. I offer several new insights into his 1911–1912 journey to Africa, especially regarding his study of African languages. And while Greece did not define Gilbert's life, I reveal that his American School experience always remained personally meaningful to him and helped shape the rest of his career.

In her biography of the pioneering Cambridge classicist Jane Harrison, Mary Beard writes of rejecting "that tone of assured certainty in which most biographies strive to be written." The often-fragmentary record of John Gilbert's life means that, from the start, I have accepted uncertainty, sometimes down to basic issues of chronology. Throughout the book, I foreground the challenges of interpreting ambiguous, conflicting, or missing sources. And I try to emphasize points in his life where Gilbert might have taken different paths. Beard also raises the question of "the biographer's personal investment in their chosen subject." Beard's answer is to note how much she and Harrison share, particularly in their deep connections to Cambridge University. My life and John Gilbert's life, in contrast, are vastly different. Born into slavery, Professor Gilbert spent most of his life in segregated Georgia. I grew up in multicultural Hawaii, the grandson of immigrants from southern China and eastern Europe. What brought us together, improbably, was Greece, where I was a student at the American School a century after Gilbert. Exploring Gilbert's sojourn in Greece drew me onward to discover a world of African American history that, as a historian of ancient Greece and Persia, I otherwise might never have encountered, and it led me to appreciate the centrality of both Classics and Christianity in the black intellectual tradition. Whether you already know him as teacher or archaeologist or missionary or you are meeting him here for the first time, I hope that reading about the extraordinary life of John Wesley Gilbert will lead you to new horizons.[7]

I

NURSED IN THE ARMS OF POVERTY

The boy was determined to write. It was Monday, the first of May, 1871, and he had come with his mother to open an account at the Augusta, Georgia branch of the Freedman's Savings and Trust Company. The clerk opened his account register and took down the new customer's information. Age: 7. Residence: Corner Center and Telfair Streets—just two blocks from the bank office on Broad Street. Occupation: Go to school to Miss Chesnut. Father: Tom Dasher. Mother: Sarah Dasher. Uncles: Gabriel, Simon, Jim, William, John, in that order. Then, as he usually did with young or illiterate patrons, the clerk wrote the boy's name on the signature line, added the notation "his mark," and offered the page for an X. The boy, however, insisted on signing for himself. He ran out of space on his first try but succeeded on his second. The register (Figure 1.1) still survives today in the National Archives in Washington, DC, bearing a shaky but legible signature: Wesley Gilbert.[1]

Given that just a few years before it had been illegal in Georgia to teach a black person to read or write, this vivid testimony of young Wesley's progress toward literacy is deeply moving. But that is not all. The names listed on this humble document enable us to reach decades back from 1871, into the darkness of slavery, to restore to light the origins and the family of John Wesley Gilbert. Few seven-year-olds make such a contribution to writing their own history.[2]

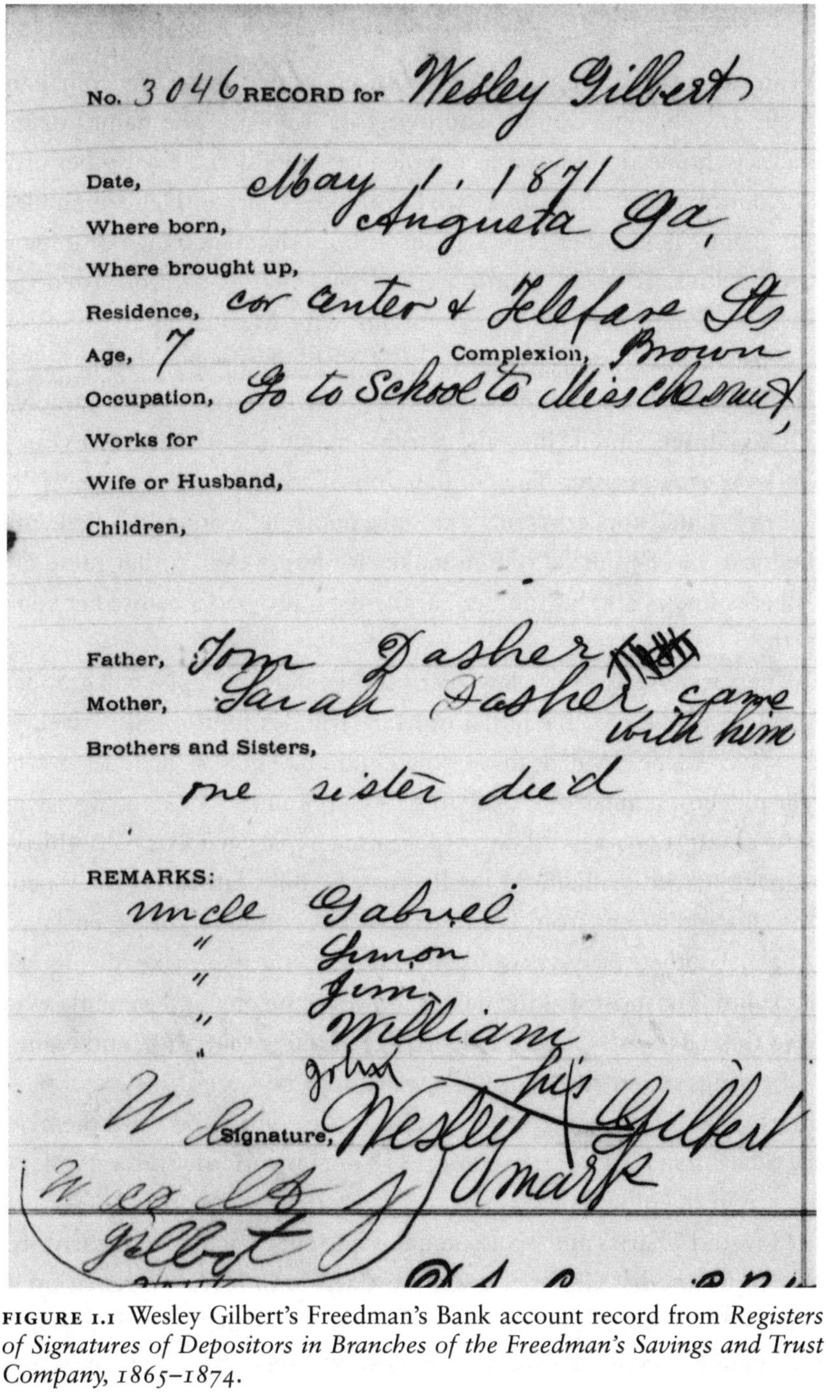
No. 3046 RECORD for Wesley Gilbert

Date, May 1, 1871

Where born, Augusta Ga,

Where brought up,

Residence, cor Center & Telfare Sts

Age, 7 Complexion, Brown

Occupation, Go to School to Miss Chesnut,

Works for

Wife or Husband,

Children,

Father, Tom Dasher

Mother, Sarah Dasher came with him

Brothers and Sisters,

one sister died

REMARKS:

uncle Gabriel

" Simon

" Jim

" William

" John

Signature, his Wesley Gilbert mark

FIGURE 1.1 Wesley Gilbert's Freedman's Bank account record from *Registers of Signatures of Depositors in Branches of the Freedman's Savings and Trust Company, 1865–1874.*

National Archives and Records Administration, Microfilm M816.

Hephzibah Origins

As an adult, Gilbert reported his birthplace as the village of Hephzibah, in rural Richmond County, southwest of Augusta. The names of his uncles (who need not have been biological uncles) and his mother provide our first clues there. In 1858, Dr. Samuel Clark of Hephzibah filed suit against landowner Henry Johnson for a decade's worth of unpaid medical bills. To show Johnson could pay, Clark's petition listed the property Johnson held in trust for his wife Mary Rhodes Johnson. The list included land just north of Hephzibah along a stream called Grindstone Branch and the names of ten slaves. Five of those names—John, Gabriel, Simon, Jim, and Sarah—match the names from young Wesley's bank register. The conjunction of so many names, especially Gabriel, which appears rarely as a slave name in Georgia, coupled with the location of Johnson's land, makes it almost certain that these are Gilbert's uncles and his mother Sarah, just a few years before her son's birth.[3]

There is more. An 1850 lawsuit over the estate of Hephzibah grandee Absalom Rhodes Sr., the father of Mary Rhodes Johnson, lists twenty-six slaves to be divided among his children. This list includes a ten-year-old boy named Bill, probably Gilbert's uncle William, who was born about 1840 according to post-Emancipation records. A thirty-year-old named William on the list may be Bill's father, for the repetition of male names from father to son was common among enslaved people. Another thirty-year-old, Jim, could be the namesake of Gilbert's uncle Jim. The most striking names, however, belong to the couple who head this 1850 list: Charles Gilbert, age about seventy-five, and Nancy Gilbert, age about seventy. While we cannot be sure of the exact relationship of "Old Charles and Nancy," as the court papers call them, to the others named in the 1850 and 1858 documents, they are very likely the origin of Gilbert's surname.[4]

How did Charles and Nancy acquire the Gilbert name? The early history of Methodist Christianity in the Caribbean reveals a remarkable possibility. In 1757, a wealthy planter from the island of Antigua sailed for England, accompanied by three enslaved servants. The planter had read a pamphlet by Anglican priest John Wesley, whose followers were known as Methodists for their methodical pursuit of Biblical holiness, and wanted to meet Wesley in person. The planter's name: Nathaniel Gilbert. In January 1758, Gilbert and his servants met Wesley near London. Wesley records the encounter in his diary: "I preached at Wandsworth. A gentleman, come from America, again opened a door in this desolate place. In the morning I preached at Mr. Gilbert's house. Two negro servants of his and a mulatto appear to be much awakened. Shall not His saving health be made known to all nations?" At the end of the year, Wesley baptized two of the slaves, describing one as "the first African Christian I have known." Gilbert and his three companions, whom later sources name Mary Alley, Sophia Campbell, and Bessie, returned to Antigua, where they built a Methodist community that still thrives today. Old Charles Gilbert, born about 1775, may well have gotten his name from that community and been brought from Antigua to Georgia as part of the thriving post-Revolutionary trade in slaves from the West Indies; perhaps Nancy, too, came from Antigua. The possibility of this Caribbean connection is bolstered by the fact that at least one white Gilbert certainly went from Antigua to Georgia: Nathaniel Gilbert's youngest son William, who moved to Augusta in 1810 and lived near the city until his death in 1824.[5]

If Antigua was in fact the ultimate source for his surname, then John Wesley Gilbert bore a name about as Methodist as could be. While we cannot prove that Gilbert and his family had an Antigua origin or even that they were aware of the surname's significance, his mother used the name after Emancipation and young Wesley found it particularly meaningful: he insisted on having it on his bank register in 1871, even though his mother had taken Tom Dasher's surname and even though some adults called him Wesley Dasher.[6]

We can follow the trail back in time from the 1850 Rhodes estate lawsuit, through court cases, tax registers, census slave schedules, probate records, and newspaper advertisements, as several multigenerational family groups were brought together, intertwined, and sometimes pulled apart. While the repetition of names from generation to generation and the lack of age figures in many documents makes tracking specific individuals very difficult, some ancestors of the enslaved people listed in Samuel Clark's 1858 petition can be glimpsed as far back as 1822. The most important source is the 1831 will of Mary Rhodes McTyeir, elder sister of Absalom Rhodes Sr. and aunt of Mary Rhodes Johnson. To Mary and her six siblings, McTyeir bequeathed seven slaves—Sarah, Solomon, Simon, Gabriel, John, Miranda, and Rachael. Given the overlap with the names on young Wesley Gilbert's 1871 bank register, these are very likely another set of his ancestors. The Sarah on this list might even be Gilbert's maternal grandmother. After her 1832 marriage to Henry Johnson, Mary Rhodes Johnson brought one or more of these seven with her to live along Grindstone Branch near Hephzibah, where they were joined by others Mary inherited from her father through the 1850 lawsuit.[7]

Sarah Gilbert was probably born at the Johnson property around 1843, and it was probably there that she gave birth to her only son on July 6, 1863, a few days after the battle of Gettysburg. By then, the war had come home to the Johnson property: the oldest Johnson son had been killed in battle at Malvern Hill, Virginia, in July 1862, and two of the three remaining sons were away in the Confederate army.[8]

Though he appears as simply "Wesley" on his 1871 bank register and in the 1870 census, the boy was probably christened John Wesley. The Johnson family had a connection to the Methodist Episcopal Church, South (MECS), a pro-slavery denomination that had split in 1844 from the original Methodist Episcopal Church founded by John Wesley's followers in 1784. In the 1850s, MECS congregations in Richmond County and neighboring Burke County included many enslaved people. Gilbert's name suggests his mother was part of such a congregation and had the ability to choose her son's name. Not all mothers were so lucky. Frederick Douglass recounts "once seeing a colored babe at the altar ready to be baptized. The old preacher took him in his arms and asked his mother what the name was to be. 'I want him called John Wesley,' she answered. 'Oh, pooh!' he exclaimed, 'no John Wesleys here,' and he began to hastily pour on the water, saying, 'I baptize thee Pompey.'"[9]

Gilbert did not live long in Hephzibah. With the Confederacy collapsing, Sarah took her baby a dozen miles north to Augusta. Nearly a century later, Augusta-born Lucius C. Harper, editor of the famed *Chicago Defender* newspaper, recorded an oral tradition about this journey: Gilbert's mother, "when freed, walking all the way, brought him as a child in a clothes basket on her head to Augusta where kindly residents took them in." When Gilbert and his mother left Hephzibah is unknown, but in October 1864, Augusta's mayor noted that the city's black population had tripled over the past year. Union General William Sherman's march from Atlanta toward the sea spurred an even greater influx of black and white refugees, especially after Sherman's cavalry raided Waynesboro, less than twenty miles south of Hephzibah, in December 1864.[10]

In Augusta, Sarah and her baby found disorder, confusion, and crime. The Confederate surrender in April 1865 led to riots and violence. Federal forces, including units of black soldiers, arrived in May to restore order. Administrators, teachers, and others soon followed. Freed servants deserted en masse, leaving their bewildered former masters and mistresses to hire new arrivals just in from plantations in the surrounding counties. Sarah probably found work as a servant in one of these households, enabling her to feed, clothe, and shelter her little boy. Even if she found a kindly employer, it was no easy life. Years later, Gilbert would recall being "nursed in the arms of poverty."[11]

While later legend named his father Gabriel, young Wesley seems to have known nothing about his biological father. Instead, his Freedman's Bank register lists Tom Dasher as his father. Sarah Gilbert had met Dasher some time after arriving in Augusta. Seven years older than Sarah, Tom was something of a rake, at least as far as the newspapers portrayed him. In June 1866, he was fined for disorderly conduct. A few months later he was back in court for discharging a pistol within city limits, though he convinced the judge he had shot at a dog in self-defense. Just before Christmas 1868, Sarah made her own court appearance, as a plaintiff against Pauline Johnson, a rival for Tom's affections. Sarah had hurled a brick at Pauline, knocking out a few teeth, at which Pauline assaulted Sarah. During the proceedings, it was

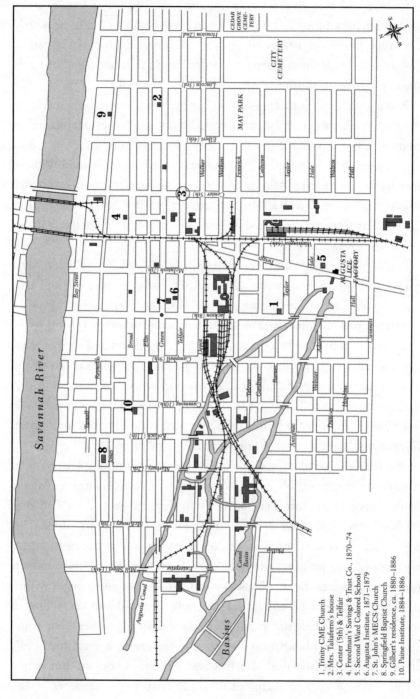

1. Trinity CME Church
2. Mrs. Taliaferro's house
3. Center (5th) & Telfair
4. Freedman's Savings & Trust Co., 1870–74
5. Second Ward Colored School
6. Augusta Institute, 1871–1879
7. St. John's MECS Church
8. Springfield Baptist Church
9. Gilbert's residence, ca. 1880–1886
10. Paine Institute, 1884–1886

MAP 1 Augusta, Georgia, circa 1870–1886

alleged that Pauline and Sarah were just two of Tom's no less than six lovers. "When this was clearly shown," claims a news report, "both consented to give up the investigation and Dasher too."[12]

In the end, though, Sarah and Tom settled down. They may have had a baby together, for Gilbert's bank register notes "one sister died," though it is possible Sarah had the child before meeting Tom. Either way, Wesley's sister died young, leaving not even her name behind. By June 1870, census records show Sarah, Tom, and Wesley living on Augusta's Greene Street (see Map 1) in a prosperous white neighborhood. Sarah worked as a servant for the widow Mrs. Taliaferro (pronounced "Tolliver") and her family, while Tom hired out as a laborer. Almost next door to the Taliaferros was the Houghton Institute, a city-run free school that enrolled several hundred white children, and, for a time, Mrs. Taliaferro's sister ran a private school in a nearby house. Though the census indicates Tom was completely unlettered, it also indicates Sarah could read but not write. How well she could read and where she learned is unknown, but her influence, coupled with the presence of so many students so close by, must have shaped Gilbert's life-long interest in education. Sarah and Tom made sure Wesley attended one of the new community schools for black children. Nearly all the other black parents in the neighborhood did likewise.[13]

Mrs. Taliaferro died in February 1871, and her household split up. By May 1871, Sarah, Tom, and Wesley had moved a few blocks west from Greene Street to the corner of Center (today Fifth) and Telfair Streets. Seven-year-old Wesley was now living in the heart of Augusta. At the southwest corner of his new intersection was one of the city's best-known houses, an extravagant mansion dubbed "Ware's Folly" after its builder, Augusta mayor and US Senator Nicholas Ware. Ware's Folly had a new owner in 1871: cotton broker and industrialist William Sibley, who moved in around the time Wesley arrived in the neighborhood. Other prosperous whites lived around the intersection, their homes interspersed with quarters for black servants and laborers. Handsome new residences were starting to fill up vacant lots, and the air soon rang with "the noise of the hammer and saw and the clatter of brick." A block west along Telfair from Ware's Folly were

City Hall, the Academy of Richmond County, the Medical College of Georgia, and Augusta's synagogue. On the blocks after that came a Presbyterian church and then a Catholic church, convent, and school. Across from the Catholic church was a school for black teachers and preachers called the Augusta Institute. It was closed when Wesley got to Center and Telfair, but the rumor was it would soon reopen. How long the family stayed in this neighborhood and on which side of the intersection they lived we cannot say, but they seem to have found a measure of stability, for Tom and Sarah formalized their marriage in August 1873.[14]

The Public Schools of Augusta

While the Civil War still raged, thousands of newly free black Americans, young and old, had thrown themselves into learning. Many more followed after the war. Their spirit was immortalized in 1868, when former Union Army general O. O. Howard visited Atlanta. Howard was commissioner of the Bureau of Refugees, Freedmen, and Abandoned Lands, better known as the Freedmen's Bureau, established in 1865 to assist former slaves and poor whites in the South. "What shall I tell the children in the North about you?," Howard asked a lecture hall full of young black students at the Storr's (or Storrs) School in Atlanta. A twelve-year-old boy, Richard Robert Wright, cried out the answer: "Tell them, General, we're rising!" Wright's response inspired a famous poem by John Greenleaf Whittier and became a rallying cry for black education. Although some African Americans emphasized practical, industrial training—a stance in later years most often associated with Booker T. Washington—for Wright and many others the pinnacle of education was the classical liberal arts curriculum, including Greek and Latin. As minister and poet George C. Rowe would put it in an 1890 ode to black achievement inspired by Wright, "Within the class-room is his place / Greek, Latin, criticizing."[15]

Young Gilbert was fortunate to grow up in a city uniquely committed to education, whose free black population of less than four hundred had sustained at least one secret school throughout the Civil War.

When Emancipation came, Augusta was one of a few places in Georgia that had many literate black people. Black Augustans quickly organized community schools and soon got help from northern missionaries. More schools were set up by the Freedmen's Bureau. In 1867, the Bureau turned its schools over to the black community, which operated them until 1872 with funds from the newly created Richmond County Board of Education. Visiting Augusta in January 1870, Freedmen's Bureau representative J. W. Alvord judged the city's schools "among the best I have seen, not so much in advancement as in high tone and enthusiasm."[16]

Wesley Gilbert started school in 1869 or 1870. By 1871, he was in class at Trinity Church in Augusta's Second Ward, less than a mile southwest of Center and Telfair. Trinity had been organized in 1842 as an all-black offshoot from the biracial St. John's Methodist Episcopal Church. Its congregation included some of Augusta's elite free black families, notably the Harpers and Ladevezes. Gilbert's future wife, Osceola Pleasant, came from another of these families; it may be the two first met as children at Trinity. About the time Wesley was starting school, Trinity became part of a new independent denomination, the Colored Methodist Episcopal (CME) Church, created by black members of the white-dominated MECS. In January 1871, twenty-nine-year-old Lucius Holsey became Trinity's first CME pastor. Though no record survives to prove it, the pastor and the schoolboy must have crossed paths early on. Gilbert might even have watched Holsey's ordainment as a CME bishop at Trinity in March 1873. Little did they realize how closely their lives would intertwine in years to come.[17]

Gilbert's teacher at Trinity, listed on his account register as "Miss Chesnut [sic]," was seventeen-year-old Cecelia E. Chestnut. Born in South Carolina, Miss Chestnut had lived for a time in Philadelphia, where her mother was a shopkeeper. Her older sister Anna was married to Daniel Gardner, one of Augusta's few black grocers, who was active in local politics and at Trinity Church. Cecelia Chestnut was one of several educated young black women and men who played key roles in the early development of black schools in the city. Thanks to the surviving records of the Augusta branch of the Freedman's Bank, we can tell that her interest in her students extended well beyond the classroom.[18]

In January 1871, Cecelia Chestnut opened her account at the Freedman's Saving and Trust Company on Broad Street. Congress had created the Freedman's Bank, as many called it, in 1865, to help freed slaves and their descendants build financial security. The Bank rapidly expanded and soon had offices from Texas to New York, welcoming business from anyone. Newspapers in Augusta told black depositors the bank would keep their savings "perfectly safe." The community poured in money, depositing more than 70,000 dollars by 1872. The bank's agents visited black schools across the country to extol the virtues of saving, but Augusta's teachers were unusually active in signing up students. Indeed, the Augusta branch's first cashier, Charles H. Prince, for a time also had charge of northern missionary teachers in the city. The result was that schoolchildren opened a quarter of Augusta's Freedman's Bank accounts. In the months after Cecelia Chestnut opened her account, her students one after another followed suit, all giving their occupations as "go to school to Miss Chesnut [or Chestnut]." By 1872, at least fifteen including Wesley Gilbert had signed up. Judging from the regular intervals at which her students opened accounts, Miss Chestnut might even have gone with them to the bank office one by one.[19]

Miss Chestnut's classroom and Augusta's other black community schools were gradually merged during 1871–1873 into Richmond County's new public school system. Georgia's 1868 constitution guaranteed all children a thorough, free education, but white opposition had in most places stymied the development of publicly funded black schools. Augusta was different, not least because the county's Board of Education, uniquely in Georgia, had the power to set its own taxes. Although white schools always got more resources, black and white Augustans worked together to build a school system for black children. At first, there were only primary and intermediate "colored schools," comprising five years in total. In 1876, two years of grammar (secondary) school were added. Until 1880, only white students could go on to three years of high school. The Board used its funding to hire black teachers, including Augustus R. Johnson, the very first licensed black teacher in the entire state. Johnson, an early graduate of the Augusta Institute, began his career in another part of town from Gilbert, but the two would cross paths before decade's end.[20]

By 1872, Gilbert was at the new Second Ward colored school, a few blocks south of Trinity Church. Nearby lay the Augusta Ice Factory and its noisy, smelly ammonia cooling equipment. Gilbert's school probably resembled the one R. R. Wright Jr.—whose father had shouted out "we are rising!" in 1868—attended in Augusta in the early 1880s. "The buildings," Wright recalled, "were of rough boards, and equipped with blackboards and desks. The principal usually had a huge bell (which we all longed to ring), that was used for calling the children to school in the morning and at recess. Abundant switches, straps, and paddles were at hand for punishment." South of the Ice Factory, a new black settlement was growing in the open fields called Verdery's Territory; sixty years later, "the Terry" would be the boyhood neighborhood of singer James Brown, the Godfather of Soul. To the west of their school, young Wesley and his fellow students could see black workmen, soon joined by Chinese immigrants, digging to enlarge the Augusta Canal, a project that would transform the city.[21]

The Ice Factory school, as it was popularly known, had two teachers. One was Cecelia Chestnut, who would soon marry Thomas Harper of the influential Harper family. The other was John F. Quarles, whose father Frank Quarles had founded the First Colored Baptist Church (today Friendship Baptist Church), Atlanta's oldest independent black congregation. John Quarles had learned to read and write while enslaved. After Emancipation, Massachusetts Senator Charles Sumner, a strong supporter of black civil rights and education, helped him go north to Westminster College in Pennsylvania. After graduating, Quarles worked in Sumner's office and studied law at Howard University before coming to Augusta. John Quarles was the first college-educated black man Gilbert ever met. Having studied Greek and Latin at Westminster, he could have given Gilbert his first exposure to these languages. Quarles did not stay long—soon after becoming Augusta's first black lawyer in January 1873 he left to pursue a career in diplomacy and politics—but remained a familiar figure in Augusta and was an important early role model for young Wesley.[22]

1873 was the year Wesley Gilbert turned ten. It was also the year of one of the worst economic crises in US history. That September, fanned by the failure of the Jay Cooke banking house in New York, financial panic swept the nation. In Augusta, there were bank runs; cotton prices plummeted and local businesses advertised "panic prices." The Augusta branch of the Freedmen's Bank survived the initial run by temporarily freezing withdrawals. There were attempts at reform in Washington, and, in March 1874, Frederick Douglass stepped in as the Bank's president. The cashier of the Augusta branch reassured the community the crisis had passed, but the effects of poor management, speculative investing, and executive fraud became increasingly clear. Congress voted to close the Bank at the end of June. A few days later, Augusta's Broad Street office halted business. At the end of October it closed for good. Like a hundred thousand other black depositors across the country, Wesley Gilbert had placed his trust in the Freedman's Bank. His mother and stepfather could have deposited their earnings in his account, too. We can only imagine their hopes and dreams for those hard-won savings. Now, that money was gone.[23]

The Bank's failure was just part of the malaise that gripped the United States for the rest of the decade. As Augusta's economy struggled, dark shadows re-emerged. At the end of 1873, a monument listing the city's Confederate dead went up on Greene Street. This modest memorial, reportedly the first of its kind in the nation, was followed in 1878 by a seventy-two-foot-tall marble pillar that still stands today on Broad Street in downtown Augusta, flanked by statues of Confederate generals and bearing the inscription, "No nation rose so white and fair, none fell so pure of crime."[24]

The mid-1870s were perhaps the most difficult period in Gilbert's life. Just before Thanksgiving 1875, his stepfather Tom Dasher died. Gilbert had probably been working since he was a little boy; with his stepfather's death, he shouldered ever more responsibility. Now growing tall and strong—as an adult he would stand more than 5 feet 9 inches—he earned money as a field laborer. As he later put it, "six months of the year, I ploughed, hoed, picked cotton, split rails and spent the other six months in the public schools of Augusta." Picking cotton was exhausting, but at least it was over by the end of September, in time for school to begin. January was for hauling wood and splitting fence rails. Ploughing and hoeing could pull Gilbert out of class as early as March or April, well before the official end of the school year. Meanwhile, one white Augustan judged four months' school a year plenty enough for black children, writing "it is not wise to offer inducements to a class of inferior mental capacity to enter into competition with the higher race, much less to pay their expenses in making the effort."[25]

With so much time out of school, only the most dedicated students managed to complete the entire course. Gilbert would become one of them, but he could not have succeeded without great teachers. He was fortunate that Augusta's public schools in the 1870s attracted a dedicated, highly skilled corps of teachers. A few were older whites, notably Susan A. Hosmer of Massachusetts, who had come as a missionary in 1866 and would stay until she left for Atlanta University in 1886. The majority, however, were young black men and women. A half-dozen women came from Atlanta University's teacher training program, or Normal School. The first to arrive was Lucy Craft Laney of Macon, a member of the inaugural Normal School graduating class of 1873, who would go on to become one of Georgia's most influential educators. Many of the other women came from Augusta's educated black elite. Almost all the men were graduates of the Augusta Institute, a Baptist academy just up the street from Center and Telfair.[26]

Teachers were assigned to schools by ward, and students were supposed to attend school in the ward where they lived, but, as late as 1883, the residency rule was not enforced because Augusta's population distribution and school locations were mismatched. Wherever he lived in the city, it is possible that Gilbert remained at the Ice Factory school until he finished the intermediate grades in 1876. After John Quarles left in early 1873, a succession of star teachers rotated through this school: Miss Hosmer, then Harrison Bouey, an Augusta Institute graduate who would go on to become a missionary to Africa, and then, in 1874 or 1875, no less than Lucy Craft Laney, in her first attested school assignment in Augusta.[27]

The possibility that Miss Laney taught young Wesley Gilbert is particularly tantalizing when we consider how and when he began learning classical languages. John Quarles had studied Greek and Latin at college in Pennsylvania, but Miss Laney had become skilled in Latin by age twelve. When she arrived in the Second Ward in 1874 or 1875, Gilbert would have been eleven or twelve. In an era when studying the Classics had powerful political and cultural resonance for African Americans, Gilbert must have leaped at any opportunity to learn Greek and Latin. Miss Laney had begun her Latin studies by reading Caesar. It may be that Gilbert did likewise. Indeed, the Paine College archives preserves one of his early class exercises, a halting translation of a passage from Caesar's *Gallic Wars*, a text commonly used for Latin teaching. If he in fact began learning classical languages in the mid-1870s, he was well ahead of the official school curriculum, which for white students introduced Latin in the first year of high school, and, for white boys only, Greek in the second year of high school. Whether he got his first exposure from John Quarles, Lucy Laney, or someone else, Gilbert would become a "linguist of pure distinction," learning French, modern and ancient Greek, German, Biblical Hebrew, Latin, and the African languages Tshiluba and Otetela.[28]

It is here that A. R. Johnson, Georgia's first licensed black public school teacher, re-enters the story. In fall 1876, Johnson was appointed to run Augusta's first public colored grammar school. The opening of this school reflected both black community pressure and the Board of Education's commitment to continue funding black public schools. During the 1870s, Richmond County's all-white Board of Education rejected proposals to dump its black schools into a separate system and resisted other white attempts to avoid paying for black education. Against this opposition, Superintendent A. H. McLaws declared, "The prejudice against the colored schools has been diminished by the excellent conduct of both the teachers and pupils."[29]

In July 1876, Gilbert turned thirteen, becoming eligible for two years of grammar school. Since there was only one black grammar school,

Gilbert must have gone to study with Johnson no matter where he lived in the city. Johnson's school began in the Second Ward but, by the next fall, had relocated east into the First Ward. When we are next able to locate Gilbert and his mother in Augusta through the 1880 census, they are in the First Ward. They may well have followed the grammar school there. There was also family in the neighborhood: Gilbert's youngest uncle Simon, who had become a railwayman (he would die in a train accident in 1881), had moved to the First Ward around 1878.[30]

Thanks to A. R. Johnson, Gilbert was able to complete grammar school. During these years, Gilbert became interested in teaching. In 1921, black community leader Silas Floyd, who as a boy in the 1880s lived on the same street as Gilbert, recorded "the first school [Gilbert] taught in his life was in Richmond County as an assistant to Dr. C. T. Walker, who taught school in this county some forty years ago." During 1876–1879, Walker taught summer school at Franklin Covenant Baptist Church near Hephzibah, so Gilbert must have assisted him during one or more of those summers. Franklin Covenant Church was (and still is) just about six miles south of Henry Johnson's property, where Gilbert had been born into slavery in 1863.[31]

Augusta to Atlanta

When Gilbert finished grammar school in 1878, he had gone as far as the city's public education system could take him. He turned next to the Augusta Institute. Founded in 1867, thanks in large part to the leadership of minister and journalist William J. White—often dubbed Augusta's "father of Negro education"—the Institute began as a night school for men and women at Springfield Baptist Church. The school struggled with lack of funds, rapid teacher turnover, and threats from the Klan but got support from some white Baptist ministers and received police protection.[32]

In 1869, the Institute came under the sponsorship of the New York–based American Baptist Home Mission Society (ABHMS), which appointed Rev. W. D. Siegfried the school's president. Siegfried refocused the Institute toward educating preachers and teachers and made it men-only. He acquired several run-down buildings on Telfair Street and began renovations. Word of the school spread beyond Augusta. One man walked twenty-six miles for the chance to attend class. Said another, "I have a hungering and a thirsting after education; and this school is the only thing that satisfies that desire. Just as I hunger for bread and meat, so do I hunger for knowledge. Once I was forbidden to study. For that I was not responsible. But if I fail to study now, I *am* responsible."[33]

The Institute's new visibility inflamed whites opposed to black education. In December 1870, an unidentified assassin shot dead one of the students. The next day, Siegfried sent an emotional letter to New York describing the murder of "a dear, devoted, inoffensive" man and denouncing Southern racist violence as "a reign of terror." After extracts from this letter were published, an outcry from white Augustans, some of whom had supported the school and insisted the killer must have been an outsider, forced Siegfried to suspend classes and leave town early in 1871, just about the time young Wesley Gilbert was moving to the corner of Center and Telfair.[34]

To restore the situation, the ABHMS turned to a white South Carolinian, Joseph Thomas Robert. The son of a Baptist pastor, Robert attended Columbian College (today George Washington University) before studying at Brown University under its president Francis Wayland. At both schools Robert earned top marks in Greek and Latin. Graduating from Brown in 1828, Robert finished medical school in South Carolina but soon turned to the Baptist ministry; his first congregation was majority black. He held posts in Georgia, Kentucky, Ohio, and South Carolina, earning a reputation as a gifted conciliator. Robert also became strongly anti-slavery. He emancipated his own slaves after entering the ministry and left the South in 1857 because he "did not wish to rear his children where slavery existed." Robert spent the Civil War teaching at Iowa Agricultural College (today Iowa State). While his wife Adeline remained pro-slavery and most of his family fought for the Confederacy, his second son, H. M. Robert, a West Point graduate later famous as the author of *Robert's Rules of Order*, served in the Union Army. Adeline died in 1866, and, in 1871, Robert returned south to lead the Augusta Institute. His daughter Mattie, a teacher who had studied at Holyoke Female Seminary (today Mount Holyoke College), joined him.[35]

When Robert took over in August 1871, most white Augustans viewed the Institute with "intense odium." He turned things around. With help from the city's black Baptists, he gradually rebuilt relationships with white Baptists and raised money to refurbish the Telfair Street buildings into classrooms and dormitories. A growing stream of dedicated young black men, many from beyond Georgia, arrived to study with him. Most had been born in the 1850s; some had learned to read and write clandestinely while enslaved. Mattie Robert writes movingly of the students' eagerness for education and of the enormous sacrifices they made to remain in school. In 1874, an Indiana minister who came to speak about his travels in the Holy Land marveled that afterward the students asked him questions for nearly three hours. Among those students was Charles T. Walker—the same C. T. Walker whom Gilbert assisted at Franklin Covenant Church a few years later. Walker would go on to achieve national renown as a preacher. By 1877, Robert hired two of his best students as assistant instructors. Collins H. Lyons of Alabama taught mathematics, while William E. Holmes of Augusta handled English grammar. Both men continued to study rhetoric and Greek with J. T. Robert. That year, the Institute appeared in the Augusta city directory, a mark of white acceptance.[36]

Young Wesley Gilbert must have had his eyes on the Augusta Institute throughout these years. His turn to enroll came in fall 1878 or spring 1879, when he was not yet sixteen. He was probably the school's youngest student and seems to have overstated his age to get in. Despite the great number of applicants, the teenaged Gilbert clearly impressed J. T. Robert enough to be admitted, perhaps even enough to receive a scholarship to pay the monthly tuition of a dollar. Still, he may have had to leave school early in May to help with the harvest.[37]

Even as Gilbert began his studies in Augusta, momentous change was under way. In late 1878, there was news the Institute might relocate to Atlanta, and, by March 1879, the Telfair campus was up for sale. Over the summer, Robert moved the Augusta Institute to Atlanta, where it became the Atlanta Baptist Seminary. W. E. Holmes accompanied Robert as his personal secretary and assistant instructor.[38]

Somehow, Gilbert scraped up the money to follow Robert and Holmes. It was a big step for a sixteen-year-old, but he did not go alone: at least a half-dozen other students also made the move from Augusta to Atlanta. With the seminary's new building on the corner of Elliott and Hunter Streets still under construction in October 1879, the school held its first classes in Friendship Baptist Church, whose pastor Frank Quarles—father of John Quarles who had taught school in Augusta—had been a major force in bringing the school to Atlanta. When the new building was finally ready in December, the speakers at the packed opening ceremony included Georgia governor A. H. Colquitt.[39]

The fanfare belied difficult conditions. While no expense had been spared on the building, furniture and books were scarce. Worse, Atlanta's rapid growth had resulted in a rail yard and a lumber mill springing up next to the school. The din of trains and machinery invaded the classrooms, even with the windows shut tight. There was no dormitory. Gilbert was one of ten students, roughly a third of Atlanta Baptist's initial enrollment, who found rooms in a boarding house on West Mitchell Street, close to Friendship Baptist and just a few blocks from the Seminary building. Gilbert, who was most likely the youngest in the group, was one of only two Augustans and one of the few not planning to enter the ministry. The crowded quarters made it hard to concentrate, and the students had to prepare their own meals. Outside, the distractions of Atlanta beckoned.[40]

For all that, Mitchell Street offered young Gilbert his first taste of independent life and a chance to refashion his identity. The 1880 Atlanta city directory lists him at the boarding house as "John W. Gilbert, student." This is the earliest known document to give this form of his name. As a child in Augusta, he seems always to have been just "Wesley," and his mother apparently called him that even when he was grown. Now, in Atlanta, Gilbert chose to use the full name by which he would be known for the rest of his life.[41]

Sometime during the school year, John W. Gilbert moved a few blocks west from Mitchell Street to board at the home of the Easley family with W. E. Holmes and two other young Augustans, James H. Bugg and William D. Johnson. Isaac Easley was a blacksmith; his daughter Elizabeth, an 1878 Atlanta University graduate, had just been hired as one of the first five black women to teach in the Atlanta public schools. Bugg was interested in medicine, and Johnson seems to come from a teaching stint in rural Georgia. All in all, Gilbert must have found the Easley home more congenial and intellectually stimulating than the crowded Mitchell Street boarding house.[42]

Accounts of John Gilbert's life typically skim quickly past the Augusta Institute and Atlanta Baptist Seminary. Gilbert himself in later years said little about these schools. Yet they were crucial stops on his intellectual journey. While Gilbert was probably exposed to ancient languages early on through Lucy Laney or John Quarles, the Augusta Institute is the first place he certainly studied Greek and Latin under the guidance of an experienced scholar who had taught these languages at the college level: J. T. Robert. Because Robert aimed unwaveringly at educating ministers first, Gilbert's early Greek lessons focused on the New Testament—a good reminder that for many people, black and white, in the late 1800s, Greek was above all for reading the Bible not the Classics. Even so, Robert did not entirely neglect Classical texts. Furthermore, Robert's rigorous and inspiring teaching methods set an early example for Gilbert. Last but not least, Gilbert benefited from the training J. T. Robert offered in public speaking and parliamentary procedure, aided by H. M. Robert's donation of a thousand copies of *Robert's Rules of Order* to the Augusta Institute in 1877. Gilbert was among the very first Americans of any race to employ this now iconic handbook. His early practice in public speaking laid the foundation for a lifetime of powerful oratory.[43]

W. E. Holmes also played a key role in this phase of Gilbert's life. Gilbert took classes from Holmes, and in Atlanta the two lived together for part of the school year. Holmes was esteemed as a teacher, and students often consulted him for personal advice, too. While most of the black students Gilbert met during this period were focused on preaching, Holmes provided an example of a different path, one toward scholarship. Conversations with Elizabeth Easley may also have inspired Gilbert toward teaching. Last but not least, the relationship of Holmes and Robert provided Gilbert a model of what a black scholar and a white scholar could achieve together in the common cause of education.[44]

Despite its early challenges, Atlanta Baptist Seminary survived. J. T. Robert died in 1884, but Holmes, who married Elizabeth Easley in 1885, kept up the work. The school moved to a more congenial neighborhood in 1889, where it took root and grew. In 1897, it was renamed Atlanta Baptist College. In 1898, a young black scholar named John Hope, who had studied with John Gilbert in Augusta and followed in his footsteps to Brown, became a Classics professor at Atlanta Baptist and, in 1906, its first black president. Under Hope's leadership, in 1913 the school became Morehouse College, the alma mater of Martin Luther King, Jr. and many other illustrious African Americans.[45]

John Gilbert wanted to stay in Atlanta, too, but like so many of the eager students who came to the Seminary in 1879, he could not afford to pay his own way and there were too few scholarships to go around. By the summer of 1880, he was back in Augusta, living on Reynolds Street with his mother and facing an uncertain future.[46]

Augusta Again

The 1880s were promising times for Augusta. The expanded Augusta Canal had helped the city recover from the depressed 1870s and spurred a cotton processing boom. Existing textile mills expanded and mammoth new factories sprang up, using the canal's waterpower to run their machinery. By the end of the 1880s, a quarter of the cotton produced in the South went to Augusta, filling the warehouses that lined Reynolds Street by the Savannah River. Black and white workers found new jobs in the textile industry, though only one mill hired black machine operators. Whites and blacks rode together on the city's horse-drawn streetcars and in some neighborhoods lived alongside each other. Black entrepreneurs prospered. Perhaps the best known was Lexius Henson, whose Broad Street restaurant was whites-only and served alcohol. In 1881, thirteen-year-old John Hope left school to work as a wine steward at Henson's; the money was good. Between 1880 and 1890, the city's population jumped from 21,891 to 33,300, about evenly divided between black and white. There were also a few Chinese immigrants, some of whom married local women (white and black) and settled down as shopkeepers.[47]

Dark shadows persisted, embodied by the looming Confederate monument on Broad Street. The annual Emancipation Day celebrations, exuberant outdoor affairs in Gilbert's boyhood, became more subdued during the 1880s, with parades now ending at black churches rather than at City Hall as they once had. Even so, Augusta earned a reputation for good race relations. Black Augustans voted, and their votes counted. They took pride in educational and cultural progress along with economic prosperity. Thanks to community advocacy, Ware High School, Georgia's first publicly funded high school for African Americans, opened in 1880. Its principal and sole teacher was R. R. Wright, Sr., whose boyhood cry of "tell them we're rising!" had become a clarion call for black education. Wright had studied Greek and Latin at Atlanta University with William Henry Crogman and William Sanders Scarborough, both eminent classical scholars by 1880. Lucy Craft Laney, who had left Augusta in 1880 to teach in Savannah, returned in 1883 to open a new school, named the Haines Institute after a wealthy Northern donor. Laney's protégé Robert Bradford Williams set a shining example of the educational possibilities beyond Augusta. After prep school in Massachusetts, Williams entered Yale in fall 1881. That same year, W. J. White established the *Georgia Baptist*, which W. E. B. Du Bois would later describe as "probably the most universally read Negro paper in the South."[48]

Future leader of the National Association for the Advancement of Colored People (NAACP) Channing Tobias, born in Augusta in 1882, remembered this era of the city's history as special: "There was something in that atmosphere. I cannot say just what it was. . . . John Hope and I used to talk about it at times. . . . It was possible for a Negro in the Augusta" of this time "to aspire to the heights and to receive encouragement from white people in so doing." Tobias credited the *Augusta Chronicle*, the South's oldest newspaper, with keeping the city informed of the world beyond, making its people less provincial and therefore less prejudiced.[49]

For John Gilbert, though, the early 1880s were a low point. Lack of money had forced him home from Atlanta Baptist Seminary, and he was unable to return. Men who had attended the Augusta Institute before him, such as C. T. Walker, had already made names for themselves. Some of his Atlanta classmates were also advancing: by 1882, his old roommate James Bugg was off to medical school in North Carolina. And it was not just men. By 1881, Gilbert's future wife Osceola Pleasant was in Nashville studying at Fisk University. Younger black women and men in Augusta had Haines, Ware, and other new opportunities. But for Gilbert, whose education had progressed beyond what Augusta could offer, there seemed no way forward. Unlike Robert Bradford Williams, he had no influential connections. Unlike John Hope, who had family resources despite his father's death, John Gilbert could expect little if any financial support from his uncles and cousins. And, while John Hope might be content with his job at Henson's restaurant, John Gilbert ardently desired more learning.[50]

Given the training he already had, Gilbert might have made a successful career as a preacher. Yet, unlike so many of his classmates at Augusta Institute and Atlanta Baptist, he did not choose that path. Indeed, it is unclear whether he belonged to a church at all during these years. Nor did Gilbert settle for life as a craftsman, servant, or laborer, the sort of employment that a black man, even one with some education, was expected to take. That would have been the easy path. After all, he was young and strong, and there were jobs to be had in booming Augusta.[51]

Instead, Gilbert found work as a teacher. At first, he taught in one of the city's public schools or in one of the small private academies that had sprung up to accommodate the many black children who could not find a place in the overcrowded public schools. In 1882, he won a teaching post back in Hephzibah. Teaching pay was meager, and

Gilbert may sometimes have had to take side jobs to make ends meet. Nonetheless, he kept on as best he could, working by day and studying at night. The publication in 1881 of W. S. Scarborough's *First Lessons in Greek*, certainly the first foreign language textbook and possibly the first textbook on any subject written by an African American, may have cheered him. Perhaps he was even able to find a copy through R. R. Wright, Sr., who ran a bookstore for Augusta's black community. Yet without a proper teacher there was only so much he could do on his own. Little wonder that Gilbert later remembered these difficult years as a time when he "began to despair of securing a liberal education."[52]

Except for his work in Hephzibah, between 1880 and 1883 Gilbert lived on Reynolds Street in a racially and economically mixed neighborhood adjacent to the main business district on Broad Street and just a block from the Savannah River. Almost next door was Charles Ladeveze, whose French father had left Haiti in 1794 and settled in Augusta in 1803; Ladeveze's mixed-race mother had come from Santo Domingo. Ladeveze ran a fashionable art and music store on Broad Street. Just down from the Ladevezes were a prominent black family, the Osbornes. Mary Osborne had owned her own home since before the Civil War; her son Henry ran a prosperous harness and saddle business. A few houses further on lived young Silas Floyd, a laborer's son who would become a prominent black journalist and community leader. Down by the river, less than a block away, was the home of wealthy white merchant Josiah Sibley. Gilbert at first shared quarters with his mother Sarah and several young friends or relatives. Later, Sarah moved in with the Osbornes. Little did Gilbert know it, but just blocks away from Reynolds Street, at St. John's Methodist Episcopal Church on Greene Street, plans were brewing for a new school in Augusta, a school that would change his life.[53]

Paine Institute

St. John's, founded in 1800, was the oldest church in Augusta. In 1844, the congregation put up a new brick building, replacing an old wooden chapel that was moved on logs down to Reynolds Street to become the home of Springfield Baptist Church, where the Augusta Institute held its first classes in 1867. The same year St. John's new church was built, the Methodist Episcopal Church endured bitter schism, with pro-slavery Southerners splitting off to form the Methodist Episcopal Church, South (MECS). Tens of thousands of black people, most of them enslaved, remained members of the MECS. Black membership in the MECS fell dramatically during and after the Civil War as many left to join the northern-based African Methodist Episcopal (AME) and African Methodist Episcopal Zion (AMEZ) denominations. In the late 1860s, the remaining black members of the MECS determined to organize their own independent denomination, the Colored Methodist Episcopal (CME) Church. Some of the initial planning for this new denomination was done in early 1869 at Trinity Church, where Gilbert went to school with Miss Chestnut. By 1870, the separation was formally complete, although MECS and CME remained closely linked.[54]

Lucius Holsey, Trinity's pastor from 1871 to 1873 and from 1873 a CME bishop, had early on broached the idea of a school where Southern white instructors would train black ministers and teachers. Nothing came of it until 1882, when an interracial group led by Holsey and MECS minister Atticus Haygood began planning for a school that would not only prepare black preachers and teachers but also offer a liberal arts education to both men and women. Holsey and Haygood chose Augusta because of its central location amid CME congregations in Georgia and South Carolina, as well as its distance from a new CME high school (later called Lane Institute) in Jackson, Tennessee. In November 1882, Holsey, Haygood, and a group of trustees met for the first time at St. John's Church. They decided to name their school the Paine Institute to honor late MECS bishop Robert Paine, who had presided over the CME's first general conference. A month later, Emory College vice president Morgan Callaway, a Confederate veteran and former slaveholder, was elected Paine's first president. Callaway was so well-known and popular that Atticus Haygood believed his election meant "the beginning of a new chapter" for the MECS.[55]

Haygood was wrong. Even Callaway could not overcome MECS and CME opposition. Some whites rejected any attempt to offer black students a full literary and classical education rather than just enough training to teach "plain, common school" basics. MECS bishop George Pierce called higher education "a calamity" that would increase racial friction, produce endless strife, and "elevate Negro aspirations far above the station he was intended to fill." CME members worried, as Holsey later recalled, that "other Negro organizations would reproach us" for subservience to the MECS and its plans "to remand the freedmen back to abject bondage." Still the founders pressed forward, hiring young MECS minister George Williams Walker as Paine's first teacher. Callaway, Holsey, and Walker took up quarters at St. John's parsonage. They spoke at black and white churches in Augusta to promote the school. By summer 1883, newspapers were reporting Paine Institute might start up in October. Although a generous few were moved to contribute—among them an anonymous black servant who reportedly left the school 600 dollars in her will—lack of money would delay the school's opening until January 1884.[56]

After three long, hard years on his own, John Gilbert must have welcomed the promise of Paine Institute. He also had questions: What was the curriculum? Who would teach? Could he afford it? According to a famous account that exists in several variants, Gilbert went to St. John's in fall 1883 looking for answers. There he met the church's young pastor Warren A. Candler, a member of Paine's board of trustees. When Candler asked why he was interested in Paine, Gilbert supposedly replied he wanted to become a doctor, to which Candler suggested the ministry instead. This portion of the story has some verisimilitude: Gilbert probably knew his Atlanta roommate James Bugg was in medical school, and, with only two or three black physicians to serve a community numbering more than ten thousand, Augusta in 1883 could certainly have used another black doctor.[57]

Candler is then said to have introduced Gilbert to George Williams Walker. Yet the earliest rendition of this episode dates from 1930. In contrast, both Walker in 1901 and Gilbert in 1911 recounted first meeting each other on the streets of Augusta, with no mention of Candler's intercession. Whatever the truth behind the Candler story, all sources agree that on Wednesday, January 2, 1884, when Paine Institute opened in rented rooms above a grocery store on Broad Street, John Wesley Gilbert was the first to enroll. Later legend transformed Gilbert into a "slim brown youngster" or "a little brown fellow" who pushed his way forward through an eager crowd of well-scrubbed children, but by now he was nearly twenty-one years old.[58]

There was no crowd either. Lucius Holsey later recalled that popular feeling in Augusta "among white and black, was widespread and bitter" against Paine. Holsey enrolled his teenaged daughter Kate and managed to convince about thirty others to sign on, promising some he would pay their way. Most of these first students were poor, and many of the younger ones were ill-prepared, as even poorer families did not want to send their best. John Gilbert was very likely the oldest of the school's first group of students. His choice to attend Paine despite such great community hostility suggests that his thirst for education outweighed all other considerations.[59]

Gilbert found an extraordinary teacher in George Williams Walker (Figure 1.2). Born in Augusta but raised in South Carolina, Walker was of eminent family. His father Hugh A. C. Walker helped found South Carolina's Wofford College, and his maternal uncle William Wightman was an MECS bishop. Another uncle, George Williams, after whom Walker was named, was reputedly the richest man in South Carolina. At age fifteen in 1863, Walker enlisted in the Confederate army but did not see combat. After the war he went to Wofford College, graduating in 1869; in 1874, he would receive an MA from Wofford. Walker excelled at languages. Friends remarked he often spent his afternoons and evenings reading Greek for pleasure. He was also deeply interested in English literature, particularly Shakespeare. From 1869 to 1873, Walker taught classical languages in Kentucky and South Carolina. Entering the Methodist ministry in 1874, he held positions in South Carolina and Missouri before coming to Augusta in 1883.[60]

Walker took the post at Paine despite objections from family and friends. "My own mother," Walker later recalled, "said that it was a noble work but that she wished deep down in her heart that God had called some other mother's son to do the work." Walker's fiancée refused to marry him unless he gave up on Paine. Instead, he broke

FIGURE 1.2 George Williams Walker, Paine's president from 1884 to 1911.
Courtesy of Collins-Callaway Library, Paine College.

off the engagement. In a sign of how closely he was identified with the school and how much some white Augustans disdained him, for several years the city directory marked Walker's name with a "c" for "colored." Even in later years, some white parishioners would walk out of St. John's when Walker came to preach.[61]

On the other hand, Paine had strong backing from several leading white Augustans. Chief among them was Charles G. Goodrich, whose contractor father had built St. John's brick church in 1844. As cashier of the Georgia Railroad Bank, the most powerful institution in Augusta, Goodrich wisely stewarded the school's finances for decades. In the black community, crucial support came from James S. Harper, a younger brother of the Thomas Harper who married Gilbert's primary school teacher Cecilia Chestnut. The Harper brothers, whose father had helped found Trinity Church in 1842, were nephews of Charles Ladeveze, Gilbert's neighbor on Reynolds Street. James Harper himself had been prominent in the community activism that led to the establishment of Ware High School in 1880. Goodrich and Harper were original members of Paine's board of trustees and both would serve the school for decades, Goodrich as treasurer until his death in 1911 and Harper as secretary until 1918.[62]

Channing Tobias, a 1902 Paine graduate, recalled that Walker "believed in a single standard of citizenship and in the sacredness of all personality, white and black." According to a black journalist, while Walker was a white man and a southerner to boot, it would be impossible to find someone else with "such broad ideas and liberal opinions as to the worth and deservedness of the Negro. He is not a man of words, but of deeds." From the start, Walker held fast to the principle that Paine would provide a liberal, classical education. He also accepted women students, a remarkable contrast with many schools across the country. Walker addressed black women as Miss and Mrs., titles most southern whites refused to use, and gave extra tutorials for promising women students. James Harper's younger sister Caroline, who attended Paine in the late 1880s, considered Walker "the most Christlike man I ever knew."[63]

Walker quickly discerned John Gilbert was exceptional and began to mentor him. From January 1884 until June 1886, Gilbert threw himself into books. "I studied all the time I was not asleep," he later said. He seems to have received some financial support, which he probably supplemented by teaching summer school. For Gilbert, Walker would grow to become a father figure as well as a teacher and colleague.[64]

Paine's early going was a "painful and pitiful" struggle for existence. There was no set curriculum. Books were in short supply, and the instructors sometimes went unpaid. Morgan Callaway spent his time traveling to give lectures and raise funds, with little success. The school's future seemed in doubt. Still, Paine soon drew national praise. "I shall not soon forget," wrote a northern visitor who met Gilbert and his classmates early in 1884, "the aspect of these earnest colored youth as I saw them at their morning devotions, or the emotions and the hopes that stirred my heart in their presence." In a series of speeches delivered as far north as Wisconsin, the prominent black classical scholar W. H. Crogman of Atlanta University hailed Paine as "the lone star of Southern Methodism, but it shines with an auspicious light. It will be the brightest star in a constellation of similar schools by and by."[65]

Augustans took notice, too. Among them was John Hope, drawn from his job at nearby Henson's restaurant. Hope was more interested in one of the students, Sarah Curry, than in books, but during his visits he must have met John Gilbert, whom he would later describe as one of the greatest teachers he had ever known. By fall 1884, Paine's enrollment had grown to about seventy. A new Southern white teacher, Sallie G. Davis, took charge of the younger students. Her arrival was an important step in the black community's acceptance of Paine, as local CME ministers began sending their children to her classroom. When Morgan Callaway abruptly resigned in November 1884, George Williams Walker took over as president. He would hold the office until a few months before his death in 1911.[66]

Sallie Davis's brother, Rev. W. C. Davis, joined the faculty in early 1885. He and Walker preached at black churches in Augusta to build up support; Walker also took part in black literary societies. In May

1885, Walker felt able to write "the sky has been very dark, but thank God, I see the break in the clouds." By then, some one hundred forty students had enrolled. John Gilbert, now almost twenty-two, was their leader and "commanding personality." Given his age and experience, Gilbert must have helped teach classes. Walker in later years required advanced students to do just that in order to hone their classroom skills. When recalling the school's early struggles, Walker often remarked, "I just could not have made it by, were it not for Mr. Gilbert."[67]

Later in 1885 came a decisive stamp of approval. In a *Georgia Baptist* editorial, W. J. White, Augusta's "father of Negro education," praised Paine and its teachers effusively. That the MECS, wrote White, a denomination "composed largely of slave-holders in the past, should at this early day of freedom undertake such a work, giving not only of their means for its support, but also putting at its head some of the best minds of their own number, is an illustration of the power of the grace of God in the human heart that cannot be gainsaid, and that must cast a beam of cheering hope on the future of our common country." Walker considered White's endorsement so crucial he quoted it verbatim in fundraising letters and featured it in Paine's printed catalogues for more than a decade.[68]

White's endorsement boosted enrollment that fall. Amongst the new students were two men Gilbert would know for years to come. Charles A. Dryscoll, a drayman's (beer delivery man's) son, had excelled in grammar school, graduated from Ware High School in 1883, and worked as a printer at the *Georgia Baptist*. Dryscoll had attended Clark University in Atlanta for a year but, like Gilbert, had been forced to return home to Augusta. Thomas L. Cottin had been Ware's only 1885 graduate and was as interested in classical languages as Gilbert. Cottin's father Lorenzo, originally from Mississippi, had come to Augusta at the end of the Civil War as a soldier in the 136th US Colored Infantry Regiment, then settled in town after mustering out.[69]

Paine Institute was also on its way to a permanent home. Millionaire landowner and MECS minister Moses U. Payne of Missouri promised 25,000 dollars if the school could secure itself suitable quarters. Helped by donations from as far away as Texas, Paine's supporters raised enough money to buy a run-down ten-acre property in the Woodlawn area, at the western outskirts of town. When the sale closed in January 1886, Gilbert moved out to Woodlawn. He and his classmates cleaned up the old stables, installing partitions and windows to make classrooms and setting up the hay loft as a dormitory. MECS minister W. C. Dunlap, who had led the fundraising effort, quipped "we have proven our humble origin and kinship with Jesus by being cradled in a manger." The main cottage became Walker's residence. An illustration of these original buildings would adorn the cover of Paine's catalogues for years to come. By March, the new campus was up and running, and in May CME leaders and MECS representatives came for a tour. Walker and his "eloquent corps of teachers and students," Gilbert among them, were there to greet the visitors.[70]

A few weeks later, Gilbert became one of Paine Institute's first seven graduates. Ella Burdette, Sarah Curry, Kate Holsey, and Carrie Wigfall would stay in Augusta as teachers. Thomas Cottin was headed to Clark University in Atlanta, where he would read Greek and Latin with W. H. Crogman. Charles Dryscoll was on his way to a music conservatory in Boston. John Wesley Gilbert, who had been nursed in the arms of poverty, come home disappointed from Atlanta Baptist, and once despaired of ever obtaining a liberal education, would continue his studies in Providence, Rhode Island, where he had won a scholarship to Brown University.[71]

THIS YOUNG MAN DESERVES SPECIAL MENTION

Mrs. Dickie L. Bridges was cleaning out her parents' attic in Alabama when she found the brittle sheets. Where her mother and father had acquired them, she could only guess—perhaps at a Nashville auction years ago. The pages had lain folded so long the creases were disintegrating. Carefully opening the old newspaper, she read the name and date at the top: *Paine Institute Herald*, May 1887. An avid antiques collector, Mrs. Bridges could not bear to throw her find away. She researched the school online, made contact with Paine College historian Mallory Millender, and mailed him the paper. "To me," she wrote Dr. Millender, "it is a treasure for someone who has interest in your school." Mrs. Bridges did not know how right she was. She had saved one of the two known nineteenth-century issues of Paine's student newspaper, which had a monthly print run of just a few hundred copies. On top of that, the entire front page of the May 1887 issue is devoted to an essay sent home from Brown University by John Wesley Gilbert.[1]

Going Up North

Brown University had long been a favorite of white southerners, so much so that, in 1845, the school refused to admit a black student for fear "southern patronage would be withdrawn." Another black applicant was similarly rejected just before the Civil War. Brown's first black students, George Washington Milford and Inman Edward Page, who had been born into slavery in Virginia, enrolled in 1873. Milford and Page came to Brown from Howard University in Washington, DC, founded in 1867 through the leadership of Freedmen's Bureau commissioner O. O. Howard; they were among the first graduates of Howard's college preparatory department. The two initially met considerable prejudice at Brown. By 1875, though, Milford wrote abolitionist William Lloyd Garrison that "I have to say that I shouldn't wish to be treated better than I am now by all the students," even if "there are some things which I could wish were otherwise." Milford got top marks in Greek and Latin. Page won fame in 1876, when he was selected as junior class orator, and again in 1877, when his classmates chose him as a graduation speaker. Milford went on to success as an attorney, and Page became nationally known as an educator. Yet after they graduated no black students followed them to Brown.[2]

Black southerners had heard of Brown University in the 1860s and 1870s through its former president Barnas Sears, who for decades led the Peabody Education Fund, endowed by banker George Peabody. Although Sears strongly advocated for black education, his acquiescence to segregation did not reflect favorably on Brown. The University got further attention in 1882, after president E. G. Robinson argued for black equal rights in a widely disseminated speech. Asserting that "Christianity . . . knows no distinctions among races," Robinson spoke of the duty to give black Americans "equality before the law and all [their] civil rights under the Constitution." Even so, he described blacks and Chinese as "races . . . that will never contribute their share to make up the typical American" and considered emigration the only real solution for race discrimination. Black lawyer and journalist George Washington Williams responded: "Well, we came here against our will, but now we're here we'll stay." The solution, Williams averred, was education, prosperity, and upward mobility, not emigration.[3]

Against this backdrop, Brown was not Gilbert's inevitable destination. He might well have returned to Atlanta. Indeed, early on, Paine had been envisioned as a feeder for Clark University, exactly where Gilbert's fellow Paine graduate Thomas Cottin was headed. Gilbert, though, dreamed bigger. To go north and succeed at a "white school" was, as R. R. Wright, Jr. would later put it, a way "to show the white people that a black boy could learn as well as a white one." Still, there were other northern schools Gilbert might have considered. There is no evidence he had contact with Milford or Page. Why Brown, then?[4]

The answer must lie at least in part with J. T. Robert, Gilbert's teacher at the Augusta Institute and Atlanta Baptist Seminary. Robert had been a favorite student of Francis Wayland, Brown's president from 1827 to 1855, and six of his nine half-brothers also attended Brown. George Williams Walker, though he took pride in having helped prepare Gilbert for Brown, never claimed he chose the school. It seems likely that Gilbert first heard of Brown from J. T. Robert and that his link with Robert played some role in his admission. Although Robert died in 1884, he was remembered in Providence, as was his daughter Mattie, who had assisted her father and must have met Gilbert. A Baptist connection through J. T. Robert would also explain why Gilbert was awarded a Brown scholarship endowed by Rhode Island Baptist minister Henry Jackson and originally meant to support students headed for the Baptist ministry. That Gilbert was coming from a Methodist institution was no bar, for President Robinson in 1886 took pains to stress that Brown was not narrowly denominational.[5]

Another possible source of information was Rev. John L. Dart, who came to Augusta in February 1886 from Providence's Congdon Street Baptist Church. Charismatic and sometimes controversial, Dart, during his six-month stay in Augusta, presided over a revival at Union Baptist Church that drew in John Hope and many others. John Gilbert was not swept up in the revival but could have heard from Dart about Providence's flourishing African American community. Dart was also reportedly "on intimate terms" with unnamed Brown professors, and John Hope would later credit Dart for pointing him toward school "up north." Dart may have provided Gilbert with connections, but Gilbert already had his eyes set on Brown before Dart arrived.[6]

Applicants for "advanced standing" at Brown in the 1880s—today we might call them junior transfers—had to take exams in Greek, Latin, French, English literature, and mathematics. Together, Gilbert and Walker read as much of Brown's required Greek and Latin list as they could, though they always preferred Greek and especially the Bible. Walker also shared with Gilbert his love of English literature, especially Shakespeare. Walker's colleague W. C. Davis may have helped with mathematics. French was especially important, as students who failed this portion of Brown's entrance exams were placed on a "select course" until they made up the deficiency. Where Gilbert learned his French is unknown, but it would become one of his best languages.[7]

Probably by June 1886 Gilbert had been offered admission based on his academic record and the "suitable testimonials of good moral character" Brown required. By then, Thomas Cottin and Charles Dryscoll also knew they were going north for school. So, too, did John Hope, who had been accepted at Worcester Academy in Massachusetts. It is tempting to picture these four young men together in the summer of 1886, full of plans and hopes for the future, excited to leave Augusta and prove themselves. John Wesley Gilbert, who had come home disappointed from Atlanta six years before, was doubly determined to excel. This time, though, he would go with the support of G. W. Walker and the promise of a scholarship if he did well on his Greek exam.[8]

Gilbert left Augusta for Providence early in September 1886. Although Dryscoll and Hope were heading in the same direction as Gilbert, and Hope's fall term at Worcester began at almost the same time as Gilbert's at Brown, whether the three men traveled together is unknown. It is difficult to imagine that G. W. Walker was not at the train station to see Gilbert off. Gilbert's mother Sarah may also have been there. She must have been proud of her son's achievement, yet we know little of their relationship at this time except that he had not been living with her for at least a year. A few weeks after he departed, Sarah married a recently widowed baker, David Thomas, who had an eleven-year-old son. Perhaps it is a sign of strain between Gilbert and his mother that she waited until after he left. After 1910, a story arose that Sarah, "an old Negro washerwoman," mailed her son a crumpled dollar bill each week to help him at Brown. Although it is certainly possible his mother helped her son with whatever she could afford, the dollar amount suggests this particular story is a later invention: in 1886, Gilbert's living expenses were seven dollars a month, and Sarah could not have provided the majority of that. Amid the mix of emotions at leaving home, Gilbert may have felt relief. Days before, an earthquake had shaken South Carolina and Georgia. Augusta suffered relatively minor damage, but the tremor had derailed trains, toppled chimneys, and left people sleeping nervously in the streets. It was a propitious moment to depart.[9]

Travelers heading north from Augusta often took the train to Charleston or Savannah, then went up the coast by steamer. Gilbert instead took an inland route through Nashville. The earthquake had briefly cut the rail lines to Charleston and Savannah, but they had been quickly restored. The most likely explanation for his route is that Gilbert went to see Osceola Pleasant, who had been in Nashville at Fisk University's college preparatory program since 1881. Osceola brought Gilbert to dine with her classmate Rachel Lester and Rachel's brother John Angelo Lester, also a Fisk student. When Gilbert died in 1923, Lester, who had become a noted physician and professor at Nashville's Meharry Medical College, still vividly recalled this first meeting: "I knew young Mr. Gilbert in his early student days, when he was a young man, vigorous and strong. He had just finished his literary course at Paine College, and was en route to an eastern institution to further pursue his studies. He stopped in Nashville and was a guest at my table. From then in the early eighties to the day of his death we were in close touch. He was fond of study and delighted in the work of the class-room." It would not be the last John and Osceola saw of each other.[10]

As he rode onward from Nashville toward Providence, Gilbert might have pondered what the contemporary southern novelist George Cable called the "special and offensive restrictions, laid upon them not for any demerit of person, dress, or manners, but solely and avow-edly on account of the African tincture in their blood, however slight that may be," that black travelers faced in the south. These restrictions fell away as he went north. Soon, the segregated train cars were gone and the dining car was open to him. The nearly thousand-mile journey to Providence was Gilbert's first taste of long-distance travel and it must have exhilarated him, for travel—by train, by ship, and on foot—would become one of the defining features of his life.[11]

Brown University

A century older and nearly four times larger than Augusta, Providence was unlike anything Gilbert had previously experienced. While textiles had brought Augusta prosperity in the 1880s, Providence had become the nation's leader in jewelry manufacturing. Compared to Augusta's roughly equal proportions of blacks and whites, less than 4,000 of Providence's more than 100,000 people were black, but this community had a proud history stretching back before the Revolution. Schools had been desegregated since 1866. Rhode Island had recently (1881) repealed its ban on interracial marriage and passed its first civil rights law (1885), prohibiting discrimination "on account of race, color or previous condition of servitude." Mahlon Van Horne, the state's first black legislator, had just been elected. Race relations in Providence were generally good: blacks and whites marched together in parades, served together in the militia, cooperated in politics, and sometimes mixed socially. Southerners were amazed at the equality they found. A visiting black minister from the Midwest, on the other hand, compared Providence unfavorably to cities he knew back home. Blacks remained segregated in certain neighborhoods and in many social settings. Black applicants for white-collar jobs often encountered "contemptible prejudice" from employers.[12]

Uphill from the city center lay Brown University. In 1886, it had fewer than two dozen faculty and staff, some 240 students, and a handful of buildings. Hope College, one of the three dormitories, would be Gilbert's home for the next two years. After finding his room, Gilbert was drawn immediately to the library. With more than 65,000 volumes, stacks open for browsing, and reference books conveniently arranged, the library must have seemed to him like a dream fulfilled.

One dormitory even had a reading room stocked with newspapers and periodicals. Some students complained about Brown's facilities, but they were opulent compared to anything Gilbert had known before. The library's surviving circulation records show he became a regular visitor.[13]

Gilbert took his entrance exams on September 13 and 14. He did particularly well in Greek, earning his promised scholarship, and he passed the French portion. Even so, his name is marked in Brown's catalogues as admitted "under conditions, or not fully examined," reflecting the limits of his preparation in Augusta, especially in mathematics. Three of the four entering junior transfer students, Gilbert included, carried this mark. He would be the only one of those three who made it to graduation.[14]

The Class of '88

The first known photograph of John Wesley Gilbert, taken sometime during 1886–1887, shows him on the steps of Manning Hall, Brown's chapel (Figure 2.1). Gilbert sits closely surrounded by his fellow juniors. One of them, Arthur Bentley, seems to rest his hand on Gilbert's left shoulder. While several men adopt formal portrait poses, Gilbert looks directly, almost earnestly, at the camera. In his right hand he holds up a stack of books and papers, as if to ensure the photographer will capture them, too. Gilbert was joining a hard-luck class: illness, death, or lack of cash had winnowed its original 64 freshmen down to just 42 by fall 1886. Gilbert and the other new arrivals brought that number up to 46, several of whom would drop out or die during the year ahead. Most of the men were New Englanders, but others came from California, Kansas, Nebraska, Wisconsin, England, and Sweden. Gilbert was the only southerner. Among his classmates in this photo are Clarence Augustus Barbour, later Brown's tenth president (1928–1936); Charles E. Dennis, the holder of Brown's first Latin doctorate (1895); Frederick E. Whitaker, its first Greek doctorate holder (1899); and Eli Whitney Blake III, a descendant of the inventor of the cotton gin.[15]

FIGURE 2.1 The Brown University Class of 1888 during 1886–1887.
Courtesy of Brown University Archives.

At twenty-three, Gilbert was among the oldest in his class. Unlike John Hope, who would come to Brown in 1890 with a cohort of Worcester Academy alumni, Gilbert arrived alone. He had no easy way into a student society that was sharply divided along fraternity and club lines. The young, wealthy set was often more interested in socializing than academics. References to their card-playing, drinking, and pranks abound in the *Liber Brunensis*, as the school's yearbook was called, and in alumni reminiscences. One group formed an Anti-Aquarian Society, pledging "to abstain . . . from the use of water as a beverage." Other students struggled to make ends meet. Indeed, Brown's catalogue offered advice on finding jobs in Providence, and professors complained students often missed class for work. President Robinson decried the "display and extravagance" that infected campus, "distracting the attention of those whose funds are ample, and burdening with anxiety those whose means are slender."[16]

Gilbert's scholarship, supplemented by money that Walker (and perhaps his mother) sent, put him in a better position than some, but he still had to work. During his years at Brown, he would take any job he could get, from teaching night school and doing the accounts for a local barber to shoveling snow—the great blizzard of March 1888, which dumped several feet of snow on Providence, would give him ample opportunity for the latter. According to Walker, Gilbert trimmed his expenses to seven dollars a month, at a time when Brown's catalogue estimated the average monthly board at twelve to fifteen dollars.[17]

The big question at Brown in fall 1886 was whether or not to admit women, a debate that other Ivy League schools sidestepped by creating separate women's colleges. While Robinson was reluctant to see "men and women of a most inflammable age . . . sit side by side," many students were enthusiastic. One wit proposed a set of rules for co-education, beginning with "each and every student is hereby required to carry a fire extinguisher." The whole discussion must have amused Gilbert, whose Paine graduating class counted more women than men.[18]

Did Gilbert's arrival also spark controversy? On the one hand, he must have had administration and faculty support to be on campus at all. Many of the professors had taught Milford and Page in the 1870s, President Robinson had advocated publicly for black education, and prominent trustee Joseph Hartshorn had recently helped found Hartshorn Memorial College in Richmond, one of the nation's first black women's colleges. On the other hand, none of the students in fall 1886 remembered Milford and Page. They knew black men as the waiters in their dining clubs, the vendors who came to sell fruits and vegetables, the janitors who maintained their buildings. They called the university staff, both black and white men, "slaves" or "servi." As far as the students were concerned, Gilbert was Brown's first black student. A careful look at Brown's catalogues shows that some in Gilbert's dormitory, Hope College, did not welcome him.[19]

Built in 1822, Hope College lacked modern plumbing, hot water, central heating, and gas light. It was known as the place for "students of brains and muscle, though possessed of less cash." The building's four floors were split vertically into unconnected South, Middle, and North Divisions, each with its own staircase. On each floor of a division, four rooms clustered around the stairwell. Gilbert's room, Hope 45, was on the east side of the North Division's top floor. This floor had long been popular and, since 1874, was almost always fully occupied, with students typically moving in as freshmen and staying until graduation (they had to furnish their own rooms, so moving was expensive and inconvenient). When Gilbert arrived, however, all seven men who had lived there the previous year moved out. During 1886–1887, Gilbert's only floor mate was another junior transfer, Frank Hawes. Hawes dropped out in 1887, and in 1887–1888 Gilbert had only two floor mates, both incoming freshmen. This departure from the floor's previous pattern is all the more striking when compared to Milford and Page's experience. From 1874 to 1877, Milford and Page had also lived in Hope, on the first floor, but none of their neighbors departed when they arrived.[20]

On Campus and Off

Brown in the 1880s had no dining facilities, so students formed dining clubs or paid to eat with local families. Where Gilbert took his meals is unknown, but they may have sometimes been as solitary as his lodgings. We catch a glimpse of what might have been his typical lunchtime in a candid snapshot taken by a classmate. The photo (Figure 2.2) shows Gilbert striding purposefully across the grass at the north edge of campus, the houses of Waterman Street visible in the background. A book in his right hand, he takes a bite from a quick meal held in his left. Judging from the orientation of the buildings behind him, he is making a beeline southeast across campus, perhaps toward a classroom in Sayles Hall.[21]

There is no sign Gilbert took part in any campus group as a junior. Instead, he looked to Providence's vibrant African American

FIGURE 2.2 John Wesley Gilbert walking on the Brown University campus,
1886–1888.
Courtesy of Brown University Digital Repository.

community for his social life, as would John Hope a few years later.
While the city did not yet have a black-owned newspaper, a regular
correspondent for the influential and nationally circulated New York
Freeman (renamed The Age in October 1887) chronicled community
doings in Providence.[22]

Much activity centered on the city's black churches, of which there
were at least eight in fall 1886 and nearly a dozen by the following

spring. Gilbert certainly went to church, for in addition to their daily morning chapel on campus, Brown students were required to attend Sunday services and report their church to President Robinson. Two black churches lay within a few minutes' walk of Gilbert's dorm. Just downhill to the northwest was Congdon Street Baptist Church, whence John Dart had come to Augusta. A few blocks to the northeast was Bethel African Methodist Episcopal (AME) Church on Meeting Street, founded in 1795. Gilbert may have made contacts at Congdon Street through Dart, but the Meeting Street church, whose roof he might have been able to glimpse from his fourth-floor Hope College window, became his church in Providence.[23]

Bethel's minister, Arthur W. Upshaw, was also new in town. Upshaw had graduated from Atlanta University in 1878, studied theology and medicine at Howard University, and worked for the federal government in Washington, DC. His classmates in Atlanta had included Augusta's James S. Harper, a key supporter of Paine Institute, and it is possible Harper helped Gilbert connect with Upshaw. In 1881, Upshaw had been a founding member of the Bethel Literary and Historical Association at Washington's Metropolitan AME Church. He was the group's first presenter, giving a paper on ancient Egypt. Bethel Literary soon became famous as the nation's premier black intellectual venue. It featured speakers such as Frederick Douglass and Mary Church Terrell, and its meetings drew audiences in the hundreds. Arriving in Providence in fall 1886, Upshaw soon founded a Historical Literary Society at Bethel AME, modeled on the Washington group. The Meeting Street church thus offered Gilbert not only a spiritual home but also a lively intellectual and social community led by a pastor with close ties to the black elite of the nation's capital.[24]

Beyond church were other attractions: literary and social clubs, amateur theatricals, and art exhibitions by Edward M. Bannister, a prominent black painter who had helped found the Rhode Island School of Design. Black veterans and militia companies regularly held parades, drills, and reunions, often with white veterans. There was also a veterans' historical association with public readings of papers. Gilbert even had the opportunity to hear Harriet Tubman speak during her Thanksgiving 1886 visit to Providence.[25]

A Thirst for Knowledge

School, however, was always Gilbert's focus. The junior curriculum was heavy on physics, chemistry, and astronomy, plus English literature, European history, and public speaking. Thanks to Brown's new elective system, though, juniors had more freedom to select courses than ever before. Among those electives was surveying, which Gilbert may have studied without being formally enrolled. While he certainly took lectures on zoology and political economy, above all he chose languages, especially Greek and Latin.[26]

Brown's three Classics professors were old hands. The youngest, William Carey Poland, had been hired in 1870 after graduating from Brown in 1868. Poland in 1886–1887 only taught freshmen and sophomores, so Gilbert probably had little contact with him. John Larkin Lincoln had taught at Brown from 1839 to 1841, then studied in Europe before returning as professor of Latin in 1844. Revered by generations of students, the seemingly unflappable Lincoln was famous for his literary enthusiasm and often addressed his classes in Latin. With Lincoln, Gilbert read the Latin poet Horace, the playwright Terence, and the satirist Juvenal. But it was with Albert Harkness, his Greek professor, that Gilbert formed the closest relationship.[27]

Born in Massachusetts to a farming family, Albert Harkness had entered Brown at age sixteen in 1838. From 1842 to 1852, he was a teacher and then principal at Providence High School. In 1854, he became the first American to receive a doctoral degree at the University of Bonn in Germany, a year after Basil Gildersleeve and a year before William Goodwin—two other prominent American classics scholars—got their degrees at Göttingen. Harkness was on his way to Greece for the first time in 1855 when he got word of his appointment as professor of Greek at Brown, a post he would hold until 1892.[28]

Ironically for a Greek professor, Harkness was more famous for his Latin grammars and readers than for his Greek textbook. Eulogizing him

in 1907, Yale's Thomas Seymour guessed a million young Americans—
including Seymour himself—had gotten their first Greek or Latin from
a Harkness text. Harkness also had unusually broad interests for a
classical scholar. While many of his contemporaries had little use for
history and archaeology, Harkness began incorporating these topics in
his Greek language classes as early as 1869. He introduced students
to the debates over the authorship, date, and composition of the *Iliad*
and *Odyssey*, the so-called Homeric Question. The study of Greek
and Latin, he wrote in 1880, must be integrated with history, linguistics, and comparative philology. By 1886, he emphasized that students
reading the Athenian orators Aeschines and Demosthenes, staples of
college and university curricula across the United States, needed not
simply command of the Greek language, but also "great familiarity
with Athenian history."[29]

Harkness also played a key role in professionalizing classical studies
in the United States. He helped found the American Philological
Association (today the Society for Classical Studies) in 1869 and served
as its seventh president in 1875–1876. He also became a member of
the Archaeological Institute of America (AIA) soon after its creation
in 1879. In 1881, he joined an AIA committee set up to explore the
possibility of an "American School of Classical Literature, Art, and
Antiquities" in Greece. Harkness became one of the first six members
of the Managing Committee of this school, which opened in fall 1882
as the American School of Classical Studies at Athens (ASCSA). He was
even elected director of the American School in 1884 but declined the
position, saying he lacked the archaeological knowledge and experience needed to lead students in Greece.[30]

When John Gilbert met him in 1886, Albert Harkness was one
of the preeminent classical scholars in the United States. At Brown,
though, Harkness suffered in comparison to John Lincoln. Students
loved "Johnny Link," who always seemed young at heart. "Stimulating
and inspiring," they invariably called him. Harkness, in contrast, was
considered a drillmaster, "insistent on accuracy of form and statement,
impatient of slovenly preparation or recital." He sometimes found
it hard to comprehend "the undergraduate mind." If students found

Harkness polite and patient, his exacting style deterred many. "I have a theory about the dead languages," remarked a freshman; "I think they were killed by being studied too hard." The *Liber Brunensis* lampooned "Harkey" and his attempts at humor: "His jokes he has noted upon every page / They are awfully stale and moth eaten with age."[31]

John Gilbert, though, was no typical undergraduate. Devoting more time to study was the very reason he had come to Brown. He must have found Harkness's insistence on preparation and accuracy especially appealing. Years later, Gilbert's own students would remark that he displayed these same qualities. In turn, Harkness found in Gilbert a dedicated, focused student who could meet the most exacting standards.[32]

Gilbert and ten other juniors read Greek with Harkness in 1886–1887: Euripides's *Alcestis* in the fall, Plato's *Apology* and *Crito* in the spring. Plato had been Harkness's standard junior offering for decades, but he had only begun teaching the *Alcestis* regularly in the 1880s, partly to have his students compare Euripides and Goethe. Harkness pushed Gilbert and his classmates to "appreciate and enjoy the thought in the original without translating it," a particularly challenging task considering they were reading carefully composed written literature rather than vernacular Greek. He also taught them about Greek literature and history, linguistics, and the history of classical philology.[33]

Produced in 438 BC at the height of Athenian imperial power, Euripides's *Alcestis* presents the myth of King Admetus of Thessaly and his devoted wife Alcestis, who gives up her life so her husband can live beyond his fated time. Admetus promises Alcestis he will spend the rest of his life in solitary mourning but breaks his promise to welcome the visiting hero Heracles. In turn, Heracles brings Alcestis back from the dead and enables the couple to reunite. *Alcestis* found new popularity in American colleges and universities, including Howard University and Atlanta University, during the late 1800s. The short, readable text helped students learn the conventions of Athenian theater. It was also becoming a favorite choice for collegiate revivals of Greek drama. Across the Atlantic, an 1887 Oxford production would become famous for featuring classicist Jane Harrison as Alcestis after

Oxford's chancellor insisted "the ladies' parts should be played by la-dies." A few years later, a young African American actor named Charles Winter Wood would make his name playing Heracles in an *Alcestis* at Beloit College.[34]

With its themes of marital love, wifely duty, and family relationships, the *Alcestis* may have had a certain appeal for many of Brown's undergraduates, who hoped or were expected to marry soon after graduation. Yet while his classmates came, as far as we can tell, from conventional and respectable families, Gilbert had never known his biological father, had lived with one stepfather as a boy, and with his mother's recent remarriage now had another stepfather. We can only wonder how these aspects of Gilbert's personal history might have shaped his response to the *Alcestis*. Whatever the reason, the play seems to have been particularly meaningful to Gilbert, if nothing else because it was the first classical Greek work he read at Brown. Though he never taught the play in his later career, he held on to his *Alcestis* textbook for decades afterward. The well-worn volume survives today in Paine's archives.[35]

Along with Greek and Latin, Gilbert took German and French. German was particularly popular among Brown students, and he would later teach the language at Paine. French, though, would become Gilbert's forte. During his 1911–1912 mission with W. R. Lambuth to the Belgian Congo, Gilbert penned several official letters in French to the Belgian authorities. Lambuth later met a Belgian colonial official in Brussels who asked about the author of the letters, remarking "they were the most correct and elegantly expressed among those received at his office from one who was not a native of either France or Belgium."[36]

Gilbert studied European history with Elisha Benjamin Andrews, who would become Brown's president in 1889, and English literature with Timothy Whiting Bancroft, who had given up a business career to devote himself to teaching. Bancroft's survey focused on authors such as Chaucer, Shakespeare, and Milton. Brown's library records show Gilbert regularly visited to check out books for these courses. He also devoted precious funds to buy books of his own, among them a standard reference on Shakespearean grammar. Bancroft required his students to write biweekly essays, then prepare and present orations based on their literary studies. One of these written assignments became the basis for Gilbert's earliest known publication, the essay that ended up on the front page of the newspaper Mrs. Bridges found in her parents' attic.[37]

Paine had acquired a printing press around the time Gilbert left for Brown. In March 1887, students published the first issue of the monthly *Paine Institute Herald*. Gilbert soon heard about the paper and along with Charles Dryscoll in Boston took an active part in enrolling northern subscribers. The essay Gilbert sent back from Brown, entitled "Did Bacon Write the Plays Known as Shakespeare's?," reflects the intense interest in this subject during the 1880s. The Francis Bacon Society, many of whose members advocated for Bacon's authorship of Shakespeare's works, had just been founded, and Professor Bancroft doubtless devoted attention to the question in his English literature classes. Indeed, Shakespeare was seemingly everywhere at Brown in the 1880s: the admission exams asked questions about his plays and student humor often involved quoting (or deliberately misquoting) him.[38]

In his essay, Gilbert carefully employs literary analysis, historical reasoning, and logic to build a powerful case for Shakespeare over Bacon. As he puts it, "if it is true the greater can contain the less, Shakespeare, and not Bacon, wrote Shakespeare's plays." Behind Gilbert's formal academic language, though, we discern his deeply personal investment in the question. Responding to the charge that Shakespeare, "a boy who had no advantages of study except at a country grammar school which he left at the age of fourteen" could never have obtained the knowledge displayed in his plays, Gilbert writes, "the solution of this seeming problem is found in the fact that during the Renaissance knowledge of every kind was imbibed by every one, and that Shakespeare learned, at least, enough in the grammar school to create a thirst for knowledge of all that came his way." It is hard not to see in these sentences a reflection of Gilbert's own ceaseless striving for education.

Around the time he sent his essay to Augusta, Gilbert was thrust into the public eye, when Samuel Chapman Armstrong, the white president of Virginia's Hampton Normal and Industrial Institute, stopped in Providence on a fundraising tour. Hampton had been founded in 1868 to provide practical training for black people and had recently begun enrolling Native Americans as well. One of the school's early graduates, a young man named Booker T. Washington, had in 1881 become principal of the Tuskegee Normal and Industrial Institute, a new school in Alabama modeled on Hampton. On March 22, 1887, Samuel Armstrong and several Hampton students spoke to a full house at Providence's Music Hall, in what was billed as a meeting "in the interest of negro and Indian education." Several prominent locals also spoke. One of them, Brown president Robinson, highlighted Gilbert's presence on campus, declaring, in the words of the New York *Freeman*, that "the University is open to any colored man who is competent to pass an examination, and that there is at present one colored student there."[39]

The next morning, Armstrong and his group attended chapel at Brown and addressed the assembled collegians. Someone, probably Armstrong, cited Inman Page's 1876 selection as class orator as evidence the university possessed "a generosity not to be found at every institution." Many of Brown's students, who had but a vague idea of the educational challenges confronting African Americans and Native Americans, found this event eye-opening. Gilbert understood these challenges better than anyone on campus. Yet however much he appreciated the attention Armstrong was bringing to the issue, Gilbert also knew that Armstrong's emphasis on "industrial education" represented the opposite of the classical liberal education that he was pursuing at Brown and that so many other African Americans also desired.[40]

Armstrong's visit stirred Gilbert's classmates. The next week's issue of the student paper, *The Brunonian*, featured a front-page editorial invoking the spirit of Inman Page. Brown men, the editors asserted, had been "remarkably democratic and free from false feelings toward men and their circumstances," unlike students at certain other unnamed schools. At Brown, they continued, "it is pleasant to feel that every person is respected in proportion to his own worth." Even so, the editors cautioned, "Nothing can so break the spirit of a man as the thought that he is not appreciated, that accidents of his condition withhold from him his completest freedom. At present there is no indication here of any such restraints; they should never be tolerated, and it is to be hoped that they may never exist at Brown." Though they never referred directly to Gilbert, the editors, who included three of his fellow juniors, were clearly writing about and for him. Their declaration reveals that, before the end of his first year at Brown, Gilbert had won acceptance and support from at least some on campus.[41]

All too soon, spring classes were over. Final exams arrived in the first week of June, and Gilbert left Providence as soon as they were finished. While the Class of '88 party crowd was celebrating with a boozy river cruise to Newport, he had already made it to Boston and boarded a Savannah-bound steamer. John Hope left Worcester Academy for Augusta about the same time, but he and Gilbert did not travel together. Gilbert's decision to return south is noteworthy, for he might easily have found summer work in Providence or at a seaside resort in nearby Newport, as John Hope later would. Newport also had an active black social scene, and Gilbert could have made connections through A. W. Upshaw, who left Meeting Street in June to lead a church there. Instead, Gilbert most likely devoted his summer to teaching school in Augusta or Hephzibah, sharing the fruits of his year's study with a younger generation of black students.[42]

Seniors

When he returned to Providence in September 1887, John Gilbert met Bethel AME's new pastor, John Thomas Jenifer. Born into slavery in 1835, Jenifer escaped to freedom in the 1850s. He pursued a business career in Massachusetts before going to California in 1862 and becoming involved in the AME Church. In 1866, Jenifer enrolled at Ohio's Wilberforce University, recently reorganized by the AME. In 1870, he was one of Wilberforce's first three theology graduates. Jenifer's eloquent preaching and peerless financial acumen quickly made him a church leader. Indeed, as pastor of Washington's Metropolitan AME Church, he would deliver the main eulogy at Frederick Douglass's

1895 funeral. Jenifer also had a great interest in church history and later wrote a history of African Methodism. Taking up his new post in July 1887, Jenifer began planning for the upcoming centennial celebration of African Methodism and drew Gilbert into the preparations soon after the young Augustan returned to Providence. Gilbert also kept in touch with Rev. Upshaw, who preached occasionally at Bethel in 1887–1888.[43]

Going into his senior year at Brown, Gilbert had required courses in US and British history, Christian theology, and philosophy, leaving plenty of room for electives. Again, he filled up on languages. John Lincoln was on leave in Europe, so Gilbert took William Carey Poland's Latin classes: the philosopher Lucretius in the fall, the historian Tacitus in the spring. With Albert Harkness, Gilbert and a group of seniors including Charles Dennis and Fred Whitaker—later Brown's first Greek and Latin doctoral degree holders—read Demosthenes's oration *On the Crown*, parts of Aeschines's competing oration of the same name, and Plato's *Gorgias*. Harkness was unusually effusive about the performance of Gilbert and his classmates, noting "they have done a large amount of excellent work, and are entitled to high praise." These senior courses were key for Gilbert, as he would repeatedly teach the same authors and texts in years to come.[44]

It was not all hard work. Gilbert also took a geology elective with entomologist Alpheus Packard, who, in one student's words, "united extraordinary biological attainments with extraordinary indifference to discipline." Packard used the same exam questions year after year, graded leniently, and took little notice when students came to class late and left early. Geology was unsurprisingly popular among seniors. More than half the senior class took it in fall 1887 and nearly a third, Gilbert among them, stayed on through the spring. Packard's course may have been easy, but Gilbert found it valuable enough that he would later teach a geology course himself. In all probability he demanded more of his students than had Packard.[45]

Packard had long included discussions of prehistoric artifacts in his geology classes, but the spotlight at Brown in the 1880s was firmly on the growing fields of Mediterranean and Near Eastern archaeology.

Late in Gilbert's junior year, Italian scholar Rodolfo Lanciani had come to present illustrated lectures on recent archaeological work in Rome. In the fall of Gilbert's senior year, Harvard's David G. Lyon, the first Assyriology professor in the United States, delivered a series on Assyria, Babylonia, and Persia. Lyon emphasized Assyriology's importance for understanding the Bible and highlighted recent discoveries such as the Cyrus Cylinder, a football-sized clay oblong from Babylon inscribed with a cuneiform edict of Cyrus of Anshan, founder of the Persian Empire. His lectures drew large crowds.[46]

On campus, Greece got constant attention. Professor Poland had long wanted to offer a Classical archaeology course and had started a fund to purchase plaster casts of antiquities for classroom use. Poland's hopes got a boost in spring 1888, when a wealthy Brown alumnus, with John Lincoln's help, arranged to buy numerous casts of Greek sculpture from museums in Europe. The first of these cast purchases, a copy of the so-called Hermes of Praxiteles from Olympia, was on its way to campus by June 1888.[47]

Students also heard regularly about the new American School of Classical Studies at Athens. *The Brunonian* carried news of Harkness's attendance at Managing Committee meetings in the United States and of the British, French, and German archaeological institutes in Greece. During Gilbert's senior year, the paper ran stories on the American School's first excavations at Thoricus near Athens and at Sicyon in the Peloponnesus, its plans for the newly discovered site of Icaria near Marathon, the hiring of "a famous archaeologist" from Cambridge University as director, and the construction of its new building in Athens. As a founding member of the Managing Committee, Harkness was eager to see the fledgling ASCSA succeed. He shared the latest news about the School soon after returning from his meetings, promoting the benefits of studying in Athens to Gilbert and other students. Harkness was so enthusiastic about the ASCSA he made it the centerpiece of his graduation address in June 1888, inviting "all the alumni if visiting Athens to be sure and visit the school."[48]

People off campus knew about the American School, too. Among them was Gilbert's junior year pastor, A. W. Upshaw. In Washington,

Upshaw had been friends with young Wiley Lane, Howard University's first African American professor of Greek and a rising star on the DC scene. The two were active in the Bethel Literary Association and appeared together at public events. Lane planned to attend the American School and had even received federal funding to study abroad, but he died suddenly of pneumonia in February 1885. Upshaw certainly was aware of Lane's plans and likely attended the public memorials held for Lane in March 1885, during which speakers repeatedly mentioned Greece and the American School. It is difficult to believe Upshaw did not mention Wiley Lane to Gilbert. Perhaps he even encouraged Gilbert to fulfill Lane's dream.[49]

There was also someone in Providence who had actually been to the American School: a Providence native and University of Michigan graduate, Annie S. Peck. Peck had spent 1885–1886 in Athens as the School's first officially enrolled woman student. She was at Smith College teaching Latin during 1886–1887, but returned to Providence in 1887 and began offering private lessons. Annie Peck knew Albert Harkness—indeed it was the possibility that Harkness might direct the program in Athens that had first drawn her toward Greece—and she may well have talked about the American School with John Gilbert during 1887–1888.[50]

By fall 1887, Gilbert's class was down to forty-three men. One got scarlet fever and dropped out a month into the term; another left soon after. The remainder hung together. "Our band is few, but tried and true," the *Liber* would assert at year's end. While Gilbert had appeared nowhere in the 1887 yearbook except in the junior class roster, the 1888 edition names him several times, showing he took some part in campus social life. These mentions often play on inside humor whose meaning has been lost, but it is notable that a list of the year's memorable quotations features a Shakespearean quip from Gilbert.[51]

Sometime in 1887–1888, the seniors gathered on the Manning Hall steps for another photograph. At the left of the photo, a confident-looking John Gilbert, bowler hat in one hand and book in the other, sits on the steps surrounded by classmates. The image (Figure 2.3) would be unremarkable except that Brown's archives preserve a second group

FIGURE 2.3 The Brown University Class of 1888 during 1887–1888, with Gilbert.
Courtesy of Brown University Archives.

shot taken moments later, from which Gilbert is missing. In this second photo (Figure 2.4), a conspicuous empty space remains where Gilbert was seated and a half-dozen of his classmates pointedly cast their eyes or turn their heads in that direction. Like the inside yearbook jokes, the meaning of the dual images is obscure. At first glance, it is tempting to assume someone demanded a Gilbert-less photograph. Yet the empty space and his classmates' sideways glances in the second photo deliberately invite attention to his absence rather than hiding or obscuring him. Perhaps the second photograph was his classmates' way of saying the Class of '88 was incomplete without Gilbert.[52]

Gilbert by now had friends on campus, but his social life remained anchored at Bethel AME on Meeting Street. There he helped Rev. Jenifer with preparations for the centennial of the 1787 founding by Richard Allen and Absalom Jones of Philadelphia's Free African Society,

FIGURE 2.4 The Brown University Class of 1888 during 1887–1888, without Gilbert.

Courtesy of Brown University Archives.

forerunner of the AME Church. AME congregations across the United States marked the anniversary with speeches, music, and festivities. Rhode Island's celebrations began in Newport early in November and continued in Providence, where Jenifer organized a week-long program of speeches, music, and festivities that drew in the city's five hundred AME members and many others from the community. On November 17, 1887, Gilbert addressed a large crowd at Bethel. He was by far the youngest of the evening's six speakers, who included Rev. Jenifer's wife Alice and the prominent newspaper editor William H. Bonaparte. Though we have only the title of Gilbert's talk—"Our Children: What Are They Doing and What Are We Doing for Them"—it is enough to reveal his continued interest in education and teaching.[53]

A week later, on Thanksgiving evening, Gilbert spoke to a packed gathering at Allen Chapel, a Bethel AME offshoot in western Providence, across the river from Brown. The event was part of a month-long fundraising drive for Allen Chapel, and Rev. Jenifer, who had a knack for reducing church debts, probably organized it. The *New York Age*'s Providence correspondent, noting the variety of musical and literary presentations, pronounced Gilbert's oration "the feature of the evening."[54]

By spring 1888, Gilbert was a well-known speaker at black community events. By then, he seems to have been bringing friends from campus to visit his church. When Jenifer went to Indianapolis in May to attend the AME General Conference, Gilbert and several other Brown students filled in at Bethel's pulpit. John Gilbert's devotion to interracial cooperation and understanding, which would become a defining aspect of his life and career, is already evident in his invitation to white classmates to join him on Meeting Street.[55]

He Will Teach in the South

Even as Gilbert was making a name for himself in Providence, trouble was growing back in Augusta. In January 1887, a new professor, Carville Hynson Carson, Jr., joined George Williams Walker at Paine Institute. Carson was an 1883 Emory College graduate and had trained as a printer. Indeed, he had supervised the creation of Paine's print shop, the very press that produced Gilbert's May 1887 essay on Bacon and Shakespeare. News reports praised Walker and Carson as "true, efficient men" who worked well together, and Carson even went to represent the school at Methodist Episcopal Church, South (MECS) events. Yet Carson was inexperienced and, by his own admission, knew little about Paine Institute before arriving. Opposition to Paine remained strong within certain MECS contingents, and Carson met the same sort of hostility Walker had. His response was unfortunately self-serving.[56]

In November 1887, Carson sent a letter to the Macon-based *Wesleyan Christian Advocate* to convince readers to abandon their "unfavorable prejudice and repugnance" toward Paine. Hoping "to relieve his conscience," Carson downplayed suggestions that Paine was a threat to white supremacy. "Social equality," he asserted, "is an expression never heard within the walls of the Institute. My observation is that the more cultured our pupils become the more adverse to the idea they get to be." Instead, Carson went on, "we meet with our pupils in the classrooms, and nowhere else . . . and in our dealings with them try to inculcate the principle of *spiritual* equality." Carson stressed that white faculty never ate or boarded with black students. What is more, he declared, "There are no colored teachers connected with the Institute, and never will be, I presume, unless some of the white teachers resign to make way for them." His letter appeared on the *Advocate*'s front page just before Christmas.[57]

Carson meant to assuage white concerns. Instead he ignited a firestorm. Black editor A. E. P. Albert of the New Orleans-based *Southwestern Christian Advocate* denounced Carson for "the most disgusting and nauseating apology for doing missionary Christian work, that we have ever read from the pen of any man." The *Advocate*'s wide readership among both blacks and whites helped spread news of Carson's letter quickly across the south and north to New York. The official Colored Methodist Episcopal (CME) publication, the *Christian Index*, remarked that Carson "ought to respect the feelings of the intelligent negroes of the south and let social equality take care of itself—be it in Paine Institute or Yale College." Tennessee CME minister C. E. Alexander wrote that Carson had "disgraced our civilization" with his "silly letter." If Carson indeed spoke for the MECS, others added, the CME church wanted nothing more to do with Paine. CME members in Augusta pressed Bishop Holsey for a full explanation in writing before they would give the school any further support.[58]

George Williams Walker, writing to Warren Candler in late February 1888, judged Carson's action "injudicious and entirely unnecessary." Carson had blindsided Walker by publishing the letter and had directly contradicted Walker's principle of "avoiding any thing that would hurt our colored patrons." The Institute had been assailed from pulpits and in newspapers, and CME members were still up in arms. The worst was over, Walker hoped, but he warned "the waters are still rolling." Walker judged he could not continue working with Carson. Fortunately, Carson was already planning to leave. Walker remained optimistic as ever, writing "the school is doing its best work and we are weathering our first severe gale. God is with us." He asked Candler to attend the next full meeting of Paine's trustees in June.[59]

Walker's mention of Carson's imminent departure suggests a plan for replacing him was already developing in February 1888. It is unclear whether Paine's founders had envisioned an interracial faculty, but Carson's letter had the unintended effect of spurring calls for just that. Around the time Walker wrote Candler, Bishop Holsey told Augusta's R. R. Wright, Sr. that "we as trustees of the school, would put in colored teachers." "I went so far," added Holsey, "as to inform him [Wright] that we had a young man in view that we would put in at the beginning of another term." That young man's identity is not hard to surmise. Walker, Holsey, and the school's other leaders knew the CME would not continue supporting Paine Institute without a black faculty member. The absence of black faculty was also drawing notice from northern black visitors. And not just any black professor would do. It had to be someone respected and known in Augusta, and someone with stellar academic credentials. There was only one real choice: John Wesley Gilbert.[60]

Walker probably raised the possibility of a job at Paine to Gilbert soon after the discussions Holsey refers to. We, of course, know John Gilbert forged a lifelong connection with Paine. Yet, just as Brown was not inevitable in 1886, returning south was not Gilbert's sole option in 1888. Two years in Providence had given Gilbert new connections and possibilities. Thanks to his academic performance and his relationship with Albert Harkness, he might have continued his Greek studies at Brown. Indeed, Harkness had already suggested to Gilbert that he do graduate work. Upshaw and Jenifer, Gilbert's pastors at Bethel AME, had close ties to the nation's black elite. Through them he could easily have found a position in Washington or elsewhere, especially with a Brown graduate degree. Going back to Paine meant foregoing these opportunities. But John Gilbert also knew George Williams Walker had helped make possible his journey north, and he knew other young black men and women back home yearned for learning as much as he did. Love for Walker and duty to community must have shaped Gilbert's decision to return home.[61]

Official action came earlier than Walker anticipated. In May, Candler convened a meeting in Nashville, where he introduced a motion authorizing Walker, "if the needs of the Institute in his judgment requires another teacher, to employ John Wesley Gilbert, a recent graduate of the Paine Institute and now recently graduated from Brown University." Since Carson had not yet resigned, Gilbert was not named to replace him. Instead, Candler also proposed that Walker hire a new white teacher, R. L. Campbell, in case Carson quit. Both resolutions passed unanimously. The word may have reached Gilbert in Providence in mid-May, as his final semester at Brown was winding down.[62]

A month later, Paine's trustees met in Augusta. Walker explained "why he needed a colored teacher as a member of the faculty in the school." The minutes do not record his words, but MECS minister W. C. Dunlap in a letter relates Walker's "utmost confidence" in the ability of "Mr. Gilbert"—note the honorific so often denied black men in the South—to "do a work that no white man can do in advancing the interest of the school among the colored people." The trustees then formally accepted Carson's letter of resignation while explicitly refusing his characterization of Gilbert's hiring as an "evil" and "revolutionary measure." It was an unprecedented moment: a Southern interracial group, over a white professor's opposition, had formed a consensus to employ a black scholar. Fifty years later, Paine's white president E. C. Peters still judged Gilbert's hiring "almost unbelievable."[63]

On June 20, 1888, John Wesley Gilbert and thirty-six other seniors became the hundred and twentieth graduating class of Brown University. It was sunny for the first time in days and a cool breeze kept back the heat. In dress suits, the men of 1888, preceded by underclassmen and a brass band, trailed by faculty and alumni, marched down from Manning Hall to Providence's First Baptist Church. There were speeches. Then, "in Latin of classic construction and continental pronunciation," President Robinson summoned Gilbert and his classmates to receive their sheepskins. It helps to put this moment into perspective. In 1888, there were nearly seven and half million black people in the United States. About eighty black men and women received college degrees that year, mostly from segregated schools in the South. Among them was W. E. B. Du Bois, who graduated from Fisk University in May 1888. Gilbert was one of only about forty black students who graduated from a northern college or university between 1885 and 1890. At the same ceremony, Robinson conferred two master of arts degrees, the first awarded under Brown's new graduate education system. In a few years, Gilbert, too, would have his Brown master's degree, becoming the first African American to earn an advanced degree from the school.[64]

From First Baptist, the procession returned uphill to campus, where dinner for 450 guests awaited at Sayles Hall, with women relegated to a gallery. At the back of the hall stood a mysterious veiled object. After the banquet, the cover was thrown off to reveal the long-awaited cast of the Hermes of Praxiteles, just off the boat from Europe. In less than three years Gilbert would see the real thing at Olympia. The distinguished dinner guests included Rhode Island's governor and chief justice, but two others may have drawn Gilbert's attention: Francis Wayland III, the dean of Yale Law School, and his brother Herman Wayland, a leading Baptist minister and educator. They were sons of Francis Wayland, who, as Brown's president in the 1820s, had mentored Joseph Thomas Robert, Gilbert's teacher at Augusta Institute and Atlanta Baptist Seminary.[65]

John Gilbert had arrived at Brown University in 1886 alone and unheralded. When he graduated two years later, his name was known in Providence and beyond, thanks to newspaper coverage of events such as Armstrong's visit and the AME centennial. If some students never reconciled themselves to his presence, others accepted and supported him. Gilbert apparently did not make lifelong friends at Brown and never attended reunions, but his experience was nonetheless positive enough that, for years after graduation, he kept in touch with classmates through the alumni association. He probably recommended the school to other black students, notably his fellow Augustan John Hope.

In contrast to the long hiatus after the 1877 graduation of George Milford and Inman Page, Gilbert's success quickly inspired other black students to enter Brown University. These students literally walked in his footsteps. In fall 1888, Frank Levi Trimble of Nashville moved into Hope College, Room 45. Several white classmates joined him on the fourth floor. Another classmate later recalled that Trimble's arrival caused "no particular stir" on campus. In fall 1890, John Hope became Trimble's roommate. After Trimble fell ill and died, Hope shared Room 45 with Heita Okada, Brown's first Japanese student. Hope kept the room until he graduated in 1894, making it a study space for black students who lived off campus. From there, Hope 45 passed on to Edward Delano Stewart and David Elliott Tobias, then to John Hope's younger brother Thomas, and to others after that. For nearly two decades after Gilbert left campus, his old dorm room was a center of black student life. In a sense, John Wesley Gilbert became the foundation of the African American presence at Brown University (see Figure 2.5).[66]

FIGURE 2.5 John Wesley Gilbert, circa 1888.
Courtesy of Brown University Digital Repository.

In June 1888, all that was in the future. Shortly after Gilbert left town, *The New York Age*'s Providence correspondent, who had chronicled Gilbert's advance into public prominence, offered a fitting closure and an augury of things to come: "Among the graduates of Brown University who have received the degree of Bachelor of Arts is Mr. John W. Gilbert of Georgia. This young man deserves special mention as he is a pushing, energetic fellow. He will teach in the South and no doubt make his mark in the world."[67]

3

NOTHING LESS
THAN GLORIOUS

John Gilbert's first year as Paine Institute's new Professor of Greek, Latin, and English had a soggy start. On September 10, 1888, the rain-swollen Savannah River began overflowing into the lowest-lying neighborhoods of Augusta. By next morning, the city center was several feet under water. The floodwaters broke a record set in 1840, killed ten people, and stranded many on upper floors or rooftops for days. Hundreds were left homeless, the canal and cotton mills damaged, bridges knocked out. The great flood swept away preparations for an October grand exhibition meant to showcase the city's prosperity. Nobody thought much about history at the time, but the water also destroyed precious sources for Augusta's black community, including back issues of the *Georgia Baptist* and *Augusta Sentinel*. Floods in 1908 and 1912, along with a 1916 fire that destroyed much of the city, thinned this record yet further. Today but a single 1885 issue of the *Sentinel* survives, and nothing of the *Baptist* before 1898. These two papers certainly reported on Gilbert's 1888 hiring, his early work at Paine, and his journey to Greece in 1890. They even published letters he sent home after arriving in Athens. Thanks to the advent of digitization and searchable online databases, we can recover some of this lost evidence second- or third-hand, through scattered quotations and summaries in other newspapers from Alabama to Minnesota to New York.[1]

A Bright Day-Dawn

Paine Institute, located on high ground away from the river, escaped the Great Flood of 1888. Its fall term began as scheduled on October 1, a bright spot in the city's scramble to rebuild (remarkably, the exhibition would be held in November). Enrollment had grown while Gilbert was away, as Walker gained the trust of black leaders in Augusta and beyond. To assist with the younger students, Walker in 1887 had hired another white teacher, Mary Zenobia Hankinson. A divorced mother of three, Hankinson had studied at Wesleyan Female College (today Wesleyan College) in Macon, Georgia, the first college in the United States chartered to grant degrees to women. She would teach at Paine until her retirement in 1913.[2]

Gilbert was one of three new faculty members in fall 1888. Charles Dryscoll returned from Boston to teach piano and voice, while Robert Lafayette Campbell became Professor of History, Mathematics, and Biblical Studies. Campbell, a minister's son, had served as a teenager in the Confederate artillery. A comrade remembered him as "one of the few . . . who carried his religion into the army, lived it there, brought it home with him and has lived it ever since." After the war, Campbell went to Emory College (today Oxford College of Emory University), where he was three years ahead of Warren Candler and got his preacher's license from Atticus Haygood, both key figures in Paine's founding. Campbell was candid about his Civil War service, telling students, "Yes, I did all in my power, fighting under General Lee in Virginia, to keep you in slavery." "But," he continued, "when I found I couldn't I set to educate you." He earned a reputation as a patient, insightful teacher and took pride in seeing his students prove "what so many white Southern people thought impossible: that Negro students could learn higher mathematics." Campbell and Gilbert would be colleagues for more than thirty years. When Campbell and Colored Methodist Episcopal (CME) bishop Lucius Holsey died within days of each other in 1920, black journalist Silas Floyd eulogized them together as "valiant men, [who] accomplished a great work for the glory of God and the uplift of the people—especially the colored people."[3]

While some white Methodists still fretted Paine would become a venue for "social equality, miscegenation, political control, etc.," George Williams Walker's deepening connections with Augusta's respected Goodrich family counterbalanced white opposition in town. In February 1888, architect Lewis Goodrich, a younger brother of the school's treasurer Charles Goodrich, took over as carpentry instructor from C. H. Carson, whose letter had opened the way for Gilbert's hiring. And, on June 7, 1888, the day after Paine's trustees accepted Carson's resignation, G. W. Walker married Charles and Lewis's only sister, Susan. If some whites ostracized the new couple, the *Augusta Chronicle* praised Walker as "a gentleman of fine mental endowments and high character" and his bride as "a worthy representative of a worthy and influential family." Even whites who did not interact with Paine became aware of its existence as the rural Woodlawn area began to be developed.[4]

In summer 1888, Methodist Episcopal Church, South (MECS) minister W. C. Dunlap heralded "a bright day-dawn to Paine Institute," but the school's budget was strained after paying off the mortgage on the Woodlawn campus. The CME Church stepped in to cover Gilbert's entire salary for two years. It was a clear sign of the CME leadership's confidence in the young professor, especially since the denomination faced competing financial demands from its other school, Lane Institute in Jackson, Tennessee. When Gilbert attended a Georgia CME meeting in November to describe his first term's progress, he got an enthusiastic reception. F. M. Hamilton, editor of the CME's *Christian Index*, was there and reported church members were "highly pleased" with the school, promising to support it "with great zeal." Paine Institute, Hamilton concluded, "is destined to become a great factor in diffusing light and intelligence among our people." Visiting Paine soon afterward, Hamilton found "everything looking bright and cheerful."[5]

The three new instructors greatly expanded Paine's curriculum. While Dryscoll focused on music and Campbell introduced advanced mathematics, Gilbert's contribution was particularly significant. In 1888–1889, Paine offered for the first time a four-year Higher Normal or collegiate course. Its curriculum, especially in years three and four, was closely modeled on Brown University's, often using the same textbooks. In addition to Greek, Latin, German, and English literature, Gilbert taught several science courses he had taken at Brown, including botany, chemistry, geology, and physics. Before 1888, Paine had offered no sciences beyond geography and chemistry.[6]

Gilbert had just three Higher Normal students during 1888–1889. The youngest was twenty-year-old John Hope, on hiatus from Worcester Academy in Massachusetts. Though he spent only a few months at Paine in winter 1889 before returning to Worcester, the experience led Hope to regard Gilbert as "among the greatest teachers he had ever known." The other two students, George Claudius Taylor and Randall Albert Carter, had just finished Paine's normal course. Taylor, an eloquent young preacher, would soon depart to pursue his ministerial career, but Carter stayed on, becoming Paine's first college-level graduate in 1891. Something of Gilbert's intellectual influence on Carter may be glimpsed in an oration, replete with references to Greek and English literature, that Carter delivered at Paine a few years after graduating. Carter would go on to become a CME bishop and a towering figure in the denomination's spread north during the Great Migration, helping found more than two hundred and fifty churches.[7]

In addition to building the collegiate curriculum, Gilbert added classes on rhetoric and English composition to the Normal (high school) program, bringing his Brown education to a new generation of young black Augustans. Among those students was Gilbert's stepbrother William C. Thomas, who began the high school program in fall 1888. Ten students, the largest class yet, graduated from the Normal course in June 1889, with four planning to go on to the collegiate course. In his annual report, Walker remarked that Paine had "passed through its most prosperous year."[8]

Graduate Study

With guidance from Albert Harkness at Brown, Gilbert also pressed forward with his own education. Gilbert does not appear in the 1888–1889 Brown catalogue, but Harkness in June 1889 reported Gilbert and fellow 1888 graduate Charles Edward Dennis, Jr. had "been reading

Greek during the year for the degree of Master of Arts." Harkness later emphasized Gilbert began his MA studies immediately after gradua- tion. By 1889–1890, Gilbert and Dennis were on Brown's rosters as graduate students in Greek.[9]

Undertaking graduate work *in absentia* at Brown was so common at the time that the school had regulations for nonresident study. In 1889–1890, five of its nine graduate students, Dennis and Gilbert among them, had addresses outside Providence. Charles Dennis lived in Connecticut a hundred miles west of campus. Gilbert was nearly a thousand miles south, but that distance only underscores his determi- nation to pursue advanced studies and illustrates Harkness's ongoing interest in his progress.[10]

When Gilbert began his MA studies, Brown was in the process of formalizing its inchoate graduate programs, following a path other US universities were taking. For decades, Brown had awarded various honorary graduate degrees, as well as a vaguely defined "in course" MA with no fixed standards. In 1887, the university published new regulations that would take effect in June 1890. Henceforth, an MA would require "a thorough course . . . of liberal graduate study, suffi- cient in amount to constitute a fifth year of college work," with either a year in residence or at least two years nonresident study. A doctoral degree would require two years in residence and a thesis. The first two MA degrees under this new system were conferred in 1888, the same day Gilbert received his BA; the first two PhDs followed in 1889. Gilbert's classmate Charles Dennis received Brown's first MA degree in Greek in 1890 and five years later became Brown's first PhD in Greek. In 1891, Gilbert would become Brown's second Greek MA, thanks in part to the thesis he wrote on the urban demes (neighborhoods or districts) of Athens. Had Gilbert resided in Providence for two years, that thesis would have counted for a PhD.[11]

The Gentle Partner of His Life

Amid the bustle of school, John Gilbert renewed his relationship with Osceola Pleasant, Ola to her family and friends. Ola did not need Miss

Chestnut's help to open a bank account, for her family was as well-known as Gilbert's was obscure. Her mother Margaret's father was Peter Johnson, a successful blacksmith who appears in the 1860 census as the only free black slaveowner in Augusta. Her father Robert's mother, Eliza Pleasant, had also been free before the Civil War and owned her own home. So, too, did Robert Pleasant, who was among the few black people listed in city directories in the 1860s. Ola, the middle of Robert and Margaret's seven children, was born around 1864. In 1870, her family lived on Broad Street in the First Ward, with both sets of grandparents and several uncles just houses away on Reynolds Street. Her Johnson uncles had followed their father into the blacksmith business and were prospering. Ola and two older siblings were at school, while her eldest sister Sarah worked briefly as a teacher at the Augusta Institute.[12]

Family and money could not save the Pleasants from disease. Ola's two-year-old sister Isabella fell ill and died in 1871. Her father followed in 1874, her mother in 1876, her younger brother Robert in 1879. Ola and her surviving siblings must have moved in with family after their parents died, though we cannot tell exactly where they went. In 1878, her older sister Martha Ann (Mollie) married a young school teacher named Wesley S. Dixson and returned with him to Barnwell, South Carolina, forty-five miles southeast of Augusta. Dixson was soon appointed Barnwell's postmaster and would later rise to prominence in South Carolina Republican politics.[13]

By 1880, when Gilbert came home broke and disappointed from Atlanta, Ola Pleasant was off to Fisk University in Nashville. From then until 1886, she studied in Fisk's Common English (high school) and Normal (teacher training) Departments, although she dropped out for at least one year. In 1885–1886, she may have encountered W. E. B. Du Bois, then in his first year of Fisk's collegiate program. Ola and John apparently kept in touch during her years in Nashville and he visited her there in September 1886, on his way north to Brown. John Angelo Lester, who recorded that visit and subsequently became Gilbert's close friend, was the brother of Ola's classmate Rachel Lester.[14]

Ola Pleasant left Fisk late in 1886 to teach at Union Academy in Gainesville, Florida. Founded in 1865 by the Freedmen's Bureau, Union Academy in the 1880s was a mainstay of black education in the city, enrolling several hundred students. Its principal, M. J. Maddox, was an Augustan and may have recruited her as a teacher. Pleasant left Gainesville sometime in 1887. After a brief stint teaching in Millett, South Carolina, southwest of her sister Mollie's home in Barnwell, she returned to Augusta to teach at the First Ward colored primary school, probably around the time Gilbert came home from Brown.[15]

Ola and John were soon engaged. Gilbert sent a letter to the Brown student newspaper to share the news, suggesting he still had friends up north. In December 1888, the *Brunonian*'s alumni column reported "Gilbert is teaching in Franklin College, Tennessee [*sic*]. He expects to be married soon." On March 13, 1889, George Williams Walker officiated at John and Ola's wedding in Augusta. Fittingly, the young couple's first trip was to the annual meeting of the Colored Teachers' State Association in Columbus, Georgia, where Mrs. J. W. Gilbert was on the list of speakers. By late summer, the Gilberts were expecting their first child. Though we have no direct evidence for the couple's personal relationship, William Crogman ends his 1898 profile of John Gilbert with a glowing description of Ola that may well derive from Gilbert's own words, since it casts her in Shakespearean terms: "to close this sketch without referring to the gentle partner of his life would be like leaving Hamlet out of Hamlet. . . . To this true and affectionate helpmeet, the fond mother of his children, he is indebted for no small degree of his success, for every true wife is an inspiration to her husband."[16]

American Greek

"Why should our young men go to Athens to study Greek? Is not American Greek good enough for Americans?" So began an 1882 *New York Times* editorial, ostensibly lampooning "the ardent but mistaken Hellenists who are trying to establish an American school of classical studies at Athens." Chief among those ardent Hellenists was Charles Eliot Norton, Harvard's first lecturer on fine arts. In 1879, Norton spearheaded the foundation of the Archaeological Institute of America (AIA) to "increase the knowledge of the early history of mankind, to quicken the interest in classical and biblical studies, to promote an acquaintance with the pre-historic antiquities of our own country, and to enlarge the resources of our universities and museums."[17]

Despite this broad ambit, Norton's own interest lay mainly in Greece. Before founding the AIA, he had tried to convince the Greek government to let Harvard dig up ancient Delphi. In 1881, he formed an AIA committee (Brown's Albert Harkness was a member) to explore the creation of an "American School of Classical Literature, Art and Antiquities" in Athens. It would be a place for young American scholars to "devote themselves, under the guidance of eminent masters, to studies and research in archaeology," enabling them to engage in "honorable rivalry" with the French School, founded in 1846, and the German Archaeological Institute, founded in 1874. The new school was to be a national intellectual venture, the first American university consortium, run by a Managing Committee of professors from its member institutions. By 1882, the Managing Committee had settled on a name: the American School of Classical Studies at Athens.[18]

There were skeptics. Columbia's Frederick Barnard opined that "if only classical knowledge is to be acquired, students can be instructed fully as well . . . in this country as in Athens," a remark that prompted the Times's tongue-in-cheek "American Greek" jab. More astute observers noted that the School had no permanent endowment, forcing it to rely on annually appointed directors from its member institutions, and no facilities in Athens. Nonetheless, in a rush of enthusiasm the School held its first session during 1882–1883, as eight students, two already holding doctoral degrees, joined director William W. Goodwin of Harvard in rented rooms in Athens.[19]

In the American School's first annual report, Goodwin skillfully promoted the new institution. While it welcomed the few Americans qualified to conduct research in archaeology or art history, most of the School's students would be classical scholars who would "come rather for general cultivation in Greek studies than for special research in a particular department." For such scholars, who already had "the book learning commonly deemed necessary for their professions," there was no better preparation for teaching than to experience the topography and monuments of Greece firsthand. Being on the spot would bring new vividness and understanding to Greek literature. Even using Greek as a spoken language would help teachers keep "ancient Greek alive as a real tongue, which it must be if it is to be taught with success." Beyond all that, enthused Goodwin, "no one can dwell in daily sight of the . . . Acropolis, crowned with the stately Parthenon . . . without feeling that merely to live under its shadow is an education." The ASCSA was thus "the last and boldest step" toward improving classical education in the United States.[20]

Goodwin also astutely assessed the ASCSA's challenges. Without a permanent director and facilities, the Americans could not compete with the French and Germans, much less the British, who in 1884 opened their own school in Athens. Facilities proved the easy part. Spurred on by the rapid completion of the British School's building, the Americans by 1887 raised money enough to begin construction on land gifted by the Greek government, adjacent to the British School. The new ASCSA building opened early in 1888. Funding a permanent directorship proved tougher. Through the 1880s, a series of annual directors of varying quality, some appointed at the last minute, led the School.[21]

Meanwhile, the search for a permanent director continued. Some thought the ideal choice was Yale's Frank Tarbell, later annual director in 1888–1889, but Tarbell was not prominent or well-connected. Instead, the Managing Committee tried to engage Charles Waldstein, a young German Jewish New Yorker with a position at Cambridge University, connections in Athens, and a reputation as an archaeologist, but the committee had difficulty raising money for his salary. Only in 1888 did Waldstein sign on for a three-year term as Permanent Director. Under this agreement, Waldstein only had to reside in Greece from January to April, so the School had to continue selecting annual directors. This awkward setup caused problems, especially regarding the School's new building, which was not designed for two directors.[22]

Perhaps the greatest challenge was getting students to Greece. Few American colleges or universities offered classical art and archaeology courses that might turn a student's interest toward on-site study. Greece had formally won its independence from the Ottoman Empire in 1830 and since 1863 had been a constitutional monarchy under King George I, a Dane elected by the country's National Assembly from a list provided by the European powers. In the 1880s, though, Greece still seemed very far away from the United States and only a few hundred Americans visited each year. There was no rail link with western Europe, steamer fares were expensive, and the threat of cholera often forced quarantines on Greek ports. If Athens was earning a reputation as an up-and-coming European city, travelers in the countryside still met dogs and bandits. In 1886, American School student Walter Miller was robbed and beaten while on a solo trip through Attica. With the help of a company of Greek cavalry, Miller found and arrested the robbers, but his experience still gave reason to be wary.[23]

For Albert Harkness, John Gilbert's mentor at Brown, the question of students was particularly pressing. Harkness was an ardent proponent of the School and a Managing Committee stalwart. Yet Brown had still not sent a student to Greece. Suitable candidates were not lacking. Between 1888 and 1890, Harkness had at least five graduate students in Greek. Three were 1888 men: John Gilbert, Charles Dennis, and Fred Whitaker. Another was Adrian Scott of the class of 1872, later a distinguished Germanic philologist. Seemingly the obvious candidate was Albert Walker Hinds, an 1887 Brown graduate who had gone to Harvard for a master's degree, then returned to Brown to study archaeology with William Carey Poland. All five must have heard similar things about the School, yet there is no indication any of them except Gilbert ever considered going.[24]

Gilbert's interest in the American School reflects the thirst for knowledge and eagerness to travel that had already propelled him to Atlanta in 1879 and Providence in 1886. He clearly began talking about the

School with Harkness while at Brown and must have corresponded regularly with him about the possibilities after returning to Augusta. The decisive factor was money. Sometime in 1889, Harkness secured a Brown fellowship for Gilbert. By June 1889, Gilbert had made plans to go, for his name appears on a Managing Committee list of eight proposed students for 1889–1890.[25]

Since his absence would put the brakes on Paine's new collegiate curriculum, Gilbert conferred with George Williams Walker before making his decision. Walker was characteristically encouraging. "I never expected to see Athens," he recalled, "but I gave to that boy all my sainted father gave me—the best opportunities and advantages within my reach." Beyond his genuine personal interest in Gilbert, Walker likely concluded Gilbert's travel would bring Paine long-term benefits far outweighing any short-term difficulties. John and Ola must also have discussed how going to Greece might affect their marriage. It is even possible the couple considered traveling abroad together, as several students in the School's early years brought along their wives. Ola's pregnancy, however, must have changed things, for Gilbert did not go to Greece in fall 1889.[26]

It was a lucky delay. The 1889–1890 director, Samuel Stanhope Orris of Princeton, seemed ideal on paper: he had spent eight months in Greece and spoke fluent modern Greek. Indeed, like a number of other classical scholars of the day, he maintained ancient Greek "should be taught as a living language with the modern living pronunciation." More attractive to the Managing Committee than his Greek skills was Orris's bachelorhood, which the committee hoped would "relieve our finances" and forestall conflict with Charles Waldstein over housing at the School. Unfortunately, no one noted that Orris had last visited Greece in the early 1870s and had suffered such severe sunstroke he now hid perpetually beneath an umbrella. In Athens, he proved ineffectual. "Princeton," complained William Goodwin, "played us a most shabby trick in putting off upon us, at such a critical time, a thoroughly incompetent man of the very smallest caliber. . . . [Orris] misunderstood everything and always did the wrong thing when he did anything at all."[27]

In fairness to Orris, he hardly had anyone to direct. One of the two students who actually made it to Athens in fall 1889 (others turned back before getting there) quickly got sick and left, while the other did not live at the School and rarely visited. Worse, the awkward dual directorship put Orris at odds with Charles Waldstein from the moment the latter arrived in December 1889. University of Minnesota professor Jabez Brooks observed the situation firsthand and dryly remarked, "the utility of this arrangement is not apparent." A few more students trickled in during the winter, only to fall ill. Waldstein's departure in March 1890 for a conference at Troy added more disruption. Although the school year was supposed to last until June, Waldstein's comings and goings meant that, as Goodwin lamented, "even now, before the middle of April, the school is practically broken up and the building in charge of a servant."[28]

Back in Augusta, Paine's 1889–1890 school year began with great promise. John Gilbert taught four Higher Normal students, including Anna L. Gardner, the first woman to enroll in the college-level program (at Brown, they were still debating whether to admit women). His step-brother William Thomas continued in the Normal course, which was drawing students from as far away as Alabama, Florida, and Kentucky, and Ola Gilbert finished the classwork she had left undone at Fisk. His wife's studies may have encouraged Gilbert to do some additional work of his own in mathematics and surveying with the assistance of his colleague R. L. Campbell.[29]

Events forty-five miles southeast of Augusta overshadowed this progress. On December 28, 1889, a mob of masked men broke into Barnwell Courthouse, abducted eight black prisoners awaiting trial, shot them in the head, and tied their bodies to trees outside town. The "Barnwell Massacre" made national headlines. Even some white Southern papers joined in expressing outrage over the "cruel, cowardly, brutal deed." For weeks afterward Barnwell was on edge. There were disturbances in Augusta, too. The *Georgia Baptist*'s W. J. White tried to calm tempers: "The good people of Augusta, white and colored, have too much at stake to allow a crowd of drunken roughs, either white or colored, to destroy the peace and good order of the community." Even after peace returned to Augusta, the Gilberts had reason to worry about Barnwell, where Ola's sister Mollie and her husband Wesley Dixson lived.[30]

Against the grim news of this atrocity, A. E. P. Albert of the New
Orleans-based *Southwestern Christian Advocate* arrived at Paine
Institute early in January 1890. Less than two years before, Albert's
exposé on C. H. Carson's incendiary letter had spurred Gilbert's hiring
at Paine. Now, seeing the school firsthand, Albert was impressed. He
called the visit a "rare treat," praising George Williams Walker and the
school's faculty. Albert closed by noting Gilbert had won from Brown
"a Greek scholarship at Athens, Greece. He is now preparing to leave
for Greece." This is the first extant published notice of Gilbert's journey,
and it indicates he had made his final decision before Albert's visit. By
now, Ola was about five months pregnant; their daughter Alma would
be born in April or May 1890.[31]

A thousand miles north of Augusta, planning for the American
School's 1890–1891 session was under way. After the Orris debacle, the
Managing Committee needed an active, effective annual director and,
more importantly, someone who could get along with Charles Waldstein.
The Committee chose Dartmouth College's Rufus Richardson. Chair
Thomas Day Seymour wrote to assure Waldstein that Richardson was
"a genial gentleman, and familiar (more than most of us professors) with
vernacular French and German. Mrs. Richardson is . . . accustomed to
Society. I have no doubt that they will prove agreeable associates." There
was also the question of students. Around the time A. E. P. Albert visited
Paine, Seymour wrote Waldstein to explain the Managing Committee'
efforts to publicize the ASCSA, remarking "few Americans who are in-
clined to such a year of study and have the means for it are ignorant of
the situation. We have reason to expect more next year."[32]

The ASCSA at this time had no set requirements for its members.
Charles Waldstein thought the only necessary preparation was "an ordinary good college education and the reading of some general book [on
Greek sculpture], and some acquaintance with [Greek epigraphy]. . . .
[W]e only want some intelligent interest in the subject." It also seems
to have been left to individual Managing Committee members to recruit and select students. By early May, Seymour had news of three
students for 1890–1891: Carleton Brownson of Yale, Herbert De Cou
of Michigan, and "John W. Gilbert, Brown, '88." When the Managing

83

Committee met in Boston on May 23, 1890, Seymour announced
Bowdoin's John Dinsmore also planned to attend and that "a young
lady from Smith" and another from the Harvard Annex (precursor
of Radcliffe College) were interested, too (the ASCSA had accepted
women since Annie Peck in 1885). The official minutes do not name the
students, suggesting the committee was more focused on numbers than
individuals. The minutes do reveal that the issue of race came up, for
Gilbert appears as "one (a colored student) from Brown University."[33]

Confederate veteran Basil Gildersleeve, who scorned "the idea of
non-Caucasians as 'brothers,' " was a Managing Committee member in
1890. He had little interest in the School's affairs, however, and in ten
years attended just one committee meeting. Two whites-only schools, the
University of Virginia and the University of Missouri, briefly contributed
to the School in the 1880s, but neither had Managing Committee representatives. Meanwhile, as early as 1885, Howard University's Wiley
Lane had planned to attend the ASCSA. Massachusetts Senator G. F.
Hoar even appropriated federal funding for Lane's study in Greece.
Tragically, Lane died suddenly before departing. Though his correspondence with the Managing Committee is not preserved, Lane's
plans suggest the School was open to black scholars from the beginning. Had he survived to become the ASCSA's first African American
student in 1885–1886, Lane would have been classmates with Annie
Peck, the first officially enrolled woman student.[34]

A year after Lane died, prominent black classical scholar William
Sanders Scarborough explored possibilities for the ASCSA with
Managing Committee chair John Williams White. White sent
Scarborough a packet of information, adding that "if you will make
the facts which I have communicated to you known to any eligible
person among your friends I shall be greatly obliged to you." White
certainly knew who Scarborough was, and his letter shows the ASCSA
actively welcomed black American scholars. Scarborough wrote back
enthusiastically, declaring "I shall spend a year at Athens. This is fixed."
White in turn replied, "I am much interested in your proposed attendance." In the end, though, Scarborough could not find the funding to

get to Greece. With the help of Albert Harkness, Gilbert would fulfill Lane's and Scarborough's dreams.[35]

Well before the May 1890 Managing Committee meeting, people across the country knew Gilbert was going to Athens. The large circulation of the *Southwestern Christian Advocate*, a paper that was read both north and south, ensured the news spread widely. Other newspapers quickly picked up the story. On March 22, the *Indianapolis Freeman*, the nation's first illustrated African American newspaper, announced that "Prof. J. W. Gilbert, a colored man holding the chair of Greek at the Paine Institute, Augusta, Ga., will spend two years at the American School of Ancient Languages in Athens, Greece, this treat being a fellowship won from his Alma Mater, Brown University." The mention of "two years," absent from the *Advocate* piece, suggests the *Freeman* got its information elsewhere, possibly from a January or February report in the *Georgia Baptist*. The *Cleveland Gazette*, that city's first African American paper, probably followed the same source, for on March 22 it published a nearly identical announcement. Wherever the story originated, the *Freeman* made the unusual move of reprinting it at least thrice in subsequent months. Similar announcements soon popped up in Alabama, Virginia, and elsewhere. The most visible one was in the nationally circulated *New York Age*, which had previously highlighted Gilbert's accomplishments at Brown. E. A. P. Albert, who had first broken the news, also reprinted the "two years" announcement in early September 1890.[36]

The "two years" is a puzzle. It may be that Gilbert and Harkness initially expected Brown would provide two years of funding, as the ASCSA had envisaged member institutions would offer fellowships "for a residence of not less than two years at the School, to be obtained as the reward for distinguished proficiency in Classical studies during the undergraduate course." Or, Gilbert may have reduced his planned time abroad once the reality of being a father hit home at the end of April 1890. Whatever the explanation, Harkness's June 1890 official report to Brown states simply that "Mr. Gilbert will continue his studies next year at the American School of Classical Studies at Athens."[37]

Gilbert had read the School's annual reports and gotten additional information from Harkness. In Providence, he may have talked with Annie Peck. From these sources Gilbert would have known the School had conducted its first excavations in 1886, had dug at Plataea early in 1890, and had high hopes of securing the rights to explore Delphi. Yet archaeology was probably not foremost in his mind. Indeed, in mid-1890, the School had no firm excavation plans for the year ahead. While the topography and monuments of Athens must have attracted him, Gilbert may have looked forward above all to the American School's library, where he could focus on reading for his master's degree. The list Harkness assigned him survives as a handwritten entry in Brown's records: "1. Homer. The whole of the *Iliad* and of the *Odyssey*. 2. The Homeric Question. 3. Plato. *Phaedo*. 4. Demosthenes. Three Orations." Gilbert's 1888 classmate Charles Dennis had just completed a very similar master's degree program. As undergraduates, Gilbert and Dennis had learned about the debates over the date, authorship, and composition of the *Iliad* and *Odyssey*—the "Homeric Question." Heinrich Schliemann's excavations, starting at Troy in 1870 and followed by Mycenae and elsewhere in the 1870 and 1880s, had expanded this discussion beyond philology, as archaeologists used the Homeric texts to interpret newly unearthed remains of Bronze Age Greek civilization. Gilbert would now have the chance to meet Schliemann in Athens and to see Mycenae and other Bronze Age sites for himself.[38]

To Go Abroad Temporarily

Paine Institute's year ended on June 4, 1890, with commencement at Trinity CME Church, where twenty years before young Wesley Gilbert had gone to school with Miss Chestnut. Now, Professor Gilbert watched as his students, six women and two men, graduated from the Normal course. Five of the eight would be starting the collegiate program while he was in Athens. Three weeks later, Gilbert delivered a commencement address at Ware High School, Georgia's first and only public high school for black students. More than five hundred people attended. His was not the only speech, but he certainly fired up the crowd. In the audience was twelve-year-old R. R. Wright, Jr., the son of Ware's principal. More than a half-century later, Wright still credited Gilbert for stirring his own educational ambitions and setting him on the path to school "up north."[39]

School done, Gilbert prepared to travel. Paine's trustees granted him a leave of absence and authorized Walker to hire a temporary replacement: Thomas Cottin, who would come back from his Greek and Latin studies at Clark Atlanta University. In a striking testament to the trustees' confidence in him, Gilbert would receive his full salary for 1890–1891 plus several months in advance and additional CME support, some seven hundred and fifty dollars all told. How much Gilbert received from Brown is unknown, although in 1890 Brown's new president optimistically suggested five hundred dollars could support a student for a year in Europe, at a time when just crossing the Atlantic and getting to Athens cost between one and two hundred dollars. Gilbert first had to budget for his family. In addition to Ola and baby Alma, he was supporting his stepbrother William. He may also have been helping his mother Sarah. In an age before the widespread use of travelers' checks, he would take the remaining money abroad in the form of a letter of credit, enabling him to draw funds at banks in Greece.[40]

Sometime in July, Gilbert began filling out a passport application in Augusta. From this seemingly humdrum form emerges a complex set of invaluable clues and unsolvable mysteries. To begin with, although the Department of State recommended passports, they were not required for travel to Europe and the American School's guidance for students did not even mention them. Gilbert's decision to apply for a passport probably reflects advice he got from Harkness and possibly Annie Peck. Foreigners in Greece found passports useful for travel in the interior and receiving mail, among other things, and most of the School's previous students had gotten them. Gilbert may also have been thinking about travel to the Holy Land or study in Germany, both of which would require a passport.[41]

Beyond these practicalities, getting a passport was laden with symbolic meaning for black Americans. Until 1864, the US government had routinely withheld passports from free black people on the grounds that they were not citizens (ironically, slaves traveling abroad were sometimes listed on their masters' passports). In the post–Civil War years, passports were a means for black travelers to display their citizenship and express their American identity in the face of continued racism. Frederick Douglass, who was notoriously denied a passport by the US minister to Britain in 1859, was, by the 1880s, the last man in the world to need an identity document. Nonetheless, Douglass made a point of getting one before his 1886 trip to Europe.[42]

After completing the portion of the form that asked him to declare why he was "about to go abroad temporarily," Gilbert confronted the section labeled "description of applicant," with blanks for different physical characteristics. The handwriting shows Gilbert filled out these blanks himself: nose "straight;" mouth "evenly-cut, thin lips;" complexion "mulatto." These responses must reflect Gilbert's self-perception. Yet they may also suggest how he wanted to be perceived by the clerk in far-off Washington who would process his application. Even more striking is Gilbert's response to the part of the form reading "my father is a ___ ___ citizen of the United States." In that blank space, where applicants often wrote "native" or "naturalized," he wrote "native white." Had he actually learned something about his biological father since the 1870s? Was it another way to minimize any potential for a racist response from that far-away clerk, in an age when white officials easily took physical characteristics—hair, nose, lips, complexion—as foolproof markers of blackness? Or did he hope having those words on his passport would grant him the protective mantle of white Americanness abroad? Whatever the reason, neither Gilbert nor anyone else ever again refers to a white father. In later passport applications he lists his complexion as "dark" or "colored" and his mouth becomes "with mustache" or "medium," although his nose remains "straight" or "aquiline."[43]

After filling out the form, Gilbert had G. W. Walker sign as a witness to his identity in Augusta on July 23. The timing is significant. Travelers of the day often applied for passports at the last minute, sometimes even having the documents sent to a steamship office at their port of departure. The process was surprisingly speedy. An application mailed from New York or Philadelphia could result in a passport issued the next day in Washington. Even an application sent from Augusta could be received and processed in two to four days. Once a passport was issued, the postal service could get it back to Augusta from Washington in about thirty hours. Unless Gilbert was displaying an abundance of caution, the date of Walker's signature on his form suggests he planned to depart around the beginning of August. Since the American School would not open until October 1, Gilbert, like other School students before him, must have intended to travel in northern Europe before heading to Athens. The School's permanent director, Charles Waldstein, would soon recommend students "study the European museums during the greater part of August and September before they enter the School in the autumn." In fact, by July 1890, the School's annual director, Rufus Richardson, and the other students Gilbert would meet in Athens were already in Europe doing exactly that.[44]

Not until August 20, though, did Gilbert complete the final portion of the application: swearing the oath of allegiance before a notary public. He did so not in Augusta but in Barnwell, with his brother-in-law Wesley Dixson as the notary. The location suggests his wife and daughter would be staying with the Dixsons while he was in Greece, but the month-long delay is inexplicable. Was baby Alma sick? Had funding not come through? Whatever the reason, Gilbert then put his notarized application in the mail to Washington, asking that his passport be sent to Barnwell. Again, a mysterious delay: his passport was not issued until September 3.[45]

After what may have been a nail-biting wait, Gilbert's passport reached Barnwell in time for him to set off on Saturday, September 6. His departure got the attention of the local weekly, the *Barnwell People*, which reported Gilbert "left Barnwell on Saturday for Greece, via New York." "He expects," the article added, "to finish the two years course in one term and get back next June"—information most likely derived either from Gilbert himself or a family member. We can only imagine the scene as Gilbert took his leave at Barnwell. He had probably already said his goodbyes to G. W. Walker and others in Augusta. Possibly there was just a small group to see him off from Barnwell: Ola, baby Alma, stepbrother William, and his Dixson in-laws. Perhaps he saved his last kiss for little

Alma, not yet five months old. Then he turned north, toward the train for New York and the steamship that would carry him across the Atlantic.[46]

Atlantic Crossing

In 1890, Americans made some ninety thousand trips abroad, mostly to Europe. These travelers represented a fraction of the nation's sixty-three million people. They included a small but growing number of African Americans. Some went to study at schools from Glasgow to Berlin to Rome. Among them was classically educated Mary Eliza Church (later Mary Church Terrell), who spent 1888–1890 in Europe, returning home just months before Gilbert left for Athens. Others were clergymen, musicians, singers, or artists. A few were wealthy elites going to Europe for business or vacation, such as Washington lawyer and financier William Matthews.[47]

Black or white, American travelers stuck largely to western Europe. After his highly publicized 1889–1890 trip to the Holy Land and Greece, Brooklyn mega-preacher Thomas Dewitt Talmage claimed that "Out of the sixty-four millions [sic] of our present American population and the millions of our past only about five thousand have ever visited the Holy Land. Of all those who cross to Europe less than five per cent. ever get as far as Rome, and less than two per cent. ever get to Athens, and less than a quarter of one per cent. ever get to Palestine." A few black Americans had gotten to the Holy Land before Talmage. African Methodist Episcopal (AME) minister Daniel P. Seaton made his first visit in 1877–78 and returned in 1889 with African Methodist Episcopal Zion (AMEZ) minister Alexander Walters and others. Seaton and Walters, however, skipped Greece entirely, as travelers to the Holy Land often did before 1890. Although two black Americans are known to have gone to Greece before the US Civil War, in the three decades before Gilbert's trip just one recorded African American traveler went there: Frederick Douglass, who with his second wife Anna spent a week in Athens during March 1887.[48]

Departing from Barnwell, which lay just off the main rail lines, Gilbert could easily have caught an express train north. With luck, he might have reached New York by the evening of September 8. We know Gilbert was in Athens by September 30 and can trace his route there thanks to two letters he sent home to Augusta. Only a summary of the first letter remains. Just after reaching Athens, Gilbert wrote C. T. Walker, whom he had known since his first work as a teacher's assistant in the 1870s. In 1890, Walker was among Augusta's most prominent black leaders, the pastor of Tabernacle Baptist Church and new editor of the *Augusta Sentinel*. Walker probably published Gilbert's letter in the *Sentinel*, for the *Indianapolis Freeman* in late October reported "Prof. J.W. Gilbert writes Rev. C.T. Walker from Athens, Greece, that he had a safe passage, stopped in London, heard Mr. Spurgeon preach, visited Westminster Abbey, London Tower, House of Parliament, went to Paris and many other places of note." A second letter, datelined "American School, Athens, Greece, Dec. 8, 1890," initially appeared in the *Georgia Baptist*. Part of this letter survives because the *New York Age* reprinted an excerpt in late January 1891, under the title "A Georgian in Greece: An Augusta Student Gives His First Impressions of a Trip to Athens."[49]

In New York, Gilbert hurried to book his Atlantic crossing. Fortunately for him, the summer tourist rush to Europe was over. While incoming ships were crammed, outbound tickets were plentiful. Here Gilbert's letter to C. T. Walker provides crucial clues. To visit Parliament, which was only open on Saturdays, and hear Mr. Spurgeon—the renowned preacher Charles Spurgeon—on a Sunday, Gilbert must have spent the weekend of September 20–21 in London. To do so, he had to have taken one of the seven steamships that left New York between September 9 and 13 and arrived in England before September 20. He is not on the passenger lists of the two that went to Southampton, so he must have gone to Liverpool, where the five others all arrived on September 19. Unfortunately, we cannot tell which of those five Gilbert took, for Liverpool's incoming September passenger lists have perished.[50]

The Guion Line's *Nevada* sailed the earliest, on September 9, but even if Gilbert reached New York in time to catch her, *Nevada* was old, slow, and no bargain. Instead, he could easily have found an economical second-class or even first-class berth on any of the other four ships, all of which sailed less than half-full. Perhaps he scored a spot on the Cunard liner *Gallia*, departing on September 10, or better yet on Cunard's speedy, steel-hulled, electric-lighted *Etruria*, which left on September 13 with barely a third of her cabins occupied. Frederick Douglass on his 1845 voyage to England on a Cunard ship had been forced to travel in steerage. He endured similar racial discrimination on his 1847 return, prompting such outrage in England that shipowner Samuel Cunard publicly apologized, declaring "nothing of the kind will again take place." By Gilbert's day the Cunard Line had earned a reputation as a friend to black travelers. John Patterson Green, one of the first African Americans to hold elected office in Ohio, recalled of his trans-Atlantic trips in the 1880s and 1890s that "for fear of being discriminated against, on account of being a colored man, I had shipped, both when alone and with my family, on a Cunarder, where I felt sure, no proscription would be made." Whichever ship he took, whether in first or second class, Gilbert could expect courteous treatment from the officers and crew. Pleasant conversations with fellow travelers may have marked his week's voyage across the Atlantic, unless he encountered a white Southerner. As Harlem minister H. A. Monroe observed after his summer 1890 trip to Europe, "Why is it that your average Southerner cannot travel without exposing his most ridiculous weakness—his fear and hatred of the Negro?"[51]

Liverpool did not rate high in guidebooks, but arriving there was exhilarating for African Americans. Journalist Ida B. Wells remarked in 1894: "To a colored person . . . it is like being born into another world, to be welcomed among persons of the highest order of intellectual and social culture as if one were one themselves . . . [to] ride in any sort of conveyance in any part of the country without being insulted, stop at any hotel, or be accommodated at any restaurant one wishes without being refused with contempt; wander into any picture gallery, lecture-room, concert hall, theater, or church and receive only the most courteous treatment from officials and fellow sight-seers." John P. Green felt overcome by a new sense of national belonging: "I immediately forgot that I was a colored American citizen, and . . . presto, I had changed to a full-fledged citizen—abroad, still under the Aegis of my dear native land." Similar feelings may well have filled Gilbert's heart, but he had little time to savor them. After disembarking at the sprawling Mersey docks and passing through the cursory customs inspection, he hurried to catch a train for the five-hour ride to London.[52]

Gilbert's route is revealing. According to the American School's official travel advice, the quickest and cheapest routes to Athens lay through Le Havre, Antwerp, Bremen, or Hamburg. Given the press of time, Gilbert might well have headed straight for Greece, yet he clearly considered London worth the extra time and expense. It is a good reminder of his interests in English literature, particularly Shakespeare, and of the English history he had studied at Brown. Gilbert spent a Saturday taking in the sights: Parliament, Westminster Abbey, the Tower of London, and whatever else he could fit in. Perhaps the highlight of his weekend was hearing Baptist minister Charles Haddon Spurgeon speak before an audience of thousands at the Metropolitan Tabernacle on Sunday, September 21. Born in 1834, Haddon had won renown as "the Prince of Preachers" for his spellbinding oratory and ministerial activism. Although his health was failing, Spurgeon in 1890 was still the most famous preacher in world. Among African Americans, he was particularly known for his outspoken opposition to slavery, a stance that had incited white Southerners to burn copies of his sermons before the Civil War. After the war, Spurgeon welcomed black students to his Pastor's College. Hearing Mr. Spurgeon was high on the list for black American travelers, including Frederick Douglass, who attended a sermon in June 1887.[53]

London to Athens

Gilbert's stay in London was all too brief. He now had about a week to reach to Athens, a journey the guidebooks said required more than four days of continuous travel even without stopovers or delays. Traveling solo would be particularly grueling, although Gilbert's knowledge of French and German probably served him well as he crossed the continent. The evidence of his first letter takes us as far as Paris, which he could have reached in about twelve hours from London via Dover and Calais. If he saw nothing else in Paris, Gilbert must have marveled at the brand-new addition to the city's skyline: a thousand-foot-tall wrought-iron tower named after its builder, Gustave Eiffel. From Paris, the trail disappears save for a fleeting mention in Gilbert's second letter of passing through the mountains of Switzerland and Italy. Whichever rail route he took, he reached the port of Brindisi in southern Italy, some 1,200 rail miles from Paris, before midnight on Friday, September 26, in time to catch the weekly steamer across the Adriatic for the Greek port of Patras. Arriving at Brindisi, Gilbert may have been reminded of the tradition that the poet Virgil had died there after arriving from Greece. The voyage to Patras took at least twenty-four hours, broken only by a brief mid-day layover at the island of Corfu. On the way down from Corfu, the steamer passed Odysseus's home island of Ithaca and then the coastal town of Missolonghi, scene of Lord Byron's death in 1824. A weary John Gilbert finished this final sea leg of his odyssey and landed at Patras in Greece (see Map 2), probably early on Sunday, September 28.[54]

MAP 2 Greece in 1890–1891

The surviving excerpt from Gilbert's second letter begins with his arrival at Patras after the twelve-hour trip from Corfu. His description of Patras, "seat of the nomarch [prefect] of Achaia-Elis and of a Greek archbishop," comes straight from Baedeker's 1889 guidebook to Greece. The ensuing paragraph, though written months after his arrival, vividly conveys the sense of culture shock Gilbert still remembered about that landing: "Such a horde of dirty Greeks and even Turks as one meets when he steps ashore at Patras baffles all attempts at description. At a veritable Babel of tongues you are in the hands of people whose very looks make you feel for your watch, and catch a tighter grip upon your satchel." Gilbert's Orientalist language is similar to that many American travelers employed, yet between the yelling, pushing boatmen looking to ferry passengers from steamer to wharf, the peddlers, beggars, and baggage touts, and the surly customs inspectors, Patras was indeed overwhelming. While the inspectors were mostly on the lookout for imported cigars, Gilbert likely piqued their interest. They had probably met black merchant sailors, but never a black American scholar. If Gilbert faced questions about his identity, his passport now proved its worth. Unlike most foreign travelers, he knew some modern Greek, "just enough to be understood" as he puts it. We can only imagine how the customs inspectors might have reacted when they discovered this particular American spoke their language, though it is a good guess his language skills were even more helpful than his passport.[55]

The food on the Brindisi steamers was atrocious, and Gilbert's first stop in Greece was to eat. Judging it "injurious to your health and dangerous to your belongings to go to any small restaurant or cheap place," he found his way to the Hôtel de Patras, the only hotel in town with a restaurant. There, he "breathe[d] a sigh of relief" and enjoyed his first Greek meal: "some boiled weeds, grapes, chestnuts, bread, meat and . . . a glass of goat's milk." The "boiled weeds" were *horta*, the dandelion, amaranth, or other wild greens that still grace Greek tables today.[56]

Thus nourished, Gilbert was soon on his way. By mid-morning, he was on a train east toward Corinth and Athens. He was among the first

Americans to take this route, as the line between Patras and Corinth had just opened in November 1888. A veteran rail rider, Gilbert was unimpressed by what he called the "narrow-gauge, dog-trot railroad" that would take about eight hours to chug just 137 miles to Athens. On the other hand, the slow pace made for splendid sightseeing.[57]

The Patras–Corinth line ran along the north edge of the Peloponnesus, skirting the Gulf of Corinth, through a fertile agricultural region thick with luxuriant grape vineyards, olive groves, and mulberry plantations. Above the narrow coastal plains rose low hills, all cultivated, and behind them Mount Cyllene, famous in mythology as the birthplace of Hermes. Across the blue gulf shimmered more mountains including snow-capped Parnassus, towering above the ancient site of Delphi. "All along the route," he enthuses, "picturesque mountains . . . shoot their craggy summits beyond the cloud, or let torrents of crystal waters leap with a mighty roar throughout their deep gorges."[58]

The flourishing agriculture also drew Gilbert's eye. He says nothing of olives—growing up in Georgia, he may have never before seen an olive tree—but the vines captivated him. "We cannot pass on," he insists, "before reverting to the vineyards which are filled with pretty, scantily clad maidens, and mountain bred lads." From the train, he could hear these workers "pouring out sweet melody in song." The sight conjured up the ancient world he knew through texts. "It is not a strain for fancy," he continues, "to picture here an age many centuries past, in which history overtasks itself in trying to follow the thread of truth through a labyrinth of mythical legends; for here we see the wine press, the fruit, the sheepskin bottles and all the concomitants fit for a festival of Bacchus." Gilbert's description, though romanticized, was no mere literary flight. Others who traveled same route at the same time of year report much the same sights, including the wine skins and the fields busy with men and women. Gilbert's wine presses, though, were probably hogshead barrels for dried currants. American minister Nathan Hubbell, passing through in September 1889, saw men "standing in the half-filled casks, stamping energetically with their heavy shoes to make room for more of the fruit then being brought to them."[59]

The vast vineyards Gilbert saw from his train represented the heart of Greece's economy. In the 1860s and 1870s, the *phylloxera* aphid had devastated western European vines. Nearly two-thirds of France's vineyards were hit, causing French wine prices to skyrocket. Although they spread as far as California and Australia, the aphids spared Greece. The country's grape production exploded, with 90% of the crop being dried for export as Zante currants or *raisins de Corinthe*. France alone was importing 69,500 tons a year by 1889, much of it for brewing artificial wine. The sweet little nuggets also became political players: in 1886, Greek premier Charilaos Tricoupis hinted the French might gain the rights to excavate ancient Delphi if only they would cut import taxes on Greek currants. France's vines were recovering by 1890, but when Gilbert passed along the Peloponnesian coast that September day, currants still comprised the majority of Greece's exports. Otherwise, the country remained underdeveloped. Indeed, just one of the massive textile factories back in Augusta ran more cotton spindles than the entire nation of Greece put together.[60]

Afternoon wore on. As the train chugged east, the coastal plain broadened out, offering vistas of the Gulf of Corinth to the left and the mountains of the Peloponnesus to the right. But Gilbert's attention had shifted from landscape to history. "Before you reach Athens," he writes, "you will pass a number of places connected with Bible story, chief among which is Corinth of Pauline fame." He could now see the enormous rock of Acrocorinth, the fortress-crowned peak of the ancient city. Below Acrocorinth, he could make out a handful of temple columns on a low hill. "Those ruins which you see over there," he observes, "mark the spot where ancient Corinth stood." The train stopped at New Corinth, founded after an earthquake destroyed the old village in 1858. Although Gilbert remarks that "until to-day the inhabitants of this plain like to point out the traditional place where St. Paul established 'the church at Corinth,' " it is not clear whether he had the time to visit the ancient site, which lies several miles southwest of the modern town.[61]

From New Corinth the train huffed on, crossing over the still unfinished canal that would link the Gulf of Corinth to the north with the

Saronic Gulf to the south. As his rail car crossed the new iron bridge two hundred feet above the canal line, Gilbert could see in the day's fading light the deep trench stretching out to the sea at both ends of the isthmus of Corinth. It was a stupendous sight compared to the canal that had brought his home town prosperity in the 1880s. While Chinese laborers had helped dig Augusta's canal, much of the Corinth canal's 1,200-strong workforce consisted of Armenians, Italians, and Montenegrins.[62]

Crossing the canal and turning south, the train ran east along the edge of the Saronic Gulf, the tracks clinging dramatically to the cliffside above the water. Like other educated American travelers passing this spot, Gilbert probably thought of the mythological bandit Sciron, who delighted in kicking travelers off the precipice into the gulf—until the Athenian hero Theseus slew him. Then came places Gilbert knew from Herodotus and other ancient authors: Megara, once a trade power-house and fierce rival to Athens, now a dusty village; the island of Salamis, where the Athenians sought refuge from Persian invasion in 480 BC; Eleusis, home of the sacred rites of the Eleusinian Mysteries. The train arced out from the coast, skirting Mount Aegaleion, where the Persian king Xerxes had sat watching from his throne as the Greek fleet scattered his armada, and at last made the final turn toward Athens.[63]

John Wesley Gilbert had traveled more than 6,200 miles by foot, horse, rail, and sea to reach Athens. It had been three weeks since he set out from Barnwell, but in another sense his journey had begun in Miss Chestnut's Augusta schoolroom almost twenty years before. As his train came around the shoulder of Mount Aegaleion and descended into the plain of Attica, Gilbert caught his first glimpse of the Acropolis. We can do no better than to relive that moment in his own words: "The sun is setting and we have been traveling well-nigh the whole day; but tired as we are, how glad it makes us feel to see in the distance that as yet undistinguishable collection of marble buildings upon a very high table land. A flood of golden light upon the marble columns, friezes, architraves, etc., makes a sight never to be forgotten, a sight nothing less than glorious."[64]

4

THE AMERICAN
SCHOOL

As John Gilbert watched the sun's last rays light up the Acropolis that clear September evening, other Americans were completing their own journeys to Athens. Their paths and Gilbert's would join at the new American School of Classical Studies at Athens building, below rocky Mount Lycabettus on the eastern outskirts of the city. Official reports name Gilbert's fellow students—Carleton Brownson, Andrew Fossum, John Pickard—and Professor Rufus Richardson, along with Mrs. Richardson, the first spouse ever to accompany an Annual Director to the School. Those reports also mention "Miss Harris and Miss Potter," the only official hint that Pickard brought family: his wife Jeanie, her first cousin Edith Harris, their friend Emma Potter, and Jeannie's mother, Caroline Gerrish. During 1890–1891, Caroline and Edith wrote several dozen letters home from Athens to family in Portsmouth, New Hampshire. Nearly all these letters survive today, offering priceless inside glimpses of the American School group and of everyday life in Athens, material no official source would ever think to include. Caroline Gerrish could not have known how prescient she was when she asked her sister Harriet "to keep my letters, because I have no journal and they may sometime be of interest."[1]

They Will Do Good Work

When Gilbert left the United States, he already knew Annual Director Rufus Richardson would lead the School during the fall. Permanent Director Charles Waldstein was not expected from England until January 1891. Albert Harkness may have told Gilbert the names of other students who were expected to attend, but the Managing Committee's lists had little certainty: only two of the four men formally announced in spring 1890 actually showed up in Athens that fall. John Gilbert was one; Carleton Brownson was the other.[2]

In his later career, Carleton Lewis Brownson was a distinguished Classics professor and dean of the City College of New York. His translation of the *Anabasis*, the famous war memoir by the Athenian writer Xenophon, remains widely used today. In 1890, Brownson was just twenty-four, slight and unassuming. The son of a respected physician from New Canaan, Connecticut, Brownson attended Yale, where he overcame severe illness to excel at ancient languages. His Greek professor, Thomas Day Seymour, found him "enthusiastic and docile." Graduating in 1887, Brownson traveled in Europe with his father before returning to Yale for graduate work. Yale had been among the American School's original sponsors, and, with Seymour now chair of the Managing Committee, campus interest in the School was growing. Between 1888 and 1890, three Yale students, all holding generous fellowships, went to Athens. Now it was Brownson's turn. He left Connecticut in late June or early July 1890, spent the summer in Europe (the details are a blur), and reached Athens around the same time as John Gilbert. Brownson must have looked forward to a busy year at the American School. Little did he know he would meet his future wife there.[3]

If Brownson represented the established northeastern elite, Andrew Fossum represented one of the new waves of immigrants reshaping the United States. Aged twenty-nine when he arrived in Athens, gray-eyed and intense, Fossum grew up on a farm in northeast Iowa. His parents and three of his eight siblings had come from Norway in the 1850s; the family spoke Norwegian at home. Fossum graduated in 1882 from

Luther College, a school founded to train ministers for Iowa's growing Norwegian Lutheran community. He followed several Luther alumni to Johns Hopkins University in Baltimore, where he studied Greek, Latin, Sanskrit, and ancient history. Fossum wrote a dissertation on Plato under the supervision of Basil Gildersleeve. He got his PhD in 1887, making him one of the first half-dozen Norwegian Americans to obtain doctorates.[4]

For the next two years, Fossum taught at a New York preparatory academy, the Drisler School, run by Frank Drisler, a son of Columbia professor and American School trustee Henry Drisler. Fossum's main impetus toward the School came from another Columbia professor, Augustus Merriam, who had been Annual Director in 1887–1888. By early 1889, Fossum was determined to go to Greece. He and John Gilbert show up together on the student list for 1889–1890, but Fossum had trouble financing his trip. He even wrote Iowa Senator William Allison to ask whether he could be made US Consul in Athens, in hopes that holding the consular position would enable him to attend the School. In summer 1889, Fossum made it as far as Paris before lack of money forced him back to the United States. After a year teaching Greek and Latin at the Hill School in Pennsylvania, he finally scraped together enough cash to embark on what a girlfriend called "the dream of [his] life."[5]

Fossum left New York in late June 1890, spent time in Berlin and Dresden, and reached Athens at the beginning of September. An account he scrawled in pencil around 1937 illuminates his early days in Greece. Fossum found the School empty except for the caretaker, Constantinos Ioannides. Costi, as the Americans called him, apparently had no list of students and refused to let Fossum stay in the building before October 1, the School's official opening date. After a few days at a boarding house in Athens, Fossum went off to explore the Peloponnesus. He got as far as the remote mountaintop Temple of Apollo at Bassae, then rode down on horseback to Olympia. At the end of September, he caught the train at Pyrgos near Olympia and returned to Athens just a day or two after John Gilbert landed at Patras.[6]

Having "bummed around for almost a month with all kinds of people in a strange country living in the manner of the land and talking the best I could the native lingo," Fossum became intent on perfecting his Greek. That meant avoiding other Americans. As he put it, "if two or more go together they invariably talk their own language and resort to the native language only when they have to. They might as well stay at home." He was also conscious of holding a doctoral degree from what was then the leading graduate research institution in the United States, obtained under the direction of the country's leading classical scholar. When he was not off on his own, Fossum gravitated to the company of professors. While the other students would come to appreciate his fluent Greek, none became close with him.[7]

The student with whom John Gilbert became closest in Greece shows up nowhere in the Managing Committee's lists. Tall, mustached, and bespectacled, John Pickard celebrated his thirty-second birthday soon after reaching Athens. His father, a descendant of Huguenot refugees, was a cabinet maker who prospered enough to buy a farm near Concord, New Hampshire, and educate his sons. After excelling in public school, Pickard received private tutoring from Amos Hadley, New Hampshire's first public school superintendent. In 1880, the same year that lack of money forced Gilbert to leave Atlanta Baptist Seminary, Pickard enrolled as a sophomore at Hadley's alma mater, Dartmouth College.[8]

While two of his brothers became doctors, Pickard turned toward ancient Greece under the influence of John Henry Wright, his Greek instructor at Dartmouth. Wright had lived in Persia (today Iran) and studied Sanskrit at Leipzig. His older sister Lucy Wright Mitchell was the first American ever to publish a book on ancient sculpture, and Wright was keenly interested in Greek art and archaeology. He even convinced Dartmouth's skeptical president to contribute to the newly founded American School. Wright's case for supporting the ASCSA gained strength in fall 1882, the start of Pickard's senior year, as Dartmouth finally filled a long-vacant chair in Greek language and literature. Greek was optional for Dartmouth seniors, but Pickard nonetheless got to know the new professor: Rufus Richardson.[9]

After graduating in 1883, Pickard taught in Vermont. In 1885, he moved to Portsmouth, New Hampshire, to become principal of the city's integrated public high school. Pickard won praise for his leadership of the school. Like John Gilbert, he was deeply interested in English literature and often taught English courses as well as Greek and Latin. He became active in state teachers' associations and Portsmouth community groups, and kept up close ties with Dartmouth. Around the time Gilbert went to Brown in 1886, Pickard received his Dartmouth master's degree, awarded upon payment of five dollars to "graduates of three years' standing who had sustained good characters and been engaged in literary pursuits."[10]

In Portsmouth, John Pickard met Jeanie Gerrish, the granddaughter of a prosperous and respected apothecary, or pharmacist. Jeanie's mother Caroline had married Boston attorney George Gerrish. George was wounded in the Civil War and died in 1866, after which Caroline Gerrish took five-year-old Jeanie and baby brother Arthur back to Portsmouth. They moved in with Jeanie's grandparents and her aunt Harriet McEwen Kimball, a noted composer of hymns and devotional verse. Another aunt, Lucy Kimball Harris, and her children Edith and Mary often visited, while Lucy's engineer husband Robert Harris was away building railroads in the United States and Mexico. John and Jeanie seem to have met around 1888. They were married in Portsmouth on July 15, 1889. "A brilliant society wedding," the newspapers called it. Among the guests was Illinois Congressman John Farnsworth, a close friend of Abraham Lincoln. The newlyweds departed straight from the reception for an unusual honeymoon: two years in Europe.[11]

Whether John Pickard had the American School on his agenda when he and Jeanie left Portsmouth is unclear, but he clearly meant to study Greek antiquities because the couple headed first to the University of Leipzig, home of preeminent classical art historian Johannes Overbeck. During winter 1889–1890 at Leipzig, John Pickard met several Americans with recent experience of Athens. Walter Miller, one of Overbeck's most dedicated students, had spent 1885–1886 at the American School and directed the first US excavation in Greece. Another student, Carl Buck, had just come from two years in Greece, where he, too, had conducted excavations. If Pickard did not already have plans for Athens, conversations with Miller and Buck likely pushed him that way. The news that his old Dartmouth professor Rufus Richardson would be the School's Annual Director for 1890–1891 may have clinched Pickard's decision.[12]

In April 1890, the Pickards moved to Berlin. There, John attended classes with famous German archaeologists including Ernst Curtius, the excavator of ancient Olympia. By early June, he met up with Rufus Richardson, who had brought his family across the Atlantic and left them to vacation in Germany's Harz Mountains while he went to Berlin to prepare for the coming year. Richardson and Pickard spent their days studying Greek vases in the Berlin archaeological museum. They also got advice about Athens from the Managing Committee's Augustus Merriam, who was in Berlin that summer.[13]

In mid-June, Jeanie's mother Caroline Gerrish (Figure 4.1), cousin Edith Harris (Figure 4.2), and friend Emma Potter joined the Pickards in Berlin. The only daughter of a wealthy Boston merchant, Emma Potter had been a bridesmaid at John and Jeanie's wedding and was fresh off an eight-month-long round-the-world trip with her father and stepmother. Since the School building could not accommodate his family, John Pickard had to make other living arrangements for Athens. He turned to a young Greek student, Francis Demetrios Kalopothakes. Frank, as his American friends called him, had graduated from Harvard in 1888, spent a year back home in Athens as a member of the American School, and came to Berlin in 1889 to begin his doctoral studies. His father, Presbyterian minister M. D. Kalopothakes, was a pillar of support for the American School and often boarded American visitors at his home in Athens. With Frank's help, Pickard arranged for his family to spend the coming year with the Kalopothakes family.[14]

The Pickards left Berlin for Dresden in mid-July, about the time John Gilbert was filling out his passport application in Augusta. After several more weeks in Germany and more than a month in Switzerland, they took ship at Marseilles and arrived in Athens on September 23, while Gilbert was still dashing across the continent from Paris to Brindisi.

FIGURE 4.1 Caroline Gerrish, circa 1895.
Courtesy of the Portsmouth Athenaeum, Portsmouth, New Hampshire.

"We have at last reached our, or rather John's Mecca," Caroline Gerrish remarked in her first letter from Athens.[15]

Meanwhile, Rufus Richardson and his family were also on their way from Germany to Athens. Richardson's path to academia had not been easy. His father, a Massachusetts farmer, died when Richardson was three, leaving his mother to raise five children. Young Rufus apprenticed as a shoemaker. Just shy of his seventeenth birthday in

FIGURE 4.2 Edith Harris, September 1890.
Courtesy of the Portsmouth Athenaeum, Portsmouth, New Hampshire.

1862, he lied about his age and enlisted in the Union Army with his older brother Alfred. Typhoid killed Alfred in Virginia, but Rufus survived and after the war was able to enroll at Yale. He graduated in 1869, then went on to Yale Divinity School and two years of theological study in Berlin, but his interests shifted toward Greek literature after he returned to Yale in 1874. In 1877, he married Alice Bowen, sister of a graduate school classmate. After getting his doctoral degree in 1878, Richardson taught in Massachusetts and Indiana before going to Dartmouth in 1882. He became renowned as a teacher. Yale students respected him for his knowledge, courtesy, and willingness to listen, while a Dartmouth alumnus noted he had "known many teachers . . . but never one more genuinely gifted." Richardson even incorporated student feedback into his school text of Aeschines's oration *Against Ctesiphon*.[16]

The Managing Committee's choice of Richardson reflected not only his teaching ability but also his wife's social status, which it hoped might smooth relations with the American School's Permanent Director, Charles Waldstein. Alice Linden Bowen Richardson was a descendant of Benjamin Franklin and her family often welcomed US presidents to its Connecticut estate. In 1839, her grandfather Lewis Tappan, a successful New York merchant and prominent abolitionist, had raised money to assist the Africans of the slave ship *Amistad*. Her father Henry Chandler Bowen helped found *The Independent*, a church weekly that was a key anti-slavery voice before the Civil War and retained a national circulation for decades afterward. Her older brother Clarence—Rufus's classmate—earned Yale's first History PhD and was a founder of the American Historical Association. Alice herself had traveled widely in Europe and studied in Germany. There was another benefit to this family connection: during 1890–1891, *The Independent* would publish some twenty American School–related items, including an article by John Gilbert.[17]

After a week on Corfu, the Richardsons reached Athens about the last day of September. Along with them came their young children Lucy, Gardner, and Dorothy, an unnamed German governess, and twenty-one-year-old Ethel Moore, the fiancée of Alice Richardson's younger brother John. John Bowen had died suddenly in January 1890, just four days before the wedding, but the Richardsons considered Moore a sister-in-law.[18]

While the Pickards settled in with Reverend Kalopothakes, the Richardsons moved into the School building and the other students soon arrived. In early October, Rufus Richardson sent his first update to Permanent Director Charles Waldstein at Cambridge University: "Four students reported to me at the beginning of the year. Pickard, Fossum,

Brownson, and Gilbert. They are men who with good guidance will do good work."[19]

Into the School

Today, the American School's campus sits amid the concrete apartment blocks and car-clogged streets of Kolonaki, Athens' ritziest neighborhood. When John Gilbert first set eyes on the brand-new School building in fall 1890, it lay nearly alone below the slopes of Mount Lycabettus (Figure 4.3). Next door was the British School. Beyond that, the closest neighbors were the old Asomaton monastery (recently converted into military barracks) a few hundred yards east and the new Evangelismos hospital to the south. To the west, scattered houses and construction sites marked the rapid expansion of urban Athens. Rumor had it the Italians might soon build an archaeological school nearby.[20]

FIGURE 4.3 The American School of Classical Studies at Athens under construction, circa 1888. Structures of the former Asomaton monastery are visible to the left of the American School building.
Courtesy of the American School of Classical Studies at Athens.

The main attraction of the School's location was the view, an "unrivalled panorama" stretching east, south, and west. The architect optimistically predicted "the open ground on all sides promises to leave [this view] to us forever." There was plentiful clean water from a nearby aqueduct, built by the Roman emperor Hadrian, that still supplied much of Athens. On the other hand, the School was so far from the city center that guidebook maps did not even show the neighborhood. The nearest shops were a half-mile away. The dirt roads around the School were, Edith Harris observed, "awful, in dry weather as well as in wet, and bad for a pedestrian as well as for a carriage." When it rained, the gully at the east edge of the property became a torrent. And, in contrast to the British School's tidy garden, the American School grounds were "a bare hillside, unplanted, unfenced, and overrun with goats and dogs."[21]

The building itself was a four-level showcase of American technology and industry, with everything from windows to flush toilets imported from the United States. The construction was less impressive. Part of a balcony would fall off in spring 1891, nearly taking along Ethel Moore, and the roof would leak for years. The ground floor entry led to two wings of bedrooms: one for Richardson and his family, the other for students. Downstairs were the kitchen, laundry, and quarters for the Greek staff—Costi the caretaker, Nikolaki the cook, Katrina the maid—and the anonymous German governess. Upstairs were a dining room, a drawing room, and a library, and on the top floor two more bedrooms and a shaded terrace. Through the summer and fall Richardson, Waldstein, and the Managing Committee had conducted a lengthy, sometimes contentious correspondence about housing. They finally agreed Waldstein would get the top floor to himself, that they would have joint use of the dining and drawing rooms, and that Richardson's children would not come to meals.[22]

For Gilbert, the building's key feature was its large, comfortable, well-lit library. Its rapidly expanding collection, sixteen hundred volumes and counting, was worlds beyond anything he would ever have access to back in Augusta. For the latest scholarship on Greece, it was better than the library at Brown or indeed most other American universities. Anything the Americans did not have, Gilbert could find in the British School library next door.[23]

Soon after moving in, Richardson wrote Waldstein that the ground floor offered "ample sleeping room for [my family] and the students with something to spare." Andrew Fossum was probably first into the student wing, for he recalls having his pick of its four rooms: "Prof. Merriam had told me to take the south-west room which had a view of Hymettus and the sea with Aegina and so I did." Judging from Richardson's first update to Waldstein, Gilbert arrived around the same time and took one of the remaining rooms.[24]

Prejudice?

Or did he? In a 1901 speech to a Methodist missionary conference in New Orleans, Gilbert's mentor George Williams Walker asserted that when Gilbert arrived at the American School, "there he met prejudice, for in that school they didn't want a Negro to board, so they put the price so high that my boy, John Wesley Gilbert (a good Methodist name, you see), couldn't go into the school and board. But he had been trained with the Southern Methodist people, and he knew what was expected; and so he turned aside and, without breathing a sigh or shedding a tear, went into a Greek home, got a modern Greek grammar, studied the language, and talked with the family."[25]

Gilbert himself wrote home to Paine Institute in fall 1890, but all we have is a second-hand report that "he enjoys his position very much." Of more significance is a notice *The Independent* printed early in January 1891: "One colored young man, John Wesley Gilbert, of Georgia, has gone to Athens to enter the American School there. He will find very little race prejudice in that classic land." The use of Gilbert's full name and home state, neither of which appears in 1890 news reports, suggests the source may have been someone at the School, if not Gilbert himself, very possibly Rufus Richardson, who regularly sent dispatches to his father-in-law's paper. Somewhere in the gap between this contemporary evidence and Walker's later story rests the reality of John Gilbert's experience.[26]

Could Gilbert's fellow students have objected to boarding with him? John Pickard, as we will see, developed a close relationship with Gilbert, but Pickard was not living at the School. We have less to go on with Brownson and Fossum. Neither mentions Gilbert in their later reminiscences of Greece, suggesting they did not become close with him. Nonetheless, Brownson and Fossum clearly worked with Gilbert throughout the year and shared very close quarters with him during the winter 1891 Eretria excavations. Fossum, it is true, got his doctoral degree at all-white Johns Hopkins under the unapologetic racist Basil Gildersleeve, but that does not prove he imbibed Gildersleeve's views. Instead, Fossum remembered that after he reached the School, "three more students arrived and the work was organized," suggesting he did not set Gilbert apart from the others.[27]

Even if Brownson or Fossum objected to Gilbert, only Rufus Richardson could exclude him from the building. Richardson's first update to Waldstein lists the students as "Pickard, Fossum, Brownson, and Gilbert." In an essay he mailed to Dartmouth later in the fall, Richardson described his "four regular students [who] have completed the full courses of classical study at Dartmouth, Yale, Johns Hopkins, and Brown University." Careful readers will note Gilbert comes last in both texts, but that hardly proves Walker's story. It is also difficult to believe Albert Harkness, who had worked so hard to get Gilbert to Athens, would have countenanced such an action. Other members of the Managing Committee, Henry Drisler for one, had vociferously rejected race prejudice in the 1860s and earlier. And, during the 1880s the School's leadership had actively welcomed black scholars Wiley Lane and William Sanders Scarborough.[28]

It is also important to consider here Scarborough's experience with the American Philological Association (APA) during the 1880s. "The men and women of those days," he later recalled, "thought more of scholarship and less of prejudice; the color of a man made no difference with them. It was his standing as a scholar and as a representative of American scholarship that counted. The Harvard, Yale, Columbia, New York, Cornell, and even some of the Princeton men vied with one another to make me, the only [active] Negro member of the Association at that time, feel at home. It was then that I felt an American scholar was an American scholar, be he white or black." Among those Yale men was Rufus Richardson, who saw Scarborough at three APA meetings in the 1880s and served with him on a committee. Hosting the Dartmouth gathering in 1884, Richardson took Scarborough and other members on an excursion to Lake Memphremagog in Canada. On this trip, Scarborough formed lasting friendships with men "who ever after made me feel that I was one of their number and gave courteous attention with no hint of prejudice."[29]

It is possible, therefore, that Walker misremembered something Gilbert wrote from Athens. Recall that Andrew Fossum reached the School early, was turned away by the caretaker Costi, and had to find a room elsewhere. Gilbert got to the School several days before its official opening and was probably also turned away, an event that could have formed the basis for Walker's later story. Indeed, in the same speech Walker erroneously describes "some Boston ladies" hiring Gilbert as a tour guide, suggesting an imperfect memory of events a decade past. If Gilbert did in fact live with a Greek family, the obvious place would have been with Reverend Kalopothakes, but John Pickard and company were already there. The next choice might have been a family from Kalopothakes's church or from Athens's tiny Baptist congregation, which had also helped American School students in years past. Yet no trace of a Greek host family survives. That silence alone proves nothing, but if he had lived with a Greek family for several months, it is hard to believe Gilbert could still write about encountering "a horde of dirty Greeks" at Patras. In the end, the balance of contemporary evidence suggests that even if we cannot definitively disprove it, we should not accept Walker's story.[30]

A Thoroughly Modern City

During his first days in Athens, Gilbert must have made the short walk up from the American School to Mount Lycabettus. From the summit, he enjoyed a spectacular view of the city (Figure 4.4), free of the concrete and smog that greet visitors today. To his left were

FIGURE 4.4 Looking southwest from the lower slope of Mount Lycabettus toward the Athenian Acropolis, 1895. Many of the houses in the foreground were not yet built when Gilbert arrived in Athens.

Library of Congress, https://www.loc.gov/item/2018650437/.

the scrub-covered ridges of Mounts Hymettus and Pentele, famous for their marble. Below him sat the American and British Schools. Beyond them, he could trace the streambed of the Ilissus, along whose banks Socrates had strolled. Following the line of the Ilissus rightward toward the city center, he could not miss the squat royal palace of King George I. Beyond the palace rose the tall columns of the Olympieion, the Temple of Olympian Zeus. Gilbert might just have been able to see the Arch of Hadrian adjacent to the Olympieion. Across the street from the Arch, almost in the shadow of the Acropolis, lay the home and church of Reverend Kalopothakes.[31]

The Acropolis itself, less than two miles away, dominated the center of Gilbert's view. Its bright marble temples, unsullied by pollution,

glowed rich amber in the sun. The modern city was spreading rapidly north and east from the Acropolis, but the plain south and west
remained largely unspoiled. Right of the Acropolis was the low rock
of the Areopagus or Mars Hill, where the apostle Paul had once stood.
In the distance lay the port of Piraeus, home to what little industry
Greece had. Smoke from new factory chimneys was starting to smudge
the skies, but Gilbert could still see the islands of Aegina and Salamis in
the distance and on the horizon the mountains of the Peloponnesus. As
his gaze swung on to the right, into view came the French School and
the German Archaeological Institute, the mansion of famed archaeologist Heinrich Schliemann, the University of Athens, and then the new
National Archaeological Museum, almost at the northern limits of the
city.[32]

Gilbert descended from Lycabettus into an Athens of dizzying
changes. Between 1879 and 1889, the city's population had grown
from some 63,000 to more than 107,000. Now, Greeks in traditional
dress rubbed shoulders with others sporting the latest Parisian fashions
and with immigrants from the eastern Mediterranean and beyond. One
visitor observed that most of the city's bootblacks were Persians. Time
itself was poised between old and new: official publications and many
newspapers still used the Julian calendar, running twelve days behind
the Gregorian calendar. Meanwhile, stately new public buildings, French
and neo-classical mansions with gardens, paved streets, sidewalks, and
electric lights had sprouted in place of mud brick. Orange trees graced
Syntagma (Constitution) Square, just below the royal palace. Well-
appointed hotels, restaurants, and shops clustered around Syntagma. If
some lamented the blinding glare of unpainted marble and the lack of
"verdure" (greenery), Athens invariably impressed visitors as "a thoroughly modern city of the best type." The contrast between romantic
expectation and reality surprised some. "Can this be Athens?," marveled one of what he called "this painfully fresh . . . North-German
town." Twenty-first century guidebooks often advise tourists to escape
Athens as soon as possible. In contrast, the 1889 Baedeker guidebook
(its first English edition) pronounced "the stay in Athens in every way
the finest part of a visit to Greece."[33]

It helped that mass tourism had not yet flooded the city. In 2018, Greece welcomed some thirty million visitors, most during the summer. In 1890, nobody went to Greece for the beaches, and the Greek government kept no visitor statistics. We get some idea of the numbers from an 1889 US consular report: in twelve months, just three hundred Americans stayed at the best of Athens' ten hotels. British School student R. A. H. Bickford-Smith, who reached Athens a few months before Gilbert, judged Greece "the least betoured of all the interesting countries in the world." "If an American goes to Greece," noted Massachusetts author Franklin Sanborn of his spring 1890 stay, "it is generally (unless he is merely touching there, on his way to Constantinople, Jerusalem, or Egypt) because he either has or wishes to have some acquaintance with Greek art or literature." Sanborn judged the Americans he met in Athens the "gifted few" rather than the "general average."[34]

If Gilbert encountered prejudice in Greece, it was most likely from "nomad Americans," as one black journalist called them, "whose snobbery is only more pronounced than their lack of culture and toleration." From Greeks, he most likely received the mix of courtesy and curiosity black Americans met elsewhere in Europe. Gilbert's fellow Augustan C. T. Walker, who visited Greece in April 1891, noted that Europeans "do not see many colored people, and they go wild over you." Although, or perhaps because, it was not yet a world power, the United States was especially well regarded in Greece. Older folks who remembered the aid American charities had sent in the 1820s, during the Greek struggle for independence from the Ottoman Empire, must have been especially pleased to discover Gilbert was American. Though the great wave of Greek emigration had not yet begun, a few people might have shared stories of relatives in America. There were also African American expatriates in Greece. Black minister John J. Smallwood, visiting Athens sometime between 1889 and 1892, even met a "native black Greek" named John Bennett, whose father had come to Greece from North Carolina by way of Scotland in the 1850s. Nothing more is known of Bennett and his family, but the possibility Gilbert forged links with a local black community in Athens is tantalizing. More evidence may someday emerge to illuminate this part of his experience.[35]

Gilbert's earliest interactions with Athenians probably revolved around food, for the American School provided no meals beyond the rolls and coffee Costi delivered each morning. Indeed, the Managing Committee could scarcely believe the British School fed its students from the director's kitchen. Gilbert soon got accustomed to Greek cooking, which some Americans judged too laden with olive oil and others found delightful. He could easily have taken lunches and dinners in central Athens, as many foreigners did. Andrew Fossum, for instance, became a regular at a hotel restaurant on Syntagma. There were also less expensive eateries near the university and cafés throughout the city where he could sip what Athenians of the day called "Turkish coffee," served thick in tiny cups. Or he could explore the narrow, winding side streets around the Acropolis, where little shops offered fried sardines or fluffy hotcakes. The latter, eaten with the marvelous Attic honey, were a breakfast "fit even for an American," as Annie Peck, the American School's first woman student, later recalled. Gilbert may even have enjoyed what Caroline Gerrish called "a preparation (I have forgotten its name) of milk, artificially soured. . . . It is thicker than cream and just as thick as the cheese that I make, and can be eaten with powdered sugar or with a little honey or some fruit as one prefers." Gilbert would have remembered the name: *giaoúrti*. Not until nearly a century later would this exotic delicacy become familiar to health-conscious Americans as yogurt.[36]

That Gilbert already spoke some modern Greek when he stepped ashore at Patras reveals his interest in the country's living people and language. Classics scholars today often turn up their noses at modern Greek, but attitudes differed in Gilbert's day. Several of the American School's early students focused on the modern language. Wiley Lane, who would have been the School's first black scholar had pneumonia not felled him in 1885, had planned to do the same. Minnesota professor Jabez Brooks, after spending winter 1890 at the ASCSA, came back so convinced of the importance of the living tongue he began offering modern Greek classes alongside ancient Greek. Even those mainly interested in archaeology or ancient literature made a point of learning modern Greek.[37]

Like many classically educated foreigners, Gilbert could easily read Greek newspapers and books written in literary *katharévousa*, with its heavy reliance on ancient forms. He probably also could follow a Greek Orthodox church service. Conversing in *demotiki*, the everyday spoken language, was tougher, not least since it required unlearning the artificial pronunciation American classrooms usually taught. Like other scholars who sojourned in Athens, Gilbert may have come to see modern Greek as especially useful for helping teach students Biblical Greek. By the end of his stay in Greece, he was at ease with the modern language. Indeed, years later in Nashville, African Methodist Episcopal (AME) minister John Q. Johnson would pay tribute to Gilbert's Greek abilities. If the notoriously racist South Carolina senator John C. Calhoun were to "rise from the dead and come to this General Conference," Johnson declared, "we would show him a negro who could not only read the ancient classics, but who is a master in modern Greek. Our Professor, J. W. Gilbert, would teach him many things about the Greek verb."[38]

The Luther of Greece

The first Greek with whom Gilbert conversed at length may have been Reverend Kalopothakes (Figure 4.5). Michael Demetrios Kalopothakes was born in 1825 in the rugged Mani region of the southern Peloponnesus. As a schoolboy, he was introduced to evangelical Christianity by Virginia Presbyterian teachers. In 1850, while studying medicine in Athens, he met Congregationalist missionary Jonas King. When an Athenian court, influenced by the powerful Greek Orthodox Church, found King guilty of preaching "false doctrines," Kalopothakes set aside his medical career to devote himself, as he later described it, "to the cause of religious liberty and reform, and to the propagation of evangelical truth amongst my fellow countrymen." Kalopothakes's boyhood teachers helped him go to the United States, where he graduated from Union Theological Seminary in New York, finished his medical training in Philadelphia, and was ordained in Richmond. He returned to Athens in 1857 to assist Jonas King and

FIGURE 4.5 Michael Demetrios Kalopothakes, circa 1886.
Courtesy of the Greek Historical Evangelical Archive, Athens.

after King's retirement took charge of Greece's evangelical movement.
By 1872, Kalopothakes had built a church and home just across from
the Arch of Hadrian. The Greek Evangelical Church still stands there
today, welcoming a diverse congregation that includes many African
immigrants to Greece.[39]

In 1858, Reverend Kalopothakes married a Massachusetts sea
captain's daughter, Martha Blackler. They were partners in evangelism

until her death in 1871. Canadian-born Margaret Kyle (Figure 4.6), who first came to Greece to assist Martha, became Kalopothakes's second wife in 1877. Margaret helped raise his three children: Maria would study medicine in Paris and become Greece's first woman physician; Daphne stayed home with her father; and Francis, whom John Pickard met in Berlin, would go on to a career as diplomat and journalist.[40]

FIGURE 4.6 Margaret Kyle Kalopothakes in her garden, 1903.
Courtesy of the Greek Historical Evangelical Archive, Athens.

Kalopothakes's renown grew as more Americans traveled to Greece. Some compared Kalopothakes to the Apostle Paul; one hailed him as "the Luther of Greece." Among his guests in the 1880s was Greek American Michael Anagnos, who introduced Helen Keller to her teacher Anne Sullivan. By the time John Gilbert got to Athens, Kalopothakes was a beacon for visitors. Those who did not know his name when they arrived were drawn in by the neatly lettered sign in English outside the church: "Gospel preached every Sunday. Seats free." "This house seems to be the headquarters of all the English and American[s]," Caroline Gerrish remarked; "they all come to Mr. and Mrs. K. for aid and advice, indeed Mr. and Mrs. K. seem to be quite indispensable to foreigners."[41]

The American School in its early years had particularly close links with Mr. and Mrs. K. Before the School building opened in 1888, professors and students rented rooms near the Greek Evangelical Church. Harold North Fowler, an 1882–1883 student, recalled that "some, perhaps most, of us often went to hear Dr. Kalopothakes preach, partly at least because it was good for our modern Greek." A few students, notably Annie Peck in 1885–1886, lived with the family. When student Walter Miller was beaten and robbed in 1886, he went first to Reverend Kalopothakes, then to the police. Managing Committee documents repeatedly highlighted his assistance, while Kalopothakes regularly mentioned the ASCSA in his newspaper, *The Star of the East*. His son Francis was a student at the School in 1888–1889, and his daughter Daphne would study there from 1894 to 1896.[42]

John Gilbert probably first met John Pickard's family during an early October service at Kalopothakes's church. Caroline Gerrish first saw him from a distance. She wrote her sister Harriett in Portsmouth: "there are only four students all told at the American School, John [Pickard] included. I imagine that John is the best pre-pared of any because he has had the advantage of study in Germany and access to fine museums. . . . One student is a colored man—a fine looking young fellow, with a remarkably handsome profile." Caroline might have had more interactions with Gilbert if she had not been confined to the Kalopothakes home for much of fall 1890. During that time, she and the other women in Pickard's family were frequently ill with what Caroline calls dysentery. Jeanie Pickard suffered the worst, being bedridden through most of October and November.[43]

Gilbert, like other Americans in Athens, may have found Kalopothakes's Sunday services a comforting touch of home: if the hymns were in Greek, the melodies were familiar. The missionary aspect of Kalopothakes's work may also have intrigued him. Since the 1870s, black missionaries had been going from Augusta to Africa. Harrison Bouey, an elementary school teacher of Gilbert's, had spent 1879–1883 on a Baptist mission in Liberia. Missionary fervor, alive at Paine Institute before Gilbert left for Greece, blossomed while he was away, thanks to the February 1891 visit of a white Methodist missionary from Kobe, Japan. Soon afterward, George Williams Walker proposed a joint mission of the Methodist Episcopal Church, South (MECS) and the Colored Methodist Episcopal (CME) Church to Africa. Paine's students immediately formed an Afro-American Mission Society and elected honorary members, among them "J. W. Gilbert of the American School, Athens, Greece." We can only imagine the conversations Gilbert had with Reverend Kalopothakes, but they may well have influenced his later endeavors. Twenty years after leaving Greece, Gilbert would fulfill Walker's vision by undertaking a co-operative interracial mission to the Belgian Congo. His white Methodist partner, Walter Russell Lambuth, was none other than the missionary from Japan who visited Paine in 1891.[44]

Our Learned Consul

Among the regulars at Kalopothakes's church was US Consul Irving Manatt, perhaps the first American Gilbert met outside the ASCSA group. A classical scholar and 1873 Yale PhD, Manatt had until recently been chancellor of the University of Nebraska. To escape a fight with Nebraska's trustees, Manatt tried wrangling an appointment as US Minister Resident and Consul-General to Greece, Romania, and Serbia, touting his "unusual acquaintance with the language, literature, and history of Greece." The job went to a better-connected Pennsylvanian, Archibald Loudon Snowden, but as consolation prize

Manatt got the Athens consulship in fall 1889, the very post Andrew Fossum had asked his senator about that spring.[45]

Today, the massive, fortified US Embassy in Athens is impossible to miss. In the late nineteenth century, Greece ranked so low in US foreign affairs that Congress in 1878 forgot to appropriate funds for the Athens legation. For several years after that, the United States did not even have a minister to the country. The American diplomatic presence was better established when John Gilbert reached Athens, with Snowden ensconced in a rented mansion, but Manatt still had to make do with a hotel room office.[46]

Snowden's poor health and preference for Bucharest meant he was often absent from Athens. Meanwhile, Manatt thrived. He became fluent in modern Greek, befriended Greek scholars and politicians, assisted American tourists, made himself a familiar figure in the city's international community, and explored the countryside. He produced reports for the State Department on subjects such as Greek mining and metallurgy, often placing the modern industries into ancient context. To make extra money, he published newspaper and magazine essays mixing bucolic scenery, mythology, and ancient history with assessments of Greece's economic potential. Manatt was an especially ardent booster of the American School, often bringing visitors to see the School building and attend lectures. "The consulship . . . seems just the place for him," observed Caroline Gerrish.[47]

By the time John Gilbert got to Greece, Manatt had been joined by his wife Arletta and two children (four others stayed in Nebraska with an aunt). The family lived at the Hotel des Etrangers on Syntagma Square, "the best consular location in Athens," where Arletta managed affairs when Manatt was off exploring. Seventeen-year-old Winifred (see Figure 4.7), who turned heads everywhere she went—Heinrich Schliemann dubbed her "Artemis"—often accompanied her father and later wrote about her travel experiences. Meanwhile, Winnie's four-year-old little sister had the run of the hotel, speaking Greek with the porters and picking up Cantonese words from a Chinese worker.[48]

For Gilbert and other American newcomers, Manatt was an important source of information about Greek government and politics.

FIGURE 4.7 Winifred Manatt, American bicyclist Thomas Allen, and US Consul Irving Manatt, March 1891.
Courtesy of the William Lewis Sachtleben Papers (Collection 1841). Library Special Collections, Charles E. Young Research Library, University of California, Los Angeles.

To begin with, there was King George I. Just eighteen when he became King of the Hellenes in 1863, George presided over what the Greeks called a "crowned democracy." The king, Russian-born Queen Olga, and their children—"a royal family without a scandal," Manatt remarked in a letter to his friend Jesse Macy, a leading American political scientist—were popular and visible in Athens. During his first weeks in the city, Gilbert may have encountered the royal family walking in the streets. While he cannily forged ties with the great royal houses of Europe (his son Constantine married Sophia, a younger sister of Kaiser Wilhelm II), King George also kept up with American affairs. He helped the American School obtain land for its building and made a point of welcoming American visitors. Ordinarily, Manatt or (when he was in town) Snowden arranged such introductions, but George even cordially received "a group of rustic Americans" in straw hats and dusters who knocked on the palace door one morning looking for "Mr. King." John Gilbert had no time for a royal audience in fall 1890, but in January he would meet George when the king visited the American School.[49]

King George provided valuable continuity for a country that saw frequent, divisive changes of administration. In the 1880s, Greece's leadership oscillated between two rivals. French-educated Charilaos Tricoupis, son of an Independence War leader, pushed to modernize, westernize, and industrialize. Populist Theodoros Deliyannis, giving voice to concerns that modernization would usurp traditional values and make Greece subservient to foreigners, famously declared himself against everything Tricoupis stood for.[50]

Tricoupis had been prime minister during most of the 1880s, and much of what Gilbert saw on the ride from Patras to Athens, from the currant fields to the Corinth Canal to the railway itself, reflected Tricoupis's economic development program. The invisible companion to those sights was the exploding debt that would drive Greece to bankruptcy in 1893. From his earliest days in the country, Gilbert discerned the effects of the high taxes Tricoupis had put on everything from wine to donkeys in hopes of raising revenue. Matches, made by a government monopoly, had become so expensive that Athenians went to tobacco shops for a light rather than buying their own. "The people are groaning" under heavy taxation, commented Rev. and Mrs. Kalopothakes.[51]

When John Gilbert arrived in Athens, the country was ramping up for an October 26 general election. Parades and rallies thronged the city's streets daily. Gilbert soon learned to recognize the competing emblems: for Deliyannists, a cord or string (*kordóni*) symbolizing united effort; for Tricoupists, the olive branch (*elyía*) of prosperity. Loud choruses of *kordóni!* and *elyía!* resounded late into the night.

"In liveliness and loudness," Manatt observed, "the Greeks leave us away back among the Sunday school processions." A few nights before the election, Tricoupists and Deliyannists collided in Syntagma. The police tried to intervene, shots rang out, and four men were carried off with bullet wounds or sword cuts. Observing the intense campaign activities, Gilbert must have been reminded that elections were also coming up back in the United States, although he could not have foreseen how disastrous those elections would be for black political progress in Georgia.[52]

Even as he took stock of his classmates Brownson, Fossum, and Pickard, and of Professor Richardson, as he settled into life in a foreign city, and as he learned more about the culture and politics of modern Greece, in the end John Gilbert had come to the American School to study the classical past. He and the other members of School were fortunate to have the advice and assistance of the Kalopothakes family and Consul Manatt as they began their explorations of the ancient remains of Greece. In the months ahead, Gilbert and his fellows would experience the country as few travelers of the era ever did.

5

NO STONE
UNTURNED

In the fall of 1890, John Hope of Augusta was a freshman at Brown University, living in his former teacher John Wesley Gilbert's old dorm room. Early in October, Hope picked up a copy of the student newspaper, *The Brunonian*. There, in the alumni column, he read: "Gilbert is at the American School in Athens." Thanks to the *Providence Journal*, the whole city soon knew that Gilbert, one of Brown's first graduate students, was studying abroad for his master's degree in Greek. John Hope did not have a class with Gilbert's mentor Albert Harkness that fall, but he was reading the Greek historians Herodotus and Thucydides with William Carey Poland, soon to be named the American School's annual director for 1891–1892. Hope may have assumed his fellow Augustan would devote himself to reading classic texts in Athens. Harkness, who assigned Gilbert a hefty MA list for the year, certainly seems to have expected as much. The reality was more complicated.[1]

In its ad hoc early years, the American School relied on annual directors of disparate interests and inclinations. If the first director, William Goodwin, stressed the value of seeing Greece's topography and monuments up close, his successors often had other ideas. In 1885–1886, Frederic De Forest Allen, who stepped in at the last minute when Harkness declined the directorship, hated archaeology and showed little interest in ancient sites. Martin D'Ooge in 1886–1887 judged excursions in Attica "only supplementary to the more serious

and regular work" of reading Greek in the library. To further compli-
cate matters, the School's early students, a fifth of whom already had
doctoral degrees, often preferred to pursue their own interests rather
than follow a formal program in Greece.[2]

Even as the School's archaeological aspect gradually increased,
starting with its 1886 excavation of the ancient theater of Thoricus,
its leaders continued courting literary scholars, architects, and artists
in hopes of enticing more Americans to Athens. In his correspondence
with African American scholar William Sanders Scarborough, for example, Managing Committee chair John Williams White highlighted
the attractions of reading classical Greek "under the quickening
influences which surround one who is resident in Athens." White's successor T. D. Seymour also played up the literary connection. "This contact with the land and air of Greece," he remarked, "this personal study
of the monuments and topography, promises a better appreciation of
ancient life and history, and thus a better appreciation of the literature
of the ancient Greeks." Albert Harkness probably pitched the School to
Gilbert in similar terms.[3]

Rufus Richardson had a distinctly less chair-bound vision. His main
influence seems to have been 1887–1888's Augustus Merriam, whom
he met in Berlin on his way to Greece. Though Merriam still devoted
much time to the classroom, he had placed new emphasis on topographical study, in other words walking the countryside in search of ancient
remains, especially those mentioned in classical texts. His explorations
led the School to excavate at the rural Attic deme, or district, of Icaria,
site of the earliest Athenian festivals to the god Dionysus. Merriam
also expanded American participation in field trips and museum tours
led by foreign scholars, above all Wilhelm Dörpfeld of the German
Archaeological Institute.[4]

Richardson went well beyond Merriam in emphasizing the outdoors.
"Some people suppose," he remarked in an essay he sent to Dartmouth,
"students come here to continue their reading of Greek authors, much
as . . . at home. The fact is, that while we make the Greek authors our
constant companions, we use them only as literary information on the
topography and monuments of Greece." During fall 1890, Richardson

would lead Gilbert and the other American School students through Athens, into the surrounding countryside of Attica, and beyond. As he put it: "we aimed to leave no stone unturned, unless it was too big to allow it."[5]

Walking with Jane

October in Athens was sunny and pleasant. Gilbert and his fellows went out early each morning to search the modern city (see Map 3) for traces of the ancient, then returned to the School library for afternoon reading and discussion. Their guide was the travel writer Pausanias (ca. AD 115–180), who had seen Greece when it was a province of the Roman Empire. Some nineteenth-century philologists dismissed Pausanias as dimwit or liar, but his stock rose during the 1880s as archaeology and tourism developed in Greece. Toting their Pausanias

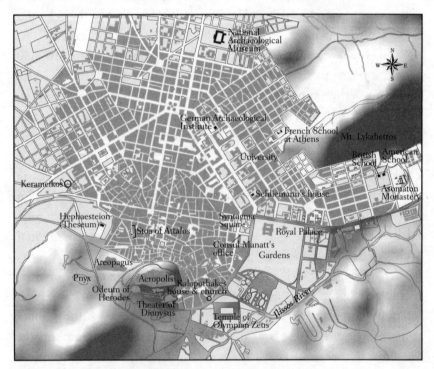

MAP 3 Athens in 1890–1891

texts as they pursued the monuments he described and reading him aloud in Greek on the spot, Gilbert and his fellows became what one British traveler dubbed "Pausaniacs." The School's Pausanias volumes got such heavy use that by year's end their bindings would be in tatters.[6]

1890 was a great time for Pausaniacs. German archaeologist Wilhelm Gurlitt published his decisive refutation of charges that Pausanias had made it all up. British anthropologist J. G. Frazer, fresh off completing *The Golden Bough*, went to Greece to research what would become a six-volume commentary on Pausanias. The biggest splash came from two other Britons, Jane Harrison and Margaret Verrall. Their *Mythology and Monuments of Ancient Athens*, hot off the presses that spring, combined Verrall's translation of selections from Pausanias with Harrison's lengthy introduction and commentary. Despite Verrall's name on the title page, it was Harrison's book. Some reviewers groused about errors; others raved. British archaeologist Ernest Gardner called it "incomparably the best guide to . . . ancient Athens generally, which has yet appeared." Aided by glowing newspaper coverage on both sides of the Atlantic, the book became a best-seller and helped make Jane Harrison's reputation; she would become perhaps the most famous female classicist ever.[7]

Mythology and Monuments was soon on the American School's reading list and became a defining presence in Gilbert's first months in Greece. Edith Harris observed that "there is a good deal of joking about [Harrison] and her books. The students go out to walk with 'Jane.' At present, we have her in the house and often you hear the cry, 'Where's Jane?' 'Have you got Jane?'" The Americans did not need Verrall's translation, nor were they much interested in Harrison's mythological analyses. Instead, they were after archaeological information, not least the unpublished speculations Harrison had collected from Wilhelm Dörpfeld (he checked her proofs to make sure his views were accurately represented).[8]

Even with Jane's help, finding Pausanias's Athens was not easy. In 1890, much of what he described was still buried. One place Pausaniacs could see was the northwest entry to the ancient city, fortuitously discovered in the 1860s by workers mining sand. By the time

Gilbert reached Athens, Greek archaeologists had in fits and starts cleared portions of the ancient fortification wall, two gates (Dörpfeld said there was just one), and the Kerameikos cemetery beyond. In a sign of the times, the area had recently been fenced to deter looting. Gilbert and his fellows strolled through the foundations of the Dipylon Gate—perhaps the very gate through which Pausanias had entered Athens—and out along an ancient street lined with beautiful sculpted tomb reliefs still in situ. It was like stepping back in time twenty-four centuries. Somewhere nearby was the Demosion Sema, the burial ground of Athenian war dead and site of Pericles's famous funeral oration. A few months before, the Greeks had resumed work in the Kerameikos. US consul Irving Manatt, with his avid interest in archaeology, had been there as the digging began and "had the pleasure of handling an old Greek skull, which had not seen the sun since Pericles's time, it may be."[9]

Southeast from the Kerameikos, a nearly intact temple sat serenely atop a low, flat hill. Casual visitors still called this building the Theseum, or Temple of Theseus, after its sculpted friezes of the legendary Athenian hero. Among them was Frederick Douglass, who recorded his impressions in March 1887: "solemn and grand with its many pillars, stood out the form of the Temple of Theseus, one of the most perfect and striking of all the fallen architectural ruins left to tell us the wealth, pride, ambition, and power of the ancient people of this famous city." From *Mythology and Monuments*, Gilbert and the others learned the building was in fact the Hephaesteion, the temple of the blacksmith god Hephaestus, mentioned by Pausanias.[10]

Used as a church from the seventh century AD until 1834, the Hephaesteion was the best-preserved temple in all Greece. Its tall, slender Doric columns had influenced nineteenth-century Greek Revival architecture across Europe and North America. Looking at the temple façade, Gilbert was reminded of a familiar sight back home: the Medical College of Georgia, whose graceful Doric portico had been inspired by the Hephaisteion. The Medical College lay less than a block west of where he lived on Telfair Street as a boy and less than two blocks east of the Augusta Institute where he studied as a teenager.

Stepping inside the Hephaesteion's colonnade, Gilbert and his fellows looked up to marvel at the sunlight filtering through the translucent marble ceiling coffers.[11]

Twenty-first century visitors to the Hephaesteion enjoy a view east over the tree-shaded expanse of the Agora, the ancient civic center and marketplace, excavated by the American School beginning in 1931. When John Gilbert stood at the temple, the area to the east was covered by the residential neighborhood of Vrysaki. The civic buildings Pausanias described were nowhere to be seen, so scholars kept busy debating where the Agora might be and indeed what exactly he meant by "Agora." Jane Harrison was sure the buildings lay south of the Hephaesteion, rather than east as many argued. The temple hill offered Gilbert and his fellows a vantage point for considering the competing theories. Meanwhile, below the hill's northern edge workmen were digging a new rail line eastward into the modern city. Little did the workers know they were cutting right across the northern sector of the Agora.[12]

Descending into Vrysaki's winding streets, the Americans came first to a mysterious half-buried jumble of ancient blocks, the "Stoa of the Giants." Neighborhood children scampered around the colossal serpent-legged statues that gave the structure its name. Pausanias said nothing about it and no one living knew what the building had been. If Gilbert stopped to practice his Greek with the children, he might have learned they called the statues "dragons." A few steps further on were the remains of another stoa (colonnaded portico), partially built into modern houses and bisected by a narrow lane. In 1862, Greek excavators had found an inscription identifying this stoa as the gift of King Attalos II (r. 159–138 BC) of Pergamon in Asia Minor, who had had studied in Athens. As they poked about the unassuming ruins of what was essentially an ancient shopping mall, Gilbert and his companions could never have imagined how important the place would become for American archaeologists in Greece. Rebuilt between 1953 and 1956, the Stoa of Attalos serves today as headquarters for the ongoing Agora excavations, a central component of the American School's work.[13]

More substantial sights awaited elsewhere. East of the Stoa of Attalos, Greek archaeologists had partly excavated a columned hall built by the Roman emperor Hadrian (r. AD 117–138). Until a fire in 1885, the hall's ruins had housed Athens' main bazaar. Twenty-first-century tourists mostly hurry past in search of cheap eats and souvenirs, but in Gilbert's day the imposing west wall and Corinthian columns of this hall were a popular landmark known as the Stoa of Hadrian (nowadays often called the Library of Hadrian). Nearby lay the Gate of Athena Archegetis ("the Leader"), dedicated in the time of the emperor Augustus (r. 27 BC–AD 14). Here the Greeks were just starting to uncover a peristyle marketplace, soon to be identified as the Roman Agora. Next door was the Tower of the Winds, an ornate octagon built in the second century BC that functioned as water clock, sundial, and weathervane. East and south of the Acropolis were Hadrian's Gate and the gigantic columns of the Temple of Olympian Zeus, the Theater of Dionysus, the Odeum (Music Hall) donated by a super-rich Athenian contemporary of Hadrian named Herodes Atticus, and more.[14]

Gilbert, whose studies at Brown had emphasized Periclean Athens as the pinnacle of classical civilization, probably found the Roman monuments less evocative. Edith Harris caught the prevailing mood: "archaeologists don't care much about [anything] of Roman date. Anything Roman or of Roman period the Greeks sniff at, and . . . students of ancient remains give their attention naturally to the older objects." The neglect of things Roman was evident at the Temple of Olympian Zeus, across from the Kalopothakes house. One visitor noted, "the boys who play about these ruins amuse themselves with breaking off pieces of the fillets of the fluting. . . . The volutes from the fallen columns have disappeared and the sculpture of the capitals will soon be destroyed."[15]

The Acropolis was another story. Between 1885 and 1889, Greek archaeologist Panagiotis Kavvadias had stripped away the last remnants of Roman, medieval, and Turkish construction on the Acropolis, turning over every inch of earth down to bedrock. The classical buildings now stood bare and gleaming in the October sun. The American Schoolers entered through the Roman-period Beulé Gate, climbed up the long stone steps below the Temple of Winged Victory, made their way past the uniformed guards lounging in the marble gateway of the Propylaea, and emerged onto the blue limestone rock of the Acropolis to stand before the Parthenon and the Erechtheion. Around them in neat rows lay freshly excavated marble blocks, some still bearing traces of paint and gilding.[16]

John Gilbert's Acropolis was hardly the site that greets twenty-first-century eyes. The tourist hordes that these days crowd the rock year-round were absent, and there was no entrance fee. Visitors roamed in and around the ancient buildings, lingering where they liked. The buildings themselves looked different. It would be several more years until Greek architect Nikolaos Balanos began reconstructing the Erechtheion and Parthenon with iron clamps, concrete, and misplaced marble fragments, in the process inflicting damage that is still being repaired today. Although the Acropolis was the place Gilbert and the other students most wanted to see, and its recently renovated museum was packed with sculpture and other finds from Kavvadias's excavations, Richardson knew Permanent Director Charles Waldstein considered it his preserve and tactfully limited the group's time there.[17]

Walking with Jane was challenging for Gilbert. He may have read some Pausanias at Brown but probably had no copy of the text in Augusta. Even if he first encountered Pausanias in Athens, Gilbert could handle the Greek. The real issue was archaeology. In Augusta, he had little or no access to the specialized texts on ancient art and architecture the American School recommended as advance reading. Furthermore, his late start for Athens meant he had not spent summer 1890 studying Greek antiquities in European museums as the others had. John Pickard noticed, remarking to Caroline Gerrish that "Gilbert is not as well prepared as the others." Pickard nonetheless found Gilbert "a good, diligent student," and the two men seem to have bonded early on. Together they began writing papers based on their walks in Athens, choosing interrelated topics inspired by *Mythology and Monuments*.[18]

The Shores of Salamis

Richardson also took the students beyond Athens, noting in his official report that "one feature of the School's work made quite prominent this year has been the securing of an acquaintance with the soil of Greece outside Athens." Andrew Fossum put it more bluntly: "Professor Richardson was fond of hikes and we went on several." In preparation, the men had new shoes custom-made in Athens. Waterproof and thick-soled, they may have been the best shoes Gilbert had ever owned. He would need them.[19]

First up was a day trip to the Salamis straits, where in 480 BC a Greek fleet of triremes (war galleys) had defeated the invading Persian armada of Xerxes. *Mythology and Monuments* only covered Athens proper, so the Americans turned for directions and practical advice to "the invaluable Baedeker [guidebook]," as Richardson called it. They reviewed the paper William Goodwin had written on the battle during the School's inaugural year and studied the ancient sources: the *Histories* of Herodotus, the *Persians* of Aeschylus (a veteran of Salamis and of the battle of Marathon, too), and Plutarch's biography of the Athenian Themistocles, mastermind of the Greek victory.[20]

The Attic coast of the straits has today disappeared under shipyards, refineries, a massive Chinese-owned container port, and block after concrete block of apartments, yet we can still trace the Americans' route on the *Karten von Attika*, an exquisite set of detailed maps German topographers compiled in the 1870s and 1880s. After a short train ride through open fields from Athens down to the Piraeus, Gilbert and his fellows enjoyed an easy hour's walk toward the coast, crossing almost untouched countryside before descending along a new dirt road to the little bay of Keratsini. According to a legend Plutarch recorded, it was from here Theseus had departed for Crete to slay the Minotaur.[21]

From Keratsini, the road ran west along the seashore below the slopes of Mount Aegaleion, where Xerxes had watched from his throne as the Greeks scattered his ships. Less than a mile across the wine-dark straits sat Salamis Island. Andrew Fossum remembered vividly: "we all together spent a day on the place trying to locate the scene of the battle, the seat of Xerxes, etc. and the movements of the fleets with Herodotus and Aeschylus in hand wandering up and down the beach." As American School groups still do, Gilbert and his fellows probably read aloud from Aeschylus's *Persians*, with its stirring rendition of the Greek rallying cry: "On, you men of Hellas! Free your native land. Free your children, your wives, the temples of your fathers' gods, and the tombs of your ancestors. Now you are fighting for all you have!" There was so much to see that the group returned for a second look several days later.[22]

The Mountains Look on Marathon

In the last week of October, as scattered clouds and rain showers signaled the end of summer, Richardson and the students made a three-day trek to northeast Attica and the battlefield of Marathon (see Map 4). Visiting this region remained expensive and inconvenient. While rural bandits had largely disappeared, dogs remained a real danger. Only two previous American School groups had taken the trouble to visit Marathon. Tourists were sometimes told they could see the battlefield from the top of Mount Lycabettus, sparing themselves an eight-hour carriage roundtrip that cost as much as a week of dinners in Athens. Irving Manatt had been out in September, escorting a wealthy American lawyer who paid for the ride, but Richardson and the students were not going by carriage. Instead, they would follow the footsteps of Augustus Merriam; of German topographer Arthur Milchhöfer, who had recently explored the area for the *Karten von Attika*; and, although they did not know it, of George Frazer, who had gone through in May researching his Pausanias commentary.[23]

Gilbert and his fellows set off before sunrise for Athens' central station, where they caught the first train out of town. Buildings and streets soon gave way to rural Attica. Morning's light shone on wheat fields, gnarled olive trees, and fruit orchards, today all long vanished under urban sprawl. Less than an hour after leaving Athens, the Americans disembarked at the leafy village of Kephissia, where wealthy Athenians kept summer homes and gardens. Then they set

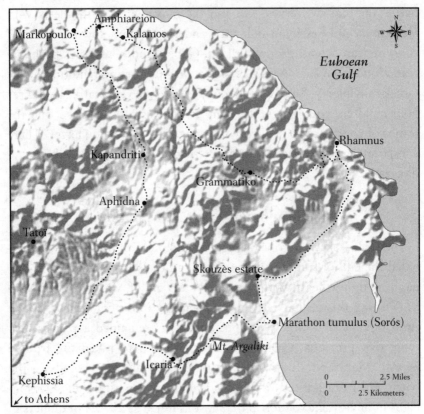

MAP 4 The American School hike through Attica, October 1890

off cross-country, looping north and east around Mount Pentele on their way to ancient Icaria seven miles away. It was a two-hour hike, first through fields sprinkled with pistachio and arbutus shrubs, then up into a broad valley lined with scraggly pines. The unpaved road sparkled with nuggets of Pentelic marble, the same stone used for the Parthenon. The group may have gone the entire way from Kephissia without seeing anyone, save perhaps a lone goatherd with his flock.[24]

As they walked, the Americans had time to discuss the previous Sunday's Greek elections. John Pickard had managed a peek into a polling station, where the voters cast their ballots by placing round lead bullets into boxes, in a manner strikingly similar to that of classical Athens. Results were still coming in, but it was already clear Prime

Minister Tricoupis had suffered an unexpected rout, even losing his seat in the Boulé (Parliament). Tricoupis and his allies had expected an easy win, as had foreign observers, but Deliyannis won voters with promises of lower taxes and, in Athens, of a better water supply. Deliyannists were soon replacing Tricoupists everywhere, in what Irving Manatt called a "clean sweep" of ministers, officials, even teachers.[25]

There was more. Charles Eliot Norton, instrumental in founding the Archaeological Institute of America and the American School, had long dreamed of excavating ancient Delphi, seat of Apollo's oracle. During the 1880s, Norton led a drive to raise money for the project. Meanwhile, the French, interested in the site since the 1860s, renewed their quest for excavation rights. Tricoupis had dangled Delphic possibilities to both sides. Although the US Secretary of State committed in 1889 not to compete with France, Norton, now working with Permanent Director Waldstein and US minister Archibald Snowden, did not give up. Both Waldstein and Snowden, though, were absent from Greece for most of 1890, while the French maintained a continuous diplomatic and scholarly presence. The French had nearly locked down the deal even before the election, but the Americans judged Deliyannis's victory the crushing blow. The day after the election, Richardson conferred with the Greek archaeologist Kavvadias, then sent Waldstein a gloomy report. Meanwhile, Waldstein was already confiding to his diary that Tricoupis's downfall had "shattered all my hopes." Waldstein would mount renewed efforts for Delphi after he got to Greece in December, but to no avail.[26]

Whether or not Richardson shared with them what he knew, Brownson, Fossum, Gilbert, and Pickard understood the election as a turning point for American archaeology in Greece. Even Caroline Gerrish recognized it, writing "there now seems very little chance of the Americans being able to buy Delphi, as the new prime minister here, Deliyanni, is a great friend to France." Visiting Delphi in November, John Pickard would lament: "if not for the want of a few thousand dollars, American engineers would now be excavating, and American scholars would be publishing their results to the world. Will this glory go at last to France, I wonder?"[27]

Disappointment also waited at Icaria. Named after the legendary Icarius, whom Dionysus first taught the art of winemaking, the deme (district) of Icaria was reputedly the home of Thespis, inventor of Greek tragedy. During the classical period, dramatic performances were held in the deme's sanctuary of Dionysus. The sanctuary's remains, partly built into a ruined Byzantine church, had been excavated in 1888–1889 by the American School's Carl Buck, whom John Pickard had met at Leipzig in winter 1889–1890. Among Buck's finds was a fifth-century BC inscription detailing the local theater's finances, a crucial source for the history of Attic drama. Later in the fall, Gilbert and his fellows may have studied this stone in Athens. If so, they were among the last to see it for a very long time: at some point after 1889 the inscription disappeared, only to be rediscovered in 1999 in the basement of the National Museum.[28]

Having read Sophocles and Euripides at Brown, Gilbert probably found the prospect of a visit to the birthplace of Greek drama compelling. The others must have felt likewise, and Merriam's idyllic description of Icaria's natural setting could only have heightened expectations. A visitor in March 1890 had indeed found the place "full of woodland beauty, of ever-flowing water (which is more rare in Attica than wine) and of ancient plane-trees forming a shade above the rill." But a very different sight greeted Gilbert and his fellows. Forest fires in August had swept down into the valley, burning the excavations. The woodland beauty was gone, the surrounding slopes scarred black.[29]

The Americans continued northeast, down along the Rapedosa ravine and then up onto the rocky slopes of Mount Argaliki. Suddenly, the plain and bay of Marathon stretched out before them. Returning to Marathon in 1927, this time by Cadillac with his wife, Carleton Brownson still remembered this moment, remarking in his travel journal that "I thought I could see the very spot where we came over the shoulder of Argaliki from Kephisia in the Fall of 1890." In 1937, Andrew Fossum remembered, too: "we followed cross-country till we saw the plain of Marathon from the mountains with the words of Byron in mind." It is not hard to imagine someone in the group, perhaps Gilbert himself, reciting aloud from Byron's "Isles of Greece" the opening lines of the famous third stanza: "The mountains look on Marathon—And Marathon looks on the sea."[30]

Marathon was a magical word to classical scholars of the day; Irving Manatt celebrated 1890 as the 2,380th anniversary of the battle. For John Gilbert, Marathon had even more powerful resonances. During the 1880s, influential African American writers had presented the Greco-Persian Wars as emblems of the age-old struggle for liberty and emancipation. In two best-selling books, Civil War veteran Joseph Wilson positioned the black soldiers of the Revolution and the Civil War as "the Black Phalanx," the true heirs of classical Greece's citizen hoplites (armored spearmen). George Washington Williams, "the greatest historian of the race" according to W. E. B. DuBois, gave historical context to the enlistment of freed slaves in the Union Army by claiming that "at the battle of Marathon there were two regiments of heavy infantry composed of slaves."[31]

Williams and Wilson helped shape late-nineteenth-century African American understandings of Marathon. Even if John Gilbert had not read their books, he was familiar with their themes, not least since he had talked with black Union veterans as a boy in Augusta and as a student in Providence. Having studied the ancient accounts of the battle, Gilbert knew that although Williams was wrong about the "two regiments" part, emancipated slaves did in fact fight for Greek freedom at Marathon. Pausanias had even seen the tomb of the freedmen who fell in the battle and were buried on the field, a mark of high honor. Looking down from the shoulder of Argaliki, Gilbert could find new meaning in the closing lines of that Byron stanza: "For standing on the Persians' grave, I could not deem myself a slave."[32]

The Americans came down into the Marathon plain about where the modern archaeological museum stands. Today, greenhouses and homes crowd the landscape, tavernas cluster along the seashore, and the rowing facility built for the 2004 Olympics sits decaying at the north end of the plain. In 1890, there was hardly a house in sight and the north end was a marsh. New vineyards were spreading across the south of the plain. Marathon's grapes were destined for Greece's nascent wine industry, which was expanding to slake French thirsts. As one visitor noted, "the wines most valued in France are all made near Marathon, or on the road to it from Athens," among them the Clos Marathon, available "pure and cheap" in Athens.[33]

A two-mile walk through the vineyards brought Gilbert and his fellows to an irregular knoll little more than thirty feet high, with a wild pear tree growing out one side (Figure 5.1). The afternoon sun hung low in the sky as they climbed up the sandy soil to take in the view. For decades there had been debate about this mound, the *sorós*. Some believed it the burial place, mentioned by Pausanias, of the 192 Athenian citizens killed in the battle (no one knew where the freed slaves were buried). Others discounted it as a prehistoric grave tumulus that predated the battle by centuries. Heinrich Schliemann, the discoverer of Troy, had dug into the mound's top in 1884, only to conclude "the theory of its being the burial-place of the fallen Athenians must be given up forever." In spring 1890, though, Greek archaeologist Valerios Staïs had dug further down, revealing ashes, bones, and

FIGURE 5.1 The tumulus (*sorós*) of the Athenians at Marathon, circa 1898. Public domain image. Rijksmuseum, Netherlands.

funeral offerings that seemed to confirm the *sorós* as the resting place of the Athenian dead. A commission of noted archaeologists verified the results on-site and Schliemann accepted the verdict. John Gilbert was thus among the very first American scholars to visit Marathon after the *sorós* achieved official status as an icon of Greek freedom. There were plans afoot to restore the mound to its "original shape," and one enterprising vintner was even marketing a "Soros" wine in Athens.[34]

The American Schoolers had the benefit of Schliemann's very personal perspective on the mound. During the group's first week in Athens, Rufus Richardson and the students had met Schliemann, who had recently returned from Troy. Staïs's work at Marathon, Richardson later recalled, came as "a great blow to Schliemann, who had never suffered such a defeat from such a young rival." Even so, Schliemann was upbeat. "I thought the great goddess Athena had deserted me," he told Richardson, "but she has just given me good luck at Troy." Less than three months after that conversation, Gilbert and his fellows would attend Heinrich Schliemann's funeral.[35]

It had been a long day. Following their morning train ride, Richardson and the students had hiked more than fifteen miles from Kephissia to the *sorós*. Fortunately, Irving Manatt had helped them arrange to stay the night at the country estate of the prominent Athenian financier Paulos Skouzès, near the village of Beï two miles north of the *sorós*.[36]

The Americans may have reached the cypress-shaded villa at Beï after sunset. Skouzès was not there to greet them personally, but his staff helped the visitors settle in for a comfortable night. Greeks outside Athens were less familiar with the United States, so Gilbert and his companions might have experienced an exchange like the one Irving Manatt had with an Attic schoolmaster in 1892: "So you are Americans?" "Yes." "Of North or South America?" The staff probably told the Americans that Skouzès had vineyards and a winery down in the plain. In fact, a French guidebook marvels that the estate's wine was already being served, "sous le nom brillant de cru de Marathon, dans les grânds hotels de Paris!" Little did anyone know the Skouzès winery lay nearly on top of the marble *tropaion*, or victory monument, the Athenians had set up some decades after the battle of Marathon. Not until 1965 would the American School's Eugene Vanderpool excavate the remains of the *tropaion*, built into a medieval tower just south of the winery buildings.[37]

Before dawn the next day, the Americans were back on the road for a seven-mile hike, following an itinerary of Pausanias: "about sixty stades from Marathon as you go along the road by the sea to Oropus stands Rhamnus." There, they explored the tumbled blocks of the sanctuary of Nemesis, where Pausanias had seen a famous statue of the goddess. Allegedly the statue was carved from a marble block the overconfident Persians had brought to Marathon for a victory monument. Valerios Staïs, fresh off success at the *sorós*, had dug at Rhamnus in September 1890, discovering sculpture fragments that matched Pausanias's description of the base of the Nemesis statue, plus a nearly intact statue of the goddess Themis and another well-preserved statue of a priestess. The new finds were now on display in Athens. Richardson regretted the Americans had not tried for permission to excavate at Rhamnus. As he wrote Waldstein soon afterward, "I suppose anybody could have had it for the taking. The work of excavating the [illegible word] temples in which the two fine statues were found must have been almost nothing."[38]

Half a mile downhill from the temples lay the ancient coastal fortress of Rhamnus, still unexcavated. Here the group took time to enjoy what would become an American School tradition of swimming after site visits. "It may sound trivial to mention it," Richardson wrote home, "but a swim in the Euripus, with the fortifications of old Rhamnus at your back and the mountains of Euboea in front of you, is a method of studying classic lands that is not without its exhilaration." As a boy in Augusta, John Gilbert had swum in the Savannah River. Rhamnus may have been his first experience of the salt sea.[39]

Refreshed by their Aegean dip, Gilbert and his fellows headed northwest for the Amphiareion, sanctuary of the mythical Argive seer Amphiaraus, near the village of Kalamos. Their exact route is uncertain, but however they went, it was some fifteen to twenty miles over hilly ground from Rhamnus to the Amphiareion. Little wonder the only previous American School group to visit both sites had gone by steamer. The hike offered splendid views: to the west, the ridges of Mount Parnes and perhaps even a glimpse of the Saronic Gulf beyond Athens; to the east the Euripos strait, with the island of Euboea stretching out in the distance. Gilbert and company did not yet know that in a few months they would be excavating at Eretria on Euboea. Although they took pride in being able to walk almost as fast as guidebooks said horses could travel, they were still slogging when darkness fell.[40]

The group probably found quarters for the night at the store of Aleko Kiousis in Kalamos, mentioned in Baedeker's guidebook as a travelers' lodging place. According to a story John Pickard later told his mother-in-law, the American Schoolers made their beds "on the floor of a country shop." Having covered somewhere between twenty-three and twenty-eight miles on foot since leaving Beï, the men were worn out. They rolled themselves up in their blankets at 10 PM, "but the Greeks sat and talked and smoked until midnight, and at 3 AM, the proprietor was up again and the business of the day began." The lack of sleep apparently played havoc with the men's memories of this portion of the trip. Rufus Richardson's official report does not even mention it. Andrew Fossum, so vivid in his recollections of the first day, could barely recall even the place names: "From Marathon we went to Ramnus and to the Ampiaraon."[41]

The trip's final day began with a two-mile early morning walk through wooded hills to the Amphiareion. The site lay in a shaded glen alongside a dry streambed. During the 1880s, Greek archaeologists had excavated a temple, a colonnade, and a small theater, along with numerous inscribed statue bases. Gilbert and his fellows read aloud Pausanias's description of the monuments and the ancient rites to Amphiaraus, then quickly inspected the remains. They were especially interested in the theater because the School had recently excavated theaters at Thoricus and Icaria. Then they set out back for Athens.[42]

Rather than returning the way they came, the American Schoolers walked about two miles west from the Amphiareion to the village of Markopoulo. There, they picked up a good track heading south, a main route since antiquity. Another ten miles across rolling country, perhaps with a brief stop at the village of Kapandriti, brought Gilbert and his fellows to the site of ancient Aphidna. Identified in the 1830s by British antiquarian George Finlay, Aphidna lay on a flat-topped hill overlooking a verdant plain. Below the hill a small stream, water gurgling even in late summer, wound east toward the Marathon plain. From the hilltop, Gilbert and his fellows could just see Marathon in the far distance. The view from the summit looks rather different today, for in 1931 much of the stream was submerged behind a concrete dam built to improve Athens' water supply.[43]

Gilbert and his fellows knew that the place loomed large in myth: Theseus had carried off young Helen (before her Trojan days) from Sparta to Aphidna, until her brothers Castor and Pollux came to rescue her. They also knew that during the classical period Aphidna was an important rural deme (district) whose fortified acropolis guarded the northern reaches of Attica. Perhaps its most famous demesman was Kallimachos, the Athenian *polemarchos* (war leader) at Marathon. Richardson had recently published a school text of Aeschines's oration *On the Crown* and may have been particularly interested in Aphidna because several men from the deme figured prominently in the disputes between Aeschines and his rival Demosthenes. The site, though, offered nothing but rubble walls and potsherds. In 1894, Swedish archaeologist Sam Wide would begin excavations around Aphidna, revealing tombs dating back to the Middle Bronze Age, but it would be many more years before another American School group visited the site.[44]

From Aphidna, it was eleven miles along an easy road to the train station at Kephissia. Richardson, though, hoped for a last stop at the deme site of Dekeleia, mistakenly believing it was "from where Aeschylus, the Marathon-fighter, hailed." In the final decade of the Peloponnesian War (431–404 BC), the Spartans had occupied Dekeleia as a base for ravaging the Attic countryside. The ruins of an old fortress thought to be the deme's center lay near the royal summer residence at Tatoï, about ten miles west of Aphidna. From there, it was another six miles downhill to Kephissia. Given that the group had already covered some fourteen miles since morning, and with the sun already hanging low in the sky, Richardson may have had to forego Dekeleia, at least on this trip. In later years, he would delight in bicycling out from the American School through Dekeleia and up Mount Parnes, stopping just long enough to savor the view from the heights of Parnes before racing back to School in time for dinner.[45]

If they were lucky, Gilbert and his fellows reached Kephissia in time to catch the last evening train back to Athens. Otherwise, they had another nine miles on foot before reaching the American School building at the outskirts of the city. Either way, it was probably after dark when an exhausted, dust-covered John Gilbert at last tumbled back into his own bed. In just three days, he and his companions had hiked at least sixty-five miles.[46]

Library Time

Less than a week after returning from the trek through Attica, Richardson was off again. Between November 5 and 15, he led a slog from Athens to Delphi, north to Thermopylae, then back through the region of Boeotia to Athens. Aside from brief train, steamer, and carriage rides, more than 170 miles of this journey was on foot, including a non-stop twelve-hour march of some 35 miles from Amphissa to the Spercheios river crossing west of Thermopylae. It was the American School's first official trip into central Greece, and John Gilbert was not part of it. While the School's annual report makes no mention of this fact, a contemporary handwritten account by John Pickard, preserved among the family papers of Pickard's great-granddaughter Katherine Tenthoff, reveals that Gilbert did not go.[47]

Pickard does not explain his classmate's absence, but we must consider matters from Gilbert's perspective. If the Americans were not going to get the rights to Delphi, the prospect of visiting the unexcavated site was less appealing, especially since archaeology was not his main interest. Thermopylae might have tempted him as another icon of the age-old struggle for freedom, but he had already seen Salamis and Marathon. And, the hike through Attica had already given him plenty enough experience of tramping through the Greek countryside. Most importantly, there was his Brown graduate reading list: the entire *Iliad* and *Odyssey*, Plato's *Phaedo*, several of Demosthenes's orations. With the fall term already half over, Gilbert needed to focus on this reading. If he did not finish his master's work in Athens, he might never have time to complete it back in Augusta.

Something else added urgency to his work: Ola was pregnant again, with a baby due in the spring. Gilbert may already have known his wife was expecting when he left home in September. That might explain the *Barnwell People* report that he planned "to finish the two years course in one term." Otherwise, he got the news by letter soon after reaching Athens.[48]

With a graduate degree, Gilbert could expect a higher salary at Paine. An advanced degree would also open the doors to opportunities elsewhere. As disappointing as it may be to learn that Gilbert did not participate in this milestone trip in the American School's history, staying in Athens was for him the better decision. While Richardson, Brownson, Fossum, and Pickard trudged through the rain across central Greece, subsisting on boiled eggs and *retsina* (wine flavored with pine resin), losing their way in the dark, and being tormented by bedbugs, Gilbert was enjoying a scholar's dream: nearly two weeks of quiet, uninterrupted time in a comfortable, well-appointed library (Figure 5.2).

By the time Gilbert's fellows returned to Athens, splashed with mud from head to foot, a cold, wet winter was setting in. The distant mountains of the Peloponnesus were snow-clad and soon the Attic hills bore a sprinkling of white atop fresh greenery. The indefatigable Richardson took the men out for one last day trip, to the mountain fortress of Phyle, where they met rain, snow, and fog. After that, the entire group headed for winter quarters in the library. For the rest of November and on into December, Richardson met the students only once or twice a week for class sessions, affording Gilbert plenty of time to focus on his reading list.[49]

It was also the season for holidays. Though President Harrison's official Thanksgiving proclamation had not reached Athens, Mrs. Kalopothakes invited all the Americans she knew in Athens to join her for a celebration on November 27, the last Thursday of the month according to the calendar in the United States (on the old Julian

FIGURE 5.2 The American School library circa 1896, looking much as it did in 1891.
Courtesy of the American School of Classical Studies at Athens.

calendar still used in Greece, it was only November 15). Some twenty-five guests came, including John Gilbert and the other students, John Pickard's family, the Richardsons, and Arletta and Winnie Manatt. Consul Manatt and Minister Snowden did not attend, probably because they were hosting an official US government function elsewhere. After decades of welcoming American visitors, Mrs. Kalopothakes had her Thanksgiving routine down. In a letter home, Edith Harris marveled: "You probably have thought we were not to have the dinner, but we did, a delicious one, turkey, potato, squash, plum-pudding (fine), nuts, fruit [emphases in original]." John and Jeanie Pickard had a special contribution: the last remaining piece of their wedding cake, carefully saved for almost eighteen months.[50]

Caroline Gerrish, who had not spent much time with the American School group during the fall, remarked on Gilbert's presence. Again, she focused on his appearance, commenting: "He is less than a mulatto—perhaps a quadroon, is quite handsome and has gentlemanly manners. He was here Thanksgiving evening and appeared as well as any of the students." Edith Harris, who along with Emma Potter had begun making occasional visits to the School library, enjoyed speaking with "the students of the Amer. School . . . a Mr. Fossom [sic], Mr. Bronson [sic], and Mr. Gilbert (the last, a negro.). They are quite pleasant." After a delightful dinner and desserts, the group turned to singing patriotic anthems and college songs. Beyond the good food and good company, Thanksgiving 1890 in Athens affirmed to John Gilbert that Mrs. Kalopothakes and her guests saw him as no less an American than any other. At the Kalopothakes's table, they were all fellow Americans. Even if back home some "fellow Americans" would not deign to sit for a meal with him, for Gilbert it offered a vision of what was possible.[51]

The Living Rock

A week after Thanksgiving, Gilbert sat down in the American School library to write home a long essay reflecting on his early months abroad. The full text of this essay, published in the now-lost *Georgia Baptist*, so far eludes us. Perhaps a yellowed, brittle copy sits in an attic somewhere, waiting to be found. Meanwhile we have only the excerpt *The New York Age* printed in late January 1891 under the title "A Georgian in Greece." We have already encountered this excerpt in retracing Gilbert's track to Athens. The final surviving portion offers us a deeply moving glimpse of his response to the city.[52]

Gilbert caps his journey to Athens with his first sunset view of the distant marble-crowned Acropolis, "a sight never to be forgotten, a sight nothing less than glorious." Then, he whisks his readers imme- diately to the heart of the classical city: "This is Athens where we are now, and the high table land is the Acropolis." "Let us go upon the Acropolis," he continues, walking his readers through the Beulé Gate and up the Pentelic marble steps, past the Temple of Athena Nike and through the Propylaea gateway to emerge before the Parthenon and the Erechtheum, just as he had walked up with his fellow American

School scholars, one of them clutching the group's copy of Jane. Even as he evokes his own physical experience of the place—"a hundred steps, I think"—his use of the plural "let us go" invites readers back in Augusta to join him in climbing those steps.[53]

On the Acropolis, Gilbert's response is intellectual, aesthetic, and precise: the Propylaea is "far-famed," the Parthenon "the master piece of Phidias' architectural skill," the Erechtheum adorned by its "beautiful Caryatid porch." He places the surrounding fortification walls into chronological context, "to the ages of Pericles, Cimon, the Pelasgians, and Turkish possession." W. E. B. Du Bois would later famously write, "I sit with Shakespeare and he winces not." John Gilbert might have said the same about sitting on the Acropolis: the ancient marbles offered no color line, no scorn or condescension. Even more than that, the shared experience of place—of the Acropolis, the other monuments of Athens, and the sites of Attica—provided Gilbert common ground (literally) with his white professor and classmates. These shared experiences, and others throughout his year in Greece, made their mark. He would return to the United States more keenly interested than ever in interracial cooperation and understanding.[54]

While he admires the ancient glories of the Acropolis, Gilbert devotes the final lines of his account, at least in the excerpt that survives for us, not to the classical past but to the Christian past of the nearby Areopagus, or Mars Hill (Figure 5.3). "Northwest of the Acropolis," he writes, "is Mars Hill, where St. Paul made his famous speech." Gilbert was hardly unusual in focusing on this unassuming rock, which according to the generally accepted reading of the Book of Acts was where Paul had stood before the Athenians to explain the tenets of Christian faith. Many nineteenth-century European and American visitors, including the most ardent classical scholars, considered Mars Hill the most important site in Athens. As Rufus Richardson put it, "not a few, preferring a trace of Paul to the monuments of Pericles, will seek . . . the bare hill of the Areopagus as the spot where Paul stood and spoke, starting from common ground with his Athenian audience, but carrying them up to spiritual heights which Pericles in his oratory never reached."[55]

FIGURE 5.3 Looking north from the Acropolis toward the Areopagus (Mars Hill), March 1891. The Hephaisteion is just visible at far right. In the left distance is the National Observatory.

Courtesy of the William Lewis Sachtleben Papers (Collection 1841). Library Special Collections, Charles E. Young Research Library, University of California, Los Angeles.

The Areopagus had yet greater meaning for African Americans. Now, on the one hand, Paul's admonitions to slaves to obey their masters made him in the antebellum United States "the patron saint of the master class" in the eyes of both slaveholders and enslaved. On the other hand, Paul's Areopagus sermon and above all his declaration that God "hath made of one blood all nations of men for to dwell on all the face of the earth" was from the eighteenth century onward a touchstone for all who asserted the common humanity of black and white people in the face of slavery and race prejudice.[56]

Although others probably visited without leaving a trace, only two African American travelers before Gilbert recorded their visits to the Areopagus. Both men's accounts reveal the place's symbolic power. David Dorr, an enslaved servant accompanying his master on a tour through Europe, was there on May 29, 1852. Sitting atop the hill, Dorr mused on the contrast between living Christianity and the dead classical monuments. "On Mars Hill where St. Paul thundered," he later wrote, "though nothing to designate the spot, there the Christian of to-day would rather stake his salvation than from the most sacred abode of Jupiter and Juno." Frederick Douglass climbed up on March 24, 1887, his final day in Greece after a week of visiting the classical monuments and enjoying the Attic countryside. Although he blasted the pro-slavery use of Paul, Douglass had for years ranked Paul's Areopagus speech alongside the Declaration of Independence, the Sermon on the Mount, and the Constitution as documents of civil rights. He recounts in his diary: "Today I took my last look at the Acropolis—and stood for the first time on Areopagus, and heard read Paul's famous address to the Athenians 18 hundred years ago. I tried to imagine the state of mind incited. . . ." He did not finish the thought in his diary, but Douglass later wrote that the experience was cause for "intense gratification."[57]

For Gilbert, the Areopagus was similarly meaningful. Paul's words helped ground his later advocacy of interracial harmony. Years later, he referred in speeches to the hill, noting that while he had "as well as he could walked in the footsteps of St. Paul," he was "more proud of being a humble worker in the colored ranks [as an educator and civil rights activist] than he was of his experience in Athens."[58]

By the time Gilbert climbed up the sixteen steps roughly cut into the south face of the Areopagus, it was common for visitors atop the hill to read aloud from Acts, hold impromptu prayer meetings, and conduct services. The peak of Areopagus veneration came in November 1889, when Presbyterian minister Thomas De Witt Talmage, the preeminent American mega-preacher of the day, stopped in Athens en route to the Holy Land. Accompanied by an entourage that included publisher Louis Klopsch (later the inventor of red-letter editions of the Bible, which print the words of Jesus in red), Talmage conducted a service on the Areopagus, an event that made headlines in seemingly every news-paper across the United States. He also visited the American School, where he would have met John Gilbert had Gilbert gone to Greece in 1889–1890. As it was, Gilbert almost certainly read accounts of Talmage's Athenian visit in the Augusta papers.[59]

Not content with preaching on Mars Hill, Talmage decided to bring it home with him. With Consul Manatt's help (Minister Snowden was in Bucharest) and permission from Premier Tricoupis and Queen Olga, Talmage had a block cut from the Areopagus and shipped back to Brooklyn to be embedded in the wall of his enormous new Tabernacle mega-church, alongside two stones taken from Mount Sinai and an-other from Mount Calvary in Jerusalem. Manatt, a devout Christian himself, found some humor in the inside story behind Talmage's re-quest for a chunk of the Areopagus, a story he probably recounted to Gilbert and the other American Schoolers: "We had one hewn out and sent him—for a pulpit, warning him that while it would take a high po-lish it would not bear much pounding; try it once, and he would think the unconverted old Erinyes [Furies, i.e. goddesses of vengeance] were in it. You see, the government didn't care to whittle the surface of the rock, so we carved our pulpit out of the Cave of the Furies, which is (so to say), just under its ribs."[60]

Standing on the Areopagus in December 1890, Gilbert, too, was overcome with the power of place. He felt compelled to leave his own enduring mark. "I tried," he writes in the final preserved sentence of his essay, "to find the very spot where [Paul] stood, and, thinking I had perhaps succeeded, I roughly scratched in the 'living rock' the names of myself and my wife." With that signature, Gilbert completed an arc begun with his boyhood scrawl on a Freedman's Bank register in Augusta two decades before. The shoes of millions of visitors have worn smooth much of the Areopagus since he stood upon it, but else-where on the rock travelers' inscriptions remain legible. The words John Wesley Gilbert inscribed may still be there today

6

THE DEMES
OF ATHENS

William Sanders Scarborough, Professor of Ancient Languages at Wilberforce University in Ohio, was in January 1891 probably the nation's most famous black scholar of Greco-Roman classics. Over the past decade, he had written a dozen papers or articles on classical philology, a Greek textbook, and many other publications on literature, politics, education, and civil rights. Scarborough was at home when a letter from a young man he had never met landed on his desk. John Wesley Gilbert sent news of his studies in Greece and expressed strong hopes of meeting one day. The timing was providential. Scarborough was just then writing a response to a set of racist screeds that Southern white politicians had published on what they called "the Negro problem" (a more accurate term, he often suggested, was "the white man question"). One particularly rankling claim came from a Georgia congressman whose district, as it happened, included Augusta: "the kind of education the Negro should receive should not be very refined, nor classical."[1]

Scarborough's response took particular pleasure in highlighting Gilbert's kind of education: "Even while I write, a letter lies before me from a young colored student, a graduate of Brown University, who is now taking a post-graduate course at the American School for [sic] Classical Studies. . . . From all reports, he is making an excellent record, and will present a thesis in March on 'The Demes of Athens.'"

Scarborough, his own dream of attending the American School never realized, seems to have hung onto this letter for decades. Penning his autobiography in the 1920s, he even quoted Gilbert's words: "I am trying to walk in your footsteps by making myself, like you, an eminent Greek scholar."[2]

The thesis John Gilbert wrote at the ASCSA during winter 1891 would indeed take him further on the path to eminence. He would be the first American scholar of any race to write about the urban demes (neighborhoods or districts) of Athens. This work helped him win a master's degree in Greek from Brown University, making him one of the first dozen recipients of a Brown graduate degree in any field and one of the very first African Americans to earn an advanced degree in classical studies. On the way to completing his thesis, though, Gilbert would have to navigate his relationship with a new arrival: Charles Waldstein, Reader in Classical Archaeology at Cambridge University and Permanent Director of the ASCSA.[3]

A Man of Impetuous Mind

In later years, Charles Waldstein helped organize the 1896 Athens Olympics, where he competed in riflery for the United States. As Sir Charles Walston—he was knighted in 1912 and changed his name during the First World War—he was a noted advocate for international cooperation. When Gilbert met him in December 1890, Waldstein was a thirty-four-year-old rising star with Columbia and Heidelberg degrees. He had made his first splash in 1882 by identifying a newly acquired marble head in the Louvre as a Lapith from the Parthenon and matching it to the proper spot on one of the sculptured metopes carried off from Athens to the British Museum nearly a century before. His widely read *Essays on the Art of Pheidias* and his work at Cambridge solidified his reputation on both sides of the Atlantic. After signing on in 1888 for a three-year term as Permanent Director of the American School, Waldstein one-upped himself in January 1889 by identifying a sculpture fragment dug up on the Acropolis as the head of the goddess Iris, part of a Parthenon frieze slab in the British Museum. Never one for modesty, Waldstein pronounced his discovery "the crowning event" of the Acropolis excavations.[4]

Recent events had been hard on Waldstein. Late in 1889, he lost the directorship of Cambridge's Fitzwilliam Museum. He went to Athens in January 1890 only to meet conflict with Annual Director Orris, bad weather, illness, a dearth of students, and disappointing excavations at Plataea. By early April he was back in Cambridge. In June came word from New York: his father Henry, an optics maker and Jewish community leader, lay dying. Waldstein rushed home, but got there too late.[5]

While a dispute over his father's estate dragged on, Waldstein spent summer and fall courting Frances Johnston, whose railroad tycoon father had helped found New York's Metropolitan Museum of Art. He made the rounds of posh vacation spots, visiting Vanderbilts and Astors in hopes of raising money to excavate Delphi, but neglected American School matters. Not until late September did he manage a brief, tense meeting at Harvard with Charles Eliot Norton, Thomas Day Seymour, Albert Harkness, and a few other Managing Committee members. Waldstein lectured on Delphi at Columbia University the day before taking ship back across the Atlantic on October 1. Four weeks later, Tricoupis's electoral defeat crushed his Delphic dreams. Though his optimism about Delphi had rebounded by the time he returned to Athens on December 16, 1890, Waldstein was hardly thrilled to be back at the American School, where he and his valet Lyon took over the building's top floor. "School looks much better," he told his diary, "though [there are] things that still irritate me."[6]

With his brilliant manner and elite connections, Waldstein fulfilled the Managing Committee's hopes of raising the American School's profile in Athens. Thomas Day Seymour marveled that "the surly Kavvadias [director of the Acropolis excavations] becomes genial in his presence and would (I believe) make him a present of the whole Acropolis if it were in his power." The Committee was less happy with Waldstein's teaching. William Goodwin observed "W. is a man of such impetuous mind, that he needs a long time to get settled in any new business. He is never quiet long enough to be of real solid substantial help to the students." Waldstein's complaints at sharing the director's residence with Rufus Richardson—though Richardson was in Greece all year and Waldstein only for a few months—further soured the School's leadership. Soon after Waldstein reached Athens, committee member Frederic De Peyster asked Thomas Day Seymour whether they had "set up a Frankenstein." Seymour was not far from agreeing. For now, though, the American School could not do without Waldstein.[7]

An Unbusinesslike Set of Men

Much of December passed quietly for Gilbert and his fellows. They studied vases in the National Archaeological Museum with the British School's Ernest Gardner and began attending German Institute Director Wilhelm Dörpfeld's on-site archaeological lectures (in German, *natürlich*), but otherwise stuck mostly to the library. Waldstein, consumed with Delphic diplomacy, barely saw the students his first week in Athens. Although a Franco-Greek commercial treaty that would give France excavation rights to Delphi had been negotiated, the two nations' parliaments still had to approve the deal.[8]

Reactions to the Permanent Director varied. Andrew Fossum, impressed by Waldstein's social connections, lively manner, and knowledge of Greek art, thought he "put new life into things." Others were less taken. Caroline Gerrish found him "a society man dressed exquisitely" with "a smooth oily tongue . . . more interested in making a good impression in society than in doing good work in the lines of his profession." Waldstein seemed to underestimate the students, and John Pickard worried he would waste time covering material the group already knew. Rufus Richardson, meanwhile, made clear he was Waldstein's ardent lieutenant and did his utmost to be accommodating. Waldstein told the Managing Committee he worked well with Richardson, but the latter's "immense" family displeased him and he would take many of his meals with the head of the Russian Legation in Athens, Baron George Bakhmetieff, and the baron's American wife Mary, an archaeology enthusiast.[9]

How John Gilbert found Waldstein is unrecorded, though we might hazard a guess. During the fall, Gilbert had been part of a small, focused group of American collegians. Rufus Richardson, despite his archaeological interests, was at his core a classical Greek scholar in the mold of Albert Harkness, Gilbert's mentor at Brown. Modest, dedicated to teaching, and willing to listen, Richardson had time for Gilbert. The frenetic, cosmopolitan Waldstein, with his scattered interests in art, archaeology, philosophy, and law, his disdain for "vulgar Americans," and what one observer memorably called "an addiction to eminent persons," probably cut a less appealing figure to Gilbert. He may have been particularly surprised to discover Waldstein did not speak modern Greek well.[10]

For his part, Waldstein responded unprofessionally to Gilbert. He had known little or nothing in advance about the four students aside from their names and Richardson's October report that "they are men who with good guidance will do good work." "They are an unbusinesslike set of men [emphases in original]," Waldstein wrote after first meeting Gilbert and the others, clearly refracting Richardson's words. Months later, Waldstein would use a racial slur in his diary. Though he did not direct it at Gilbert specifically, his use of this term suggests his response to Gilbert was at least partly based on racism. His diary clearly shows he treated the four students unequally. Andrew Fossum got the most attention, probably because of his Hopkins doctoral degree. Soon after arriving in Athens, Waldstein invited him to luncheon and gave him his choice of research subjects. The next day, Carleton Brownson, a graduate student with a Yale pedigree, had a similar invitation; Waldstein found him a "painful fellow." Three days later it was John Pickard's turn. Unhappy with Pickard's topographical research on the urban sanctuary of Dionysus in Limnae ("the Marshes"), Waldstein tried unsuccessfully to get him to switch topics. A similar discussion with John Gilbert might have been expected to follow. For the next seven weeks, though, the detailed daily entries Waldstein scribbled in his diary contain no sign of a one-on-one meeting with Gilbert.[11]

Even so, Waldstein could not outright exclude Gilbert from the School's activities. On Christmas Eve, the group went to see the new sculpture finds from Rhamnus at the National Museum, then back to the library to hear Pickard's paper on Greek theater architecture. While Pickard and Richardson spent the evening with their families and Waldstein called on eminent people, Brownson, Fossum, and Gilbert headed next door for dinner with British School Director Ernest Gardner, whose wife and children had not yet reached Greece, and a few British students. "Before leaving the table," Fossum recalled, "we sang a number of songs including Auld Lang Sine [sic] and closed with God Save the King. We had an enjoyable evening, Mr. Gardner joining gayly in the general talk."[12]

Christmas Day 1890 dawned sunny and mild, a welcome break from the increasingly chilly weather. John Gilbert had been away from Augusta for Christmas before: when he was at Brown, winter break was too short and train tickets too expensive to go home. Being away from his family, though, must have made this particular day in Athens especially lonely. It was baby Alma's first Christmas, after all. Gilbert probably attended a morning service, most likely at Rev. Kalopothakes's church. After that he might have taken advantage of the weather to stroll around town or take a train out into the countryside. Gilbert's Gregorian December 25 was for most Athenians Julian December 13, an ordinary Thursday with shops open and people going about business as usual. Like other Americans in Athens, he perhaps found amusement in disproving the old saying that Christmas comes but once a year, for the dual calendar meant the holiday would arrive again in twelve days.[13]

The day after Christmas (Gregorian) was chilly again. Gilbert and the other American Schoolers went over to the British School to hear Ernest Gardner speak about his recent excavations of the theater at Megalopolis in the Peloponnesus. As they sat listening, Heinrich Schliemann, who had fallen ill on his way home to Athens after surgery in Germany, was breathing his last in a Naples hotel room.[14]

Schliemann's Funeral

Word of Schliemann's death reached Athens via telegraph late on December 26, and US Consul Irving Manatt brought the news to the School the next morning. The city fell into mourning for the man one local paper called "greatest of the Philhellenes." While Wilhelm Dörpfeld and Schliemann's brother-in-law Panagiotis Kastromenos went to retrieve the body from Naples, US Minister Snowden began organizing a memorial service. Henry Schliemann, after all, was a naturalized US citizen. He had even left a copy of his will with consul Manatt for safekeeping. No one knew Schliemann had obtained his citizenship fraudulently in 1869, a fact that would not be uncovered until the 1970s. Waldstein, though he found himself "deeply affected" by Schliemann's death, nonetheless immediately seized the opportunity to invite the international scholarly community to the American School's first open meeting, to be held in Schliemann's honor. As funeral plans went ahead, Waldstein started his lectures to the students in the library, at the National Museum, and on the Acropolis.[15]

Schliemann's body came back to Athens on January 3, 1891, and was laid out at his mansion, the Iliou Melathron ("Palace of Troy"), alongside a bust of Homer and copies of the *Iliad* and *Odyssey*. The next afternoon, John Gilbert and the other members of the American School joined the crowd of diplomats, officials, scholars, and dignitaries at the black-draped mansion. After a service in German and eulogies from Dörpfeld and Snowden, the mourners followed Schliemann's bier a mile south to the city's First Cemetery, on a hill across the Ilissus river. It was a glorious sunny day, "like one fashioned after perfection" said Carleton Brownson, and all Athens seemed to throng the streets. At the graveside, the archaeologist Kavvadias said last words in Greek, Waldstein added more in English, and the white-haired statesman Alexander Rangabé closed with a poem.[16]

Two days later, on January 6, Gilbert and his fellow students found themselves sitting in the American School library alongside King George and Queen Olga, Crown Prince Constantine and Princess

Sophia, former prime minister Tricoupis, US Minister Snowden, British and German diplomats, and a raft of Greek and international scholars. In a mark of ongoing tensions over Delphi, the French were absent. Above the building, Greek and US flags flew at half-staff. Waldstein opened with a eulogy for Schliemann, then spoke on the sculptures that Kavvadias had recently excavated at the site of Lycosoura in the Peloponnesus, identifying them as the temple statues Pausanias had seen there some seventeen centuries before. Richardson dutifully followed with a paper on an inscribed stele Waldstein had dug up at Plataea in 1890. Afterward, Gilbert and the other students were probably introduced to the King and Queen before the royals withdrew for tea with Waldstein and the Richardsons. It was the first time the King had been to a foreign archaeological institute, and the visit made headlines in the United States.[17]

An Athenian Winter

As Permanent Director, Waldstein was supposed to lead the School's winter program, but his attention was often elsewhere. The day after the open meeting he left town for a week of bird hunting with Minister Snowden and several British diplomats. When he got back, he threw himself into entertaining Whitelaw Reid, at the time US Ambassador to France and, in 1892, Benjamin Harrison's Republican Vice Presidential candidate, even bringing Reid to the National Museum and the American School. Still chasing the mirage of an American Delphi, he piled on meetings with politicians, diplomats, and the Crown Prince. At the same time, he was making plans to dig at ancient Eretria, north of Athens. His on-again, off-again long-distance relationship with Frances Johnston in New York frequently distracted him. Atop all that, Waldstein continued his library and museum talks, always arriving late and in a rush, "as if he had the work of the universe on his shoulders." John Pickard's relatives, who were now attending every archaeological lecture they could, loved Waldstein's off-the-cuff style. Other casual visitors agreed, and Waldstein's museum talks soon drew crowds. Though she found Waldstein's voice "music itself," Caroline

Gerrish had to admit that "when he has finished the student finds he has not many facts to store away in his brain." Pickard himself judged Waldstein disorganized and repetitive.[18]

Wilhelm Dörpfeld's archaeological site tours, *giri* as everyone called them, were different. "The students are crazy on Dörpfeld," wrote Caroline Gerrish. Little wonder: the genial thirty-seven-year-old director of the German Archaeological Institute seemed to know every stone in Athens. He dispensed his learning in precise, methodical, accessible German. Edith Harris, with just a few months of German lessons, found he spoke so clearly and distinctly she could follow most of each talk. Dörpfeld had a sense of humor, too. One morning below the Acropolis, he gathered Gilbert and the others round a large cloth-covered water jar as if to explain its archaeological import. When he pulled off the cloth, a man popped his head out to proclaim he lived there, in the style of the Cynic philosopher Diogenes. Dörpfeld's downside was that he could go on forever, sometimes more than four hours at a stretch.[19]

The Americans also attended lectures at the British School, most of them interesting but none as good as British School Director Francis Penrose's on-site talk at the Parthenon in late January. Though Waldstein spoke several times about sculpture on the Acropolis, he gave little attention to the buildings themselves. Instead, months after he first caught sight of the Acropolis from the train bringing him to Athens, Gilbert got his introduction to the Parthenon's architecture from Penrose. At this and other British School events, Gilbert probably met a recent arrival: Eugénie Sellers, the British School's first woman student.[20]

These talks and tours offered Gilbert an unmatched overview of the latest discoveries in Greek art and archaeology. He was fortunate to be in Greece during a year when the new National Museum (sometimes called the Central Museum) and the refurbished Acropolis Museum (today known as the Old Acropolis Museum and closed since 2007) were better organized than ever before, even if the collections were arranged to foster aesthetic reverence rather than historical understanding. Paine's 1894–1895 catalogue, the school's only extant catalogue between 1891 and 1913, does not list a Greek art or archaeology class, but Gilbert may well have incorporated archaeological material into his Greek language courses, following the model of Albert Harkness at Brown, or into the full-year ancient history course he was teaching by 1913. Gilbert would bring home some Greek artifacts and probably used them in teaching, but he would be hampered by a lack of illustrated books, photographs, lantern slides, and plaster casts of artifacts, all of which cost money that Paine did not have. Athens also influenced Gilbert's modern-language teaching. Before going to Greece, he had offered a one-term German class based on his studies at Brown. Upon returning home, he began to teach a full-year course at Paine and would continue doing so until the end of his teaching career in 1918. A winter of listening to Dörpfeld, conversing with German scholars, and reading German publications likely played some role in that change.[21]

It was an unusually rainy winter for Athens, though the sun still shone brightly some days. Throughout January and into February, the American Schoolers had just three or four academic meetings a week, leaving ample time for other activities. John Pickard and his family received the Dörpfelds, the Penroses, and other callers. They played cards with British students and dined at the School with the Richardsons and Waldstein. Edith and Emma began frequenting the School library, and soon Carleton Brownson was coming by the Kalopothakes's house to see Emma Potter. "An entertaining little fellow," remarked Caroline Gerrish, adding that "[he] sings very well." The group saw little of Andrew Fossum, who abruptly left on January 25 to start work at Eretria.[22]

With the possible exception of Carleton Brownson's twenty-fifth birthday party on January 19, Gilbert is conspicuously absent from the half-dozen gatherings Caroline Gerrish, Edith Harris, and Charles Waldstein record. If he had a social circle in Athens, a *paréa* as Greeks would say, it is invisible to us. Possibly he made friends beyond the American School and perhaps evidence of those connections will resurface someday. In any case, Gilbert had not come to Greece to socialize. With the clock ticking down on Ola's pregnancy, he stayed focused on work. He finished off his master's degree reading list, then returned to the research he had begun in the fall.[23]

Researching the Demes

The American School's regulations in 1890 required each student to "present a thesis or report embodying the results of some important part of his year's work." The best of these papers would be published to showcase the advance of American scholarship in Greece. During winter 1891, all four students gave papers on their work in Athens. Gilbert left his handwritten thesis in the School library; whether he made another copy to take home is uncertain, and no trace of the text has yet surfaced in Greece or elsewhere. For now we have only the title: "The Demes of Athens" as Gilbert wrote in his letter to Scarborough, or "The City Demes of Attica" as the American School's official report names it. While it might seem impossible to wring anything from those few bare words, they reveal a fascinating and important story.[24]

Gilbert had probably first learned about the demes (*demoi*), meaning rural districts or urban neighborhoods, while studying Athenian history at Brown with Albert Harkness. According to ancient writers, some demes predated the legendary times of Theseus, who convinced the people of Attica (the region around Athens) to join politically into the single city-state (*polis*) of Athens. From reading the historian Herodotus, Gilbert knew that the Athenian reformer Cleisthenes gave demes new importance at the end of the sixth century BC, when Athens experienced political revolution. To break up existing regional factions, Cleisthenes mixed demes from the city, coast, and inland regions into ten new civic tribes. While these tribes played central roles in Athens' political and military organization, Gilbert knew from other sources that demes became the bedrock of classical Athenian democracy, as deme identity passed down from father to son. A citizen's deme was even part of his name: Aeschylus son of Euphorion of Eleusis, Pericles son of Xanthippus of Cholargus, Euripides son of Mnesarchus of Phlya.[25]

Nineteenth-century scholars pieced together much about demes from ancient literature and inscriptions, but they were missing a crucial source: the *Athenaiôn Politeia* or *Constitution of Athens*, a fourth-century BC treatise on Athenian government attributed to Aristotle.

Brief quotations survived in other ancient authors and in 1880 a few fragments of the text had been identified among Egyptian papyri in Berlin. When Gilbert arrived in Athens, though, the *Athenaiôn Politeia* seemed lost forever.[26]

During fall 1890, Gilbert learned about the topographical side of deme studies, which focused on identifying ancient deme locations in Athens and rural Attica. Though Pausanias was not much help in this endeavor, stone deme inscriptions discovered in situ often provided decisive clues. English traveler William Leake had led the way in the 1820s with his publications on Athenian topography. Others followed, including Schliemann's brother-in-law Panagiotis Kastromenos, who wrote his Leipzig dissertation on demes. By the 1880s, German scholars working on the *Karten von Attika* had located numerous demes; one more was found even while Gilbert was in Greece.[27]

The American School also got into demes. In 1885, a student had researched northeast Attica's rural demes, though he never wrote a paper. In 1886, the School's first excavation uncovered the theater of the coastal deme Thoricus. In 1888, the Americans dug up inscriptions at Icaria that shed new light on deme institutions and festivals, while other inscriptions at the nearby village of Stamata enabled them to locate the deme of Plotheia. Augustus Merriam, 1887–1888's Annual Director, became so interested in demes that he set one of his students at Columbia to writing a dissertation on rural Erchia, the deme of the historian and philosopher Xenophon.[28]

For all that, much remained uncertain. Of the 140-odd demes scholars knew when Gilbert reached Athens, only about 30 were securely located, with another 30 or so approximately placed. The city demes were particularly challenging. Only a few, notably Melitê west of the Acropolis, had been pinned down in 1890. Although a student in 1886–1887 had made an oral presentation on the urban deme Hippios Colonus, the setting of Sophocles' tragedy *Oedipus at Colonus*, he had never written up his report. John Gilbert would be the first American scholar to write about the city demes.[29]

Thanks to the School's library, Gilbert was able to read the topographical and historical publications of Leake and his successors, with one significant exception. In 1846, Göttingen University's Herman Sauppe had written the first study devoted to city demes, but the library would not acquire Sauppe's book until years after Gilbert left Athens, and there was no copy next door at the British School. Rufus Richardson, in fact, seems to have been unaware of Sauppe. While Richardson probably provided some guidance and advice, Gilbert's main inspiration for studying the city demes was almost certainly the same book that got John Pickard into the Limnae: *Mythology and Monuments of Ancient Athens*, the American Schoolers' "Jane."[30]

For scholars of Gilbert's day, one of ancient Athens' most famous spots was Kynosarges, site of a sanctuary of Heracles and nearby gymnasium (exercise grounds). The gymnasium once had a down-market reputation as the hangout of foreigners and illegitimate sons, until the young Themistocles convinced his well-born friends to work out there with him. In 490 BC, the Athenians rushed back from victory at Marathon and took position by the sanctuary to deter a Persian landing against Athens. Antisthenes, considered by some the founder of Cynic philosophy, lectured at Kynosarges in the mid-fifth century. And somewhere nearby lay another famous sanctuary-gymnasium combination: the Lyceum, where Aristotle taught in the fourth century.[31]

Pausanias was vague about the whereabouts of Kynosarges, but passing references in other ancient authors put it in the city deme Diomeia, between the demes Alopekê and Kollytos. That meant locating Kynosarges could help pin down three city demes and possibly the Lyceum, too. In the 1820s, William Leake had suggested Kynosarges might have been in the area of the Asomaton (Holy Angels) monastery below Mount Lycabettus, with Alopekê around the nearby hamlet of Ambelokipi. Though little evidence emerged to support Leake, his suggestions gained acceptance. By the 1880s, the *Karten von Attika* had Kynosarges at the Asomaton, Diomeia stretching southwest from there toward the Acropolis, Kollytos adjoining Diomeia north of the Acropolis, and Alopekê east of the monastery at what had become the large village of Ambelokipi. In *Mythology and Monuments*, however, Jane Harrison had revived the contrary view of English antiquarian Thomas Dyer, who in 1873 had argued Kynosarges actually lay more than a half-mile southwest of the monastery, along the right (northern) bank of the Ilissus streambed.[32]

Smack in the middle of this debate sat the American School, located on land that had once been part of the Asomaton grounds. From the library windows, Gilbert could see the tree-shaded monastery buildings, recently converted into army barracks, barely two hundred yards to the east. Harrison's attention to Kynosarges, combined with the monastery's proximity, must have shaped Gilbert's interest in city demes. He may have noticed what Harrison did not: relocating Kynosarges would pull Alopekê, Diomeia, and Kollytos further south, too, radically reshuffling scholarly understanding of the ancient city's topography. That some of Athens' most famous citizens hailed from these demes—Plato from Kollytos and Socrates from Alopekê, to name a few—could only have heightened his interest. During fall 1890, Gilbert and his fellows almost certainly walked the area around the School with Jane and Pausanias in hand, looking for evidence to resolve the debate. In fact, by December, Pickard knew the neighborhood so well he had found a shortcut leading downhill behind the School, past the barracks, through a hole in a fence, and back to the Kalopothakes's house.[33]

If we can explain why Gilbert chose the city demes as his subject, we can only guess at the arguments he advanced. In his published paper, John Pickard reiterates Harrison's view (derived from Wilhelm Dörpfeld's unpublished work) that the ancient sanctuary of Dionysus in Limnae lay northwest of the Acropolis, rather than south of the Acropolis where scholars had long placed it. Perhaps Gilbert took a similar topographical tack, using Harrison's view (derived from Dyer) about Kynosarges to relocate Alopeke, Diomeia, and Kollytos. If so, he was ahead of his time. In 1895, Dörpfeld would argue that Kynosarges lay on the left (southern) bank of the Ilissus, even further south than Dyer had put it. Dörpfeld's analysis pulled those three city demes south of the Acropolis, where maps of ancient Athens still show them today. While Dörpfeld relied on sources unavailable to Gilbert, there remains the tantalizing possibility that a conversation with Gilbert during winter 1891, perhaps after one of those on-site *giri*, just might have helped spark Dörpfeld's interest in city demes.[34]

Whatever direction Gilbert's paper took, he and John Pickard clearly grew closer through their work. In addition to *Mythology and Monuments*, the two men read Baedeker's guidebook, which mentioned demes and Dionysus almost in the same sentence, and the topographical aspects of their projects took them to the same books in the library. The pair probably also explored on foot together, for Pickard mentions walking south of the Acropolis with survey instruments, work very similar to that he and Gilbert would soon undertake at Eretria. Last but not least, it is significant that Gilbert and Pickard persisted in their research despite Charles Waldstein. Though Waldstein admitted the value of topography, it did not excite him the way fine art did. Andrew Fossum and Carleton Brownson, eager to please, both took up topics he suggested: Fossum wrote about a statuette in the National Museum, Brownson on the relationship between sculpture and vase painting. In the face of Waldstein's disinterest, Gilbert and Pickard found common ground.[35]

Scooped

Winter got decidedly worse in the final days of January. Up north in Thessaly, an avalanche buried an entire village; snow drifts cut others off for weeks. Down south in the Peloponnesus, men froze to death trying to clear snow-bound roads. In Athens, wind and rain kept Waldstein from joining Fossum at Eretria. He was especially eager to escape bad news about Delphi. France's parliament had ratified the commercial treaty, leading the Archaeological Institute of America to withdraw its bid. Waldstein's last forlorn hope was that the Greek parliament would reject the deal, throwing Delphi back to the Americans. With the seas still too rough to sail, he and his valet Lyon finally set off overland for Eretria on February 1.[36]

The other American Schoolers kept up their work in the library while Athens lay cold and damp under rain showers and snow flurries. Americans accustomed to roaring fireplaces and central heating found the conditions especially hard, for Greeks preferred to put on more clothes rather than burn expensive wood or coal. Fortunately, the American School had a furnace and ample fuel. Though the furnace did not always work properly, it kept the library warm enough.[37]

We get a glimpse of library life from the diary of an unlikely eyewitness. William Lewis Sachtleben and Thomas Allen, Jr., fresh out of college in St. Louis, had set off from London in fall 1890 to ride around the globe on their new-fangled "safety bicycles." Sachtleben and Allen reached Athens the day of Schliemann's funeral, then found themselves stuck waiting for replacements for their worn-out machines. Consul Manatt, naturally, made their acquaintance. On February 5, Manatt brought Sachtleben (Allen had just left for London in search of bicycles) to visit the American School. Ever the booster, the consul claimed the School was built on the spot where Socrates was born.[38]

Sachtleben and Manatt arrived to find ten men and women seated around a library table, listening to Rufus Richardson speak about the battles of Marathon and Plataea. Brownson followed with his School paper. The academic formality bored Sachtleben. "If they could only have spoken it off hand they would have made their speeches much more attractive," he complained. Afterward, though, he found himself conversing eagerly with Gilbert, Pickard, Richardson, and Brownson, whom he described as "gentlemen . . . from all over the U.S." who were or wanted to be professors of Greek. The School's combination of books and on-the-spot study intrigued Sachtleben. He got a tour of the library and the students' rooms, too. Archaeology, the scholars told him, was "one of the most fascinating but inexact of all studies." "All is conducted in a polite and polished manner," Sachtleben noted in his diary. Before he left, the American School men invited Sachtleben to use their library whenever he wished.[39]

More interested in Manatt's attractive teenaged daughter Winnie than in professors of Greek, Sachtleben hurried off with the consul, although not before making a deep impression on Rufus Richardson. As the American School's director from 1893 to 1903, Richardson took up cycling with near fanaticism, leading students by bicycle as far as Sparta, a hundred and thirty-five miles from Athens. He once rode more than a hundred and twenty miles across central Greece in under three days, stopping just long enough to take in the view of Mount Olympus before turning home.[40]

If only Sachtleben had visited a week later, on Thursday, February 12. By then Waldstein was back from Eretria, nursing an eye so sore his ophthalmologist prescribed topical cocaine. His other eye was soon bad, too, courtesy of the stinging dust clouds the winter wind whipped through the streets of Athens. Consumed by his usual array of affairs, Waldstein devoted a single sentence in his diary to the American School's evening library session that Thursday: "Then Gilbert read his paper on the Demes of Athens." Someone at the School did send a report back to the United States, for in March several newspapers noted the event. Gilbert's topic was so unfamiliar that some papers garbled it into "the Deems" or "the Deuse."[41]

In his presentation, Gilbert may have mentioned recent news from the Greek papers: the British Museum had acquired a papyrus scroll of the long-lost *Athenaiôn Politeia* or *Constitution of Athens*. Foreign newspapers were hard to come by in Athens, but he might even have found an old issue of the London *Times*, announcing a discovery "almost unprecedented in the whole history of classical learning . . . nothing less than the discovery of very nearly the complete text of a treatise . . . attributed by every writer of antiquity who quoted it to Aristotle." The *Ath. Pol.*, to use today's academic shorthand, contains a detailed description of the history and institutions of Athenian government, including extensive sections on how the demes functioned within Athenian democracy. Access to this new evidence could have fundamentally reshaped Gilbert's research on the city demes. It would be weeks, though, before a copy of Frederic Kenyon's first scholarly edition made its way from London to Athens.[42]

John Pickard got his hands on the *Ath. Pol.*, for he cites it in the revised version of his Limnae paper he sent off for publication on April 30. John Gilbert, though, left Athens on March 27 to travel in the Peloponnese on his way home, probably without ever seeing the new text. Back in Augusta, his chances of obtaining a copy were slim. Lack of access to the *Ath. Pol.* and to the veritable deluge of new publications that followed Kenyon's first edition goes a long way toward explaining why Gilbert never published a revised version of his paper. It was his bad luck to have completed a thesis that stood on the forefront of a research field at the very moment world-changing new evidence appeared.[43]

That unfortunate coincidence could not diminish Gilbert's scholarly accomplishment, especially in one key regard. On February 14, nearly two months after arriving at the American School, Permanent Director Charles Waldstein at last sat down one-on-one with John Wesley Gilbert. Waldstein's diary barely mentions the event ("Morning saw students. Gilbert &c."), as if simply writing about it made him uncomfortable. He did not invite Gilbert to luncheon as he had invited the other students. The very fact of their meeting, nonetheless, suggests Gilbert presented a thesis of such quality that Waldstein could no longer avoid granting him the professional acknowledgement he deserved. Both Waldstein and Richardson would later highly commend the thesis to the Managing Committee. It was also clear John Gilbert would have an equal share in the next stage of the School's work: the excavations at Eretria.[44]

7

EXCAVATING
ERETRIA

The thirty-three photographs of the 1891 Eretria excavations preserved in the archives of the American School of Classical Studies at Athens are among the earliest images of American archaeological exploration in Greece. Six are publication-quality prints made from photos taken by wealthy Scottish archaeology enthusiast J. G. Gordon Oswald and by the German Institute's Wilhelm Dörpfeld. Nineteen others are 4×5-inch film sheets, ultra-modern technology in 1891. These sheets, some of them badly damaged, mostly depict Eretria's fortifications and were made with a camera belonging to Carleton Brownson or John Pickard. Then there are the fragile 5×7-inch glass plates of a type widely used in the late 1800s. These plates belonged to Rufus Richardson's camera. We are fortunate to have them at all, for Richardson nearly lost his photographic gear overboard on his storm-tossed sea journey to Eretria. Many of the photos Richardson took failed to develop and others succumbed to the ravages of time, but among the eight survivors are two showing John Wesley Gilbert. Just days before this book went into press, American School archivist Natalia Vogeikoff-Brogan identified a third, previously unrecognized glass plate showing Gilbert. Together, these three priceless images offer vivid witness to Gilbert's archaeological survey and excavation work at Eretria.[1]

Great Trouble About Fossum

Eretria lies on the south coast of the island of Euboea, about thirty miles north of Athens as the crow flies. Thanks to the work of Greek and Swiss archaeologists, today we know Eretria was inhabited in the Bronze Age (ca. 3000–1100 BC) and flourished as a city-state starting in the eighth century BC. It helped found some of the earliest Greek overseas colonies, traded with Egypt and the Near East, and was among the first places the alphabet appeared in Greece. In Gilbert's day, Eretria was best known for having joined Athens to support the Ionian Greek rebellion against the Persian Empire around 500 BC. In retaliation, the Persians sacked Eretria on their way to Marathon in 490 BC, deporting part of the population more than two thousand miles east to near the Achaemenid capital of Susa. The city recovered and lived on, enjoying prosperity in the Hellenistic period (323–30 BC) and during the Roman Empire, until it was finally abandoned some time after AD 500.[2]

Eretria was reborn in 1834, when the Greek government settled refugees from the Aegean island of Psara on the marshy, half-buried ruins of the ancient city. The move was laden with symbolism, for Psariots had struck an early blow in the independence struggle against the Ottoman Empire. Nea Psara was to be a grid-planned showcase, home to Greece's naval academy, but mosquitoes and malaria soon drove people away. Many went to the growing town of Chalcis up the coast. By 1891, Nea Psara, or Aletria as many called it, was a run-down village of some four hundred souls. Steamers from Athens usually did not stop there, forcing travelers to disembark at Chalcis, then backtrack fourteen miles over a rutted dirt road. Sometimes it was faster to go overland from Athens to Skala Oropou on the north coast of Attica, then hire a boat across the Euboean straits.[3]

Nea Psara's failure meant opportunity for some. Antiquities hunters plundered the extensive cemeteries east and west of the ancient city for gold artifacts and fine vases, especially the delicate, painted white funeral jars called *lekythoi*, to sell in Athens. Eventually armed guards were stationed and in 1885 a young archaeologist named Christos

Tsountas (later famous as the father of Greek prehistorical studies) supervised the first official dig. The Greek government also issued excavation permits to private individuals who got to keep some of their finds. Work in 1889 produced a bumper crop of *lekythoi*, including two with scenes from Homer's *Odyssey*. John Gilbert studied those vases in the National Museum with British archaeologist Ernest Gardner; Eugénie Sellers, the British School's first woman student, had just gotten permission to publish them.[4]

The American School's Charles Waldstein wanted *lekythoi*, too. Dreaming big as usual, he also hoped to find the famed temple of Artemis Amarysia, which the ancient geographer Strabo said lay seven stades (less than a mile) outside the city walls. The mounded ruin of Eretria's theater was another attraction. Theaters were big in 1891, as scholars looked to archaeology to help explain how the ancients had staged the plays of Aeschylus, Sophocles, and others. A very public dispute between Ernest Gardner and Wilhelm Dörpfeld over how to interpret the theater the British School had recently excavated at Megalopolis in southern Greece only added to the interest in drama. Lastly, there were substantial remains of the city's fortifications to study, remains that might provide clues to test another claim of Strabo's: that Eretria had been refounded at a different site (often called New Eretria) following the Persian destruction.[5]

In mid-January, Waldstein arranged with a landowner he calls Contogianni to dig on the latter's property in the village. Andrew Fossum's abrupt departure for Eretria, though, resulted not from that arrangement but from scandalous necessity. "Great trouble about Fossum," a distressed Waldstein told his diary on January 23; "This serious. Fossum will certainly have to leave the house." Though he omits specifics, Waldstein complains "this is one of the results one might have foreseen from seating him with young lady &c," suggesting Fossum had become involved with someone at the School, the most likely candidate being the Richardsons's anonymous German governess. Whatever happened, it was so bad Waldstein went straight to Kavvadias, who immediately issued the American School an excavation permit for Eretria. Two days later, Fossum was on the steamer to Chalcis, carrying five hundred US dollars and instructions to find workmen and housing at Nea Psara.[6]

Journey to Eretria

Accompanied by Vasilios Leonardos, the Greek ephor (supervisor) appointed to observe the excavations, Waldstein and his valet Lyon took a boat from Skala Oropou across the Euripos straits to Nea Psara and joined Fossum on February 3. Happy to be away from Athens and alone among Greek speakers, Fossum had made friends, including Nikolaos Belissarios, scion of an old Psariot family and a former Greek vice-consul in Italy. Belissarios, it turned out, was at odds with the demarch (mayor), G. I. Zacharias. Fortunately for the Americans, Belissarios seemed to have greater influence in the village.[7]

Fossum had already found two dozen workmen with Belissarios's help. Waldstein added Barba Spiro, a grizzled pickaxe artist with two convictions for antiquities theft who had previously dug for the Americans at Plataea in spring 1890. Housing, though, was scarce. The best Fossum had managed was to rent an empty two-room house with broken windows, with the promise of a nearby derelict house for a kitchen. Waldstein set Fossum to work excavating the theater's *skenê* (stage building), left Barba Spiro digging up graves at Contogianni's property, and rode out east along a road lined with ancient tombs to find the Temple of Artemis. About seven stades out, right where Strabo said it would be, Waldstein found several finely carved marble building blocks he decided could be the temple. Then, just two days after arriving, he took a steamer for Athens, with Barba Spiro and Lyon in tow.[8]

Back in Athens, Waldstein quickly dispatched the School's cook Nikolaki, a veteran of previous American excavations, to Eretria with a load of supplies. He spent the following week nursing his bad eyes. By February 15, the day after he finally met one-on-one with Gilbert, Waldstein was ready to revisit Eretria. Again, the weather had other ideas. Snow blanketed Mount Hymettus. Rain, driven by a gale so strong it tore off part of the American School's roof, buffeted the city.

Waldstein, Richardson, and Brownson finally left by steamer during a break in the weather on February 18. They barely got around the southern tip of Attica before a storm drove them into harbor for two days. Between that and the muddy road from Chalcis, the trio did not arrive in Eretria until late on February 22.[9]

That same day, John Gilbert and John Pickard left Athens, reaching Eretria on the evening of February 26. Why Gilbert and Pickard went later than the others is a mystery. Perhaps they were ill, for Caroline Gerrish mentions Pickard coming down with a cold, and Gilbert holds a handkerchief in all three of his Eretria photos. Or they may have taken extra library time to prepare for the topographical survey of the ancient city to which Waldstein had assigned them. Their route and why they took four days are other unknowns. One possibility emerges from the British School's 1891 report, in which Francis Penrose thanks unnamed American School students for visiting Rhamnus to check on temple orientations for an article he was researching. Fossum could not have been one of those students, as he was certainly at Eretria until the excavations ended on March 20, and Brownson appears to have been there almost until the end. Gilbert and Pickard, though, could have gone by train from Athens to Kephissia, by horse to Rhamnus, obtained Penrose's data, continued to Skala Oropou, and crossed by boat to Eretria in the space of four days. As we will see, another possibility is that the two men stopped at Rhamnus on the way back to Athens after the end of the excavations. Whichever route they took, the pair's journey together to Eretria is evidence of the bond they had formed in Athens. Sharing the hardships of four days' travel seems only to have strengthened their relationship.[10]

The Best Archaeologist

After several months in the comfortable American School library, John Gilbert may have found Nea Psara (Figure 7.1) dismal at first glance. Fishing caïques lolled in the sandy harbor awaiting better weather. The village was half-empty, with many locals wintering in Chalcis. Grass grew in the wide streets between the squat, tile-roofed stone houses.

FIGURE 7.1 Looking north toward Nea Psara village, February 1891. The acropolis of ancient Eretria rises behind the village. Beyond the acropolis are the snow-covered mountains of Euboea. In the foreground are opened graves, with ancient potsherds scattered about.

Courtesy of the American School of Classical Studies at Athens.

Some houses sat abandoned amid pools of water from heavy winter rains. There was barely a tree to be seen in the fields near the village or on the slopes above. The roofless shell of the unfinished Naval Academy, built of reused ancient blocks, sat desolately at the north edge of the village, just below the theater. Behind the theater rose the rocky acropolis and beyond loomed the snow-covered mountains of Euboea. At least it was a lovely day. The sun shone on the remains of ancient walls and towers, reminding Gilbert he had come to do work that would set him on the forefront of archaeological research in Greece.[11]

Gilbert and Pickard reunited with the rest of the American Schoolers in their two-room house near the center of the village. Nikolaki, a skilled carpenter as well as an excellent cook, had repaired the shutters (there was still no glass) and roof, cleaned the fireplace, and set up camp beds, making for dry if cramped quarters. Brownson, Fossum, Richardson, and Waldstein were already in one room, so Gilbert and Pickard took the other. "Great squeeze in our little house," Waldstein recorded, "but we were pretty jolly." On the other side of the block, along the village's main street, Nikolaki had transformed a derelict house into a kitchen complete with benches and a table of rough boards. The Americans soon dubbed their house the "dormitory" and Nikolaki's kitchen the "salle à manger."[12]

The next day, February 27, Rufus Richardson took Gilbert and Pickard for their first look around under a cold, gray sky. They may have begun at the demarch's office, tidy but—like seemingly every house in the village—unheated. The demarch, Mr. Zacharias, showed them the original 1834 plan for Nea Psara, complete with boulevards, open squares, fountains, gardens, and public buildings. The plan had been drawn by German architect Eduard Schaubert, who also helped design the new urban layout of Athens. Zacharias probably allowed the pair to trace or copy this plan, for Pickard's hand-drawn survey map, preserved in the American School archives, shows similarities with the Schaubert plan, particularly in its compass orientation and its alignment of the walls and street grid. The published version (see Map 5) retains these similarities.[13]

There was little else to see in the village aside from the makeshift museum, its inscribed stones and other finds stacked haphazardly in a courtyard. The two men did learn there was a telegraph line and postal service. Waldstein, eager for publicity, used the telegraph to send updates to Athens, where they were often published (and sometimes garbled) in the Greek papers and thence rapidly picked up by the European and North American press. The mail, in contrast, was so slow that the essay Gilbert sent in March from Nea Psara to *The Independent* in New York was not published until April 30, more than six weeks after he wrote it. By comparison, John Pickard's essay about Eretria, mailed from Athens no earlier than April 7, appeared in *The Independent* on April 23.[14]

Up at the theater, Gilbert and Pickard found Andrew Fossum supervising some thirty workmen in fluent Greek. Over the previous weeks,

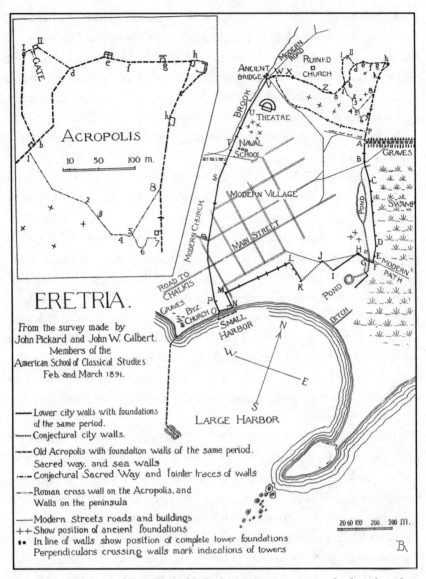

MAP 5 Survey map of Eretria, published in *American Journal of Archaeology and of the History of the Fine Arts*, December 1891.

Fossum's men had largely unearthed the remains of the stage building, using horse carts and wheelbarrows to haul away the dirt. Now they were busy clearing out a vaulted tunnel beneath the stage building. Carleton Brownson (Figure 7.2) and a few workers had just begun

FIGURE 7.2 Excavating the east side entrance (*parodos*) of Eretria's theater, March 18, 1891. Carleton Brownson stands at far left and Charles Waldstein (wearing pith helmet) at right.
Courtesy of the American School of Classical Studies at Athens.

digging into the orchestra, the choral dancing space in front of the stage. Searching for the theater's seats, they had instead come down on the top of another subterranean passage, this one leading out from the stage into the orchestra. With such important architecture appearing, ephor Leonardos spent nearly all his time observing Fossum and Brownson. Gilbert in his *Independent* essay describes with dramatic flourish his close-up view of these excavations: "It is really exciting to stand in breathless anxiety at the mouth of one of these caves when the workman had just now dug out perhaps a marble finger, a bit of the face of a fine statue, a piece of an inscription containing a few ancient Greek letters, or a part of the chair of the priest of Dionysos, and you yourself can see sticking in the earth an as yet undistinguishable something which may be the rest of the fragment you are holding in your hand."[15]

Out along the ancient road east of the village, Barba Spiro and his pickaxe were clearing out graves for a pith-helmeted Charles Waldstein. The old tomb robber, whose motto was "the pick (*kasmás*) is the best archaeologist," deeply impressed Gilbert and Pickard. Both quote him in their essays: "Dig until you reach *stereo*," or virgin soil; you can tell "by the way the earth works." Pickard likened "the picturesque old fellow" to one of Hamlet's grave-diggers, a Shakespearean reference he may have gotten from Gilbert. It may well have been Barba Spiro who pointed out to them that the Classical graves, the ones most likely to contain the fine vases Waldstein wanted, were typically covered with a layer of beach sand. Some of the other workmen were also skilled excavators, having honed their skills digging up artifacts to sell on the antiquities market. Among them was a Spartan named Giorgios Morakis, whom Waldstein soon appointed foreman.[16]

Gilbert also saw how the Permanent Director treated ordinary workmen. "These people," Waldstein later sniffed in *The New Review*, a mass-market London weekly, "have the most striking characteristic of all the Greek peasantry and people, a really childlike disposition; and they possess both the virtues and faults of children." The peasants, he went on, were so ignorant they had to be taught how to use wheelbarrows. In an account written for New York's *Century Illustrated Monthly Magazine*, he contrasts the careless, impulsive, and easily discouraged laborers with "the morally and intellectually superior archaeologist," the model of course being Waldstein himself. While Gilbert himself had written of meeting a "horde of dirty Greeks" on landing at Patras five months before, the similarities between Waldstein's attitudes and the racism he knew in the United States could not have escaped him. No stereotypes about Greek people appear in his Eretria essay. John Pickard, meanwhile, made a point of providing the workmen's perspectives.[17]

So eager was Waldstein for grave goodies that he struck a private deal with Fossum's friend Nikolaos Belissarios to excavate in the latter's fields east of Nea Psara, little knowing Belissarios was in the antiquities trade and sometimes dug graves under the cover of farm work. The land around the village, the American School men were learning, was a mosaic of tiny plots, each requiring its owner's permission to dig on. Two days before Gilbert and Pickard arrived, Rufus Richardson with a half-dozen villagers had started digging around the marble foundations

Waldstein thought might be the Temple of Artemis. When it became clear the marble was a tomb enclosure rather than a temple, one of the workers objected that the tomb was on his land. The man clearly calculated he would pocket a bigger haul from excavating clandestinely later instead of letting the foreigners dig and only getting the government reimbursement—half the estimated value of any finds. Eventually the workman relented, but his objections momentarily halted work on what the Americans soon christened the "mausoleum."[18]

Richardson preferred inscriptions to digging anyway, especially if a hike was involved. The same day Gilbert and Pickard took their first look around, Richardson followed a local guide more than four miles east and nearly a mile inland to see an inscribed stele that a tomb robber had just unearthed. If they were lucky (or unlucky, depending how they felt about Richardson's hikes), Gilbert and Pickard joined this quest, which ended at a thin blue slab of marble propped up against a farmer's hovel. On the stele was a 2,300-year-old epigram for "a boy observant and dutiful," Diogenes, son of Diodorus: "If earth is a goddess, surely I am a god, for I sprung from earth and became a corpse, and from a corpse earth again." The devout Protestant Richardson judged the verses "cold comfort" for their lack of Christian hope, but the inscription at least conferred some humanity on the people buried in Eretria's graves. Later the stone was brought to Nea Psara's makeshift museum, then lost. If they indeed hiked out with Richardson that day, Gilbert and Pickard were among the last foreign scholars to set eyes on this stone before it disappeared.[19]

A City Worthy of Mention

That evening, Pickard and Gilbert told Waldstein their plans. Early the next day, February 28, as scattered snowflakes danced in the air, they walked out to the foot of Eretria's acropolis, at the point where the grave-lined ancient road went east out of the city. From here, traces of the fortifications ran south toward the sea between marshes and ponds. These wetlands, the pair knew, had been Eretria's bane since at least the fourth century BC, when the city hired an engineer named

Chairephanes to drain the swamps. Now, the area was so rain-swollen that only a few feet of dry ground remained on each side of the wall. Gilbert and Pickard followed this line southward for almost a half-mile, measuring and recording as they went, until they reached the carefully carved stone blocks of two round towers that might once have flanked the southeast gate to the city. This stretch alone was enough to show the Greek historian Herodotus was right to call Eretria "a city worthy of mention."[20]

John Pickard and John Gilbert were only the third American team to conduct an archaeological site survey of this type in Greece. In 1882–1883, American School member J. T. Crow and visiting architect J. T. Clarke had studied Athens' Pnyx hill, the assembly place of classical democracy, with the aid of a surveyor's transit and level borrowed from Heinrich Schliemann. Henry S. Washington, an associate of the American School from 1888 to 1894 who later became one of the most important American geologists of the twentieth century, may have brought the School its first surveying equipment. In winter 1890, Washington and architecture student Herbert Hale surveyed the city walls of Plataea, site of the climactic 479 BC clash between the invading Persians and a Greek alliance. Their Plataea survey report, published in December 1890, may have reached Athens in time for Gilbert and Pickard to consult before Eretria. Pickard and Gilbert's precision, however, would far exceed that of Washington and Hale. Their careful methods would also stand in sharp contrast to Waldstein's quest for beautiful artifacts, which was more akin to plundering than archaeology. Indeed, his approach was so slapdash that when American excavators returned to Eretria in January 1892, they found ancient artifacts lying in the spoil heaps from Waldstein's digs nine months before.[21]

Two photographs taken at Eretria on March 18, 1891, by visiting archaeology enthusiast J. W. Gordon Oswald, show the surveying instrument Pickard and Gilbert employed, called an altazimuth theodolite for its ability to measure vertical and horizontal angles. In one photo (Figure 7.3), apparently the first surviving image of an American archaeologist in Greece using a scientific instrument, Pickard stands

FIGURE 7.3 The stage building of Eretria's theater, March 18, 1891. From left to right: Ephor Vasilios Leonardos (?), Charles Waldstein wearing pith helmet, Rufus Richardson (?), two unidentified Greek men, John Pickard with theodolite, unidentified Greek youth, Andrew Fossum.

Courtesy of the American School of Classical Studies at Athens.

next to the theodolite, notebook in hand. Gilbert may be at the other end, holding the stadia rod. Though its precise make and model are unclear, the device's prominent telescope and bubble level suggest it was optimized for taking elevations. Gilbert took charge of the School's twenty-meter surveyor's or engineer's chain, consisting of light steel or iron bars joined by either hinges or small oval links, with small brass tags called tellers attached at decimal intervals along the chain like marks on a ruler. The Americans also had a linen or steel measuring tape, but the chain was more accurate. With these instruments, the pair could measure wall lengths, tower dimensions, and other features. They would also use theodolite, chain, and trigonometry to calculate the height of Eretria's acropolis (116 meters), the angles of its slopes

(25 degrees at the steepest), and the distance from Eretria to sites across the Euripos straits. In keeping with the best scientific practice of the day and the United States' rapid move toward the latest global standard, their measurements would be entirely metric.[22]

Most importantly, Gilbert and Pickard knew how to use their instruments. Pickard likely had taken surveying at Dartmouth, where the subject was required until around 1880 and remained a popular elective thereafter, thanks to Dartmouth's agricultural and engineering emphases and its extensive collection of surveying equipment. Gilbert had studied surveying either at Brown or at Paine. Like other segregated schools in the south, Paine offered surveying partly because it could be presented as practical knowledge, acceptable to southern whites and to northern white philanthropists who favored Booker T. Washington's "industrial education" model. That "industrial" knowledge helped put John Gilbert at the forefront of archaeological methodology in Greece.[23]

It was perhaps on this first day of surveying, February 28, that Rufus Richardson and his glass plate camera caught up with Gilbert and Pickard by the round towers marking the southeast corner of the city walls. The photograph Richardson took shows Gilbert, Pickard, and an unidentified young Greek man standing near the towers (Figure 7.4). Visible on Gilbert's and Pickard's feet are the custom-made waterproof walking shoes they had purchased in Athens the previous fall. The young Greek man may have been Gilbert's assistant, for accurate chain-measuring, or chaining, required two people. While the "follower" stood still, holding one end of the chain at the starting point of a measurement, the "leader" paid out the chain, placing metal stakes called "arrows" at regular intervals until he reached the end point. The follower then picked up the arrows, recounting them as he went, until he rejoined the leader. Pickard's spoken Greek was the worst in the group—indeed he was the butt of jokes in this regard—so Gilbert likely did the talking with this young man and other locals. In the years after Richardson took this photo, villagers began dragging away the southeast tower blocks for landfill and construction material. Only a few remain in place today. Similar destruction occurred elsewhere around

FIGURE 7.4 John Wesley Gilbert, John Pickard, and an unidentified Greek man at the Southeast Gate of Eretria, February 1891.
Courtesy of the American School of Classical Studies at Athens.

Eretria's fortification circuit. Thanks to Pickard and Gilbert's careful survey, however, knowledge of these lost sections survives.[24]

Articles of Use and Beauty

Richardson made his second photograph of Gilbert and Pickard (Figure 7.5) a good half-hour's walk north and east of the round towers, at the "mausoleum" where Waldstein and his Spartan foreman Morakis had resumed digging on February 28. It was late when Gilbert and Pickard got there and snow was falling. Gilbert turned up his coat collar and donned a hat, while Pickard wrapped his shoulders with a blanket. Smashed limestone blocks and fresh-dug earth lay atop the marble facade of the tomb enclosure. Behind the marble, three or four workmen were picking and shoveling their way downward. Andrew Fossum stood taking notes as a village woman and a rifle-armed guard looked on. Richardson focused his camera. He slid in the glass plate

FIGURE 7.5 Excavating "the tomb of Aristotle," February 28, 1891. At left, Andrew Fossum stands with notebook in hand. At right, John Wesley Gilbert and John Pickard stand next to a village woman.
Courtesy of the American School of Classical Studies at Athens.

and exposed it just as Gilbert and Pickard glanced toward him from the edge of the excavation pit. The digging continued. The limestone top of a tomb appeared. Gold glittered as the workmen removed the heavy slabs. Inside lay a skeleton, ribs covered with a mass of gold oak, ivy, and olive leaves, a gold signet ring on one finger. Word spread and villagers gathered, led by the demarch and Belissarios. They watched as the treasures, including some two hundred gold leaves, were spread out on a cloth, then gathered up by ephor Leonardos to be taken back to the National Museum in Athens (Waldstein showed little interest in dating these finds and his vague descriptions make assigning a date to them difficult). That evening, snow and wind swirled outside as the tired American Schoolers ate dinner.[25]

It snowed for two days straight. Thirty miles south, snow blanketed the streets of Athens, a sight Mrs. Kalopothakes told Edith Harris that she had last seen in 1872. As white drifts piled up more than six inches deep in Nea Psara and the snow line crept down to the base of Euboea's mountains, the American Schoolers huddled around the smoky fireplace in their tiny house. The men had brought some books from the library and spent an afternoon discussing an 1864 travel account of Euboea and German archaeologist H. G. Lolling's 1885 article arguing that, contrary to what Strabo said about separate Old and New Eretrias, the city had always been on the same site. After that, they passed the time playing cards.[26]

By Monday, March 3, the snow had become rain and Nea Psara's streets were a slushy mess. Waldstein, "quite desperate about work," asked Richardson and the students to dig the mausoleum with him. They said yes. As John Pickard remembers, "the pleasures of camp life had been exhausted and all were sighing for a change." After a hearty meal from Nikolaki the cook, Gilbert and the other Americans shouldered tools and went off through slush and freezing rain singing college songs, followed by Morakis and three Greek workmen. Waldstein's *Century Magazine* account dramatically portrays villagers looking out from their shutters "at the crazy foreigners, for mad they certainly thought us."[27]

At the mausoleum, the men struggled in the heavy, sticky soil. Again, Waldstein elaborated for *Century Magazine*: "It was really comical . . . to see the learned Professor Richardson picking away vigorously; while another bespectacled student [Pickard] filled the baskets which were handed from one to other." Morakis, claims Waldstein, exhorted the Greek workers "to take note how the gentlemen could work." Pickard himself writes simply, "all lent a hand." Significantly, Gilbert's essay says nothing of this episode. He had done more strenuous farm labor as a boy in Georgia. For him, there was no romance in fieldwork. The American School men went on digging through mud and freezing rain until it grew dark. In a Hollywood movie, this supreme exertion would be crowned by grand discovery, but Gilbert and his fellows unearthed no treasure, just a small, empty grave.[28]

Over the next few days the weather cleared. While work continued at the mausoleum, Waldstein's attention flitted back to Belissarios's field, where tombs were disgorging beautiful gold jewelry. On March

5, workmen opened another rich grave within the mausoleum. Inside were more gold leaves, plus gold diadems, silver cups, a terra cotta statuette of a man with arms folded, two styli for writing on wax tablets, and what looked to Waldstein like a metal pen. "Splendid," he enthused; "Since Schliemann no such find." He decided the tomb must have belonged to a "poet, philosopher, priest, or statesman." On March 6, the day before he planned to return to Athens, Waldstein made a final mausoleum foray. The last two of the mausoleum's six graves produced little except for a fragmentary marble stele, its left edge damaged. The surviving portion was inscribed *[-]IOTH [-]PIΣTOTEΛOY*. Making a wild leap from the inscription, which could be restored to read "Biotê, daughter of Aristotle," Waldstein speculated that the person buried in the adjacent rich grave with pen and styli might well be *the* Aristotle, a notion scholars would soon disprove. He saved his greatest glee, though, for the beautifully painted white *lekythoi* that turned up in one of Belissarios's graves that afternoon, the very objects he told his diary he had been "praying for . . . all this time."[29]

In his later popular accounts, Waldstein embellished his diary entries into a melodramatic blow-by-blow of each tomb's opening. Writing after he returned to Athens and apparently without benefit of a diary, Pickard remembered many of the same episodes but mixed up their chronology. Gilbert, writing in the smoky lamplight of the cramped Nea Psara dig house, invoked the exhilaration of discovery he felt at the time. He vividly blends together the dizzying rush of a week's activity at both Belissarios's and the mausoleum, poetically inviting readers to "Imagine if you can—for it beggars description—the wild joy, the hearty 'hurrah!' of the directors, the students, and even the workmen, when, perhaps in the twilight of evening, the old grave-digger, with a small lantern, after removing the top slabs, crawls into a sarcophagus, and hands out vases of unique mold, terra-cotta figurines, finger-rings, ear rings set with amber, or opals in granulated gold, defying for beauty of design and excellence of workmanship those of the present day, gold leaves in imitation of grape leaves, gold crowns, alabaster boxes, and numerous other articles of use and beauty."[30]

Mapping Eretria

On March 7, jubilant over his "luckiest days ever," Waldstein left for Athens accompanied by Richardson. Brownson and Fossum were already back at the theater, Morakis back digging graves in Belissarios's fields. With the sun shining and snow melting, Gilbert and Pickard resumed their survey. Gilbert remarks: "less exciting, yet no less important, is the tracing and measuring of the city walls, noting their towers, peculiarities of construction, the quality and character of their stones, and mapping everything of archaeological significance." In his final publication Pickard would highlight Gilbert's contributions, naming him with the title so often denied black men in the United States: "Mr. John W. Gilbert is responsible for all the chain-measurements. The exceedingly rough and bushy nature of a portion of the ground surveyed rendered this work at times very troublesome." Pickard would also acknowledge Gilbert's "many suggestions," listing his name ahead of Waldstein, Richardson, Brownson, and even the great Dörpfeld.[31]

Picking up where they had left off at the southeast round towers, the two men traced the scant remains of the ancient harbor fortifications, which were obscured by brush and ploughed fields, and explored the arcing shoreline around the modern harbor (see Figure 7.6). They spent enough time by the shore to observe that at high tide the harbor's southeast peninsula became an islet. Indeed, the newly identified glass plate in the American School archives (Figure 7.7), which shows Gilbert and Pickard by the water's edge in front of a boat with crewmen at the ready, suggests the pair may have sailed around the harbor as part of their survey. In this new photo, Gilbert stands next to several ancient stone blocks. Perhaps drawing on Gilbert's geological studies at Brown, Pickard and Gilbert correctly surmised that the action of wind and waves had altered this coastline, leaving little trace of the inner and outer harbors the ancient sources described.[32]

At the city's southwest corner, Gilbert and Pickard came upon the massive semi-polygonal stones of an enormous round tower, 7.6 meters in diameter according to Gilbert's chain. The tower sat at the water's edge, guarding what was once a small fortified anchorage. Hoping to

FIGURE 7.6 Looking east across Eretria's harbor, February or March 1891. Scattered remains of ancient blocks are visible along the water's edge.
Courtesy of the American School of Classical Studies at Athens.

test German archaeologist H. G. Lolling's analysis of the figures given in ancient texts, they used the anchorage as a base point for calculating the distance from Eretria across the Euripos straits to modern Skala Oropou (site of the ancient port of Oropos) and to the ancient port of Delphinion, which Lolling had recently identified. Gilbert almost certainly talked with local sailors about the harbor and the long western mole that protected it from winds sweeping down the Euripos, for Pickard records the local tradition that a lighthouse once stood at the mole's end. Then the pair turned north and went up the city's western side toward the acropolis. Only scattered wall foundations were visible along this side, and the two men unknowingly walked right over Eretria's buried West Gate, the main entrance to the city. Not until the 1960s would Swiss archaeologists excavate this gate.[33]

En route to the acropolis, there was time for some humor. A photograph in the final publication, possibly taken either by Carleton

FIGURE 7.7 Gilbert (far left) and Pickard (far right) inspect ancient blocks in the harbor of Eretria, February or March 1891. Behind them are two of the same boats seen in Figure 7.6.
Courtesy of the American School of Classical Studies at Athens.

Brownson or John Gilbert, shows Pickard sitting near the theater, just below the southwest slope of the acropolis, examining a tortoise. Only a select few would grasp the sly reference to the philosopher Menedemus, architect of Eretrian prosperity during the late 300s and early 200s BC. Menedemus, it was said, liked to rile political opponents with his favorite lines from Achaeus, Eretria's most famous playwright: "Ere long the swift is overtaken by the feeble / And the eagle by the tortoise." The staged photo offered an implicit contrast between Waldstein's rapid progress from grave to grave and the slow, methodical work of the American students.[34]

Pickard and Gilbert devoted the majority of their time to Eretria's steep-sided, overgrown acropolis. "It was our good fortune," Pickard later remarked, "to be busied with this survey in those days of early March when the snowstorm had cleared away, followed by many days of cloudless beauty." The various construction styles here, the two men realized, told their own story, one that could be set against the ancient written sources. As Gilbert puts it, "the best remains of the walls and towers whose character represents several periods of history are those immediately surrounding the Acropolis." While little remained of the walls down in the plain, a sign that their upper portions had been mud brick, on the acropolis the roughly coursed stone walls in places survived more than two meters high. The large polygonal blocks of these walls were more irregular than the semi-polygonal masonry down in the plain. Contrasting with the polygonal acropolis wall were the remains of four large towers, built of regular courses of nearly rectangular (ashlar) blocks, each more than a half-meter high. The best preserved of these towers still stood nearly five meters tall. The massive bases of the others, one measuring thirteen meters wide, were surrounded by scatters of fallen blocks. As they scrambled through the undergrowth, measuring and observing with the help of their young Greek assistant, Gilbert and Pickard saw the ashlar towers were later additions, built up against the original polygonal wall. They also found evidence of later repairs to several sections. The men hunted unsuccessfully for evidence of a polygonal wall defending the south slope of the acropolis, though they were able to trace what they dubbed "the Roman cross-wall," a poorly built stretch of small stones held together with mortar, along that slope.[35]

Pickard's publication would distinguish four main phases to Eretria's fortifications: first, the original polygonal acropolis walls, built at some time before the Persian Wars; then, the semi-polygonal circuit of the lower city; after that the large ashlar acropolis towers, evidence of the city's recovery from Persian destruction; finally, the stone-and-mortar "Roman cross-wall." The presence of this sequence all at one site showed Strabo was wrong. In Gilbert's words, "this work has quite satisfactorily proven that Old and New Eretria occupied the same extent of territory." In making this conclusion, Pickard and Gilbert were going against Dörpfeld, who preferred to follow Strabo and thought Old Eretria might still be found further east.[36]

Subsequent work at Eretria has confirmed that Gilbert and Pickard were right about the city's location, but in 1891 the scientific study of Greek fortifications was just beginning. The two men misinterpreted some of the surface remains they saw, while subsequent excavations and library research have revealed crucial evidence to which they had no access. Their four-phase periodization has been superseded. Nonetheless, Pickard and Gilbert's careful study set the stage for the Greek and Swiss investigations of Eretria's fortifications that began in the 1960s and continue today. If John Wesley Gilbert has become recognized as "the first black archaeologist," it is important to emphasize that his most significant work was in topographical survey, a good reminder that archaeology is not just about digging.[37]

Arriving in Athens six months before, Gilbert had found his first sight of the Athenian acropolis "nothing less than glorious." Now, from the summit of Eretria's acropolis, he and Pickard shared another view during the cloudless spring days of March 1891. Close below, Brownson and Fossum's workmen were busy at the theater. Out east on the plain were the tiny figures of Morakis and his men, opening more tombs. "Beyond the town," Pickard tells us, "stretched the winding course of the Euripos with occasionally a passing sail. The snow had scarcely melted when thousands of bright anemones scattered themselves over the fields." The two men raised their eyes from the flowers to look far west to the winter-white slopes of Mount Parnassus above Delphi, south to the distant peaks of Attica, east and north to Euboea's snow-clad mountains. Each day they worked, the snow receded, the plain became greener. Though we do not have his own description of the scene, John Gilbert would doubtless have agreed with John Pickard that "the contrasts of these snow-caps and the verdure, the wide extent of sea and plain and mountain, as seen through the clear air of Greece under the soft purplish glow of a Greek sunset, made a picture of rare beauty, such as one seldom looks upon, but never forgets when once seen."[38]

Resurrecting Aristotle

Gilbert and the other Americans had heard Waldstein speculate about "the philosopher's grave" at the mausoleum. In his essay from Nea Psara, Gilbert even records Waldstein's fuzzy reasoning: "when we remember that the pen was the symbol for a philosopher, that Chalcis, which is near Eretria, was the native [ancestral] home of Aristotle, the philosopher, that the relation between the two towns was generally that of friendly intimacy, and that Eretria, like the Cerameicus at Athens, was probably a burial place for celebrated persons, it does not seem improbable that the grave of Aristotle . . . was in Eretria, and that the present excavations have brought it to light." Andrew Fossum, having written his dissertation on Plato, could have told Waldstein that Socrates judged writing and philosophy incompatible, but he owed the Permanent Director too much for rescuing him from scandal to say anything. Though the students were elated at the rich tomb finds, none of them anticipated how Waldstein's flight of fancy would grow into worldwide factoid, overshadowing their work on the fortifications and theater.[39]

Waldstein telegraphed Athens about the Biotê inscription and other finds either before leaving Nea Psara on March 7 or from Chalcis on March 8. Somehow the "daughter" part got left out. Soon after he and Richardson reached the American School on March 9, papers in Athens were running headlines about "the tomb of Aristotle." These reports, one of which credited the German Institute with the find, were generally skeptical. Even so, the headlines grabbed attention, for the city was already abuzz with the recent publication of the *Athenaiôn Politeia* papyrus attributed to Aristotle. Consul Irving Manatt, an avid reader of the Greek press, commented: "Well, we are resurrecting Aristotle. First came up his Athenian Constitution. Now the American School have found his tomb [emphasis original] at Eretria. So the papers say yesterday morning. After recovering stage of theater, our people opened a number of tombs, found a dozen golden wreaths and the like, and one tomb inscribed =*ristotelês*—all but initial." Manatt was unconvinced, since Aristotle died at Chalcis rather than Eretria and his remains were reportedly taken to Stagira in northern Greece. Still, he wrote, "Aristotle or no Aristotle, we are in luck at Eretria. I can afford to get on without Delphi."[40]

Waldstein saw the headlines and worried. "Papers premature announcement that I discovered tomb of Aristotle," he told his diary; "Must stop the report in its present stage." He sent cautioning notes to the Athenian papers and mailed a letter to New York, but it was too late. Word flashed through Europe and across the Atlantic, sped by 1891's global news giants, Reuter's Telegram Company and the Associated Press. In February, Eretria got a half-dozen mentions in US papers; in March, nearly a hundred.[41]

Athens' rich and famous acclaimed Waldstein's magnificent discovery. At an evening diplomatic ball, King George called out to him across the room, "I congratulate you." The royal family was so intrigued Waldstein got a request from the palace for a tour of the Eretria finds when they reached the National Museum. By March 13, Rufus Richardson had a cable from his father-in-law at the New York *Independent* asking for one hundred words on Eretria. Richardson sent his dispatch the next day. At Athenian telegraph rates, those hundred words cost at a minimum between twenty-three and thirty-five dollars. John Gilbert's monthly salary at Paine Institute, by comparison, was forty dollars.[42]

His head splitting with a whirl of activities, Waldstein managed to deliver an even-handed preliminary public report on March 16. Then he was off once more on the steamer, for the moment more intent on Eretria's theater than on Aristotle. Rufus Richardson, weary of Nea Psara, took his family on a trip south to the picturesque Peloponnesian harbor town of Nafplio. Back at Eretria, Waldstein again skittered from theater to graves to mausoleum, stopping in between to look over the acropolis walls and greet visitors—J. G. Gordon Oswald and his wife, come to tour the site and take the photos that would end up in the American School archives. At the mausoleum, Waldstein picked up a small marble statuette head he had missed before. "Head does look like heads of Aristotle," he mused. Running short of cash to pay the workmen, Waldstein halted excavations on March 19. By the next evening, Waldstein, Fossum, Nikolaki the cook, and the Gordon Oswalds were back in Athens.[43]

Charles Waldstein never returned to Eretria, but the American School did. William Carey Poland, one of Gilbert's professors at Brown, dug briefly in 1892, assisted by Carleton Brownson. Rufus Richardson led longer campaigns in 1894 and 1895. Under Richardson, the American School finished uncovering the theater and excavated a gymnasium, a temple of Dionysos, and other remains. The famed temple of Artemis Amarysia, though, remained elusive until the 1980s, when Swiss researcher Denis Knoepfler realized the "seven stades" (about 1,260 meters) of Strabo's text was a Byzantine copyist's error for "sixty stades," or about 10.8 kilometers. After two more decades of careful survey and excavation work, in 2017, Greek and Swiss archaeologists definitively identified the site of Artemis's sanctuary at the Paleoekklisies hill. That hill lies some 10.3 kilometers east of Eretria's city walls, counting from the spot where Gilbert and Pickard began their work in 1891.[44]

As in the beginning, so in the end: Gilbert and Pickard's return from Eretria is mysterious. Waldstein's diary does not even name Gilbert after February 28, though he was clearly there in March working on the survey. Pickard was still at Eretria on March 18 because he appears in one of Gordon Oswald's photographs that day, but he did not return to Athens until late evening on March 21, a day after Waldstein. The weather in late March was far more congenial than at the end of February. Perhaps, then, it is here we should place the travels which led the British School's Francis Penrose to thank the unnamed American students who went to Rhamnus "on purpose from Eretria." Since the timing of Brownson's return to Athens is also unclear, it might be that Brownson, Gilbert, and Pickard went back from Eretria together. Adding to the mystery, a 1923 obituary lists the ancient battlefield of Leuctra in Boeotia, more than a day's journey west from Skala Oropou, among the sites Gilbert visited in Greece. If "Leuctra" is not an error for "Eretria," it may mean Gilbert took advantage of the good weather to travel through the central Greek region of Boeotia on his own, so he could see some of the sites (such as Leuctra) he had missed by not joining the School group in November. Another possibility, suggested by the obituary's listing of several Aegean islands, is that Gilbert made a brief steamer trip through the Cyclades to the island of Syros. All we can say for sure is that he was back in Athens no later than March 26.[45]

Across the Atlantic, Richardson's cable and a long editor's commentary appeared in *The Independent* on March 19, the same day work ended at Eretria. With its boldface headlines—"Wonderful News . . . City of Tombs . . . Daughter of Aristotle . . . Much Gold Found . . . Nothing Finer Ever Discovered"—this dispatch garnered widespread attention, even as Richardson noted Waldstein "distinctly disclaims" the identification of Aristotle's tomb. Richardson also named the four students, "Messrs. Bronson [*sic*], Gilbert, Fossum, and Pickard." Newspapers across the United States quickly picked up the dispatch, occasionally under whimsical titles such as "The Remains of Miss Aristotle," and it stayed in circulation for months afterward, even reaching the sleepy seaside town of Santa Barbara, California. In the south, many black Americans first read the story in the official Colored Methodist Episcopal (CME) journal, *The Christian Index*. Editor F. M. Hamilton, who knew Gilbert personally, reprinted Richardson's entire dispatch, adding: "Mr. Gilbert is from Paine Institute. We are glad to [learn] he is connected with [so impor]tant a discovery."[46]

The American School's regulations said the academic year went until June. The 1890–1891 official report obscures what really happened: the group began to splinter as soon as the season at Eretria was done. Charles Waldstein busied himself paying social calls, dreaming up future excavations in the Peloponnesus, and showing off the Eretria finds to the royal family and other eminent visitors. Someone at the National Museum had accidentally broken off part of the "philosopher's pen"; on seeing it, King George quipped Waldstein had found "Aristotle's tooth-pick." Rufus Richardson and his family, back from Nafplio on March 20, left the next day for Constantinople, not to return until the end of March. Andrew Fossum went to the library to write up his report on Eretria's theater. Carleton Brownson visited sites around Athens. John Pickard and his family had hoped to see Constantinople but could not afford it. Instead, John and Jeannie decided to stay in Athens, while Caroline, Edith, and Emma made plans for a brief sightseeing trip to the Peloponnesus. Waldstein, accompanied by Brownson, left Athens on April 1 to see Argos and other prospective dig sites in the Peloponnesus, then headed for Paris. Richardson, Brownson, Fossum, and Pickard would reunite one last time for Dörpfeld's exhausting "Peloponnesreise" from April 9 to April 22, but by May they, too, had gone their own ways.[47]

John Gilbert would have joined Dörpfeld, too, but he was low on cash and his time abroad was running short. Back in Augusta, Ola's baby was due soon. Gilbert also knew the final public meeting of the School, scheduled for March 27, held nothing new for him. Waldstein would extemporize about the Aristotle-ish terra cotta statuette and marble figurine head he had picked up at Eretria, Fossum would talk about the theater, and Pickard would at last present his School paper on Dionysus in Limnae. Gilbert had heard enough of Aristotle, seen Fossum's excavations firsthand, and already knew Pickard's research. He chose instead to join Caroline, Edith, and Emma. Since his relatives spoke no Greek, very likely Pickard asked Gilbert to accompany them. At noon on March 27, John Gilbert and his three traveling companions left Athens for Nafplio in the Peloponnesus.[48]

When Gilbert left Athens, Waldstein's cautionary notes and Richardson's dispatch seemed to have slowed the progress of the "Aristotle's tomb" fancy. Greek scholar Margaritis Dimitsas followed up with a detailed critique of Waldstein's faulty reasoning. If Waldstein himself acknowledged the tenuous evidence in his official Greek report, he somehow turned disbelief into conviction. Three weeks after leaving Athens, he declared to a Paris newspaper that the tomb was authentic. Several US papers duly reported this declaration, spawning a secondary wave of reprints that lasted almost into 1892. In London, Waldstein dictated an account for the May issue of *The Nineteenth Century*, editing and returning the proofs in under twenty-four hours. With its come-hither title—"Is It Aristotle's Tomb?"—and simultaneous declarations that "we could not in the present day have hoped for better evidence for the identification of the grave of Aristotle" and "I do not make any final and definite statement whether this is the tomb of Aristotle or not," the article only aroused interest in Waldstein's theory.[49]

Back at Cambridge, Waldstein leaned in, even after hearing Dörpfeld had expressed skepticism during his May 5 visit to Eretria and even after Kavvadias wrote telling him that foreign archaeologists in Athens were shaking their heads at what they considered "an incomprehensible misapprehension." Perhaps praise from eminent people drove him; perhaps he needed the money. In June, he delivered a lecture confidently titled "The Discovery of the Tomb of Aristotle" at the Royal Institution in London, for a fee that was as much as John Gilbert made in a month and a half. While critics in England and Europe hoped the whole idea would go away, Waldstein was already pitching another popular account, with advance payment, to New York's *Century Magazine*. The American School's Augustus Merriam wrote Waldstein in July 1891 that the Biotê inscription was linked to previously published Eretrian grave stones, all belonging to a family clearly not *the* Aristotle's. Nonetheless, in "The Finding of the Tomb of Aristotle," published in *Century*'s July 1892 issue, Waldstein concluded: "for the present, we are justified in naming this grave, excavated at Eretria by the American School of Athens, the Tomb of Aristotle." As late as 1909, Waldstein in speaking to "a large juvenile audience" mentioned the possibility it was Aristotle's tomb. In 2016, a Greek archaeologist rejected Waldstein's claim, announcing he had found the tomb at Aristotle's home town of Stagira in northern Greece. This identification has found little support. For now, the philosopher's final resting place remains unknown.[50]

First Published Black Archaeologist

John Gilbert had already endured the bad luck of finishing his thesis on the demes of Athens just as the *Athenaiôn Politeia* was rediscovered. Although the *Ath. Pol.*'s ascription to Aristotle was fiercely debated from the start and most scholars today do not believe he wrote it, at least that papyrus was an authentic, invaluable historical document from the fourth century BC. It was far worse that Waldstein's Aristotelian fancy overshadowed what Gilbert aptly termed the "less exciting, yet no less important" work of the Eretria topographical survey. Indeed, Waldstein in his official reports and popular accounts reduced Gilbert's and Pickard's contributions to a footnote. The June 1891 issue of a new American scholarly journal, *The American Journal of Archaeology and of the History of the Fine Arts*, however, excerpted verbatim large portions of the two men's *Independent* essays about Eretria. Following the usual practice of the day, editor A. J. Frothingham omitted Pickard and Gilbert's names. John Gilbert thus became the first African American scholar to be published, albeit anonymously, in what remains today a flagship journal of ancient Mediterranean archaeology. As gratified as he was to see his essay excerpted, Gilbert may have been even more pleased to read the anonymous letter Frothingham also quoted. Waldstein's Aristotle, the letter noted, had already turned up in published inscriptions from Eretria dated to around 200 BC, more than a century after the famous philosopher died. "Hence," the letter concluded, "the philosopher theory may be safely laid upon the shelf of undigested notions."[51]

The "tomb of Aristotle" affair damaged Charles Waldstein's reputation and contributed to his not being made Permanent Director of the American School in 1893 (the post went to Rufus Richardson, who would hold it until 1903), but Waldstein finessed the gaffe. Even his harshest critics stayed on good terms with him, despite what French archaeologist Salomon Reinach later called Waldstein's aesthetic sentimentalism and tendency to philosophical gibberish. John Gilbert, though, had no margin for error. If his connection with Waldstein's alleged discovery was to some a mark of distinction, once the misidentification was widely known it would make easy fodder for white Southern racists eager to disparage Gilbert's scholarly qualifications. Responding to a request for information from Brown's alumni association in 1894, Gilbert listed his thesis, his survey work with Pickard, and his participation in the Eretria excavations, but not Aristotle.[52]

John Wesley Gilbert succeeded in Greece despite Charles Waldstein. Unlike at Brown, however, his accomplishment did not lay the foundation for a lasting African American presence at the American School. The School's original leaders, men like Gilbert's mentor Albert Harkness, had displayed a strong commitment to racial equality and

welcomed black scholars. As those leaders passed away, new generations of the School's Managing Committee did not keep up that commitment. The School's increasing focus on archaeology at the expense
of the broader range of Hellenic studies also played a role. In 1885,
Wiley Lane had planned to focus on modern Greek. In 1886, William
Sanders Scarborough, although he was interested in material culture,
would probably have focused on philological research. Gilbert under-
took both excavation and survey, but he was not primarily an archaeologist. Back at Paine, he did not have the resources and equipment
needed to offer full-fledged archaeology courses that would bring new
black students into the field. As archaeology came to the forefront at
the ASCSA, opportunities for black scholars to do literary study in
Greece became more constrained. Meanwhile, a younger generation of
African American intellectuals was turning away from classical studies.
W. E. B. Du Bois and John Hope, both of whom began their careers
teaching Greek, would by 1910 argue for reducing the role of Greek
and Latin in black higher education in favor of science, English, history, and sociology.[53]

Yet it is also worth considering how different our story might be
had Gilbert or another black scholar gone to Greece in 1895–96, when
Rufus Richardson began excavating ancient Corinth and when the
original members of the Managing Committee still led the American
School. Gilbert and Pickard's topographical survey, the most modern
such project conducted in the first decade of the American School's
work in Greece, represented a significant step in the development of
American classical archaeology, but Eretria was hardly a household
word compared to Corinth. For many African Americans, to whom
the apostle Paul's Areopagus speech was a central text, the Christian
archaeology of Greece and especially the places Paul traveled would
have been particularly meaningful. Since the 1870s, black ministers
had been traveling to the Holy Land in search of Christian sites. The
news that a black scholar was excavating at Corinth would likely have
excited far more interest among African American audiences than esoteric Eretria. At Paine, Gilbert and George Williams Walker would
likely have had far greater success raising money for books and lantern

slides to teach Biblical than Classical Archaeology. And imagine if John Wesley Gilbert or one of his students had been part of Richardson's American School team at Corinth in 1898, when an inscribed marble lintel was discovered near the city's Roman marketplace. It read [Suna]gôgê Hebr[aiôn], "Synagogue of the Hebrews" and was quickly linked with Paul's sojourn in Corinth, where "he reasoned in the synagogue every Sabbath, and persuaded the Jews and the Greeks." Perhaps today we would be speaking of the contributions of generations of black American archaeologists to the study of ancient Greece and early Christianity.[54]

8

A HUMBLE
WORKER IN THE
COLORED RANKS

In the decades after John Wesley Gilbert returned from Greece, legends spread about his travels across the Aegean. Gilbert himself may in his later years have exaggerated the extent of his travels, especially when it came to sites of Biblical resonance. By 1923, a former student of his would report that Gilbert had visited Philippi in northern Greece, the Dardanelles Strait (Hellespont), and other places "made famous by St. Paul's writings," along with islands in the Cyclades and Sporades and even "the Isle of Patmos, of St. John fame, more than once." Gilbert might in fact have seen some of the Aegean under the sunny skies of late March 1891, for the three-day steamer tour from the Piraeus through the Cyclades to the island of Syra (today Syros), capped by a visit to Delos if the weather cooperated, was easily done. He could not possibly have gotten as far north as Philippi and east to Patmos (both still part of the Ottoman Empire in 1891) during the week that elapsed between the official end of the Eretria season on March 20 and his departure from Athens for the Peloponnesus with Caroline Gerrish, Edith Harris, and Emma Potter on March 27, a trip we can trace in detail thanks to Caroline and Edith's letters.[1]

Going Home

The Peloponnesus was a six-day whirlwind. Caroline Gerrish recalled, "We were a real look-ey party, glancing at a place, then jump into the carriage and run." Gilbert and his companions spent two nights in the pleasant harbor town of Nafplio, with an excursion to the theater of Epidaurus, then hurried through Tiryns, Argos, and Mycenae to catch the train via New Corinth to Patras. They stayed a night at the Hôtel de Patras, in whose restaurant Gilbert had eaten his first Greek meal six months before. Next afternoon they headed to Pyrgos, just sixty miles south but nearly three hours by narrow-gauge rail. After a night in a dirty, inhospitable Pyrgos hotel, it was on to Olympia, a five-hour carriage ride away. The group explored Olympia American School–style, Pausanias and Baedeker in hand. "The best thing we kept for last," writes Gerrish of the museum's prized statue of Hermes and the infant Dionysus, the only surviving work of the classical sculptor Praxiteles. Three years before, Gilbert had seen a cast of this masterpiece at his Brown graduation dinner. Then it was back to Pyrgos and another night in that terrible hotel. On Wednesday morning, April 1, Gilbert bade farewell to Caroline, Edith, and Emma at Patras. Late that evening, he was on a steamer for Brindisi. We can only imagine his thoughts as he watched the Peloponnesian coast recede into darkness, though it is a good bet he would have seen more of Greece had time and money permitted.[2]

According to Rufus Richardson's official report, Gilbert left Athens early to study in Berlin. By 1902, profiles of Gilbert mentioned an entire semester at the University of Berlin. The university's 1891 student registers, though, show no sign of him. He almost certainly visited Berlin and other German cities, for he appears on the outbound passenger list of the Hamburg-American Packet Company's SS Slavonia, departing Hamburg on April 13. That port makes sense only if he went home through Germany. The Slavonia carried 8,000 bags of beet sugar, 665 mostly German immigrants (a third of them children) in steerage, and just three passengers including Gilbert in its comfortable, mostly empty first-class section. The ship took two weeks to steam the 4,400 miles across the Atlantic to Baltimore. En route, Gilbert kept up his German in conversations with Captain Schmidt and the two other first-class passengers—Frau Hundt von Hafften and her little boy Charlie. Gilbert disembarked at Baltimore on April 28. On arrival, he gave his occupation as "merchant," thus deflecting any questions about the trunkful of souvenirs he had with him. From Baltimore it was a day's train ride south to Augusta. With luck, he arrived within hours of his son John Jr.'s birth on April 30. Nearly eight months after setting off for Greece, John Wesley Gilbert was home.[3]

Wherever They Pitch Their Tents

As John Gilbert was holding his new baby boy, Charles Waldstein was back at Cambridge preparing for spring term. Waldstein would return to the American School of Classical Studies at Athens for one final season as Permanent Director in 1891–1892, during which he began important excavations at the Argive Heraion, a major sanctuary of Hera near Argos. He served a further five years as the School's Professor of Ancient Art before moving on to his many other endeavors.[4]

Rufus Richardson left Dartmouth to become ASCSA Director from 1893 to 1903. During this formative decade, Richardson completed the School's work at Eretria, began the American excavations at ancient Corinth that continue to this day, and put a lasting stamp on the School's academic program with his fast-paced bicycle-borne field trips (today conducted by bus and no less fast-paced). Richardson then retired with his family to Woodstock, Connecticut. He wrote several popular books, notably 1907's *Greece Through the Stereoscope*, which weaves photographs, maps, and text into a virtual tour of the country. Rufus Richardson died in 1914. The American School remembered him as "a man of singularly generous and lovable nature, careful and considerate of the rights of others in all the relations of life."[5]

Closing his 1890–1891 report, Richardson wrote: "It may be predicted with absolute certainty that our four students will go back in due time to America, if not trained archaeologists, at least with an interest in the Greek lands, and the life and monuments of ancient

Greece, which will make them infectious centres of interest wherever they pitch their tents." Richardson would welcome John Pickard back to the American School in 1901–1902, and he may also have seen Andrew Fossum in Greece in 1898, but he apparently never saw Carleton Brownson or John Gilbert again.[6]

Andrew Fossum returned to New York in late summer 1891. Despite his Johns Hopkins PhD and American School experience, he had trouble finding a university job. In 1892, Fossum and his bride Amelia moved to Minnesota, where he became professor of Greek at St. Olaf College. After Amelia died in 1906, Fossum raised their children Paul and Edith. He taught at Park Region Luther College in northwestern Minnesota from 1910 to 1918, then at nearby Concordia College until retiring in 1923. Like many Norwegian American scholars of his day, he found his research hampered by heavy teaching loads and poor library resources. Nonetheless, he revisited Greece in 1898 and 1921 and produced several more articles on Greek theaters. He also became interested in Viking lore, publishing *The Norse Discovery of America* in 1918. Fossum never kept in touch with the rest of the American School group. His commitment to speaking Greek, though, was lifelong. During his Concordia years, he regularly visited the owners of a Greek restaurant in neighboring Fargo, North Dakota, to keep up his Greek. Andrew Fossum died in 1943. His gravestone in Allamakee County, Iowa bears a Bible verse in Greek.[7]

Carleton Brownson, John and Jeanie Pickard, Caroline Gerrish, Edith Harris, and Emma Potter traveled together in Italy and Germany during summer 1891. While Brownson returned to the American School for 1891–1892, Pickard and most of his family spent the year at the University of Munich. Edith Harris went back to Portsmouth, New Hampshire, where she lived the rest of her life in the family home on Austin Street. Edith died in 1956, but the letters she and her aunt Caroline wrote from Greece were preserved in the Austin Street house for another half-century, then given to the Portsmouth Athenaeum in 2003.[8]

Brownson rejoined the Pickards at Munich in summer 1892 and renewed his relationship with Emma Potter. The group sailed back across the Atlantic together in August 1892, and Brownson returned to his graduate work at Yale. He and Emma were married that December; their only daughter Katherine died in infancy. After receiving his Yale doctoral degree in 1897 with a dissertation on Plato, Brownson went to teach Greek at the City College of New York. He was the first Dean of the College of Liberal Arts (1909–1926) and chaired the Classics Department from 1917 until his retirement in 1936. He and Emma returned to Athens in 1927, where they visited Rev. Kalopothakes's youngest daughter Daphne in her family home across from the Arch of Hadrian. Brownson died in 1949 and Emma Brownson in 1964. Carleton Lewis Brownson remains best known today for his Loeb Classical Library translations of Xenophon's *Anabasis* and *Hellenica*, still widely used a century after he published them.[9]

John Pickard's University of Munich dissertation used evidence from recent excavations of Greek theaters at Eretria and elsewhere to interpret what ancient texts said about the positioning of actors and chorus in classical drama. In 1892, he was hired as professor of Greek at the University of Missouri. John and Jeanie, joined by Jeanie's mother Caroline Gerrish, moved west to Columbia; their only child Caroline was born in 1896. At Missouri, Pickard quickly began offering courses—Athenian topography and monuments, Greek vases, epigraphy—based on his American School year and soon stopped teaching Greek. He expanded into surveys of archaeology and of European art history, and eventually even taught classes on nineteenth-century painting. Pickard got Missouri to acquire plaster casts, lantern slides, and photographs, the vital teaching aids such classes required. Through the thousands of students who took his courses, Pickard promoted interest in archaeology and art history across the Midwest. He helped found the College Art Association and, from 1914 to 1919, served as the group's first president. Between 1917 and 1928, he led the artistic design team for Missouri's new capitol building and by the time he retired in 1929 was famous as "Missouri's Apostle of the Beautiful." John Pickard died in 1937 and Jeanie moved to Santa Fe, New Mexico to live with their daughter Caroline. To this day, Pickard's great-granddaughter,

Katherine Tenthoff, preserves handwritten documents from John and Jeanie's year in Greece.[10]

John Pickard and John Gilbert seem not to have kept in regular contact, for in 1894 Gilbert did not know Pickard had been hired at Missouri. Yet the records of the American Philological Association (APA, today known as the Society for Classical Studies or SCS) reveal the network linking them. In the 1890s, membership in the APA required a vote of the group's executive committee. Pickard was elected in 1893 and went to his first meeting in 1894, at Williams College in Massachusetts. As a newcomer, he must have been glad to see his old Dartmouth professor John Henry Wright, now at Harvard and just elected APA president, among the sixty-three attendees. Wright probably introduced Pickard to Harold North Fowler (one of the American School's first students in 1882–1883), to Managing Committee Chair Thomas Day Seymour, and to William Sanders Scarborough, a close friend of Wright's. The American School certainly came up in conversation, for decades later Scarborough still remembered Fowler urging him to go to Greece. Gilbert's name probably came up, too: Scarborough had met him in 1893 at a Georgia State Teachers' Association conference in Atlanta. Though his memory later muddled the date and place, Scarborough never forgot his first encounter with Gilbert, calling him "a scholarly, enthusiastic young man, just returned from Greece."[11]

Pickard, Scarborough, Seymour, and Wright met again at the July 1896 APA meeting at Brown University. Also there were Carleton Brownson, Albert Harkness, Irving Manatt (hired from Athens in 1893 to fill the position opened by Harkness's retirement), and William Carey Poland (ASCSA annual director in 1891–1892). It is impossible to believe Gilbert went unmentioned in such company. What is more, among the thirty-four new members elected at Brown were two African Americans: Howard University's Lewis Baxter Moore, who had just received his Classics doctorate from the University of Pennsylvania, and former Howard professor James Monroe Gregory, now a school principal in New Jersey. The year before in Cleveland, another African American scholar had been elected: William Lewis Bulkley of South Carolina's Claflin University. People at the Brown meeting must have asked why Professor Gilbert of Paine Institute was not already a member of both the APA and of the Archaeological Institute of America (AIA). It is no coincidence that Gilbert was elected to the APA the very next year. In Augusta and Atlanta, news reports of Gilbert's election proudly claimed both him and Scarborough as native Georgians, "an honor to their state and country."[12]

Early in 1898, Gilbert and Scarborough received personal invitations to join the AIA from the group's new president, John Williams White of Harvard. In his letter to Gilbert, White complimented him as an ASCSA alumnus and highlighted the AIA's ties with the School. To Scarborough, White may have mentioned the possibility of joining the School's Managing Committee. Some years later, Scarborough confidently wrote, "the American Philological Association knows no color. The same may be said of the Archaeological Institute of America."[13]

Unlike the scholarly APA, the AIA in the 1890s was organized into local societies that welcomed nonacademic archaeology enthusiasts, a feature it retains today. Scarborough joined his friend Harold North Fowler in the Cleveland Society and would remain a member until about 1909. Gilbert's closest option in 1897 was Baltimore—Nashville would not have a chapter until 1912, Atlanta not until 1947. The Baltimore Society had members living as far away as California, and its roster included Claflin's William Bulkley, but for some reason Gilbert did not join it. In December 1900, though, he attended the AIA's second general meeting, held jointly in Philadelphia with the APA, the Modern Language Association, and three other learned societies.[14]

Gilbert's timing is unlikely to be coincidental. In July 1899, Pickard and Scarborough had met for a third time at the New York APA, where both presented papers and heard about the upcoming first-ever AIA general meeting at Yale in December. None of the three attended the Yale AIA—Gilbert, whose youngest daughter Mattie (his and Ola's fourth child) was born in July 1899, had his hands full at home—but they seem to have made plans for the following year. In December 1900, Gilbert and Scarborough met at the Philadelphia joint convention. Pickard, now president of the Missouri AIA Society, may have been there, too. The AIA's John Williams White and the ASCSA's Thomas Day Seymour were certainly there, and Scarborough must have introduced Gilbert to them.[15]

Among the speakers Gilbert and Scarborough heard in Philadelphia was Smith College's Harriet Boyd, the first American woman to lead an archaeological excavation in the Aegean, just back from her year at the American School and on the island of Crete. Scarborough gave an AIA paper on the topography of Pylos and Sphacteria, sites of a surprise Spartan defeat early in the Peloponnesian War (431–404 BC), and an APA paper on Euripides, Racine, and Goethe. Given his literary interests and his topographical work in Greece, Gilbert certainly appreciated both topics. He was probably also interested in a presentation by the American School's Arthur Cooley, who had just completed the first topographical survey of ancient Corinth. Between sessions, Scarborough and Gilbert visited the offices of the African Methodist Episcopal (AME) journal, *The Christian Recorder*, the country's oldest African American periodical. They also got the attention of a columnist for the African American *Washington Bee*, who described them as "enthusiastic students of Greek archaeology."[16]

If Pickard and Gilbert in fact saw each other in Philadelphia, it seems to have been their last meeting. Gilbert and Scarborough, though, crossed paths again in September 1901, at a Methodist conference in London. They saw each other at least once more, at Tuskegee Institute's twenty-fifth anniversary celebration in 1906. Yet, while Scarborough attended APA meetings until 1920 and remained a member until he died in 1926, Gilbert never again attended the APA or AIA, and, by 1907, his memberships in both groups had lapsed. Instead, he focused above all on the grounds where he had pitched his tent: his beloved Paine.[17]

From Institute to College

A distinguished visitor graced Paine Institute's campus in November 1891: former US President Rutherford B. Hayes, on a tour of Southern black educational institutions. After meeting George Williams Walker, John Wesley Gilbert, and the other faculty, Hayes received the latest issue of the *Paine Herald* and a copy of the school's catalogue to take home with him. These precious documents—the only other known issue of the *Herald* is the one Dickie Bridges found in her parents' attic, and just three other catalogues survive from Paine's first quarter-century—are preserved today in Ohio's Rutherford B. Hayes Presidential Center. The catalogue, published in spring 1891, proudly notes Professor Gilbert is "in Athens, Greece, prosecuting his studies." The newspaper, printed in October, notes Walker's pleasure at Gilbert's return. Behind that story lies an untold one: Gilbert considered leaving Paine soon after returning from Greece.[18]

While Gilbert was at the American School, the Georgia legislature, with federal land-grant funding from the Second Morrill Act, had approved a new segregated unit of the University of Georgia system, to be named the Georgia State Industrial College for Colored Youth. Prominent minister C. T. Walker pushed to get the school located in Augusta. Instead, it went temporarily to Athens, Georgia, then permanently to Savannah, where it flourishes today as Savannah State University. The industrial college's first president was R. R. Wright, Sr. of Augusta, its first students all alumni of Augusta's Ware High School. Wright may have encouraged Gilbert to apply for a position as Greek professor. Gilbert did so soon after returning home only to be told, in the words of University of Georgia chancellor William Boggs, that "the law does not specify that the ancient languages shall be taught in the school." Wright would end up teaching Greek and Latin clandestinely.[19]

The next year, Gilbert got a job offer from Lincoln Institute (today Lincoln University) in Jefferson City, Missouri. Founded by black Union Army soldiers at the end of the Civil War, Lincoln had become a land-grant college in 1890. While the school added industrial education classes, it kept its thriving language program, including Greek, Latin, French, and German. And, its president was Inman E. Page, who in 1877 had been one of Brown University's first two black graduates. Possibly Page himself, having learned of Gilbert's work in Greece, sought to recruit his fellow Brown alumnus. Gilbert may well have found Lincoln Institute attractive, but he probably also knew Page was embroiled in an on-campus controversy so bitter the school's regents believed the only solution was to hire an all-new faculty. Gilbert was the only one of four new recruits to decline the offer. Perhaps he would have accepted had he known John Pickard would soon arrive at the University of Missouri in Columbia, less than forty miles north of Jefferson City. It is fascinating to imagine how Gilbert and Pickard's relationship might have helped bring more African American students into the fields of art history and archaeology had the two men ended up so near each other in Missouri.[20]

Gilbert's pursuit of the Georgia Industrial College post reflects his need to support his growing family. As difficult as the conversation may have been, he surely told George Williams Walker he was applying. In 1911, Gilbert would tell Walker's widow Susan that in a quarter-century's work together Walker had never once been impatient with him, "though I know I must at times have made mistakes of the head, never of the heart. In not one instance did I ever by subterfuge or mental reservation fail to talk out of my heart of hearts." Walker well knew the financial difficulties, reminding Paine's trustees in June 1892 that "we find it very difficult to live within our salaries." The board approved a raise for Walker, Gilbert, mathematics professor Robert Campbell, and instructor Mary Hankinson. Gilbert's salary more than doubled, to one thousand dollars a year. The following year, perhaps responding to the Lincoln Institute offer, Walker supplemented Gilbert's salary with funds from the Colored Methodist Episcopal (CME) Church. Gilbert may have received another job offer after that, for in June 1897 Walker reported "it would be a great help and a deserved merit if the Board would increase the salary of Prof. J.W. Gilbert by $200." With this raise, Gilbert's pay matched that of his most senior white colleague, mathematics professor R. L. Campbell. By 1916, he would make more than Campbell.[21]

The money would see good use, for John and Ola had three more children in the 1890s: one who died in infancy around 1893, Sarah in January 1897, and Martha (everyone called her Mattie) in July 1899. Times were tight after the financial panic of 1893, but fortunately for the Gilberts, Augusta's economy did not suffer as badly as those of other Southern cities. By 1899, they were able to buy a home on

Magnolia Street (later Forest Street), in a new subdivision a mile and a half south of Paine's campus.[22]

Paine's enrollment grew steadily, too. The school had broken the 200-student mark while Gilbert was in Athens. By 1899 it had more than 260, many coming from beyond Augusta and some from as far away as Florida and Virginia. Most were in the high school (Normal) level, with a half-dozen or so in the collegiate department. There were also several dozen theological students, some attending irregularly. Though just one or two students graduated from the college course each year, their contributions to the nation's intellectual and religious life were significant. Notable among them was 1893's R. A. Carter, later a CME bishop and founder of more than 250 churches. In 1894, Fannie Jones became the first woman to complete the college course. Theological students George L. Tyus worked his way through Paine before returning to lead the CME's Haygood Seminary in Washington, Arkansas from 1894 to 1910. For a time, Tyus was the only college-educated black American in southwestern Arkansas. Channing Tobias, a 1902 collegiate graduate, went up north to Drew Theological Seminary in New Jersey. Other alumni made their marks as teachers or ministers across the South and as far north as Boston and New York.[23]

For much of the 1890s, students slept in the same unheated hay-loft and took classes in the same converted stables that Gilbert had helped fix up in 1886. Walker tirelessly sought funds for proper facilities, and, in 1897, construction began on a three-story brick building, named Haygood Memorial Hall in honor of Methodist Episcopal Church, South (MECS) bishop Atticus Haygood, an early and staunch supporter of the school. The building was in use by 1899, though it took until 1902 to complete. According to tradition, music instructor Charles Dryscoll had the idea of adding a clock to the hall's central tower. Haygood Hall would become an Augusta landmark until fire consumed it in 1968.[24]

Paine was about to get a new name, too. By 1901, the school's academic program had developed to the point that Bishop Holsey renewed a proposal he had made unsuccessfully several years before. This time, the school's leadership agreed, and in June 1903 Paine Institute officially became Paine College. Gilbert made sure the APA and the American School learned of the name change.[25]

Church and Community

If he lived by the principle that "the noblest profession is that of the teacher," Gilbert extended his energies into many other spheres. In 1892, he gave public lectures in Georgia and South Carolina about his American School year. He soon earned a reputation as "the finest Greek scholar in the South." By 1902, Southern papers often named him "the ablest Greek scholar of the race." In the 1890s, he became a regular speaker for the Georgia Teacher's Association and other educational groups, for church meetings, and for Emancipation Day celebrations. He joined the staff of Augusta's black Third Militia Battalion and got involved with the local Republican Party. He was one of the youngest delegates to the 1894 CME General Conference in Memphis, a first step in what became a lifelong role in the denomination's leadership.[26]

As Gilbert's community involvement grew, so, too, did his interest in ministry. His Nashville friend J. A. Lester recalled Gilbert "sought eagerly to find a way to help lighten the burdens of the masses of our people. His very soul went out to those whose condition was less favored than his own." During 1897–1898, Gilbert enrolled at Gammon Theological Seminary in Atlanta, studying theology and Hebrew. By 1898, he was ordained in the CME. Henry Rutherford Butler, the city's leading black physician, described meeting Gilbert in Atlanta: "like most men with brains, he is a very plain, quiet man, but he is a man with an independence of thought." At some point in this seminary year, Gilbert encouraged Bishop Holsey, whom he had known since childhood, to publish a volume of sermons and essays and even raised money for its publication. Gilbert and G. W. Walker together read the manuscript and corrected the proofs.[27]

By the time Gilbert finished his ministerial studies, the Spanish-American War was under way, and Augusta had become a training ground for troops going to Cuba. Along with other community leaders, Gilbert helped welcome the African American soldiers of the Tenth US

Volunteer Infantry Regiment, popularly called "the Immunes" because of the myth that they were immune to tropical diseases. If he had not had three little ones—Alma, John Jr., and Sarah—at home, Gilbert might have volunteered to serve in Cuba, as C. T. Walker and other black Augustans did.[28]

It is a good bet Gilbert would have gone to Cuba if he could have, for he loved to travel. In 1893, he made it all the way to San Francisco in company with Bishop Holsey's son-in-law Charles G. Dickson, a recent Paine graduate. The purpose of this trip is unclear, but Dickson, whose mother Amanda America Dickson was probably the wealthiest black woman in the nineteenth-century United States, must have financed it. With his children still young, nearly all Gilbert's other trips in the 1890s were in Georgia or neighboring South Carolina. Later, he was able to head further afield, to a Washington, DC, CME conference in November 1900 and to Philadelphia in December 1900 for the APA-AIA convention. Then, in August 1901, eleven years after setting off for Greece, Gilbert departed again across the Atlantic as a CME Church delegate to the Third Ecumenical Methodist Conference in London.[29]

A Methodist, Regardless

Gilbert and the other eight delegates rendezvoused in New York, got passports the day they applied, and on August 17 sailed aboard the brand-new *SS Potsdam*. The group, led by bishops Elias Cottrell and Robert S. Williams, also included Gilbert's former student R. A. Carter, *Christian Index* editor Charles H. Phillips, and the eloquent Henry S. Doyle, an Ohio Wesleyan theology graduate. The men landed at Rotterdam on August 28, spent a week touring Antwerp, Brussels, and the field of Waterloo, and then joined the conference in London on September 4. W. S. Scarborough, who had been traveling in France and Italy, reached London about the same time to join the AME delegation.[30]

The conference organizers had reserved rooms for many of the black American Methodists, who altogether mustered fifty-five of the five hundred total delegates, at the newly renovated St. Ermin's Hotel. While

Gilbert was still at sea and Scarborough still in Italy, an early arriving AME group checked in only to meet racism from white American tourists, one of whom whined about "the privileges granted [African Americans] in Europe generally." Hotel manager Harry Richardson told the white guests they could leave if they were unhappy. The AME group stayed, and, when Gilbert, Scarborough, and the remaining delegates arrived, the hotel received them, too, with all courtesy.[31]

A decade before, Gilbert had spent a hurried weekend in London on his way to Greece. Now, he would have two full weeks in the city. Gilbert did not speak at the conference, but he and Scarborough were mentioned prominently in African Methodist Episcopal Zion (AMEZ) Bishop Alexander Walters's opening address. If some MECS delegates muttered and a few walked out when Walters denounced lynching, he got loud cheers from the British audience, and the black Methodists were full participants in the conference sessions. As C. H. Phillips put in it his speech, "Scrape any delegate . . . and you will find a Methodist, regardless of the complexion of the skin or the texture of the hair. In Methodism all races and kindred, and people, and tongues can find common ground on which to stand." Several American speakers extolled President William McKinley as a "loyal and consistent" Methodist. Indeed, his pastor was among the delegates. The news that McKinley had been shot in Buffalo, delivered at breakfast on the conference's fourth day, was thus an especially awful shock. H. S. Doyle, who had met McKinley as a student in Ohio, spoke movingly that morning. "I do not know," said Doyle, "what worse thing could have happened" for McKinley "is such a President that all peoples and all races of our common country can claim a part of him." William Sanders Scarborough, who had also known McKinley personally, helped the AME delegation write a message of sympathy to the White House. Over the next week, until McKinley died on September 13, there were daily prayers for the President, followed by a memorial service on the conference's last day, September 17.[32]

London, which had recently shed its mourning for Queen Victoria, was soon black-draped for McKinley. Despite the subdued mood, Gilbert and his fellow delegates found time between conference sessions for sightseeing, bookstores, and receptions. Each delegation also posed for photographs before John Wesley's tomb. The CME's group shot (Figure 8.1) is a portrait of the men who would lead the denomination into the new century: R. A. Carter, J. C. Martin, C. H. Phillips, and G. W. Stewart all became bishops; Gilbert and H. S. Doyle might have joined them had they not died young, while J. F. Lane would lead the CME's Lane College from 1907 to 1944. In the photo, a dapper Gilbert seems almost lost in thought as he stands before the grave of his namesake.[33]

Gilbert probably talked with a number of MECS delegates, including J. D. Hammond, a future president of Paine College. The one who most interested him, though, was the General Secretary of the MECS Board of Missions, Walter Russell Lambuth. Born in Shanghai,

FIGURE 8.1 Colored Methodist Episcopal (CME) Church delegates to the Ecumenical Methodist Conference in London, September 1901. Seated left to right: R. A. Carter, C. H. Phillips, Bishop R. S. Williams, Bishop E. Cottrell, J. C. Martin. Standing left to right: G. W. Stewart, H. S. Doyle, J. W. Gilbert, J. F. Lane.
Courtesy of Bishop Othal Lakey.

Lambuth had followed the path of his missionary parents. Except for college in Virginia and medical school in Tennessee, he had spent almost his whole life in China or Japan. In February 1891, while Gilbert was in Greece, Lambuth had spoken at Paine about missionary work and become friends with George Williams Walker. Indeed, Lambuth had just seen Walker at an April 1901 MECS missionary conference in New Orleans. A major theme of the London conference was the need for trained missionaries at home and abroad, and Lambuth's closing address to the delegates was a call to mission work. Gilbert had first met Lambuth in the mid-1890s, and the two men must have conversed in London. Gilbert clearly drew inspiration from Lambuth's speech and became increasingly interested in mission work. Neither man could have predicted that almost exactly ten years later they would meet again in London, en route to the Belgian Congo.[34]

On their way home, the CME delegates sailed through one of the last storms of the 1901 Atlantic hurricane season. Most of the men were seasick the whole way, one so badly he vowed never to make the crossing again. C. H. Phillips later recalled that John Gilbert was the only one unaffected. Yet the Atlantic tempest was a ripple compared to the racist storms sweeping across the United States.[35]

Into the Nadir

Gilbert's personal success, the progress at Paine, and the congenial welcome in London took place against a grim backdrop: the South's descent into the legalized, institutionalized apartheid of Jim Crow. As the federal government abandoned them, African American citizens lost their basic rights. Lynching became epidemic in Georgia, peaking in 1899, when mobs murdered twenty-seven black Georgians. Augusta, which had prided itself on good race relations, took longer to succumb than other places. Nonetheless, the special atmosphere Channing Tobias remembered from his childhood, in which black Augustans could "aspire to the heights and to receive encouragement from white people in so doing," was gone by 1897, when President McKinley's nomination of respected black lawyer Judson Lyons as the city's postmaster ignited

white reactions so hostile that Lyons withdrew; he would instead become Register of the Treasury in 1898, the highest ranking African
American in McKinley's administration. Daily life for black Augustans
began to carry an undertone of violence. By 1908, Gilbert would say
that he "never rode on the [street]car with his wife, lest some cheap
conductor might insult her, and he would do as any other man, defend
her, and a mob would be the result."[36]

Many black Americans sought hope in Booker T. Washington's
accommodationist September 1895 speech, the so-called Atlanta
Compromise. Coming just seven months after Frederick Douglass died,
this speech got national attention. Gilbert was not there, but a week
later he wrote Washington to praise "the most opportune speech ever
made before a Southern mixed audience." Gilbert was not alone: W.
E. B. Du Bois telegraphed Washington to congratulate him on his "phe-
nomenal success at Atlanta," and W. S. Scarborough later asserted he
followed Washington's advice to "let down your bucket where you are."
Gilbert's former student John Hope, recently graduated from Brown
and now teaching at Roger Williams University in Nashville, heard
Washington in person and had a very different reaction. As Hope asked
in a speech several months later, "If we are not striving for equality, in
heaven's name for what are we living?" Ironically, in later years Du
Bois would emerge as Washington's leading critic, while Hope would
be dismissed as one of Washington's disciples.[37]

If Gilbert agreed with Washington about the need to work closely
with Southern whites, "whom we *must make our friends* [emphasis in
original] upon grounds which brook no compromise of Negro manhood on the one hand, nor breathe an incendiary spirit of race an-
tagonism, socially speaking, on the other," he rejected Washington's
strident advocacy of industrial training over liberal education. Soon
after writing Washington, Gilbert published a letter in the New York
Independent—the same paper that had featured his 1891 dispatch
from Eretria—dismantling the claims of W. C. Steele, General Secretary
of the MECS's Epworth League, that liberal education "will be the ruin
of the African." Gilbert later publicly criticized Washington himself for
his "narrow and erroneous" promotion of industrial training, saying it

would condemn black people to lives of "drawing water and hewing wood." For his part, Washington in 1899 admitted Paine was "one of the best colleges for our people," and the two men remained on good terms into the 1900s.[38]

White Augustans, meanwhile, were abandoning African American education. With Augusta's "colored" schools already overcrowded and underfunded, the Richmond County Board of Education voted in August 1897 to shutter Ware High School, one of a handful of publicly funded black high schools anywhere in the South. Leading black citizens, including Paine trustee James S. Harper, tried to save Ware. Their struggle went all the way to the Supreme Court, which in a landmark 1899 decision upheld the Board of Education's action. That same year, Augusta's Democratic Party began excluding blacks from voting in primary elections. Since the Democrats dominated Georgia politics, the whites-only primary effectively disenfranchised black voters. By 1903, many whites questioned the very existence of black public education and not until 1945 would the city again have a four-year public high school for African Americans.[39]

Augusta's black elites despaired. A few escaped north or west; Bishop Holsey turned to black separatism. Others refused to give up. Lucy Laney built Haines Institute into an educational, cultural, and community center that nurtured generations of black Augustans. At Paine, with its biracial faculty and board of trustees, John Gilbert carried on. Some of Ware's younger students completed their degrees at Paine in 1898–1900. In the years that followed, Paine, Haines, and C. T. Walker's Baptist Academy filled the gap left by Ware's closing. Through it all, Gilbert and many others found inspiration and hope in George Williams Walker. William A. Bell, who graduated from the Normal course in 1901 and the college course in 1906, vividly remembered making his way through a white neighborhood with Walker one Sunday, on the way to Trinity Church. A group of white youths blocked their path. "We never get off the sidewalk for dogs," one sneered. Stepping into the street alongside Bell, Walker replied, "We always do."[40]

Like others during this dark period, Gilbert stressed black self-reliance as a way forward. Soon after returning from London, he wrote an essay on this theme for a widely read compendium, *Twentieth-Century Negro Literature*, edited by Daniel Culp, a graduate of Princeton Theological Seminary and successful Florida physician who had met Gilbert in Augusta during 1891–1892. Gilbert was among the youngest of the hundred nationally known African American women and men, among them Mary Church Terrell, Mary Burnett Talbert, Booker T. Washington, and William Sanders Scarborough, who contributed to the volume. Unsurprisingly, "education" was his first answer to the question "How can the Negroes be induced to rally more to Negro enterprises and to their professional men?" Education, Gilbert argued, must highlight black Americans' achievements and their contributions to the United States, to overcome slavery's most destructive legacy, "lack of confidence and race pride." Yet school alone was not enough. Churches, social groups, and civic organizations together had to unify the community into steadfast support of black-owned businesses and professionals. At the same time, added Gilbert, "no man should expect or receive patronage solely because he is black." Black businesses and professionals had to exceed the average, white or black. One shining example of such a business was Augusta's Pilgrim Health and Life Insurance Company, founded by four black teenagers as a mutual aid society in 1898. True to his essay's word, Gilbert was among Pilgrim's earliest supporters. Pilgrim was incorporated in 1905 and would grow by 1948 into a multimillion-dollar enterprise that employed hundreds of African Americans in Augusta and beyond.[41]

Of the many speeches Gilbert delivered during these years, one is of particular note because its complete text survives. On January 1, 1904—Emancipation Day—he took the pulpit before a packed crowd at Augusta's Tabernacle Baptist Church. Newspaperman Silas Floyd, who had known Gilbert since boyhood, introduced him. Gilbert's oration was a response to Atlanta's notorious John Temple Graves, who the previous summer had publicly proposed lynching be legalized, called black people "unwholesome, helpless, unassimilable," and argued the only solution to "the problem of the races" was to deport African Americans from their own country. Gilbert's speech was so well-received that *The Augusta Chronicle* judged it "masterful and thorough," and *The Georgia Baptist* decided to publish it. The only known surviving copy, bearing a dedication from Gilbert himself, was given to Howard University in 1912.[42]

Gilbert's text begins by reviewing with pride the accomplishments of African Americans. "Whether as slaves, freedmen, or freemen," he remarks, "we have contributed as much to the birth, growth, power, and perpetuity of the Stars and Stripes as any other people in the country." Then he turns to the racist present exemplified by Graves: "a white-hot prejudice, bereft of the fear of God . . . as merciless and unreasonable as it is unjust," by which "the door of hope is shut in our faces." Gilbert brings in history, logic, statistics, and well-placed sarcasm to systematically demolish Graves's claims. He lifts the Bible against the color line, noting that the name Adam in Hebrew connotes neither black nor white, but red-colored. And, he displays his classical erudition, asking rhetorically, "Wherein does this essential inequality of the races actually, or potentially lie? Is there some conjuring talisman, some Eleusinian mystery which the white man has and the Negro has not and can not get?" Gilbert saves his strongest denunciation for Graves's lurid fantasies of "black fiends of lust" assaulting white women, noting that "there is another womanhood whose virtue we wish you to help us protect— another woman for whose outraged virtue we have never been avenged either by mobs or courts. I speak of the black woman of the South."[43]

Even as he decried prejudice, legalized discrimination, and mob violence, Gilbert's address carefully appealed to the better natures of Southern whites. He notes that 180,000 black Americans fought bravely during the Civil War, but also remarks that "five thousand Negroes served in different ways in the Confederate Army" and takes pains to emphasize that slaves did not desert or revolt en masse. While stressing the close ties of Southern whites and blacks, Gilbert emphatically distances himself from "social equality," the era's code words for integration. He also dismisses any notion of wholesale black emigration from "our country, ours by our fathers' sweat and blood which still fertilize its roots of liberty." Let us "drive away the ghosts of hate," he says in closing, for "we have too much in common to agree about and live for."[44]

Gilbert's oratory was increasingly in demand beyond Augusta. In 1905, he traveled to Denver, Colorado to address an interracial Epworth League convention. A local paper described the event as the first to bring "any considerable number" of African Americans to the city. More than three thousand people came to hear his January 1906 Emancipation Day speech in Macon, Georgia. Quoting President Theodore Roosevelt's favorite slogan, Gilbert insisted African Americans deserved "'a square deal' in all the relations of life" and argued "negroes ought to be allowed by law to serve on juries where negroes were being tried in the courts." When a white reporter put words in his mouth, Gilbert calmly set the facts straight in writing. A month later, he was back in Macon as one of two hundred delegates to the Georgia Equal Rights Convention, where he saw his former student John Hope, soon to be appointed first black president of Atlanta Baptist College, as well as W. E. B. Du Bois of Atlanta University and many others. Gilbert did not speak at this convention, but he appears tenth on the list of conveners, and portions of the meeting's final resolution echo his 1904 Emancipation Day oration. In April, he went to Alabama for Tuskegee Institute's twenty-fifth anniversary. At the end of August 1906, he shared the stage with W. E. B. Du Bois, Mary Church Terrell, and Booker T. Washington at the Ohio State Colored Educational and Industrial Exposition.[45]

Just weeks after Gilbert got home from Ohio, the white population of Atlanta erupted in racist barbarism, incited in part by John Temple Graves. Dozens of black Atlantans were murdered, many more injured, black-owned businesses looted or destroyed. While Gilbert's daughters were enrolled at Paine, fifteen-year-old John Jr. was about to start the college preparatory course at Atlanta University. Had the massacre begun a week later, he would have been in the midst of the riot. In the aftermath, Gilbert may have kept his only son home for the year. Augusta escaped violence, but tensions ran high. When the *Georgia Baptist*'s W. J. White condemned the rioters, he received death threats and had to leave the city. Soon afterward, Gilbert, Bishop Williams, C. T. Walker, and other black leaders met with a group of white ministers. Gilbert and his colleagues had little choice but to present a conciliatory front. They asked whites to distinguish between "good negroes and bad negroes," deplored "social equality," and hoped simply for justice before the law. Silas Floyd later commended the "conservative, level-headed, educated colored men" who helped Augusta maintain a semblance of good race relations, but the national environment remained poisonous. Gilbert would probably have agreed with Howard University's Kelly Miller, who lamented "almost every reflecting Negro of my acquaintance is growing prematurely gray."[46]

Keeping the Dream Alive

Paine's association with the MECS proved both blessing and curse during the nadir. If some in the MECS turned away from the school, several key allies held steadfast. Among them were W. R. Lambuth, elected a Paine trustee in 1904, and J. D. Hammond, leader of the MECS Board of Education. MECS women's groups also provided important support. Seed money from a Pennsylvania coal baron helped fund a new divinity (DD) program, and Channing Tobias came back in 1905 from New Jersey's Drew Seminary to lead it. But Paine's development into a college and its strong liberal arts emphasis (after 1903, vocational training was relegated to an Industrial Annex) put off philanthropists who wanted to see industrial education. Worse, in 1907, several of the CME's regional conferences cut funding to Paine. Although the CME recognized Paine's importance, there was pressure to devote scarce funds to schools it solely controlled.[47]

Fundraising had long been part of Gilbert's job. Now, it dominated his life. In June 1907, he attended his first Paine trustees' meeting, where G. W. Walker reported "we have fallen behind." The school was running a deficit, and unpaid bills were piling up. Gilbert and J. D Hammond embarked on a fundraising odyssey, sleeping on trains and speaking to several different audiences a week. Between October and December alone, they hit MECS meetings in Arkansas, both Carolinas, Georgia, Virginia, West Virginia, and as far west as Yoakum, Texas, a thousand miles from Augusta, stopping between trips barely long enough to see their families. Hammond would do the opening pitch.

Gilbert would follow with an appeal for support, emphasizing "the historic and kindly relations" of CME and MECS, the success of Paine's graduates in ministry and teaching, and the fact that not one of the school's alumni had ever been arrested. Sometimes he noted that "he had visited Athens, Greece, and had as well as he could walked in the footsteps of St. Paul, but he was more proud of being a humble worker in the colored ranks than he was of his experience in Athens." Everywhere they went, Gilbert and Hammond passed the hat.[48]

The money they collected kept Paine going, but by June 1908 even G. W. Walker's perennial optimism was cracking. For the first time in a quarter-century, his annual report did not call the past year the school's "best ever." Paine was short of cash for faculty salaries, furnace repairs, even groceries. In recognition of his vital fundraising role, Gilbert was elected a trustee. He and Hammond made another grueling tour in fall 1908, with W. R. Lambuth joining them on at least one stop. They did it again in 1909, when the coal baron money was withdrawn and Paine had to sell land from its endowment to pay debts, and yet again in 1910. Gilbert's dignified, eloquent presence at dozens of MECS conferences during this period helped make him a legend in the denomination's later lore. Meanwhile, an exhausted Hammond told his wife Lily that "how Gilbert stands it, physically or religiously, I cannot see. He goes half the time without lying down to sleep. If I were not with him, to dash into some white restaurant and buy him a cup of coffee and something to eat, he would often go hungry. And I have never once heard him complain, or seen his Christian composure ruffled. He is doing us white people a great service, freeing us from some of our worst prejudices; and we require him to do it at this cost!"[49]

To raise money, Gilbert sometimes appealed to those prejudices. On occasion he told audiences that slavery had been "an instrument in the hands of God for preparing . . . negroes to aid their fellow men," echoing a position that other African American leaders took. In November 1909, he flattered a group of Arkansas ministers, telling them Southern whites knew better than Northerners how to address "the negro problem." When the Associated Press reported this speech, the Minneapolis-based *Appeal* scorned Gilbert as "a flunkey who deserves the contempt of every self-respecting Afro-American." *The Horizon*, edited by W. E. B. Du Bois, similarly attacked Gilbert for sidestepping the issue of "social equality" in a North Carolina speech that otherwise contained "many excellent passages." Despite such criticism, Gilbert later put these views on slavery and social equality into print. He would do whatever it took to preserve Paine and the precious educational opportunities it offered African Americans, even if that meant accepting segregation. Gilbert was not alone. As John Hope and many other Southern black leaders recognized, for the more than two-thirds of their people still living in the South, demanding immediate integration was unrealistic.[50]

Alongside his fundraising, Gilbert sought out opportunities for interracial cooperation wherever he could, even within the segregated bounds of the YMCA. He became a board member of Augusta's black YMCA in 1907. The next spring, he joined John Hope, W. R. Lambuth, and African American YMCA leaders Jesse Hunton and W. A. Moorland for an interracial meeting convened by white reformer Willis Weatherford. Tens of thousands of Southern white college students read the volume that Weatherford subsequently published, which asserted "it is not the negro that is on trial before the world, but we, the white men of the South." Perhaps as a result of his participation in this meeting, John Gilbert in 1909 was the first African American invited to address Vanderbilt University's white YMCA.[51]

Given all Gilbert was doing to keep Paine alive, he may have bridled when the school got a low ranking in W. E. B. Du Bois's 1910 study of black education. To that insult was soon added heartbreaking loss. George Williams Walker was ailing; his final handwritten annual report, in June 1910, seems brief and unsteady. By the following January, he was bedridden and math professor R. L. Campbell became acting president. Walker died on May 18, 1911. Nearly a thousand people, black and white, came for his funeral in the chapel of Haygood Hall. Bishop Warren Candler nearly broke down while delivering the eulogy. John Wesley Gilbert helped carry Walker's casket to the hearse and followed it to Magnolia Cemetery. Overcome by grief and unable to stand the sight of Paine College, where he and Walker had labored together for a quarter-century, Gilbert left town immediately after the funeral. To Walker's widow Susan, he wrote: "A score of times I've picked up my pen to drop you some lines expressive of what you have always known about me. My heart would fail me each time I attempted to write. Even now, I am in tears as I write. Dear Dr. Walker, who picked me up off the streets of Augusta nearly twenty-nine years ago to try to let the influence of Christ, whom he so closely represented, have its course in my life, was as much a father to me as he was a husband to you. . . . No man ever loved me as he did. I never loved any man as I loved him." By the time he returned to Augusta two weeks later for the election of Walker's successor, J. D. Hammond, Paine had suffered another blow with the sudden death of Charles Goodrich, the school's treasurer since 1884.[52]

Gilbert's emotion over Walker stands in contrast to the near-silence regarding his mother Sarah, who died in July 1911. Sarah Dasher (she had kept her first husband's name) had remarried in fall 1886, just weeks after Gilbert departed for Brown. Her second husband, David Thomas, died in 1901, and no trace of Sarah Thomas can be found from then until 1910, when the US Census lists her with Gilbert and his family on Magnolia Street. She may have been there since 1901; we cannot tell. Sarah must have been proud of all her son had achieved and Gilbert was clearly dutiful in caring for his mother, but beyond that their relationship remains opaque. Both Sarah Thomas and George Williams Walker, though, had something in common: before they died, both knew that John Wesley Gilbert would soon embark on another trans-Atlantic journey, this time to Africa.[53]

9

MUTOMBO KATSHI

The fall of 1956 was a busy time for Paine College's brand-new president, Reverend Eugene Clayton Calhoun. The school's enrollment was growing, its new science building was almost complete, and plans were afoot for dormitories, a dining hall, and a new chapel. For years, there had been proposals to name this chapel in honor of John Wesley Gilbert and Walter Russell Lambuth, southern Methodism's first missionaries to the Congo. That idea was gaining steam as the fiftieth anniversary of Lambuth and Gilbert's 1911 departure for Africa approached. Calhoun, who had himself once hoped to be a Congo missionary (he had instead served in China), started exploring Paine's archives in preparation for the anniversary. What began as dutiful research became the work of devotion. After a four-year search, Calhoun located Lambuth's original Congo diaries, which had lain for decades in the filing cabinet of a Methodist mission office in New York, and made contact with Gilbert's eldest daughter, Alma Gilbert Sims of Jersey City, who loaned him the surviving portion of her father's 1911–1912 diary.[1]

Against the backdrop of the Congo's sudden independence from Belgium in June 1960, Calhoun began to write whenever he could find time on weekends, sitting with the two travelers' diaries before him. His book, *Of Men Who Ventured Much and Far: The Congo Quest of Dr. Gilbert and Bishop Lambuth*, appeared in 1961. Its publication helped spur the construction of Gilbert-Lambuth Memorial Chapel, christened in February 1968. Six months later, fire swept through Paine's main building, Haygood Hall, destroying the school's archives and most of Calhoun's research materials. Amongst the losses was the typed copy of Gilbert's diary Calhoun had made before sending the original back north to Alma Sims. That original was lost after Alma died in 1980. Lambuth's original diaries have also disappeared (again), but several typed copies survive. Only thanks to E. C. Calhoun's labor of love can we can still read fragments from John Wesley Gilbert's Congo diary.[2]

I Must Go

Although Walter Russell Lambuth was born in Shanghai and spent his early life as a Methodist Episcopal Church, South (MECS) missionary in China and Japan, he had long dreamed of Africa. In 1890, the same year John Wesley Gilbert went to Greece, Lambuth, who was then living in Kobe, Japan, proposed the MECS undertake a mission to Africa. When Lambuth returned to the United States early the next year, among his first stops was Paine Institute. His February 1891 visit inspired Paine's students to form an Afro-American Mission Society whose honorary members included "J. W. Gilbert of the American School, Athens." Paine President George Williams Walker soon proposed a joint mission by the MECS and the Colored Methodist Episcopal (CME) Church. Lambuth's interest in the Congo was heightened by his April 1891 conversation in Nashville with explorer Henry Morton Stanley. The first known European to travel the entire course of the Congo River (in 1877), Stanley had spent 1879–1884 establishing outposts along the river for King Leopold II of Belgium. In 1885, Leopold had laid claim to a huge swathe of the Congo basin (about 900,000 square miles) as his personal domain, the so-called Congo Free State, in reality a brutal colonial enterprise. Around the time he met Stanley, Lambuth also learned that two southern Presbyterians—black Virginian William Henry Sheppard and white Alabamian Samuel Norvell Lapsley—had established a mission at Luebo in the Kasai region of the Congo (on their way upriver, Lapsley and Sheppard met a young Polish sailor named Józef Korzeniowski, better known as Joseph Conrad, who later fictionalized his African experiences in the novel *Heart of Darkness*).

Lapsley died in 1892, but Sheppard would help lead the interracial Presbyterian effort in the Congo until 1911.[3]

From 1892 onward, the southern Presbyterians repeatedly urged the MECS to join them in the Congo. These exhortations reached the CME, too, for its leaders were considering foreign endeavors as early as 1894 and, by 1898, judged the time had come "to start some mission work in Africa, the land of our ancestry." Paine's Afro-American Missionary Society remained active, and the school's 1894–1895 catalogue (the last one surviving until 1913–1914) reports two of its members stood "ready to go as missionaries to Africa whenever the church shall call." There was also a short-lived CME-wide group, the Vanderhorst Foreign Missionary Society. Despite these preparations, "debt and lack of conviction," as Lambuth put it, kept the two churches from action. In the meantime, Lambuth became Secretary of the MECS Board of Foreign Missions and fostered Methodism in Brazil, Cuba, Japan, and Korea.[4]

While Lambuth long had Africa on his mind, Gilbert did not. During the decade after his 1891 return from the American School of Classical Studies at Athens, Gilbert focused on teaching Greek, German, and English literature and on church leadership and civil rights advocacy at home. His mentor George Williams Walker likewise did not emphasize foreign mission work during this period. Though Gilbert certainly met Lambuth during the 1890s, he did not begin his foreign missionary turn until the 1901 Ecumenical Methodist Conference in London, where Lambuth delivered a stirring call to mission work that clearly inspired Gilbert. From that 1901 conference until their departure for the Congo in 1911, the two men saw each other regularly, especially after Lambuth became a Paine College trustee in 1904. From 1906 onward, a joint mission began to seem a real possibility.[5]

Lambuth was not the only person turning Gilbert toward Africa. In 1903, CME bishop R. S. Williams had helped three young Zulu men from Natal, South Africa, enroll at Paine. These men may have been connected with South African educator John Dube, later famous as the founder of the African National Congress, who sent a number of students to the United States for seminary or college work around this time. For the next seven years, Gilbert worked closely with the three

Zulus, learning about their culture and language in the process. His long interaction with the Zulus helps explain how quickly he picked up the Congolese languages Tshiluba and Otetela, which are distantly related to Zulu. One of the three men apparently died of tuberculosis, but the other two, William and Josiah Nyatikazi, graduated in 1910. By then, several other African students were at Paine.[6]

Gilbert's decision to emphasize foreign mission work during the early 1900s also had a very practical aspect. The decline in MECS funding for Paine, followed by the 1907 decision of several regional CME conferences to cut their support entirely, put the school in financial straits. The fundraising odysseys Gilbert made during 1907–1910 with his white colleague J. D. Hammond kept Paine alive, but something more was needed. If an interracial MECS-CME mission in Africa, on the lines of the successful Presbyterian venture, could be established, Paine College would gain new purpose as a training ground for black missionaries. White southern Methodists otherwise indifferent or hostile to Paine could become more enthusiastic, and the school's new direction might also convince reluctant CME conferences to resume their support.[7]

Meharry Medical College physician J. A. Lester, whom Gilbert frequently visited in Nashville, remarked on his friend's growing interest in Africa. Gilbert's educational and religious work at home, Lester observed, "fired his soul to usefulness to the great mass, of whom he read and heard beyond the seas." Even so, Gilbert at first did not intend to go to Africa. Paine College needed him and so did his wife and children; his youngest daughter, Mattie, had only been born in 1899. He tried unsuccessfully to find another CME representative to join Lambuth. "It pained him," Lester remarks, "because his friends could not see and feel as he did." In the end, Gilbert felt himself called to the task. "I MUST GO," he told Lester.[8]

In late April 1910, Gilbert went to Nashville for a meeting of Lambuth's Board of Foreign Missions. Stirred by Gilbert's eloquence, the Board resolved to send an MECS representative (Lambuth was not named, but it could be no one else) to Africa "to study the conditions there with reference to one or more eligible sites for a mission" and began to seek funding for the trip. A week later, Lambuth was elected an MECS bishop, with charge over the western United States, Brazil, and the proposed new African venture. In mid-May, Lambuth attended the CME general conference in Augusta, where Gilbert proposed his denomination join the MECS, with himself as CME representative. "No colored man," wrote famed black journalist Horace Slatter in covering the conference, "enjoys the confidence of the M. E. Church, South more than does Prof. Gilbert," and the CME enthusiastically approved the cooperation. Gilbert was elected the CME's first Superintendent of African Missions. Nearly twenty years after Lambuth's first visit to Paine, the CME-MECS venture to Africa was under way.[9]

But where in Africa? Neither the MECS nor the CME had specified. Paine's Zulu students, Josiah and William Nyatikazi, got Gilbert and Lambuth to consider South Africa first. At the end of May 1910, *The Augusta Chronicle* reported the Nyatikazis were to "locate a site for a Methodist mission in Zululand" under Lambuth and Gilbert's direction. Paine's trustees voted to hire a replacement for Gilbert, and, in July, friends held a farewell gathering for him in Atlanta. The next month, Gilbert accompanied Josiah and William to New York, where the Zulus boarded the liner *Oceanic.* In a letter from New York, Gilbert writes that "my heart leaped with joy, and a deep anxiety to go on the same vessel . . . seized me as I saw these two young men, the physical embodiment of the work, faith, hopes, and prayers of our two churches for the 'Dark Continent,' walk up the gangway of that steamer. But I must wait two months longer before going to join [them] in the effort to carry the gospel of the Son of God and the teachings of Paine College to my fatherland." In October 1910, Gilbert still anticipated going to South Africa, but plans changed sometime after that. Early in 1911, William Nyatikazi wrote to Paine to describe the tiny Methodist congregation he had built in Natal, adding "we are waiting for Bishop Lambuth and Rev. John Gilbert." By then, though, the Presbyterians had turned Lambuth and Gilbert toward the Congo.[10]

Even while he prepared for Africa, Gilbert continued raising money for Paine with the help of MECS women's groups. He also secured donations for two other CME schools, Lane College in Tennessee and

Miles Memorial College in Alabama. His efforts let up only briefly as he mourned the deaths of his mentor George Williams Walker in May 1911 and his mother Sarah Thomas in July 1911. Though he grieved Walker's passing, Gilbert drew strength from the memory of the man he loved as a father, with whom he had labored side by side for nearly thirty years. "As I go to the wilds of Africa," Gilbert wrote the widowed Susan Walker, "George Williams Walker will go with me, to strengthen and help me carry on his noble work. 'Though dead yet he speaketh' in the lives of the black men and women whose lives are the sheaves of the harvest of his sainted life." Of his mother, Gilbert would later say rhetorically that she bequeathed her meager estate to support his journey. To help pay for his travel and equipment, Gilbert collected donations, some of just a few dollars apiece, from friends white and black. When Gilbert's fundraising fell short, Lambuth stepped in to cover the remainder.[11]

In late summer 1911, Gilbert went to Virginia to speak with black missionary William Henry Sheppard, who in 1890 had co-founded the Presbyterian mission at Luebo. Sheppard and his wife Lucy had spent most of the years since then in the Congo, finally returning to the United States just a few months before Gilbert's visit. The two men hit it off. "I have opened my heart and life to Brother Gilbert," Sheppard later wrote. Along with practical travel advice, Sheppard offered Gilbert deep perspective on the Congo's history. Leopold II's so-called Congo Free State, established in 1885, had been the Belgian king's personal money pit, nearly bankrupting him by the time the Presbyterians got to Luebo. Leopold was saved by the invention of inflatable rubber tires and the insatiable demand for rubber that ensued (Gilbert had seen some of the first such tires in Athens in 1891, mounted on the new "safety bicycle" ridden by a visitor to the American School), for the Congo was full of rubber trees. Leopold became rich by mercilessly imposing taxes in the form of rubber, which natives had to harvest in the jungle and deliver in baskets. The king's African tax collectors terrorized the land, often killing, raping, mutilating, and torturing indiscriminately. Sheppard had been a leading critic of the king's atrocities. Facing international condemnation, Leopold in 1908 relinquished control of the Congo to Belgium. The new colonial administration made reforms but abuses continued. After Sheppard published an article condemning the exploitation of Congo's people, a Belgian rubber-trading company sued Sheppard and his white colleague William Morrison for libel. Morrison's case was dismissed. Sheppard was acquitted in 1909, only to retire in 1911.[12]

Talking with Sheppard helped Gilbert understand the tightrope he and Lambuth would be walking in the Belgian Congo. They could not condone exploitation and abuse, but in order to establish a mission they would need the support and approval of the Belgian authorities. And, although black and white Presbyterians had worked fruitfully together in the Congo for many years, Sheppard probably told Gilbert about the tensions that had arisen recently as many in the southern white leadership became wary of educated black missionaries. For his part, Sheppard was especially taken by his visitor's linguistic skills, noting that Gilbert "is even now acquiring a working knowledge of the Congo languages with remarkable aptitude and quickness" to complement his fluent French. Speaking from two decades of experience, Sheppard judged Gilbert "one of the best prepared men for [missionary] work I have ever met, regardless of color."[13]

The Native Soil of My Race

On September 26, 1911, Gilbert set out from Augusta for his third Atlantic crossing. While he was away, Paine College's new President J. D. Hammond would be setting up the new missionary training department. Gilbert boarded the Cunard liner *Mauretania* in New York on October 4 with the highest hopes. "As I see it," he wrote, "this move will help us all, both black and white, to get closer together here in America by the cooperation of our two churches, will broaden and strengthen them both, and at the same time will be a community of effort 'to go into all the world and preach the gospel to every creature.'" The *Mauretania*, the world's fastest passenger ship, took Gilbert to Liverpool in less than six days despite bad weather. Meanwhile, Lambuth was on his way from Argentina after a summer's work in

Brazil. The two men met in London and equipped themselves with tropical clothing, tents, medicines, tools, and a portable typewriter before crossing the English Channel to Antwerp, where they boarded a Belgian steamer on October 14.[14]

The voyage to the Belgian Congo, some five thousand miles south of Antwerp, took nearly three weeks. Gilbert and Lambuth spent the time studying and praying. They read Presbyterian missionary William Morrison's grammar of the Tshiluba language spoken around Luebo, along with books on Africa by explorer Henry Stanley and others. "Bishop Lambuth," remarked Gilbert in his diary, "is very devout and ever ready to study the Scriptures in French, Portuguese, and English. What a blessing his association has been to me." They got to know a Baptist missionary on board and slowly warmed up to another set of passengers: a dozen Catholic priests, friars, and nuns. "The R. C. [Roman Catholics]," admitted Lambuth after attending Mass, "have a reverential spirit while they worship. Something to be learned from everybody."[15]

After stopping in the Canary Islands, the travelers made landfall at Dakar, in what was then French West Africa. "We have at last set foot on the great continent of Africa," Gilbert wrote in a letter home. The pair's first act ashore was symbolic: "Bishop Lambuth and I, squarely facing each other shook hands on the native soil of my race." Walking through the city, Gilbert saw the bustling harbor, the mix of native and European dress, and the varied produce in the market. After Dakar came brief stops at Conakry in French Guinea and Freetown in British Sierra Leone. Freetown particularly impressed Gilbert. "I did not see a single white man in any official capacity," he notes in another letter. "It was an inspiring sight," he continues, to see educated, uniformed black men in charge of Sierra Leone's railroad: "engineer, fireman, conductor—everything black, every thing orderly and neat." From Freetown, Gilbert and Lambuth sailed on to Boma at the mouth of the Congo River, arriving on November 2 (see Map 6).[16]

Boma in 1911 was the capital of the Belgian Congo, a status it would not cede to Léopoldville (today Kinshasa) until 1926. The flags of foreign consulates flew by the harbor; wooden railroad ties and coal from

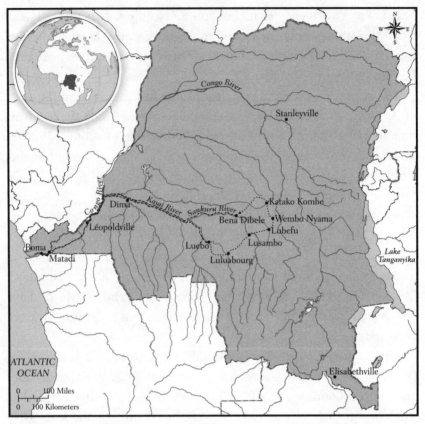

MAP 6 Route of Gilbert and Lambuth in the Belgian Congo, 1911–1912

Belgium lay on the piers. Lambuth the world traveler found echoes of northern China's Liadong peninsula in the hilly landscape around the port. The beautiful two-story bamboo houses reminded him of the Philippines, the chaotic post office of Santiago, Cuba, in the 1890s. The post office and other colonial buildings stood on iron pilings, meant to ward off moisture and insects. Gilbert's only surviving written description of reaching the Congo is matter-of-fact: "we entered the mouth of the Congo about four and one half degrees below the equator." Perhaps Boma made him think again of Patras in Greece, a port he had seen and Lambuth had not. Gilbert and Lambuth stopped in Boma just long enough to register at the US consulate and meet with several

American missionaries who warned them of the dangers of the tsetse fly and the pandemic sleeping sickness it brought. Then they continued thirty miles upriver to Matadi, where they visited the grave of William Henry Sheppard's white partner Samuel Lapsley. Above Matadi, rapids made the Congo River impassable for more than two hundred miles. A winding rail line, laid down around the same time the Corinth Canal in Greece was dug, took Lambuth and Gilbert on a two-day, two-hundred-fifty-mile chug northeast to Léopoldville, where they arrived about November 8.[17]

On the River

From Léopoldville upward, the Congo and its tributaries were navigable. Gilbert and Lambuth had expected to get a ride to Luebo on the Presbyterian-owned steamer *Lapsley*, but through miscommunication the boat left without them. Not until November 19 did the pair board a Belgian Kasai Company steamer that took them eight days and several hundred miles northeast, to the company's headquarters at Dima on the Kasai River. En route, they saw their first hippopotamuses and crocodiles and suffered their first tsetse fly bites. "Sly, persistent, and bloodthirsty as a maneater," lamented Lambuth about the flies, adding "Gilbert much disturbed tried but failed to kill a single one." The companions distracted themselves by reading the Bible in French and studying Tshiluba.[18]

Onward from Dima, Lambuth and Gilbert's only option was a cramped, dirty paddle-wheeler. Their tiny sleeping area was just feet from boxes of ammunition and explosives stacked close to the vessel's wood-fired boilers. "I pointed [the boxes] out to Gilbert," records Lambuth, "and was sorry I did it. If his hair could have uncurled it would have. I remarked, 'Gilbert we are in no hurry to get to heaven, but it is well that we have prepared for any urgency.'" As the boat churned slowly up the Kasai River, the travelers endured heat, mosquitoes, tsetse flies, rancid food, drunken Belgians, and close encounters with hippos and crocodiles. There were frequent riverbank halts so the crew could cut wood for the boilers and barter for food with locals and occasional overnights at colonial posts, some well-kept and others rank with neglect.[19]

At one post, Gilbert and Lambuth conversed with Mr. Lazarus John, an African clerk from Sierra Leone whose brother was with the Presbyterians at Luebo. Mr. John told them "he dared not bring [his] wife to the post and leave her—it would not be safe. Why?— The Whiteman!!" Further on, a fierce thunderstorm forced their paddle-wheeler to tie up for safety alongside a steamer coming downriver. Lambuth and Gilbert had thirty minutes to talk with the English couple on the other vessel: John Hobbis Harris and his wife Alice Seeley Harris, two of the most influential anti-slavery and anti-colonialist campaigners of the day. In the early 1900s, Alice Harris's graphic photographs of the atrocities perpetrated by Leopold's rubber-tax collectors had sparked outrage against the king. The Harrises told Gilbert and Lambuth that Belgian administrators had received them courteously and were trying to repair the damage Leopold had done, but colonial officials were poorly paid and sometimes inept. A Belgian doctor the Americans met a few days later had further insights on colonialism: the Europeans were killing themselves with alcohol, while disease had wiped out whole native villages.[20]

The Presbyterians

On December 7, some eighteen days and a thousand river miles from Léopoldville, Gilbert and Lambuth reached Luebo, in the lands of the Baluba and Lulua peoples. They received a royal welcome from the Presbyterians and their leader William Morrison. The Methodists admired the community the Presbyterians had built around Luebo: some 8,000 church members, including 300 mostly self-supporting teachers and evangelists, and another 20,000 adherents. With Sheppard's recent retirement, Morrison was, as Gilbert observed, "preacher, pastor, manager, and judge of the court." Gilbert was particularly pleased to meet Morrison's African American colleagues Alonzo and Althea Edmiston, recently returned from the United States. While Morrison emphasized

Tshiluba because it was a lingua franca at Luebo and across large parts of the upper Kasai River basin, Althea Edmiston was working on a less widely spoken language, Bushong. The extant fragments of Gilbert's diary do not name the Edmistons, but he clearly had them in mind when he wrote, "the kindness of these Presbyterians to us can never be forgotten. They never left a thing undone to secure our comfort, to acquaint us with the customs of the natives, to instruct us in missionary policies, plans, experiences, etc."[21]

Gilbert's long study of Tshiluba paid off at Luebo, for the local people took quickly to him. During the fifteen days he and Lambuth spent with the Presbyterians, Gilbert got to know the native church elders. Chief among them was Moses Mudimbi, originally from the Lualaba (Zaïre) River region far to the east. As a child, Mudimbi had been a captive at the court of Ngongo Luteta, a warlord who had served both Arab slavers and the Congo Free State. Mudimbi escaped around 1891 and ended up at Luebo, where the Presbyterians took him in. He became a Christian, married another refugee, and with his wife became a leader in the community. We can only wonder if Moses Mudimbi stirred Gilbert's Athenian memories of another native Presbyterian evangelist, Rev. Michael Demetrios Kalopothakes.[22]

It may have been at Luebo that Lambuth and Gilbert posed side by side for what would become an iconic photograph (Figure 9.1). If they appeared at first glance an odd couple—strong, outgoing Gilbert alongside frail, quiet Lambuth—the two men complemented each other. Stories emanating from the MECS in the 1920s and 1930s sometimes transform Gilbert into a stereotype of the faithful black servant protecting his white master. While Gilbert himself sometimes played up the "protector" angle in fundraising speeches to white audiences after 1912, the contemporary evidence shows their relationship was founded on equality and mutual respect. Even before landing in Africa, Lambuth wrote to Paine trustee Warren Candler that Gilbert "came to me as a brother—I shall ever treat him as such." Months into the mission, when a white doctor at the Belgian colonial post of Lusambo invited Lambuth but not Gilbert to dinner, Lambuth promptly declined the invitation, stating "Gilbert and I [are] on an equality here."[23]

FIGURE 9.1 Professor John Wesley Gilbert and Bishop Walter Russell Lambuth in the Belgian Congo, 1911–1912.

Courtesy of the United Methodist Church General Commission on Archives and History.

Following Presbyterian advice, Lambuth and Gilbert decided to explore northeast from Luebo into the lands of the Batetela people. In recommending this direction, William Morrison hoped the Methodists would help check the advance of Belgian Catholic missionaries. Morrison also preferred to leave the challenge of mastering Otetela, the Batetela language, to the Methodists. Gilbert and Lambuth would not go unaided. Mudimbi and his fellow elders Dufanda and Bushong, all three of whom spoke Otetela, would accompany them; Bushong would cook for the Americans. As it was planting season, Lambuth and Gilbert had trouble finding the sixty porters needed to carry their equipment and supplies—above all the salt and other goods they needed to pay for food en route—until a dozen men from the Luebo congregation stood up. Others at the mission would take care of the volunteers' families while they were gone.[24]

The March Upcountry

A crowd turned out on the cold, foggy morning of December 22 to bid the expedition farewell. "Dr. M[orrison] had to protect us from our friends," records Lambuth; "they also gave us each a name. The occasion touched our heart deeply." Gilbert received the name of a famous Baluba chief, Mutombo Katshi, who had recently died. Lambuth was given the name of another chief, Kabengele. Then they set off along the caravan route to Luluabourg (today Kananga) and thence to the town of Lusambo, a trek of about two hundred and fifty miles.[25]

It was more than twenty days to Lusambo. The group fell into a routine: Gilbert and Mudimbi leading the column, Lambuth and Dufanda bringing up the rear. This arrangement, along with the column's daily progress into what were for him unknown lands, must have made Gilbert think of a classical Greek text he knew intimately and taught every year at Paine: Xenophon's *Anabasis*, with its vivid depictions of Greek mercenaries marching through the wilds of Anatolia, the Spartan Cheirisophus in the van and the Athenian Xenophon in the rear. Perhaps he even made the comparison to Lambuth during their evening conversations.[26]

Xenophon never learned the languages of Anatolia, but with Mudimbi's help Gilbert made rapid progress in both Tshiluba and Otetela. Fragments from his diary describe conversations with natives, among them the chief Kanyoke. "Had an interesting talk with him," writes Gilbert; "a hard case. Couldn't read and didn't care to learn how. Had 10 wives and only 1 child. Wants 40 wives. . . . Conception of God is that though he created us he cares not for us any further." Gilbert also noted how native evangelists from Luebo had stimulated many villagers' keen interest in Christianity. "Sometimes," he observes, they "succeed in learning from passersby like the Bishop and myself the Lord's Prayer, etc., and these natives learn by heart and repeat what they have learned every morning . . . and on Wednesday nights in their huts. They pray to Nzambi [God], without knowing very much about him." Lambuth marveled at Gilbert's rapport with everyone they met, especially children. At one stop, Gilbert played leap-frog with a throng of youngsters, drew in their parents, and succeeded, Lambuth remarks, "so well that he even got the dignified chief at it. He simply captured the village." In a letter he wrote soon after, Lambuth called Gilbert "a providential man."[27]

Northeast of Luluabourg at Mutoto, Gilbert and Lambuth ran into a white Presbyterian making a circuit from Luebo, Joseph Pritchard of Mississippi. Sick with fever, Pritchard greeted the Methodists with racial slurs of the sort Gilbert had often heard back home but never before in Africa. Even so, Gilbert recounts Pritchard was "kind to us and to me. Gave me two pamphlets to help me with Baluba [i.e., Tshiluba]. Sent American flag to meet us." Lambuth and Gilbert took Pritchard to Lusambo, through rain so heavy the column sometimes had to take shelter for hours. Gilbert's diary records genuine concern for Pritchard, and, as the Mississippian recovered, the two men struck up a friendship based on their common interest in African languages. When they parted ways, Pritchard gave Gilbert and Lambuth his American flag. The Methodists and their Presbyterian volunteers posed for photos with the flag (see Figure 9.2) and would carry it into Batetela lands. The flag might seem an imperialist gesture, but the opposite is more likely. By displaying the Stars and Stripes, Lambuth and Gilbert hoped

FIGURE 9.2 Gilbert and Lambuth (both seated) with Presbyterian volunteers, circa January 1912.
Courtesy of the United Methodist Church General Commission on Archives and History.

to distinguish themselves from the Belgians, whose colonial banner of yellow star on blue field was all too familiar to the Congo's people.[28]

Gilbert and Lambuth stayed at Lusambo from January 13 to January 18, 1912, long enough for Gilbert to preach a Sunday sermon there. He also had time for a letter to *The Christian Index*. Remarking on the work of other black American missionaries, Protestant and Catholic, across the continent, Gilbert pledged, "I intend to do all in my power during the rest of my life for the evangelization of Africa. . . . I never expect to rest until my great Church is at work here too." He had received no news of home since a letter from Ola dated October 23, 1911. Nonetheless, added Gilbert, "don't think of me as being unhappy here in the heart of the Dark Continent. Jesus is with me as never before."[29]

Mudimbi and the Presbyterian volunteers would go with Gilbert and Lambuth the entire way, but some of the hired porters went home from Lusambo. The Methodists had to accept conscripted replacements from Lusambo's Belgian station chief. While Lambuth and Gilbert acknowledged this official's assistance and were grateful for the hospitality of other individual Belgians, they were ever more aware of the parasitic nature of colonialism. The Belgians, Lambuth wrote, "[have] not learned the art of living off the products of the soil. They live rather off the native." By 1914, his assessment of Belgian officialdom was more scathing: "uneducated, uninformed, immoral, mercenary and have no genuine interest in the development of the country or people."[30]

From Lusambo, Lambuth and Gilbert pressed on eight days and a hundred miles to the Lubefu River, encountering many Batetela villages but no suitable mission site along the way. The people were friendly. At one village Mudimbi led a Sunday service while Gilbert sat with the local chief's only son perched on his knee. Lambuth noted, "All the children love Gilbert. They crowd about him everywhere." Nature was less welcoming. "We had to wade streams infested with crocodiles," Gilbert's diary records, "walk on stick bridges which were scarcely able to sustain our weight . . . and climb up hills of 60 degree slant by pulling our bodies up by roots that jutted out from water-made and beast-made paths." Gilbert nearly took a fatal tumble when a rotten bridge broke under him. Swarms of ants and mosquitoes attacked. "Mosquitoes worst in my life," scrawled Gilbert one evening; "carriers also said same . . . . OH THE MOSQUITOES."[31]

Gilbert's linguistic skills helped him connect with villagers and defuse tensions among the porters. He also began putting Otetela on paper. "I did what I could," he later reported, "in collecting a Batetela vocabulary, formulating a grammar and writing the First Epistle to the Corinthians and the Epistle to the Romans in the Batetela language. However crudely done, a beginning was made." As he worked, Gilbert must have been reminded of Corinth, where the Apostle Paul wrote both epistles, and of the Areopagus in Athens where Paul had preached. Lambuth offers a vivid scene of Gilbert sitting at his typewriter in the middle of a Batetela village, a crowd of hundreds intently watching his every keystroke. Gilbert's work was pioneering, for the first Otetela-English dictionary was not published until about 1923 and not until 1938 would a complete Otetela New Testament appear.[32]

On January 26, the column reached the Lubefu River. It took the sixty-odd men nearly two hours to cross the swaying, two-hundred-foot-long vine suspension bridge across the turbulent water (Figure 9.3). Gilbert led the way, carrying the American flag. Lambuth and Gilbert spent four nights as guests at Lubefu's tidy Belgian outpost. Then they continued northeast with the Presbyterians and new Batetela porters, replacements for the Lusambo conscripts.[33]

As they pushed on into rolling, grassy country, Lambuth and Gilbert worried. On the advice of Mudimbi and Dufanda, they had already rejected a potential mission site south of Lubefu. Would they have to trek another hundred and fifty miles to the town of Katako-Kombe to find a suitable place? Farther? Just two days out of Lubefu, they got lost and missed the direct route for Katako-Kombe. It was a fortunate misstep—providential, Gilbert and Lambuth would have said—for the next day, February 1, they walked through rich millet fields and into the village capital of the Batetela chief Wembo Nyama.[34]

Wembo Nyama's Land

It was the forty-second day out of Luebo. For once, Gilbert and Lambuth were together up front, with Mudimbi and Dufanda far to the rear. Wembo Nyama, dressed in a European coat and white hat, was the tallest man the Americans had seen in Africa. Politely cautious, he shook hands with the Americans, asked whether they were "of the [Belgian] state or God's people," and gave them a tour of his court buildings, from which he ruled a domain of some forty-seven villages. Minutes after Mudimbi and Dufanda arrived, the chief's attitude changed entirely. "Choose any of my many villages and come among us!," he enthused, addressing Gilbert rather than Lambuth. Wembo Nyama and Moses Mudimbi, it turned out, were boyhood friends. Both had served the warlord Ngongo Luteta decades before, but while Mudimbi had fled captivity and gone to Luebo, Wembo Nyama had returned home to succeed his father as chief. Just before dinner, the chief recognized Bushong the cook as another friend from Ngongo Luteta days. As he embraced Mudimbi and Bushong, Wembo Nyama did not tell the Americans that he himself had once been among Luteta's most feared lieutenants.[35]

FIGURE 9.3 Vine suspension bridge over the Lubefu River, January 1912. Courtesy of the United Methodist Church General Commission on Archives and History.

Gilbert and Lambuth stayed four days in Wembo Nyama's home. They had no inkling of the debate that went on in the nearby council house. Several of the chief's advisors, including his brother, argued that all missionaries, Protestant or Catholic, were servants of colonialism. Wembo Nyama, citing the example of the Presbyterians at Luebo, countered that the Americans were different. He hoped the Methodists would help him build schools, hospitals, and homes and improve the economic condition of his people. His decision made, the chief began taking Otetela reading lessons with Mudimbi and begged Gilbert to stay on in his capital until more missionaries came (see Figure 9.4). Nothing survives of Gilbert's immediate response to Wembo Nyama, though he would later offer a glowing evaluation of the chief and his tribe: "One of the finest places in all Africa, one of the finest tribes to work among, affable, brave, fine of physique, acute mentally, and responsive to the gospel."[36]

Homeward Bound

Promising to return in eighteen months, Gilbert and Lambuth departed Wembo Nyama's capital on February 5, 1912. The chief clasped Gilbert's hand first, exclaiming "Hurry back! Hurry back!" in Otetela before shaking Lambuth's hand in silent farewell. Then the Methodists and the Presbyterian volunteers were on their way again, making a loop of several hundred more miles north and west through Batetela lands. They reached the Belgian post at Bena Dibele on the Sankuru River on February 19, sixty-one days and perhaps as many as nine hundred miles after leaving Luebo. After another set of farewells, Mudimbi and his Presbyterians returned home while the Americans caught a boat downriver.[37]

At Léopoldville, Gilbert composed several letters in French to the Belgian authorities, requesting a grant of land and permission to establish a mission with Wembo Nyama. Though he and Lambuth had witnessed numerous instances of brutality and repression, any mention of those events would cause the Belgians to deny their request. Instead, Gilbert embellished his letters with compliments for the colonial

FIGURE 9.4 Dufanda, Bushong, Chief Wembo Nyama, Mudimbi, and Bishop Lambuth. Photograph taken during Lambuth's second visit in 1914.
Courtesy of Bill Lovell.

régime. Years later, Lambuth remarked that "the colonial minister, upon my subsequent visit to Brussels, inquired who wrote the letters, and remarked that they were the most correct and elegantly expressed among those received at his office from one who was not a native of either France or Belgium."[38]

Lambuth sent letters from Léopoldville, too. One went to Paine president J. D. Hammond. "Such a workman we have in John Wesley Gilbert," he told Hammond. "If Paine College never turns out another man, all the expenditure of money and effort will not have been in vain. On the contrary, it will have been fully justified. He is diligent, painstaking, and consecrated. He has breadth, culture, and piety. He is a Christian at heart and in his daily life, and I have had ample opportunity of watching him under circumstances which try men's souls." Lambuth considered Gilbert so crucial to success in the Congo that he asked Paine College to give Gilbert an additional year of paid leave to fund his return to Wembo Nyama in 1913.[39]

The two men parted ways at Léopoldville, probably in late March. While Lambuth stayed on to visit the northern Congo before heading for Brazil, Gilbert headed back to Antwerp on his own. On the long return voyage, he drafted the introduction and outline for a book that would recount, as he put it, "the endeavor to find a place for the first missionary work of Southern Methodism in Africa." While he did publish brief accounts in a MECS journal and in the 1914 CME conference proceedings, Gilbert would never finish this book. From Antwerp, Gilbert made his connection to Liverpool, then took ship for New York on another fast Cunard liner, the *Lusitania*. With travelers on edge after the *Titanic* disaster just two weeks before, the *Lusitania* carried extra lifeboats, but the crossing was uneventful and the ship reached New York on May 2, 1912. Mutombo Katshi was back in Augusta a few days later. In less than eight months, he had travelled at least 28,000 miles, including nearly a thousand miles on foot. He got home in time from his African *Anabasis* in time to watch his oldest daughter Alma graduate from Paine's Normal program.[40]

THE OLD VETERAN

John Wesley Gilbert had found in Africa a salve, not only for the recent deaths of George Williams Walker and his mother, but for all the trials and challenges of the previous decade. Against the darkness that Jim Crow segregation had cast on the United States, the joint mission with Lambuth to the Congo brought light to Gilbert's life, opening his eyes to new possibilities and renewing his hopes for interracial cooperation. He was filled with eagerness to return to Africa. His friend J. A. Lester observed, "he began to tell the story of dangers and privations, and then his eyes would light up, as he told of the joy which came with these experiences." Within weeks of getting home, Gilbert was at Augusta's Colored YMCA for a lecture entitled "To the Congo for Christ." He agreed to stay on temporarily at Paine and pushed vigorously for the new missionary training department. That project went ahead, but the school was short of funds and there was no way J. D. Hammond could grant Gilbert paid leave to return to the Congo, as Lambuth had requested from Léopoldville. To raise money, for the rest of 1912 and into 1913 Gilbert spoke to audiences across the South and as far north as New York, accompanying his talks with slides made from stereopticon photos he had taken in Africa. Lambuth joined him several times in 1913. Decades later, an elderly Alabama minister told Paine president E. C. Calhoun that he still vividly remembered hearing Gilbert's address to a Methodist Episcopal Church, South (MECS) conference around 1912, remarking "that was the highest moment . . . I have known in nearly sixty years of ministry."[1]

Just as Soon as Possible

The year 1913 opened with high hopes. In February, with Lambuth coming to visit, Paine's President Hammond announced the school would be training Colored Methodist Episcopal (CME) missionaries for the Congo. News reports in the following months named Gilbert and the three MECS missionaries "who have been chosen to pioneer the work in Africa," suggesting the MECS would fund Gilbert. The MECS men planned to bring their wives, and there was talk that Gilbert's wife Ola would join the group, too. The youngest Gilbert daughters, teenaged Sarah and Mattie, could stay home with their older sister Alma, now a teacher in Augusta. John Jr., meanwhile, had moved to Nashville. Black Presbyterian missionaries were elated at the prospect of the Gilberts coming to the Congo. Lambuth and Gilbert made plans to attend the June 1913 MECS missionary conference to be held in the denomination's new facilities at Lake Junalaska, North Carolina.[2]

Just before the Junalaska conference, however, Lambuth got dire news: several wealthy, influential families had threatened to quit the MECS if any of their money was used to support black missionaries. Without this funding, the entire Congo enterprise was in doubt. Lambuth received the news in confidence, and he may well have concealed the specifics from Gilbert. Only decades later would Congolese historian M. O. Kasongo uncover the truth. Rather than taking the stage together with Lambuth at Junalaska, Gilbert was shuffled off to a separate part of the program. A fourth white missionary was announced in his place. In his conference address, Lambuth tried to make the best of the situation by promising the entry into the field "at a later date of Prof. and Mrs. J. W. Gilbert," but he could not hide the reality. If Gilbert was going to return to the Congo, it would have to be with money from the CME, whose next General Conference was slated for 1914.[3]

Meanwhile, Paine was floundering. Despite J. D. Hammond's best efforts, by June 1913 enrollment had dropped from 337 to 252, lower than it had been in 1899. The MECS was providing too little funding, students were choosing CME-controlled institutions over Paine, and the MECS refusal to support Gilbert's return to Africa cast doubt on the missionary training project. The school had also lost a crucial black supporter when *The Georgia Baptist*'s W. J. White died in April 1913. Although Paine's trustees hoped Gilbert would stay on in Augusta, he instead agreed to take over from his former student, William A. Bell, as president of Miles Memorial College near Birmingham in Alabama, while Bell came to Paine to teach mathematics.[4]

The CME leadership hoped Gilbert could rise above the faculty in-fighting that was roiling Miles, especially since he had been in Africa when it broke out. Gilbert may also have hoped to find a better living situation in Alabama for his family, as the area around their Augusta home was deteriorating. Lily Hammond, the wife of Paine's president, reports that Gilbert's neighborhood had grown to be "good enough for a white man's house of ill-fame, which he found was to be erected on the lot adjoining his own." Gilbert salvaged the situation by buying the adjacent lot, "at a cost of long saving and strain." Eventually he would own four properties along Forest Street, as Magnolia Street was renamed in 1912. But, he told Lily, "I am not safe any more. . . . There are still vacant lots there; and I can't possibly buy them all."[5]

Gilbert's first year as president brought Miles College "renewed confidence in its future," a Birmingham paper observed. By early May 1914, when he set out for the CME General Conference in St. Louis, some were putting him forward for a bishopric. While Gilbert got only a handful of votes, he had the pleasure of seeing his former student R. A. Carter elected with overwhelming support as one of two new bishops. His Congo hopes, though, were dashed. The MECS mission-aries had reached Wembo Nyama in February 1914, and two Paine students were training for Africa, but despite Gilbert's eloquent advo-cacy the General Conference would do no more than pass a vague res-olution that the CME send its missionaries "just as soon as possible."[6]

Gilbert put on a brave face. After his report in St. Louis, he immedi-ately caught an overnight train five hundred miles southeast to Atlanta to speak at the Negro Christian Student Conference (after speaking, he took the train back to St. Louis in time to catch the end of the CME meeting). The Atlanta conference's organizers included Lambuth and

John Hope, and a tenth of its seven hundred delegates were white. His former student Channing Tobias, now an up-and-coming YMCA leader, was a highlight of the program. Gilbert's address urged students toward foreign mission work with now-familiar arguments: Africa needed doctors, teachers, and ministers; black Americans were better suited to Africa than others; interracial cooperation abroad would foster better race relations at home. Yet while Gilbert had previously spoken of African "savagery and superstition," he had a new message in Atlanta: "we [American Negroes] owe it to the African to teach him that his continent and his people had proud representatives in the early morning of sacred and profane history." In a remarkable turn, Gilbert asserted that Africa's past eclipsed even the Greek and Roman classics: "Let [the African] know that Egypt was introduced to history by dynasties of Hamitic, most probably Negro, kings; that hoary Mt. Berkel and Meroe, two large cities down the Nile, peopled and governed solely by wooly haired Negroes before Homer or Virgil sang the fall of Troy, had reached the acme of the world's sculpture and architecture." The most telling feature of his speech, though, was Gilbert's unbridled criticism of the "so-called civilization" of colonialism, which exploited Africa's land and people for money, leaving behind ruin. "Instead of bread they give them a stone and instead of meat they give them a poisonous serpent," he declared. At Léopoldville in 1912, Gilbert had flattered the Belgians with the best French his pen could muster. That he did not hold back in Atlanta suggests he already knew in his heart he would never see the Congo again.[7]

The CME did not officially decide against mission work in Africa until 1922, perhaps reflecting its reluctance to close the door Gilbert had worked so hard to open, but, after 1914, there was no real chance its missionaries would join the MECS in Wembo Nyama's land. Despite the bitter disappointment, Gilbert remained close with Lambuth. The two men reunited occasionally at church conferences, and in 1918 worked together to find chaplains for African American troops going to serve in France. When Lambuth returned to the Congo in 1913 with only white missionaries, Wembo Nyama and his people wondered where Mutombo Katshi was. Nearly a decade later, villagers who had met Gilbert just once were still asking about him. In 1946, when Gilbert's former student Channing Tobias visited the Belgian Congo as director of the Phelps-Stokes Educational Fund, local leaders asked him when the CME Church would resume the work Gilbert had begun. The CME was never able to send its people, but the mission John Wesley Gilbert helped establish in Wembo Nyama's land endures to this day and the names Mutombo Katshi and Kabengele are still honored there.[8]

I Still Have Faith

Despite his success in Alabama, John Gilbert resigned the presidency of Miles Memorial in August 1914 and went back to Paine College. Most likely he realized Paine needed him more. The school's financial problems, exacerbated by chaotic accounting, were mounting and people had lost faith in president Hammond. Back in Augusta, Gilbert became Paine's first Dean of Ministerial Training and started a new theological curriculum to attract more students. He also took over as the trustees' secretary. For the next several years the minutes feature his strong, clear handwriting. The bad news continued. By June 1915, enrollment was down to 192, and MECS funding cuts forced the school to lay off faculty. J. D. Hammond submitted his resignation. So did Warren Candler, a trustee since the beginning. Hammond had told Candler in 1914 that Paine had to be "either better provided for or abandoned altogether." Candler for the moment chose the latter, although he would be re-elected in 1916.[9]

Paine limped into fall 1915 under a new white president, Donald E. Atkins, previously the college's business manager. Just weeks into the term, the Gilberts suffered a devastating loss: their eighteen-year-old daughter Sarah, a recent graduate of the college preparatory course at Claflin University in South Carolina, suddenly fell ill and died, perhaps of appendicitis. Friends remembered her as "a very bright young woman" for whom "the future held much in store." Gilbert barely had time to grieve before he had to set off again to beg money for Paine from white Methodists in Oklahoma, Texas, and Louisiana. He also began giving paid lectures on his Congo experiences. If he could not go back to Africa, he could at least use his vivid stories to bring in cash for his beloved school. The CME promised in December to renew its funding for Paine, but by March 1916 the situation was so dismal the trustees briefly considered abandoning the college program Gilbert had helped create in 1888. Rather than take that radical step, the trustees appointed Gilbert as Financial Commissioner with the task of raising money to pay off the school's debt.[10]

Gilbert was on the rails the rest of 1916. When not fundraising, he participated in interracial conferences to build support for black education. In October he journeyed by rail some 2,500 miles from Augusta through Phoenix, where a large MECS group came to hear him, and all the way to Los Angeles. He spoke at Santa Monica's CME church, founded in 1908 as the denomination's first outpost on the West Coast, at the University of Southern California, and at other venues. "I am writing this letter while on a fast moving train," he wrote Bishop C. H. Phillips on the way home, "because I cannot wait to say some things to you about my recent trip." Gilbert's letter, which praises the CME's westward growth, survives only because Phillips quoted it in his autobiography two decades later. In December, before five hundred mostly white delegates to the Federal Council of Churches in St. Louis, Gilbert spoke eloquently of the challenges facing African Americans and advocated the formation of interracial ministers' alliances to address community issues "without regard to race or color," earning loud applause, national press coverage, and even an approving nod from W. E. B. Du Bois. By year's end, there was again talk Gilbert would be up for a bishopric at the next CME General Conference in 1918.[11]

Citing "the hopeless financial outlook," Paine president Atkins tried to resign in January 1917, but was convinced to hang on until the MECS found a replacement. In the meantime, Gilbert was Paine's de facto leader (see Figure 10.1). The only break he took from Paine was to help found the Augusta chapter of the National Association for the Advancement of Colored People (NAACP). In April, he made a last-ditch plea in Nashville's *Christian Advocate*, arguing "no money spent

FIGURE 10.1 John Wesley Gilbert with some of his former students, circa 1917. Standing, left to right: Professor Gilbert, J. A. Walker (CME minister, Philadelphia), W. A. Bell (businessman, Atlanta), M. B. Gray (teacher, St. Louis). Kneeling, left to right: L. L. McKenzie (history professor, West Virginia State College), C. H. Tobias (national YMCA Secretary), H. S. Dunbar (YMCA Secretary, Detroit). Seated, left to right: L. H. Pharrow (former teacher at Paine), R. T. Hollis (high school teacher, Chattanooga), E. C. W. Gray (teacher, Paine College).

Courtesy of Collins-Callaway Library, Paine College.

to redeem a race at home or abroad has ever gone so far or done so much in the achievement of its end" and asking that "any individual, Church, Sunday School, or missionary society send at once any sum, however small it may be, to keep life in a worthy institution." Others might have given up, Gilbert concluded, but he had not: "I, who was the first one to matriculate in Paine thirty-three years ago, still have faith." Less than a week after this plea appeared came word that Albert Deems Betts, a white South Carolinian, had agreed to become president. In a sign of how crucial Gilbert had become to Paine's survival, the letter bearing this news was sent to him.[12]

In April 1917, though, the nation's attention was fixed on Europe. Like many Americans, Gilbert had at first given little thought to the war overseas. The 1915 German U-boat sinking of the *Lusitania*—the ship he had taken from Liverpool to New York on his way back from Africa in 1912—must have caught his attention, but that distant tragedy paled in comparison to the terrible March 1916 fire that devastated thirty-two blocks of central Augusta. Within weeks of the US declaration of war on April 6, 1917, Augusta was designated an Army training ground and, by 1918, hosted some 60,000 troops. The city's African American community rallied to the flag, with Gilbert's old friend C. T. Walker even giving a sermon entitled "This Is God's War." Gilbert took a leading role in the local Red Cross auxiliary, volunteered as a draft registrar, and was asked to teach French to black troops in France. In August, at a Blue Ridge, North Carolina conference hosted by white re- former Willis Weatherford, Gilbert proudly reported that the first four black Augustans to register were Paine students. Two other Paine men, he added, were in Iowa at the US Army's first training camp for black officers.[13]

Yet Gilbert did not relent in his criticism of racism and mob violence. "Black men are ready to give their lives, as American soldiers, in this world war to make the world safe for democracy," he remarked at Blue Ridge, "but they want to feel their own lives and liberties are safe in the democracy here at home." Those men included his twenty-six-year-old son John Jr., now a waiter at a private club in Muskegon, Michigan. John Jr. had his father's eloquence. Two weeks after the United States entered the war, he wrote the local Muskegon paper, declaring the pa- triotism of African Americans and exhorting readers to "lift up our hands unto the hills [and] read the writing in the skies foretelling the death of prejudice and hate wiped out by bloodshed for a nation's cause."[14]

As his war work continued into 1918, Gilbert also kept up his fund- raising for Paine in cooperation with President Betts and with white teacher Mary de Bardeleben. Just thirty-seven when he took over, Betts proved an inspiring if overly ambitious leader. Before leaving Paine in 1921, he would help set the school on a path to renewed stability and success. On top of all that, Gilbert somehow found time to keep teaching Greek, French, and German. Newspaperman Silas Floyd called Gilbert "the old veteran," a scholar who "would add lustre to any college faculty anywhere in the South."[15]

For the old veteran, another General Conference disappointment loomed. When the CME gathered at Chicago in May 1918, its leaders decided no new bishops were needed. And, though Gilbert had continued to push for training missionaries at Paine, the conference had not a word about Africa. Instead, Gilbert was elected national leader for the new Sunday School Department, intended "to perfect Bible knowledge for the moral and religious training" of CME children. Though it was no bishopric, the position offered steady pay, required less travel, and came with a stenographer. Silas Floyd did his best to compliment Gilbert, describing the Sunday School post as "a new thing, but a big thing." The job would require moving to Nashville, but the Gilberts had friends there, above all J. A. Lester of Meharry Medical College. With Alma now established as a teacher in Augusta, John Jr. on his way from Michigan to New York, and Juanita (as youngest daughter Mattie had refashioned herself) soon to graduate from Paine, John and Ola made plans for Nashville.[16]

Twilight

Sometime after 1923, a legend grew up that John Wesley Gilbert succumbed to sleeping sickness, contracted from tsetse fly bites in the Belgian Congo. Among the many who repeated this story was his former student John Hope. It is not impossible Gilbert actually was afflicted by the west African form of this disease, known as Gambian trypanosomiasis, which in rare cases can lie dormant in a person for many years before causing symptoms. But that is not the sole explanation for his doleful, lingering end.[17]

Gilbert escaped the first wave of pandemic influenza that ran through Augusta in the winter of 1918–1919 (the city had reacted quickly by closing schools, churches, and shops). In January 1919, he

had no difficulty traveling to Alabama for a Tuskegee Institute conference. John and Ola also enjoyed touring the countryside in their new
automobile. After the many thousands of miles he had covered without
incident by rail, by ship, on horseback, and on foot, a car crash was
the beginning of Gilbert's end. In February 1919, the couple got in a
wreck so bad Ola had an arm amputated and spent nearly two weeks
in the hospital. Gilbert seems to have suffered lasting effects. He largely
stopped traveling, and, by May, his once-clear handwriting appears
shaky and uncertain in Paine's records. Summoning last reserves of
strength, he and Ola went ahead with their move to Nashville. There,
in early June 1919, Gilbert made what was probably his final public
appearance, joining Bishop Lambuth at an MECS conference. Soon
afterward, Gilbert "collapsed mentally and physically" and the couple
returned to Augusta.[18]

Gilbert continued at Paine as long as he could. At his final trustees'
meeting in March 1920, he was too weak to write, so Channing
Tobias filled in as secretary. While Gilbert remained titular head of
the Sunday School Department, J. A. Lester did the work, assisted by
Gilbert's daughter Juanita. Gilbert's broken health soon forced him to
resign from Paine. Bishop Lambuth asked missionary physician D. L.
Mumpower, who had spent 1914–1918 in the Congo with Wembo
Nyama, to examine Gilbert, but Mumpower could not diagnose what
was wrong. Lambuth also obtained an MECS pension for Gilbert.
Though his condition briefly improved, by March 1921 Gilbert was
confined to bed.[19]

Walter Russell Lambuth died at Yokohama, Japan in September
1921. When the news reached Augusta, it was left to Ola to respond.
"I am sorry to say," she wrote, "that Mr. Gilbert is no better, per-
fectly helpless, and is not able to talk any." Ola, moved to tears by
Lambuth's death, lamented that "I can't tell my poor dear husband
but I am sad for him, for he loved [the] Bishop so." Other men whose
lives had entwined with Gilbert's were dying: Bishop Holsey and R. L.
Campbell in August 1920, C. T. Walker in July 1921, Silas Floyd in
September 1923. Ola nursed her husband until her own health failed.
Alma and Juanita took over, and John Jr. came home to help. Osceola

Pleasant Gilbert, weakened by the car crash and suffering from kidney disease, died in the hospital on June 20, 1922. John Wesley Gilbert lingered on, a shadow of his former self, for another seventeen months before joining Ola on November 18, 1923. Pneumonia, his death certificate said.[20]

CONCLUSION

ENDURING SPIRIT

Two weeks after John Wesley Gilbert died on November 18, 1923, an obituary by Colored Methodist Episcopal (CME) minister James Arthur Martin appeared in the white-run *Nashville Banner*. Martin knew Gilbert well. He had entered Paine's high school course in 1893, completed the college program in 1901, and over the years kept in close touch, visiting Paine as often as he could and sometimes traveling with Gilbert. In 1918, Martin and nine fellow Paine alums had even collaborated on a brief biography (unfortunately lost in the 1968 Haygood Hall fire) of their favorite professor.[1]

Martin's obituary lovingly recounted Gilbert's accomplishments from his public school days in Augusta to his studies at Paine and Brown, from his work at the American School of Classical Studies at Athens and his European travels to his Belgian Congo mission with Bishop Walter Russell Lambuth, from his three decades of teaching at Paine to his contributions as a CME minister and nationally known African American leader. Martin quoted extensively from a letter Lambuth had sent him in 1918. Apart from George Williams Walker, wrote Lambuth, few men knew Gilbert as he did: "for sincerity of purpose, high character, and noble ideals, he has few equals and surely no superior." Lambuth praised Gilbert's linguistic mastery and the way he employed "not only his brain, but his conscience" in translating parts of the New Testament from Greek into Otetela. Martin also explained how Gilbert faced the debilitating illness of his final years, "with as much fortitude and humility as characterized him in his palmy days when instructing the youth." Through his life and work, Martin concluded, John Wesley Gilbert "transcended the bounds of any one church or race and became an American contribution."

Martin was not the only one to write a heartfelt tribute to Gilbert, but his piece got the most attention. Nashville's *Christian Advocate*, the most widely circulated and influential journal of the Methodist Episcopal Church, South (MECS), published an expanded version in January 1924. In May, the NAACP's official journal, edited by W. E. B. Du Bois, reprinted parts of it. CME minister Joseph Colclough relied extensively on Martin for his hastily penned 1925 hagiography, *The Spirit of John Wesley Gilbert*. So, too, did many others who wrote about Gilbert in the years that followed. Martin himself, apparently dissatisfied with Colclough's treatment, was researching a book-length biography when he died in 1934.[2]

As much as later authors relied on Martin, they missed a key sentence. Martin had been to Gilbert's home on Magnolia Street (later Forest Street, and today 13th Avenue) in Augusta and sat in his study. Martin describes seeing his professor's souvenirs of Greece: stones from the Areopagus, the Parthenon, and Marathon, other classical relics, and "Grecian shoes." Without context the shoes were meaningless and it is no surprise later authors never once refer to them. But thanks to the pencil-scrawled reminiscences of American School student Andrew Fossum, we know that Gilbert got those shoes custom-made in Athens in fall 1890. They were the shoes he had worn as he climbed up the Acropolis and the Areopagus, as he looked out over the battlefield of Marathon, as he sat writing his thesis in the School library, as he dug in the mud of Eretria's graves and surveyed its city walls, as he explored the Bronze Age citadels of Tiryns and Mycenae and the ruins of ancient Olympia. For all that he accomplished in his later years and all the many directions his life after Greece took him, his sojourn at the American School remained for Gilbert so meaningful that he always kept his Grecian shoes.

Those shoes and stones, unfortunately, are lost. Gilbert's lengthy illness had strained the family finances. With their parents gone, the Gilbert children soon left Augusta for good. John Jr. went back to Michigan and from there moved to New York, dying in Jersey City in 1931. Juanita married dentist James Bell in 1924 and followed him to Savannah, where she died in 1971. Alma continued teaching school in Augusta until 1930, when she moved north permanently and married Jersey City realtor Eldridge Sims; she died in New York in 1980. None of the three Gilbert siblings had children. Alma and Juanita had set up a simple marble grave marker for their mother, but they were not able to do the same for their father, who was buried next to his beloved Ola in Augusta's Cedar Grove Cemetery. A guidebook writer for the Works Progress Administration, visiting the cemetery around 1937, observed Gilbert's grave was un-marked. The stone that today adorns Gilbert's final resting place was set up decades later as part of a community endeavor to commemorate the renowned black Augustans buried at Cedar Grove.[3]

Although Alma held on to her father's Congo diary, the Gilbert children's dispersion meant the loss of letters, memorabilia, and other precious evidence. Paine President E. C. Calhoun lamented, "it is all but tragic that [Gilbert's] papers were treated so carelessly that little of his writing is preserved." Whatever survived the family's scattering was burned in the 1968 Haygood Hall fire. Yet there is always the possibility that more documents of Gilbert's life await rediscovery, per-haps in an attic in Georgia or a storage box in Greece. It may be that someone reading these words will find them.[4]

Beyond his family, living memory of Gilbert was fading. Many of those who had known him best—his mathematics colleague R. L. Campbell, newspaperman Silas Floyd, Bishops Holsey and Lambuth, Reverend C. T. Walker—passed away just before Gilbert. Former Paine president J. D. Hammond died just a few weeks after him. Others were gone in the following decade: Bishop R. S. Williams in 1932, Lucy Craft Laney in 1933, J. A. Lester in 1934, John Hope in 1936. At Paine, A. D. Betts was replaced in 1921 by a new acting president, R. S. Tomlin, who had not known Gilbert well. In covering his funeral, *The Augusta Chronicle* praised Gilbert as "an exceptional scholar, a man of rare intellectual attainments, a genius and a marvel on account of his profundity and his ability to charm and magnetize," but without Silas Floyd to tell the story, the paper was short on specifics. If not for

J. A. Martin, much knowledge of Gilbert's life and work might have disappeared by the 1930s.[5]

Thankfully, we also have the loving words of J. A. Lester, who had known Gilbert since September 1886, when the young student from Augusta stopped in Nashville on his way north to Brown University. "Perhaps our friend and brother Gilbert had some faults as we all have," wrote Lester in December 1923, "but he was rich in virtues we all may well strive to possess. He was Christ-like in that he often prayed for those who could not and did not see as he saw. He had a warm heart for everybody. The poor, the weak, the ignorant, and the neglected had his first care, and he delighted to render them service. He loved his friends and counted them among all classes of people. He believed himself God's man to go where duty called and do with his might whatever his hands found to do."[6]

Paine College, of course, has never forgotten its first student, first graduate, first black faculty member, its leader in so much else. Together with George Williams Walker, Gilbert built the foundations for a unique American institution, a living example of interracial commitment to harmony and equality. As historian Mallory Millender writes, "when Martin Luther King, Jr. so eloquently articulated his dream for America in 1963—'that one day on the red hills of Georgia the sons of former slaves and the sons of former slave-owners will be able to sit down at a table of brotherhood'—actual ex-slaves and actual ex-slave-owners had already been sitting at that table at Paine College for 81 years." Gilbert-Lambuth Memorial Chapel on Paine's campus (see Figure 11.1), dedicated in 1968, stands as a physical reminder of the Christian faith and devotion to interracial cooperation that so shaped Gilbert's life and the life of his beloved school. Embedded in the chapel floor are small unworked stones from the ancient Greek city of Ephesus in Asia Minor, an archaeological touch Gilbert would have appreciated. Despite many challenges, today the people of Paine College proudly carry on into the twenty-first century the intellectual and spiritual tradition begun in rented rooms on Augusta's Broad Street in 1884. That tradition has nurtured not only America's first black archaeologist but also many other African Americans who have risen to national and international

FIGURE 11.1 Gilbert-Lambuth Memorial Chapel at Paine College.
Courtesy of Eyedew Photography, LLC.

prominence, including civil rights leader Channing Tobias, John Hope and several other presidents of historically black colleges and universities, educator and theologian Captolia Newbern, pioneering geologist Mack Gipson, Jr., United Methodist Church bishop Woodie White and other spiritual leaders, best-selling novelist Frank Yerby, and Emma Rhodes Gresham, one of the first African American women to hold elected office in Georgia.[7]

Elsewhere in Augusta, markers and monuments commemorate the places and people around whom Gilbert built his life. Among those places is Trinity CME Church, mother church of the denomination, where a little boy called Wesley went to school with Miss Chestnut in 1871. Closed in 1998 due to chemical contamination, Trinity escaped the wrecking ball and was moved in 2018 to a new location just across the street. The historic church awaits restoration.[8]

The MECS long remembered Gilbert as "the famous Negro missionary," and talks about his life featured in women's church meetings across the South for many years. In 1941, the MECS opened the

Gilbert Center at its Lake Junalaska conference site to provide separate accommodations and worship space for black visitors. Junalaska would be desegregated in 1968, and Lake Junalaska's leaders formally repented in 2017 for the site's racist past. In the north, white Methodist women as far away as Illinois and Pennsylvania learned about Gilbert into the 1940s. Gilbert's former student Emma C. W. Gray, a professor of English at Paine College, prepared materials for use in these meetings. In the 1950s and 1960s, Gilbert's teaching and missionary work continued to earn mention in African American newspaper and magazine articles on Negro History Week (the ancestor of Black History Month). To this day, his missionary endeavor with Lambuth is remembered in the Congo and in the Methodist schools Lambuth established in Japan.[9]

In the fields of Classics and classical archaeology, though, Gilbert's name and his pioneering contributions began to be forgotten with the passing of the American School's first generation of leaders in the early 1900s, especially those who had known Gilbert personally. Gilbert himself let his connections with the American Philological Association and the Archaeological Institute of America lapse after 1907, as he devoted himself to Paine and to the Congo. In contrast with his missionary adventures, there was no ready audience for stories about Gilbert the archaeologist. Again, consider how different things might be had he excavated at Bible-famed Corinth rather than at Eretria.

Gilbert fell out of touch with Brown University by 1917, but there was renewed interest in him there during the late 1920s and early 1930s, when his 1888 classmate Clarence Barbour was president and another classmate, Arthur E. Watson, talked about him with John Hope. After that, he seems to have faded back into obscurity at Brown until archivist Martha Mitchell in the early 1990s identified him as the school's first African American advanced degree recipient. Then came the work of Michele Valerie Ronnick and others on black classicists, and the Society of Black Archaeologists' recognition of Gilbert as "the first professionally trained African American archaeologist." In the years I have been writing this book, interest in Gilbert has grown rapidly. After a 2018 student-led research symposium at Brown, Gilbert's photograph was installed prominently at the entrance to Brown's Joukowsky Institute of Archaeology. And, in fall 2020, the American School of Classical Studies at Athens announced it would name a room in his honor. The American School has also created a new travel fellowship, named in honor of Gilbert's fellow classical scholar, Williams Sanders Scarborough.[10]

Paine president E. C. Calhoun described Gilbert as "Christian gentleman, professor, scholar, linguist, preacher, lecturer, churchman, missionary, writer, editor, and in that order." Calhoun's sequence (he does not specify "archaeologist," but he certainly recognized that aspect of Gilbert's work) reflects his own perspective, and each of us may choose a different ordering. If I have emphasized Gilbert's year in Greece, I have done my utmost to set that eventful sojourn into the wider sweep of his extraordinary life and to emphasize the centrality of both Classics and Christianity in his experience. I also hope that the approach I have adopted in this book, of recovering a seemingly lost history from a diverse range of scattered and sometimes fragmentary sources, will open the way to investigating other hidden figures, whether in classical studies or other fields. Meanwhile, whether in our mind's eye we picture him in Augusta or Atlanta or Providence, on the Acropolis or on the Areopagus or at Eretria, in London or in the Congo, in church or in the library or the lecture hall, before audiences black or white or interracial, John Wesley Gilbert remains forever inspiring.[11]

APPENDIX I: THE BIRTH DATES
OF GILBERT AND HIS FAMILY

JOHN WESLEY GILBERT

Ronnick (2001: 13) noted that conflicting evidence exists for Gilbert's birthdate, with 6 July 1864 and 9 January 1865 often given. With proper caution, she gave the year as circa 1864. New evidence enables us to reassess the question.

The date of 6 July appears repeatedly in documents throughout Gilbert's life. The earliest known source for 9 January 1865, on the other hand, is Colclough (1925: 79; repeated in Calhoun 1961: 9, Calhoun 1974: 1004). The January date appears nowhere in existing documents and is most likely an error. So too is the July 3, 1864 date of Terrell and Terrell (1977: 6).

Gilbert's death certificate gives his birthdate as 1865 and his burial record (Cedar Grove E149) gives his age as fifty-eight. These were probably the sources for the inscription on his grave stone, which reads "aged 58 years," but his grave was unmarked in the late 1930s (Federal Writers Project 1938: 116) and the current stone was set up sometime in the 1980s (the stone also gives his death date as November 19, actually his burial date; his death certificate states November 18). Gilbert himself sometimes gave his birth year as 1865. He is listed as age twenty-six on the passenger manifest of the ship he took home from Europe in 1891 (see Chapter 8). He also wrote 1865 on his 1911 passport application and on a 1911 consular certificate in the Belgian Congo (see Chapter 10).

The earliest known attestation of 1864 is by Kletzing and Crogman (1898: 481), probably using information from Gilbert himself. Gilbert gives the same year in his 1901 passport application. His birth year is given as 1864 in the 1900 US Census (123rd Militia District, Richmond County, Georgia, Supervisor District 10, Enumeration District 46, 18 June 1900: 12). The 1910 US Census (123rd Militia District, Richmond County, Georgia, Supervisor District 10, Enumeration District 76, 26 April 1910: 26) gives his age as forty-six. If the enumerator followed the 1910 instructions to record a person's age at last birthday prior to 15 April 1910, this would also indicate an 1864 birthdate. Gilbert and his family do not appear in the 1920 Augusta census, probably because he moved to Nashville in June 1919 to run the Colored Methodist Episcopal (CME) Church's Sunday School Department (*Nashville Banner*, 15 June 1919; the address given, 810 Broadway, is that of Capers CME Church).

Augusta's 1890 census records (along with most of the country's) were destroyed in a 1921 fire, but G. W. Walker gives Gilbert's age as twenty-seven in a letter (*Augusta Chronicle*, 04 July 1890) responding to an appeal for census information. Writing just three days before Gilbert's birthday, Walker may well have rounded up. On his August 1890 passport application, Gilbert himself twice writes his birthdate as July 1863.

Gilbert appears twice in the 1880 census (see Chapter 1). Enumerators in 1880 were instructed to record each person's age at last birthday prior to 1 June 1880. In Atlanta, where an enumerator visited Gilbert's household on 2 June, his age is given as seventeen. If the enumerator followed instructions precisely, this would indicate an 1863 birth year. That same day, another enumerator in Augusta listed Gilbert's age as eighteen.

The 1870 census lists Gilbert as Wesley Dasher (using his stepfather Tom Dasher's last name), age seven. The 1870 census asked for each person's "age at last birthday." If the enumerator followed instructions precisely, this would indicate an 1862 birth year. As it was just a few weeks before Gilbert's July birthday, the census enumerator or an informant may have rounded up. Gilbert's Freedman's Bank register, dated 1 May 1871, gives his age as seven. This number, indicating an 1863 birth year, came either from Gilbert himself or from his mother

Sarah, who accompanied him to the bank office and certainly knew when her son was born. There was no reason for anyone to misstate Gilbert's age, as several other children aged seven or younger registered for accounts the same year (Walker 1998: 224, 371–372, 407). With more than two months before Gilbert's July birthday, rounding up is less likely in this case.

The balance of the early evidence, therefore, points toward 1863. Another approach is to consider the reported ages of students at Augusta Institute and Atlanta Baptist Seminary. In mid-1878, the Augusta Institute's students were all sixteen or older (Robert 1878: 8, M. Robert 1878: 18). In September 1879, Atlanta Baptist's students all said they were eighteen or older (Robert 1879: 235). Against this evidence, an 1865 birth year seems least likely, as it would make Gilbert just fourteen when he went to Atlanta. 1864 is possible, but 1863 is most likely, as a sixteen-year-old Gilbert would have had more success convincing others he was actually eighteen. An 1863 birth year also gives Gilbert sufficient time to get through the seven years of Augusta's primary-intermediate-grammar public school sequence before entering Augusta Institute. While certainty eludes us, careful consideration of the available evidence makes it most likely that John Wesley Gilbert was born on 6 July 1863.

OSCEOLA PLEASANT GILBERT

There is more inconsistency in the birth years given for Gilbert's wife, and we have only her birth month, not a day. Her death certificate (20 June 1922) and burial record (Cedar Grove E140) list her age as fifty-eight (born 1864), but her obituary (*Augusta Chronicle*, 23 June 1922) gives her age as fifty-five (born 1867). The 1910 census lists her age as forty (implied birth year of 1870), while the 1900 census gives her birthdate as February 1866. G. W. Walker's 1890 *Augusta Chronicle* letter gives her age as twenty-five, suggesting an 1865 birthdate. I cannot find her in the 1880 census, but the 1870 census lists her as age eight, indicating an 1862 birthdate if she was born in February. The later birth dates (1867, 1870) would make Osceola Pleasant too young to go to Nashville to attend Fisk in 1880 (see Chapter 5). Given the uncertainties, I cautiously assign a birthdate circa 1864.

ALMA GILBERT AND JOHN WESLEY GILBERT, JR.

The birth dates of Gilbert's eldest daughter Alma and of his son John Jr. are important for the chronology of Gilbert's travel to and from Greece in 1890–1891. While some later records give Alma's birth year as 1891, Walker's July 1890 letter describes Alma as three months old and the 1900 census gives her birthdate as April 1890. Some later records give John Jr. an 1892 birth year, but the 1900 Census lists him as born in April 1891, and he gives his birth date as 30 April 1891 on his 1917 draft registration card.

APPENDIX 2: JOHN WESLEY GILBERT AND JOHN HOPE

Davis (1998: 104) describes Gilbert and Hope as cousins, but he may be writing metaphorically, and evidence of the two men's family relationship is lacking. They grew up in different parts of Augusta in separate social circles. Although two of Hope's sisters did marry sons of Charles Ladeveze, Gilbert's neighbor on Reynolds Street in the early 1880s, Gilbert was too poor and obscure to be part of Augusta's black elite during his childhood. Though some of his family members had links to Thankful Baptist Church, Gilbert's Methodist connection is amply documented. Hope was not a regular churchgoer until 1885, when he joined the Baptist Church. While Gilbert and Hope may have crossed paths earlier, possibly they first got to know each other during Hope's visits to Paine Institute's rented rooms on Broad Street in 1884–1886.

Torrence (1948: 70, 86–87) writes as if Gilbert went north to school before Hope, and Davis (1998: 36) cites oral histories suggesting Gilbert recommended school "up north" to Hope. In fact, Gilbert and Hope both went north about the same time in early September 1886: Gilbert to Brown and Hope to Worcester Academy. Providence and Worcester were only forty miles apart, and the two men's fall terms began within a week of each other. Possibly, then, the two traveled north together. Yet no evidence shows Hope visited Brown while Gilbert was there.

When could Gilbert and Hope have talked together about Brown? Hope and Gilbert both came back to Augusta to work in summer 1887 (see Chapter 2), so they could have talked then, but another time may be more likely. Worcester Academy's 1888–1889 catalogue, published in June 1889, names John Hope as a junior. Yet Hope is missing from

Worcester Academy's grade records for winter term (January–March) 1889. Meanwhile, Paine Institute's 1888–1889 catalogue, published in spring 1889, lists him as a first-year student in the Higher Normal department. Hope must therefore have spent winter 1889 studying with Gilbert at Paine, where the two would have had plenty of time to talk about Brown University. That also explains why William Coleman, one of Hope's roommates at Brown, says that Hope spent only three years at Worcester (*Richmond Planet*, 30 June 1894).

Hope's 1889 winter term at Paine helps date the report (Torrence 1948: 57) that Hope heard Gilbert speak during an Emancipation Day (January 1) celebration in Augusta before going to Brown. It is unlikely Gilbert was a speaker in 1885 or 1886 while still a student at Paine or that he came back from Providence in January 1887 or 1888, but, as a recent university graduate and Paine's first black professor, he would have been an obvious choice in January 1889 (*Augusta Chronicle*, 29 December 1888 and 01 January 1889 mention this celebration, unfortunately without naming speakers).

NOTES

Introduction

1. The fire: *Augusta Chronicle*, 04 August, 11 August, 15 August 1968, 16 October 1968. Loud enough: "I very distinctly remember hearing the clock ring in the Haygood Hall tower. Indeed, it could be heard all over town!" (personal communication, Mallory Millender, Paine College Class of 1964, 10 October 2020). Perished: Eskew 1992: 638, Johnson 1970, Clary 1971. Haygood-Holsey Hall: Montgomery and Speno 2010: 15. Throughout this book, I follow Paine College historian Mallory Millender in writing "black" and "white" without initial capitals. During Gilbert's life, black people also used Colored and Negro as terms of self-identification; as CME Bishop Othal Lakey notes (Lakey 1996: 18), "none of these terms are pejorative."

2. Floods and fires: Tilson 2002: 7–8. Papers: Calhoun 1974: 1004.

3. Belgian Congo: Lambuth 1915, Reeve 1921, Pinson 1925, Sheffey 1939, Calhoun 1961. John Hope: Torrence 1948, Davis 1998. No reference: Lord 1947, De Grummond 1996, Dyson 1998. African American archaeologists: Franklin 1997, Agbe-Davies 2002, Agbe-Davies 2003. Survey: Slater 1994, following Mitchell 1993. Wider attention: Ronnick 1997, Ronnick 2001, Ronnick 2004a, Ronnick 2004b, [no author] 2002; Strauss 2005 draws on Ronnick along with Haley 1989 and Haley 1993. "The first": Flewellen and Dunnavant 2012. Hawley and Speth 2016 identify two predecessors of Gilbert: antiquities collectors Benjamin Hughes and John Mallory, active in Wisconsin during the mid-late 1800s. "First black archaeologist": E.g., Millender 2012.

4. First fifty: See list in Seymour 1902: 57–69. Anywhere: Dyson 2006: 122–124 for the Mediterranean; the first US excavation in the Near East began at Nippur in 1889.

5. Interest: Greenwood 2009, Malamud 2016, Schliepake 2016. Black travelers: Lee (forthcoming b) examines Gilbert's Greek travel alongside the accounts of two other African American visitors to Greece, David Dorr and Frederick Douglass. Biographies: Beard 2000, Dyson 2004, Davis 2015, Kimberley 2017. Researchers: Former Paine professor Catherine Adams visited the ASCSA archives in 2015 and wrote a blog post about Gilbert.

6. "Providing access": Anderson 1988: 29. Touchstone: Malamud 2016: 28–30.
7. "Assured certainty" and "personal investment": Beard 2000: xi–xii.

Chapter 1

1. Account register: Walker 1998: 203.
2. Illegal: Cobb 1851: 981, Tolley 2016.
3. Filed suit: Clarke [sic] vs. Johnson, 03 December 1858, Richmond County, GA (Race and Slavery Petition no. 20685802); this database contains only three other Georgia Gabriels, all from the 1820s–1830s. Johnson owned eleven slaves in 1850 and fifteen in 1860 (Rowland 2006c: 17).
4. Lawsuit: Elizabeth Day petition, 16 March 1850, Richmond County, GA (Race and Slavery Petition no. 20685011). Slave names: Genovese 1974: 445–447, Gutman 1976: 230–256, Litwack 1979: 247–251, Cody 1982, Cody 1987. William and Jim: Men by these names registered as voters in Richmond County in 1867. Of the seven William or W. Gilberts buried in Augusta's Cedar Grove Cemetery, only one was alive and an adult in 1871: W. Gilbert, occupation fireman, born about 1844, died 21 June 1904 (Cedar Grove D147). William Gilbert, occupation fireman, appears in Augusta city directories during the 1880s–1890s; he lived in the 1880s with Jim Gilbert, when both were employed at the Georgia Chemical Works (e.g., Augusta Directory 1882: 209).
5. Nathaniel Gilbert: Smith 1964: 1–2, Vickers 1999: 241–242, Frey and Wood 2000: 104–106. Antigua to Georgia: Smith 1991: 93–101. William Gilbert: *Augusta Chronicle*, 03 July 1824, Cheshire 2018.
6. Wesley Dasher: US Census, Augusta, Ward 1, 10 June 1870: 48.
7. Mary Rhodes McTyeir: Richmond County, Georgia Wills, Vol. A–B, 1798–1853: 336–338.
8. Around 1843: US Census, Augusta, Ward 1, 10 June 1870: 48 gives Sarah's age as twenty-seven, implying a birthdate circa 1843. July 6, 1863: see Appendix 1. Johnson sons: NARA M226 (*Index to Compiled Service Records of Confederate Soldiers who Served in Organizations from the State of Georgia*), roll 32 (Charles A. Johnson), Cornell 2000: 540.
9. Christened: Culp 1902: 190–191 records a tradition Gilbert was named after his uncle John, but John Wesley was a common name for enslaved black children; two famous examples are John Wesley Cromwell (1846–1927), born into slavery in Virginia and later a leading educator and attorney in Washington DC, and John Wesley Work I (ca. 1848–1923), born into slavery in Kentucky and later the choir leader of the singers who formed the nucleus of the famed Fisk Jubilee Singers (directed by his namesake son, John Wesley Work II). Congregations: Smith 1992. "A colored babe": Blassingame and McKivigan 1992: 485; my thanks to Michele Valerie Ronnick for bringing this passage to my attention.

10. "Walking all the way": *Chicago Defender*, 22 September 1951. Tripled: *Augusta Chronicle*, 09 October 1864. Waynesboro: Burr 1990: 246–247.

11. Surrender and aftermath: Burr 1990: 260–278, Clark 2003: 48–49, Brown 2006. "Nursed": Kletzing and Crogman 1898: 482.

12. Legend: Martin 1924: 106, Colclough 1925: 25. Tom Dasher (ca. 1836–1875): *Daily Constitutionalist* (Augusta), 21 October 1868, *Augusta Chronicle*, 11 November 1872). Disorderly conduct: *Augusta Chronicle*, 27 June 1866; for the charge, see *Augusta Chronicle*, 23 May 1866. Pistol: *Daily Constitutionalist*, 08 August 1866. Sarah and Pauline: *Daily Constitutionalist*, 24 December 1868.

13. "One sister died": Walker 1998: 203; the child is not on the Mortality Schedule of the 1870 Census and therefore died before June 1869 or between June 1870 and April 1871. Greene Street: US Census, Augusta, Ward 1, 10 June 1870: 47–48 lists Thomas, Sarah, and Wesley Doscher immediately after Mrs. Sarah K. Taliaferro and her family. The census taker probably wrote "Doscher" rather than "Dasher" because he knew the prominent white Doschers of Augusta, but Tom always appears as Dasher on voter lists and other documents. Sarah's listed occupation (domestic servant) and her juxtaposition with Mrs. Taliaferro suggests she was working in the Taliaferro household. For comparison, next door to the Taliaferros, Rachel Gordon is listed as a domestic servant following the household of John E. Crocker; in her Freedman's Bank register (Walker 1998: 211), Gordon names Crocker as her employer. Augusta Directory 1867: 54 gives Mrs. Taliaferro's address as 63 Greene Street, but the city's "extremely *complete* system of *not numbering*" (Augusta Directory 1877: 5) was completely revamped in 1879–1880 (Augusta Directory 1882: 9–16, Walker 1998: vi). Comparing the 1870 census (which has no street addresses) with US Census, Augusta, Supervisor District 2, Enumeration District 96, 05 June 1880: 23–25 and Sanborn 1890: Map 34 places Mrs. Taliaferro's residence on what is today the 300 block of Greene Street. Houghton Institute: Maxwell 1878: 66, Jones and Dutcher 1890: 318–319. Private school: *Daily Constitutionalist*, 01 September 1867 and 10 September 1869. Did likewise: of the ten nearest black or mulatto households in the 1870 census, only one has school-age children not listed as "at school."

14. Mrs. Taliaferro: Magnolia Cemetery B161 (03 February 1871). Center and Telfair: Sanborn 1884: Map 14. Ware's Folly: personal communication, Erick Montgomery. Around the intersection: US Census, Augusta, Ward 1, 21 and 25 June 1870: 81–83. "Noise": *Augusta Chronicle*, 26 July 1873. West along Telfair: Telfair Street lies on the long axis of central Augusta's street grid, which runs northwest-southeast along the Savannah River. Augustans have long referred to streets on this axis as "east-west"; the cross-streets running up from the river are called "north-south" even though their actual orientation is northeast-southwest. Deeds, directories, and other documents employ this directional terminology. Formalized: Georgia, Marriage Records from Select

Counties, 1828–1978, Richmond County, Book H 1868–1875: 151; the minister was J. T. Tolbert, later pastor of Thankful Baptist Church.

15. Storrs School: Link 2013: 111–113. R. R. Wright, Sr. (1855–1947): Wright, Jr. 1965: 15–20. Wright's words are reported as "Massa, tell 'em we're rising" in 1869 newspaper accounts and appear as such in early printings of Whittier's poem, but Wright wrote Whittier in 1869 to object that he did not say "massa." Later accounts often quote Wright's response as "General, tell 'em we're rising." Wright's classmate and friend W. S. Scarborough gives a different version in his autobiography (Ronnick 2005a: 43–44), but he confused Howard's 1868 visit with an 1870 visit by J. W. Alvord (Alvord 1870: 25–27). Liberal arts curriculum: Winterer 2004, Strauss 2005: 47–50, Malamud 2016: 28–31. Many studies of black classicism note South Carolina senator John C. Calhoun's reported gibe to the effect that "if he could find a Negro who knew the Greek syntax, he would then believe that the Negro was a human being and should be treated as a man" (Crummell 1898: 11, reporting a conversation overheard in 1833 or 1834). "Within the classroom": Rowe 1890: 61–62; see also Sherman 1992: 343.

16. Secret schools: Pegues 1892: 529–530, Patton 1978: 45, Freedman 1999: 11–13. One of a few: Wright 1894: 21. Community schools: *Augusta Chronicle*, 01 July 1865, *Colored American* (Augusta), 30 December 1865, Alvord 1867: 15, Terrell and Terrell 1977: 6–7. Freedmen's Bureau: Patton 1978: 48–49, Cashin 1985: 13. Financial help: *Daily Constitutionalist*, 27 March 1867, Alvord 1867: 27, Wright 1894: 29. "Among the best": Alvord 1870: 15.

17. 1869 or 1870: The 1870 census records "Wesley Doscher" had attended school in the past year, though it marks him unable to read or write; such marks were only the census taker's selective impressions. Trinity School: *Colored American*, 30 December 1865, *Loyal Georgian*, 27 January 1866, Terrell and Terrell 1977: 6–7, Eskew 2001: 95. Osceola Pleasant: Her story is told more fully in Chapter 4. Trinity Church and CME: Holsey 1898: 20, Cashin 1995: 37, Eskew 2001: 88–100. Ordainment: *Augusta Chronicle*, 25 March 1873.

18. Cecelia Chestnut: US Census, Augusta, Ward 4, 13 August 1870: 100; for her family see Walker 1998: 46, Rowland and Rowland 2009: 102. Daniel Gardner: *Loyal Georgian*, 06 July 1867, *Augusta Chronicle*, 22 September 1872, 02 October 1872; Augusta Directory 1867: 24, 1872: 89, 1877: 175, 351.

19. Her account: Walker 1998: 46. Freedman's Bank: Osthaus 1976, Walker 1998: i–vi. "Perfectly safe": *Loyal Georgian*, 17 March 1866. Poured in: Du Bois 1907: 136, Fleming 1927: 161–162. Visited schools: Osthaus 1976: 95. C. H. Prince: Brawley 1917: 14, Osthaus 1976: 59, 230, Walker 1998: i. Nearly a quarter: Osthaus 1976: 84–95, using a limited sample from seven branches, shows children opened 23% of Augusta accounts, compared to just 6% in Charleston and less in other cities. One after another: between February 1871 and May 1872, fifteen students, ranging in age from 6 to 21, listed Miss Chesnut/Chestnut as their teacher (Walker 1998: 112, 162, 203,

224, 242, 295, 330–331, 371–372, 407, 445, 469, 530, 548, 565, 575); most use the phrase "go to school to Miss Chesnut/Chestnut," although three use "been/have been to school," perhaps to indicate they were no longer attending school. The students give addresses from all of Augusta's four wards, with most in the Second Ward. While other teachers and their students show up in the registers (Walker 1998: 48, 90, 112, 156, 183), Miss Chestnut appears most often.

20. School system: *Augusta Chronicle*, 16 February 1873, Maxwell et al. 1878: 65–78, Jones and Dutcher 1890: 321–328, Patton 1978: 49–50, Cashin 1980: 157–159, Cashin 1985: 9–10, 25, Cashin 1995: 62–63. Went to Atlanta: *Augusta Chronicle*, 20 July 1873. A. R. Johnson (1853–1908): Jones 1962: 41, 47; *Augusta Chronicle*, 22 October 1908. Johnson was teaching by 1870 (US Census, Augusta, Militia District 123, 06 June 1870: 10), he was in the Third Ward from ca. 1872 to fall 1876 (*Augusta Chronicle*, 26 January 1872, 05 October 1873, 10 October 1876).

21. Second Ward: *Augusta Chronicle*, 16 January 1873, 01 March 1873. This school lay at the corner of Twiggs and Walton Streets; it was demolished in 1911 (Augusta Directory 1877: 34, Sanborn 1904: Map 56, *Augusta Chronicle*, 10 September 1911, Jones 1962: 68–69). "The buildings": Wright, Jr. 1965: 28–29. "The Terry": Harvey 1973 uses the less-common spelling "Terri." Canal: Jones and Dutcher 1890: 188. Chinese: *Augusta Chronicle*, 05 November 1873, Ken 1972: 52.

22. T. R. Harper (1848–1905): Georgia, Marriage Records from Select Counties, Richmond County, Book H, 1868–1875: 43; Torrence Papers 3/4/149–152, Leslie 2001: 122–124. J. F. Quarles (ca. 1847–1885): Westminster College 1869–1870: 7, 17–18, Wickersham and McCaskey 1875: 169–170, Howard University 1896: 27, Smith Jr. 1999: 218, Burke 2017: 47. Quarles was teaching in the Second Ward by January 1871 (*Daily Chronicle & Sentinel*, 15 September 1871, Walker 1998: 48); Chestnut joined him by February 1872 (*Daily Chronicle & Sentinel*, 06 February 1872). First black lawyer: *Daily Chronicle & Sentinel*, 07 January 1873. Did not stay long: *Boston Globe*, 29 January 1885, *Brooklyn Daily Eagle*, 29 January 1885; Quarles returned at least once for a public lecture (*Augusta Chronicle*, 16 June 1877, 01 July 1877).

23. Panic: Foner 1988: 512–513, Jones and Dutcher 1890: 419–423, Wicker 2000: 18, 23. Cotton and "panic prices": *Augusta Chronicle*, 30 September 1873, 12 October 1873, 23 October 1873, 05 December 1873. Fell victim: Osthaus 1976: 174–200, Foner 1988: 531–532, White 2017: 265–266; *Augusta Chronicle*, 01 May 1874, 01 July 1874, 25 September 1874 (Augusta branch). Savings: The average Augusta account in 1870 had forty dollars; some children's accounts started with just five cents (Osthaus 1976: 95–97).

24. Malaise: Foner 1988: 512–524, White 2017: 266–273. Confederate memorials: Jones and Dutcher 1890: 180–182. Broad Street pillar: *Augusta Chronicle*, 01 November 1878, Whites 1992, Clark 2003: 55.

25. Dasher died: Cedar Grove B330 (24 November 1875). Tall and strong: Gilbert gives his height as 5 feet, 9½ inches on his 1890 passport application, NARA M1372359-0061 (no. 20676). "Six months": Kletzing and Crogman 1898: 482. Cotton: *Augusta Chronicle*, 07 August 1872, 09 September 1873, 11 August 1874, 25 September 1875, 13 October 1876, 10 November 1877, 17 September 1879 indicate the picking around Augusta was complete by the end of September, except in 1877, when the crop was not in until December. For the agricultural calendar and black schoolchildren as laborers, see Jones 1980: 132–134, Messick et al. 2001: 27. School year: Maxwell et al. 1878: 67–70, Jones and Dutcher 1890: 327. "Not wise": *Augusta Chronicle*, 16 April 1875.

26. S. A. Hosmer (1836–1912): Adams 1918: 8, Jones 1980. A half-dozen (by hometown and graduation date): Lucy C. Laney (Macon, 1873), Georgia M. Swift (Athens, 1874), Anna F. White (Augusta, 1876), Pattie M. Hall (Augusta?, 1877), Mildred A. Brown (Augusta, 1878); see Adams 1918: 13, 17. L. C. Laney (1854–1933): Patton 1978, McCluskey 2006, McCluskey 2014. Almost all the men: Compare the alumni list of Robert 1878 with 1870–1880 reports in the *Augusta Chronicle*'s; Augusta's James S. Harper, an 1877 BA graduate of Atlanta University, also worked as a teacher. See Butchart 2010 for more about black and white teachers in this era.

27. Supposed to attend: *Augusta Chronicle*, 27 September 1874, 10 March 1878, 18 April 1883, Jones and Dutcher 1890: 326. Hosmer: *Augusta Chronicle*, 01 March 1873. H. N. Bouey (1849–1909): Simmons 1887: 951–953, Jacobs 2011: 17–18. Laney: *Augusta Chronicle*, 29 June 1875 (misspelling her name "Lang"); *Augusta Chronicle*, 8 March 1874, reports Laney's teacher license, so she could have been at the Ice Factory by spring 1874.

28. Studying the classics: Malamud 2016: 28–39. *Gallic Wars* (*BG* 1.7): Paine Archives, Box 86. High school: Augusta *Chronicle*, 12 April 1876. "Pure distinction": Calhoun 1974: 1005.

29. Grammar school: *Augusta Chronicle*, 29 August 1876, 01 October 1876, Augusta directory 1877: 34. Out of town: *Augusta Chronicle*, 20 July 1873, Donaldson 2002: 32–34. The next fall, Miss Laney opened a second black grammar school in the Fourth Ward (*Augusta Chronicle*, 30 September 1877). Segregated boards: *Augusta Chronicle*, 11 July 1875. Avoid paying: *Augusta Chronicle*, 12 October 1875, 14 October 1875. "Excellent conduct": *Augusta Chronicle*, 09 July 1876.

30. In the First Ward: US Census, Augusta, Supervisor District 2, Enumeration District 96, 02 June 1880: 6–7. Simon: Augusta Directory 1878–1879: 198, 1880: 164, *News & Herald* (Winnsboro, SC), 26 January 1881, Cedar Grove C [unnumbered] (burial date 15 January 1881); for other uncles, see Augusta Directory 1882: 209, 1883: 242, 1886: 200.

31. "The first school": *Augusta Chronicle*, 17 July 1921, Calhoun 1961: 10. Franklin Covenant: Floyd 1902: 20–21, 35–41, Clark 1909: 119.

32. Augusta Institute: *Colored American*, 30 December 1865, *Loyal Georgian*, 16 May 1867, Robert 1878, Reed 1889: 361–363, Corey 1895: 39–41, Brawley 1917: 9–19, Jones 1967: 17–36, Terrell and Terrell 1977: 7, Davis 1998: 103–104, Donaldson 2001: 138–140, Saunders and Rogers 2004: 14–16.

33. W. D. Siegfried: Robert 1878: 4–5, Brawley 1917: 19–20. Telfair Street: *Christian Era* (Boston), 26 May 1870, ABHMS 1871: 26. Evidence from Maxwell et al. 1878: 45–46, *Augusta Chronicle*, 25 March 1879, and Sanborn 1890: Map 26 suggests the Institute lay on what is today the large parking lot on Telfair Street behind St. John's Methodist Church. A photograph in the Atlanta University Archives (http://digitalcommons.auctr.edu/mcimg/2/, accessed 18 November 2017) may show the Institute's original buildings, but the identification is uncertain. "Twenty-six miles" and "a hungering": ABHMS 1870: 23–24.

34. Letter: *Examiner and Chronicle* (New York), 29 December 1870; it is not clear if Siegfried meant his letter to be published. Outcry: *Examiner and Chronicle*, 27 April 1871. ABHMS 1871: 36, 1872: 26 elide the episode; Robert 1878: 5 refers to it only in the most delicate terms.

35. J. T. Robert (1807–1884): *Baptist Home Mission Monthly* 6.5 (May) 1884: 106–107, *Providence Journal*, 18 June 1884, Brown University 1936: 140, Saunders and Rogers 2004. Emancipated: ABMHS 1874: 36. "Did not wish": Brawley 1917: 21. Martha (Mattie) A. Robert (1833–1887): Augusta Directory 1877: 279, Mount Holyoke Seminary 1889: 61, Reed 1889: 365, Abernethy 1907: 81, 85, Antrobus 1915: 180.

36. "Intense odium": Robert 1878: 5. Turned things around: M. Robert 1878: 16–19, Reed 1889: 361–363, Brawley 1917: 21–25, Cashin 1995: 55, Saunders and Rogers 2004, 16–19. White Baptists: E.g., *Augusta Chronicle*, 26 October 1875. Growing stream: Robert 1879: 235. "Eagerness and enthusiasm": M. Robert 1878: 18. Indiana minister: ABHMS 1874: 36. C. T. Walker (1858–1921): Floyd 1892, Floyd 1902, Caldwell 1917: 683–688, Patton 1978: 47–48, Mairs 2016: 88–98. C. H. Lyons (?–1894): Robert 1878: 7, 13, Carter 1894: 216, Caldwell 1920: 243. W. E. Holmes (1856–1931): Robert 1878: 7, 13, Simmons 1887: 567–571, Carter 1894: 213–215, Kletzing and Crogman 1898: 480–481, Brawley 1917: 25. Was listed: Augusta Directory 1877: 39.

37. Gilbert's turn: Robert 1878: 14–19 (published in May 1878) does not list Gilbert, but Brawley 1917: 184 does, so he must have begun in fall 1878 or later. Kletzing and Crogman 1898: 482 write (based on Gilbert's own testimony) that Gilbert attended "for some months the Baptist Seminary, in his own city," perhaps suggesting he was not enrolled for the entire 1878–1879 school year. A yellow fever outbreak delayed the fall 1878 term (*BHMM* 1.4, October 1878: 59), so Gilbert could have begun in January 1879 (the spring term; see Robert 1878: 12). Overstated: Appendix 1. Scholarship: Robert 1878: 22. Harvest: *BHMM* 1.11, May 1879: 169–170.

38. Would relocate: *Augusta Chronicle*, 22 November 1878, ABHMS 1879: 37, Saunders and Rogers 2004: 18–19. For sale: *Augusta Chronicle*, 25 March 1879. Atlanta Baptist: *BHMM* 1.14, August 1879: 221.

39. Under construction: *BHMM* 1.15, September 1879: 225–226, *Atlanta Constitution*, 25 November 1879. After 152 years on the same site, Friendship Baptist Church was razed in 2014 to make way for a new football stadium (*Atlanta Journal-Constitution*, 26 May 2014). Opening: *Atlanta Constitution*, 19 December 1879, ABHMS 1880: 38–39, Reed 1889: 364, Brawley 1917: 34–35.

40. Conditions: Robert 1880: 159–160, Brawley 1917: 35–37; for a map of the neighborhood, see http://disc.library.emory.edu/atlantamaps/1878-atlas/, accessed 17 November 2017. One of ten: Atlanta Directory 1880: 121, 124, 141, 200, 208, 312, 340, 397; Brawley 1917: 179–193. Five of these students attended Augusta Institute before May 1878 (Robert 1878: 14–19); the only other student from Augusta was John T. Russell. Enrollment: *Atlanta Constitution*, 19 December 1879 (30 students); by January there were 75 (*BHMM* 2.2, February 1880: 35). Boarding house: Atlanta Directory 1880: 378; US Census, Atlanta, First Ward, Supervisor District 1, Enumeration District 90, 05 June 1880: 17. Enter the ministry: Brawley 1917: 179, Jones 1967: 35. Hard to concentrate: ABHMS 1881: 51–52.

41. "John W. Gilbert": Atlanta Directory 1880: 200.

42. Easley family: US Census, Atlanta, Ward 1, Supervisor District 1, Enumeration District 91, 02 June 1880: 5. Elizabeth Easley: Atlanta Directory 1879: 173, Adams 1918: 17, 38, Smith 2009: 97. The Easley home at 17 Chapel Street was close to Frank Quarles's residence on Hayne Street (Atlanta Directory 1881: 433). J. H. Bugg: Robert 1878: 14, *BHMM* 1.16, October 1879: 253, Brawley 1917: 194. W. D. Johnson: Carter 1894: 104–108, with a very confused chronology.

43. Greek and Latin: Robert 1878: 21. Unwaveringly: Robert 1878: 8. Teaching methods: Robert 1882b, *BHMM* 6.5, May 1884: 107. Public speaking: Robert 1878: 7–8, Brawley 1917: 26, Jones 1967: 34. *Rules of Order*: Robert 1878: 7. H. M. Robert published the first edition in February 1876, followed by a second edition in July. The Augusta Institute may have received a tenth of these first two editions; *The Inter Ocean* (Chicago), 10 March 1877 mentions 10,000 copies in print.

44. Esteemed: Brawley 1917: 37, Davis 1998: 107.

45. Kept up the work: Kletzing and Crogman 1898: 480–481, Brawley 1917: 25, 37, 40, 95, Davis 1998: 130–134, Donaldson 2002: 56–60. John Hope and Morehouse: Brawley 1917, Torrence 1948, Davis 1998.

46. Could not afford: Kletzing and Crogman 1898: 482. Scholarships: *BHMM*, March 1880: 52, Robert 1880: 160. Of Gilbert's nine boarding house roommates, only George Grinage, John Russell, and Cyrus Wilkins made it to Atlanta Baptist's first graduation in 1884 (Atlanta Baptist College 1897–1898: 36). Back in Augusta: US Census, Augusta, Supervisor District 2, Enumeration District 96, 02 June 1880: 6–7 lists Sarah Dasher, domestic servant, and her son Wesley Gilbert, school teacher, at 327 Reynolds Street. At

the same dwelling are listed Jeff Mason, described as Sarah Dasher's brother, and Moselle Bugg, listed as her sister; these terms need not indicate genetic relationships (Walker 1998: iv–v). Gilbert also appears on an Atlanta census record dated the same day (US Census, Atlanta, Ward 1, Supervisor District 1, Enumeration District 91, 02 June 1880: 5). Given the number of school or family connections, both reports clearly refer to Gilbert. Theoretically, Gilbert could have been present in Atlanta in the morning, then traveled to Augusta in time to be counted there, too, but more likely someone in one city or the other mentioned Gilbert even though he was not present. Gilbert's double appearance is not unique: James H. Bugg also appears in both the Atlanta and Augusta censuses, although not on the same day (US Census, Augusta, Supervisor District 2, Enumeration District 96, 08 June 1880: 39 and note 42).

47. Promising times: Augusta Bicentennial 1935: 31–32, Torrence 1948: 59–68, Cashin 1978: 62–64, Terrell and Terrell 1977: 11–15, Cashin 1980: 149–156, Cashin 1995: 66–68, Davis 1998: 30–34. Mills: Jones and Dutcher 1890: 420–423. *The Freeman* (New York), 02 April 1887 offers a vivid snapshot of Augusta's prosperous black landowners, merchants, and professionals.

48. Emancipation Day: Torrence 1948: 56–60, Cashin 1995: 63–64, Davis 1998: 33, Clark 2003. Race relations: McCluskey 2006: 84. Voting: Cashin 1985: 36, Eskew 1992: 654. Ware High School: Wright 1894: 35–37, Jones 1962: 64, 71, Kousser 1980, Patton 1978, Cashin 1980: 159–160, Cashin 1985: 19–20, Cashin 1995: 65, Donaldson 2001: 141–142. Crogman, Scarborough, and Wright: Ronnick 2006: xxiii, Ronnick 2011. Haines Institute: McCluskey 2006, Rowland and Rowland 2009: 27, McCluskey 2014, Ronnick 2016. R. B. Williams (1860–1942): Graduating from Yale in 1885, Williams worked as a teacher, toured the world with the Fisk Jubilee Singers, and eventually settled in New Zealand (Yale University 1913: 339–340, Davis 1998: 33–36). *Georgia Baptist*: Simmons 1887: 1095–1096, Donaldson 2001: 142–143, Donaldson 2002: 36–37.

49. "There was something": Torrence 1948: 59. *Augusta Chronicle*: Tobias 1953: 177–179.

50. Medical school: *Augusta Chronicle*, 13 May 1881, 14 May 1881, Whitted 1908: 158, *Savannah Tribune*, 18 June 1892, 07 August 1920. Osceola Pleasant: Fisk University 1881–1882: 12. John Hope: Davis 1998: 32. Uncles and cousins: Augusta city directories indicate William Gilbert was employed throughout the 1880s at the Georgia Chemical Works, a fertilizer factory. James (Jim) Gilbert also worked there in 1882, then found a position as a gardener and servant. Simon Gilbert is listed as a laborer in 1880, living at 323 Reynolds. Gabriel Gilbert may have lived south of Hephzibah in Burke County.

51. Expected: Tobias 1953: 179.

52. Found work: Augusta Directory 1880: 164 and 1883: 242 list Wesley Gilbert, teacher, at 325 Reynolds Street, but he is not listed as a public school teacher

in city directories or *Augusta Chronicle* reports from this period. Back in Hephzibah: *Tenth Annual Report of the Public Schools of Richmond County 1882*: 5 lists J. W. Gilbert as a teacher in Hephzibah. No directory was published in 1881, and school board reports for 1881 and 1883 do not survive. Private schools: E.g., Torrence 1948: 61. Twice as many: *Augusta Chronicle*, 17 March 1882 (732 spots for 1,132 students in the city), 03 October 1883 (300 applicants for 160 First Ward spots). Teaching pay: In the early 1880s, some teachers got as little as twenty dollars a month, with black teachers typically receiving half to two-thirds the pay of a white teacher holding a similar position (Augusta Directory 1882: 19–20, 1883: 21–22); *Augusta Chronicle*, 14 December 1879, prints a letter from fifteen black teachers asking for a salary increase. Bookstore: Haynes 1952: 69–70. "Began to despair": Kletzing and Crogman 1898: 482.

53. Reynolds Street: US Census 1880, Augusta, Supervisor District 2, Enumeration District 96, 02 June 1880: 6–7, Benson 1953: 1–6. The neighborhood was often called "Pinched Gut" or "P. G.," (*Pinch Gut Press*, 15 April 1985, Leslie 2001: 116). Charles Ladeveze: Cashin 1980: 184, Davis 1998: 33, Leslie 2001: 114. Osborne (or Osborn) family: US Census, Augusta, Richmond County, Ward 1, 16 June 1860: 32; US Census, Augusta, Ward 1, 08 June 1870: 41; US Census, Augusta, Supervisor District 2, Enumeration District 96, 02 June 1880: 7; Augusta Directory 1891: 321, Cashin 1995: 81. Silas Floyd: Caldwell 2015. Josiah Sibley: He was the father of William Sibley, who purchased "Ware's Folly" in 1871. Moved in: Sarah Dasher appears at 311 Reynolds Street in Augusta Directory 1886: 168, but she probably moved before then, as a saddle-maker named Jacob Brooks is listed with Gilbert at 325 Reynolds Street in Augusta Directory 1882: 135 and 1883: 145.

54. St. John's: Cashin 1980: 78, Garvey 1998. MECS and CME: Hamilton 1887, Graham 1954: 32–40, Lakey 1996, Owen 1998, Gravely 2005, Mills 2017. Planning: Holsey 1898: 14. In 1954, the Colored Methodist Episcopal Church became the Christian Methodist Episcopal Church.

55. Paine Institute's founding: Graham 1954, Calhoun 1961, Clary 1965, Clary 1971, Lakey 1996: 263–265, 446–450, Eskew 1992, Owen 1998: 166–167, Somerville 2004. Graham 1954 and Clary 1965 are invaluable because they quote at length from documents lost in the 1968 Paine fire. Robert Paine: Graham 1954: 65, Clary 1965: 9, Clary 1971: 25, Eskew 2001: 100. Moses Payne's 25,000-dollar gift to the school (Walker 1901: 475) led some to call it the "Payne Institute." Some early publications utilize both spellings interchangeably (Clary 1965: 9–12), but Payne himself called it Paine Institute (Payne to Goodrich, 16 May 1888, Paine 149/39). Adding to the confusion, from 1870 to 1880 there was an entirely different Payne Institute, sponsored by the African Methodist Episcopal (AME) Church, sixty miles north of Augusta in Cokesbury, South Carolina; W. S. Scarborough was its principal in 1876–1877 (*Christian Recorder*, 28 June 1877). This school moved to

Columbia, South Carolina in 1880, where it became Allen University. Morgan Callaway: Callaway 1884, Dempsey 1940: 653, Williams 1984. "A new chapter": Rubin 1959: I.77–78, 83–85.

56. "Plain, common school": *Raleigh Christian Advocate*, 31 October 1883. "A calamity": *Nashville Daily American*, 05 February 1884. "Reproach us": Holsey 1898: 25. Pressed on: Graham 1954: 67, Clary 1971: 27. Start up: *Southwestern Christian Advocate*, 31 May 1883, *Augusta Chronicle*, 19 July 1883. In her will: *Southwestern Christian Advocate*, 11 October 1883.

57. W. A. Candler (1857–1945): The brother of Coca-Cola founder Asa Candler, he later helped found Emory University; on his St. John's years, see Bauman 1981: 42–50. Variants: *Missionary Voice* 1930, Gray 1948: 28–29, Pierce 1948: 162, Graham 1954: 134, Calhoun 1961: 11 (recognizing the mythical qualities of the episode). Gray 1933: 35, McAfee 1945: 65, Peters 1945: 257 do not mention Candler. Physicians: George Davis, Augusta's first black doctor, began practice in 1879; two others soon followed, but by 1888 there were no black doctors in town (Terrell and Terrell 1977: 11–13).

58. Streets of Augusta: Walker 1901: 476, Gilbert quoted in Peters 1937. Opening date: *Raleigh Christian Advocate*, 16 January 1884; *Atlanta Constitution*, 29 November 1884, Clary 1965: 72. Rented rooms: Eighty-eight-year-old Marie Williams, who attended Paine in the mid-1880s, gave the address as 1002 Broad Street (*Augusta Chronicle*, 18 December 1966). Grocery store: *Augusta Chronicle*, 20 November 1883, 15 March 1885; Sanborn-Perris 1884: Map 10, De Bardeleben 1920: 424. The school is sometimes said (e.g., Montgomery and Speno 2010) to have occupied the floor above Claussen's Bakery, but that bakery did not open until 1888 (*Augusta Chronicle*, 14 August 1888). Pushed his way: De Bardeleben 1920: 424, De Bardeleben 1921: 31.

59. "Widespread and bitter": Holsey 1898: 29; also Eskew 1992: 650–651. Pay their way: Gray 1948: 29. First students: Walker 1901: 475–476, Graham 1954: 136. The oldest: Gilbert was born in 1863, compared to his classmates Ella L. Burdette (ca. 1866–1947), Thomas L. Cottin (1868–1905), Sarah M. Curry (ca. 1870–?), Charles A. Dryscoll (ca. 1866–1924), Kate Holsey (ca. 1868–1937), and Carrie L. Wigfall (ca. 1869–1891).

60. G. W. Walker (1848–1911): Duncan 1901: 340–341, Chi Psi Fraternity 1902: 467, *Augusta Chronicle*, 18 May 1911, 20 May 1911, *The Daily Record* (Columbia, SC), 24 May 1911, Peters 1937, Clary 1965: 53–54, 59, Calhoun 1961: 13–14, Strawn 1984: 284–291. "Richest man": Rubin ed. 1959: I.188.

61. Family and friends: *The Congregationalist*, 24 April 1884, Strawn 1984: 290. "My own mother": Walker 1901: 474. Fiancée: *Raleigh Christian Advocate*, 15 November 1917, De Bardeleben 1920: 425. Walker's name: Augusta Directory 1888: 429, 1889: 404; also *Augusta Chronicle*, 21 April 1888. Walk out: Clary 1965: 42.

62. C. G. Goodrich (1844–1911): *Augusta Chronicle*, 20 April 1882, 02 June 1911, 15 November 1911; Graham 1954: 64, 127, 141, Clary 1965: 58–59,

Clary 1971: 24. J. S. Harper (1855–1920): Graham 1954: 128, 141, 201, Clary 1965: 44–45, Kousser 1980: 21, 28, Leslie 2001: 123–124.

63. "Single standard": Tobias 1953: 181–182. Impossible to find: *Freeman* (Indianapolis), 21 June 1890; also Martin 1931: 32. Liberal education: Graham 1954: 180–181. Women: Torrence 1948: 68, Graham 1954: 138–139. "Christlike": Torrence Papers 3/4/152.

64. "All the time": Colclough 1925: 27. Kletzing and Crogman 1898: 482, counting only formal school terms, give the total time of Gilbert's attendance as eighteen months. Summer school: *Atlanta Constitution*, 29 November 1884.

65. "Painful and pitiful": Paine Institute 1894–1895: 15, Clary 1965: 89. Callaway: *Atlanta Constitution*, 26 November 1884, Clary 1971: 28. "Not soon forget": *The Congregationalist*, 24 April 1884. "Lone star": Crogman 1885: 44 (Cincinnati, mid-1884), Crogman 1896: 41 (Madison, 16 July 1884); on Crogman, see further Towns 1934, Ronnick 2000.

66. John Hope: Davis 1998: 32–34; Davis also names Georgia Foster, who does not appear in surviving lists of Paine's early students. Gilbert and Hope: See Appendix 2. Sallie G. Davis: Paine 50/1/55-57 (13 August 1884); Augusta Directory 1888: 154 and 1889: 142 mark her with a "c." Began sending: Peters 1937. Walker took over: Paine Institute 1894–1895: 15, Graham 1954: 112–113, Clary 1971: 28–29.

67. W. C. Davis: *Raleigh Christian Advocate*, 01 July 1885, Paine Institute 1885–1886: 1. Preached: E.g., *Augusta Chronicle*, 24 May and 11 October 1885 (sermons at Springfield Baptist, Union Baptist, Trinity CME). Literary societies: Torrence 1948: 68, with more detail in Torrence Papers 3/4/14. "Break in the clouds": *Southwestern Christian Advocate*, 07 May 1885. Enrollment: Paine Institute 1894–1895: 15. "Commanding personality": Colclough 1925: 33–34. Advanced students: Paine Institute 1894–1895: 19. "Made it by": Colclough 1925: 34–35.

68. Editorial: No known 1885 issues of the *Georgia Baptist* survive, but White's endorsement appears in *Christian Recorder*, 5 November 1885 (fundraising letter) and in all four surviving pre-1900 catalogues (Paine Institute 1885–1886: 4, 1889–1890: 20, 1890–1891: 25, 1894–1895: 19) and the now-lost 1886–1887 catalogue Clary 1965: 77); see also *Christian Index*, 31 October 1891.

69. C. A. Dryscoll (ca. 1866–1924): *Augusta Chronicle*, 01 July 1879, 16 June 1882, 29 June 1883, 16 June 1885, 14 October 1956, Augusta Directory 1883: 211, Atlanta University 1884–1885: 13. T. L. Cottin (1868–1905): *Augusta Chronicle*, 30 June 1885 and 06 February 1905, Brown 2017.

70. Payne: Biographical sketch in State Historical Society of Missouri C983, Payne-Broadwell Family Papers; also *Nebraska State Journal* (Lincoln), 12 August 1895, *Lincoln Star Journal* (NE), 12 August 1895, *Macon Republican* (MO), 16 August 1895. On the conditions of his gift, see Payne to Goodrich, 16 May and 21 May 1888, Paine 149/39; Walker 1901: 475. Woodlawn: *Augusta*

Chronicle, 04 June 1882 (map), Clary 1965: 78, Montgomery and Speno 2010. Texas: *Nashville Christian Advocate*, 20 February 1886. Moved up: Gilbert is not on Reynolds Street in Augusta Directory 1886: 168; his mother is still there. Cleaned up: *Southwestern Christian Advocate*, 11 March 1897, Walker 1901: 475, De Bardeleben 1920: 424; no source specifies students did the renovations, but there was no money to hire laborers. "Cradled": Clary 1965: 63–64. Up and running: *Raleigh Christian Advocate*, 10 March 1886. "Eloquent corps": *Augusta Chronicle*, 12 May 1886; also Hamilton 1887: 95.

71. Graduates: *Daily American* (Nashville), 18 June 1886, Paine Institute 1890–1891: 5. Cottin: Clark University 1887–1888: 11, Clark University 1896–1897: 62–67. Dryscoll: He is said to have attended the New England Conservatory of Music (e.g., Paine 50/1/119, Floyd 1902: 172–173, Clary 1965: 113), but the New England Conservatory's catalogues do not list Dryscoll as a student. He may have attended the Boston Conservatory, which was sometimes confused with the New England Conservatory. Due to the coronavirus pandemic, I was unable to consult the Boston Conservatory's records.

Chapter 2

1. Attic: personal communication, Mrs. Dickie L. Bridges. "A treasure": Bridges to Millender, undated, Paine College Archives. Just two: the other issue (October 1891) is preserved at the Rutherford B. Hayes Presidential Library in Ohio; Hayes probably received it during his 1891 visit to Paine. Print run: Rowell 1894: 99, Lord & Thomas 1894–1895: 55 (these are the earliest mentions in newspaper directories). Essay: Gilbert 1887.

2. "Southern patronage": *The Liberator*, 03 October 1845. Another black student: Chace 1891: 44. Milford and Page: Simmons 1887: 484–480, Brown University 1936: 273, Logan 1967: 37, Breaux and Perry 1969. Prejudice: Simmons 1887: 475. "I have to say": Milford to Garrison, 06 February 1875, Boston Public Library Rare Books Department, MS A.1.2, vol. 38, p. 8B. Won fame: *Rhode Island Press*, 07 October 1876. Milford and Page are today recognized as the first Brown University students both to identify themselves and to be identified by others as black. Franklin Henry Brown, described in some reports as "colored" and in others as the descendant of a "Spanish lady" from Demerara (British Guiana, today Guyana), entered Brown in 1871 and graduated in 1875 (*Brooklyn Daily Eagle*, 13 July 1871, *Hartford Courant*, 08 August 1871, 12 August 1871, 23 August 1871, Brown University Catalogue 1871–1872: 16, 1875–1876: 55, Brown University 1936: 264). Brown appears as "white" in the 1875 Rhode Island census, "mulatto" in the 1880 and 1910 US censuses, and "white" again in the 1920 US census. William Edward White, son of a Georgia slave owner and a mixed-race slave, attended Brown from 1879 to 1880. Though White spent his adult life

passing as white, some consider him the first black major league baseball player for an 1879 game he played in Providence (Husman 2013). Daniel Barclay Williams, Virginia's first black university classicist, is sometimes said to have attended Brown during the 1880s. Williams himself states he "matriculated in Brown University" but was unable to attend. He independently pursued the curriculum in Brown's catalogue while teaching in Virginia (Williams 1890: 8, Becker 1999).

3. Barnas Sears: Bronson 1914: 359–360, Vaughn 1964, West 1966: 5–9, Cashin 1980: 7. Speech: Robinson 1883, Chang 2004: 134–135, Chang 2010: 4–6. "We came here": *Macon Telegraph*, 13 April 1883, *New York Globe*, 14 April 1883, Franklin 1998: 135.

4. Feeder: *Southwestern Christian Advocate*, 26 June 1884. "Show the white people": Wright Jr. 1965: 30.

5. Half-brothers: *Brown Alumni Monthly* 13.1, June 1912: 188, Brown University 1936: 1515. Never claimed: Walker 1901: 476; Torrence 1948: 58 places Robert and Walker together on an undated Emancipation Day in Augusta. Remembered: Stockbridge 1882: 53, *Providence Journal*, 18 June 1884. Scholarship: Treasurer Receipts, 1757–1891. MS-1D-R1. Series I, Box 30. Scholarships, 1884–1891, Folders 3–5 (1886–1888), Brown University Archives; Brown University Catalogue 1886–1887: 56–57. Henry Jackson: *Providence Daily Journal*, 02 April 1863, Bronson 1914: 219, Brown University 1936: 123. Took pains: Brown University Annual Report 1886: 12–13.

6. J. L. Dart (1854–1915): Pegues 1892: 145–147, Caldwell 1919: 210–212, *Providence Journal*, 11 October 1884, 14 August 1885, *Augusta Chronicle*, 21 February 1886, Torrence 1948: 68–73, Davis 1998: 35–37. "Intimate terms": *Providence Journal*, 14 August 1885; also *Bulletin of Atlanta University* 36, April 1892: 5. Pointed him: John Hope Records 65/3 (autobiographical sketch, 1934), Torrence 1948: 69–70, 86–87, Davis 1998: 48.

7. Advanced standing: Brown University Catalogue 1885–86: 22–26, 29–31 (the latest catalogue Gilbert and Walker could have consulted). English literature: Walker 1884, *Augusta Chronicle*, 13 March and 10 April 1889, Torrence 1948: 68. Mathematics: the most Paine offered before 1888 was geometry (Clary 1965: 161), most likely taught by W. C. Davis since Walker is never listed as teaching mathematics.

8. Admission: Brown catalogues of this period do not give an admissions timetable, but admissions exams were held in June each year, with a secondary set in September, suggesting decisions were normally made in the summer. John Hope: Torrence 1948: 72–73, Davis 1998: 36–37. Studied together: Torrence 1948: 72–73 writes that G. W. Walker helped Hope to prepare for Worcester. Davis 1998: 37 adds that Gilbert may have helped, too; Davis suggests Robert Bradford Williams might also have helped, but Williams did not return to Augusta after graduating from Yale in 1885.

9. Dryscoll and Hope: Worcester Academy's fall 1888 term began on 12 September, Brown's on 14 September; Davis 1998: 39 reports that Hope reached Worcester a week before the term began. "Washerwoman": Forman 1913: 252, Gilbert 1913: 35, Massachusetts Reformatory 1918: 586. A version published in Texas (*Aspermont Star*, 13 February 1913) has Gilbert save the money and return it to his mother after graduating. Remarried: Georgia, Marriage Records from Select Counties, 1828–1978. Richmond County, Book O, 1881–1887: 231; the minister was J. T. Tolbert of Thankful Baptist Church, who presided over Sarah's 1873 wedding to Tom Dasher. For Thomas's first wife Laura and their son William, see US Census, Augusta, Supervisor District 2, Enumeration District 96, 10 June 1880: 44, *Augusta Chronicle*, 06 June 1886). Baker: Augusta City Directory 1886: 360. Earthquake: *Atlanta Constitution*, 03 September 1886, Torrence 1948: 73.
10. Dryscoll and Hope: New England Conservatory 1886–1887: 12 shows fall term beginning 9 September; Hope arrived in Worcester a week before the beginning of fall term in early September (Davis 1998: 39). J. A. Lester (1864–1934): Mather 1915: 175–176, *The Tennessean*, 28 September 1934. "I knew young Mr. Gilbert": *Christian Index*, 06 December 1923. Osceola Pleasant: Fisk University 1881–1882: 12, 1884–1885: 20, 1885–1886, 19, 25, 1886–1887: 19 (listed next to Rachel Lester).
11. "Special and offensive": Cable 1888: 4–8. On black rail travelers in this era, see Kornweibel 2010.
12. Providence: Bayles 1891, Gibson and Jung 2005, tables 11, 40. Black community: Stewart 1975, Rhode Island Black Heritage Society 1984, Davis 1998: 55–56. Race relations: *New York Freeman*, 14 May and 09 July 1887. Less hospitable: Bartlett 1954: 59, 63–64. "Contemptible prejudice": *New York Age*, 10 December 1887.
13. Brown University: Brown University Catalogue 1886–1887: 10–11, 21, 49–52; Brown et al. 1909: 430. Circulation records: Fries 2017.
14. Greek exam: Walker 1901: 476. "Under conditions": Brown University Catalogue 1886–1887: 14 marks Gilbert as admitted "under conditions, or not fully examined"; Brown University Catalogue 1887–1888: 14 has only "not fully examined." The student lists first feature these marks in 1885 (Brown University Catalogue 1885–1886: 14). Limits: Gilbert's Brown transcript has apparently been lost; Torrence Papers 3A/6/16 preserves an abbreviated summary of his course record made in the 1940s, probably by consulting the transcript. This summary includes several freshman and sophomore mathematics courses marked "Adm." Transfers: Brown University Annual Report 1887: 3.
15. Photograph: Class Album of Theodore Francis Green, 1887. Brown University Archives. Class of '88: Brown University Catalogue 1884–1885: 19–21, 1885–1886: 17–18, 21, 1886–1887: 14–15, 21, 25, 28; these numbers include four non-degree "select course" students. Drop out or die: *Liber Brunensis*

1887: 34–35; also *Providence Journal*, 13 April 1887. Classmates: Brown University 1936: 328–332.

16. Among the oldest: A few men were Gilbert's age or older (the oldest was Richard King Wickett, born in 1846), but most were born between 1865 and 1867. Hope's cohort: Davis 1998: 50. Sharply divided: Brown et al. 1909: 436. Anti-Aquarian: *Liber Brunensis* 1887: 85. Had to work: *Providence Journal*, 23 December 1885, Brown University Catalogue 1886–1887: 55, Brown University Annual Report 1887: 32. "Display and extravagance": Brown University Annual Report 1888: 17.

17. Scholarship: The terms of his funding are uncertain, but Brown's records show that Gilbert received twenty-five-dollar checks in October 1886, February 1887, and April 1887. He probably also received tuition and housing rebates or reductions; compare the surviving bill of an 1887 freshman (Treasurer Term Bills, 1785–1904. MS-1D-T2. Box 1, Term Bill of Edward Bartlett, Jr., 1889 October 1. Brown University Archives). Had to work: Kletzing and Crogman 1898: 482, Walker 1901: 476. The mention of a barber shop is particularly interesting, but I am unable to identify the shop. One well-known black barber in the 1880s was John W. Thompson (*New York Freeman*, 16 October 1886, Providence Directory 1887: 525); on black barbers, see Rhode Island Black Heritage Society 1984: 50–51, Mills 2013: 63–64. Blizzard: *Providence Journal*, 15 December 1888, Brown 1909: 427. Seven dollars: Walker 1901: 476. Monthly board: Brown University Catalogue 1886–1887: 52–56; the estimated total annual cost of attendance was between one-hundred-fifty and two-hundred-twenty dollars, including a one-hundred-dollar tuition.

18. Women: Brown University Annual Report 1886: 14–18, *Liber Brunensis* 1887: 10, 92. "Inflammable": *Providence Journal*, 02 July 1885. Fire extinguisher: *Liber Brunensis* 1887: 83.

19. Hartshorn: Brown University Annual Report 1891: 3–4. Waiters and vendors: Anonymous photographs and illustrations of these men appear in class albums and in the *Liber Brunensis*. Staff: *Liber Brunensis* 1887: 81, 88, Brown 1909: 406, Munro 1929: 8; named photographs of several janitors from 1886–1888 survive in Brown's archives.

20. Hope College: Renovations in 1957 completely changed the building's interior, but its 1886–1888 layout survives in a set of plans produced for an 1891 renovation (Brown University Department of Facilities Management, plan dated ca. 11 July 1891). Each division originally had two rooms per floor (Brown 1909: 170, 196), divided into four in the 1870s. Within each division, rooms were numbered by floor, from bottom to top floor (*Liber Brunensis* 1887: 46). The four rooms of the fourth (top) floor, North Division were numbered 46–49 until 1878, when they were renumbered 45–48, probably because a student died in Room 49. "Brains and muscle": *Providence Journal*, 29 April 1888. Gilbert's room: Brown University Catalogue 1886–1887: 14 and 1887–1888: 14. Since 1883, Hope's room prices had varied by desirability (Brown

University Annual Report 1883: 12). The first published price list shows Hope 45 was one of the cheapest in the building, although the lowest rents were for ground floor rooms (Brown University Catalogue 1890–1891: 108). An old pump still stands outside Hope College today, but cold water was piped to some parts of the building by 1885 (Brown 1909: 327). Furnish their own: *Brunonian*, 09 April 1887: 1–2. Seven men: Four moved elsewhere in Hope College, two to other dorms, and one dropped out for the year. One of the seven was from Tennessee and another from Wisconsin; the others were New Englanders. Hawes: Phillips Exeter Academy 1903: 125, Brown University 1936: 330.

21. Snapshot: This spot is today covered by the western part of Faunce House (originally Rockefeller Hall), erected in 1904. The photographer, Charles D. Cooke, took at least 144 photos of students and professors, often catching them in characteristic poses or attitudes; amateur photography was the rage on campus at the time and the camera club was flourishing (Brown 1909: 440–442). Beeline: Map in Sanborn 1889: 46.

22. Social life: Stewart 1975, Torrence 1948: 98–99, Davis 1998: 55–59. Newspaper: Stewart 1975: 35. *Freeman* and *Age*: Pride and Wilson 1997: 121–124, Martin 2004.

23. Black churches: *Providence Journal*, 24 June 1886, *New York Freeman*, 25 September 1886 and 23 April 1887, Providence Directory 1886: 105–107 and 1887: 669, Bayles 1891: 434–494, Rhode Island Black Heritage Society 1984: 52–58. Select a church: Brown University Catalogue 1886–1887: 51. Bethel AME: Bayles 1891: 473. Glimpse: Brown University Catalogue 1892–1893: 160 describes the view from Hope 45; Sanborn-Perris 1899: 107–108 shows the church's location. Brown University purchased the building in 1961 and demolished it; today a plaque marks the site.

24. A. W. Upshaw (?–1892): Atlanta University 1884–1885: 7, *Providence Journal*, 04 September 1886, Providence City Directory 1887: 539, Lamb 1900: 266. Bethel Literary: Cromwell 1896, Wright 1916: 367–338, McHenry 2002: 149–165, Roberts 2010. Historical Literary Society: *New York Freeman*, 25 December 1886, 1 January 1887, 15 January 1887, 19 March 1887.

25. Clubs and theatricals: *New York Freeman*, 27 November and 11 December 1886; John Hope later joined one such club (Torrence 1948: 98–99, Davis 1998: 57–58). Veterans and militia: *Freeman*, 25 June 1887; see also Gannon 2011: 46, 55, 60. Historical Association: *Freeman*, 19 March 1887. E. M. Bannister: *Freeman*, 27 November 1886, 16 April 1887, 14 May 1887, Stewart 1975: 34, Shaw 2006. Harriet Tubman: *Providence Journal*, 27 November and 28 November 1886, *Freeman*, 04 December 1886. While he was at Brown, Gilbert missed Frederick Douglass's visit to Augusta (*Augusta Chronicle*, 04 March 1888).

26. Junior curriculum: Brown University Catalogue 1886–1887: 31–33, Bronson 1914: 405–406. Surveying: Paine Institute 1888–1889: 15 lists a junior year

spring-term course on surveying, exactly the place the course had at Brown. Languages: Torrence Papers 3A/6/16; this summary lists languages (Greek, Latin, French, German), but not specific authors and texts.

27. W. C. Poland (1846–1929): *Annual Report of the President* 1887: 28–29, Bronson 1914: 440–441. J. L. Lincoln (1817–1891): Lincoln 1894: 611–618, Brown 1909: 389–390, 413–414, Bronson 1914: 435–439.

28. Albert Harkness (1822–1907): *Liber Brunensis* 1889: 51–52, Faunce et al. 1907, Bronson 1914: 438–440.

29. Most famous: *Liber Brunensis* 1889: 52. A million: Faunce et al. 1907: 33–34. Broad interests: Brown University Annual Report 1869: 30, 1879: 24, 1880: 29, 1882: 15–16, 1886: 26–27 ("great familiarity"). Homeric Question: Brown University Annual Report 1884: 28–29, Turner 1997. As a textbook, Harkness used the English translation (Bonitz 1880) of Hermann Bonitz's influential 1860 essay on the Homeric poems.

30. Key role: AIA 1881: 13, AIA 1882: 46–56, Seymour 1902: 21, Lord 1947: 4. Director: *Bulletin of the School of Classical Studies at Athens* 1885: 23; see also *Providence Journal*, 18 May 1883,

31. Harkness and Lincoln: Bronson 1914: 439–440. Young at heart: Lincoln 1894: 617. "Stimulating and inspiring": Brown 1909: 223–224. Drillmaster: *Brown Alumni Monthly* 7.2, July 1907: 30. "Polite and patient": Brown 1909: 223–224, 414. "Studied too hard": *New Haven Register*, 11 March 1887. "Harkey": *Liber Brunensis* 1887: 80; also *Liber Brunensis* 1888: 102, 111, 115.

32. Same qualities: Calhoun 1961: 17.

33. Greek: Brown University Catalogue 1886–1887: 32–33, Brown University Annual Report 1887: 20–21, Torrence Papers 3A/6/16. *Crito* and *Apology*: Brown University Annual Report 1869: 30. *Alcestis*: Brown University Annual Report 1876: 27, 1878: 24, 1883: 21, 1885: 20, 1886: 27. "Appreciate and enjoy": Brown University Annual Report 1887: 21; compare 1883: 21, 1888: 22, 1890: 24.

34. *Alcestis*: Visvardi 2016. Popularity: Winterer 2002: 95–96, Luschnig and Roisman 2003, Slater 2013: 81–86. Revivals: Plugge 1938: 13–16, 32. Oxford: Beard 2000: 47–51, Robinson 2002: 82–84. Charles Winter Wood: *New York Age*, 20 June 1953, Hill 1984: 57–61. In 1962, the first musical staged in London by an all-black company, the Ira Aldridge Players (named after the famed nineteenth-century black actor), was based on *Alcestis*; see Ronnick 2019.

35. Undergraduates: *The Brunonian*, 19 January 1889. Never taught: The surviving Paine catalogues do not list Euripides, although Sophocles's *Antigone* does appear. Textbook: Gilbert must have acquired this copy of Theodore Woolsey's 1869 revised edition of the *Alcestis* (Paine College Archives PA3975.A2) in Providence, for it includes examination marks, metrical notes, and the previous owner's notation ("finished May 27, '84"). Southern Methodists of the

time often condemned theater, but back in Augusta even Warren Candler—thunder as he did against the corrupting stage in a notorious 1887 sermon—judged it acceptable to read Euripides and his ancient fellows who were "purer than modern stage writers" (*Nashville Tennessean*, 10 October 1887).

36. German and French: Brown University Catalogue 1886–1887: 31–33, Torrence Papers 3A/6/16. Letters: Lambuth tells the story in an oft-quoted 1918 letter (e.g., Martin 1924: 106).

37. History and literature: Brown University Catalogue 1886–1887: 31–33, Brown University Annual Report 1887: 24–26, 35, Torrence Papers 3A/6/16. Bancroft: Sears 1891. Regular visitor: Fries 2017. Shakespearean grammar: Abbott 1884 (Paine College Archives PR3075.A4).

38. Printing press and *Herald*: Slater Fund 1887: 29, Paine Institute 1888–1889: 17, Range 1953: 70–71. Everywhere: *Liber Brunensis* 1887: 102 and 1888: 116–118, Bronson 1914: 400.

39. Fundraising tour: *Boston Herald*, 20 March 1887, 21 March 1887, 22 March 1887, *Providence Journal*, 22 March 1887, 23 March 1887, *Brooklyn Daily Eagle*, 02 April 1887, *New York Freeman*, 02 April 1887, *New York Tribune*, 04 April 1887. "One colored student": *Freeman*, 26 March 1887.

40. Chapel: *Providence Journal*, 25 March 1887, *New York Freeman*, 02 April 1887, *The Brunonian*, 9 April 1887.

41. Editorial: *The Brunonian*, 9 April 1887; juniors Francis J. Belcher, William A. Wilbur, and Eli W. Blake, III were on the seven-man board. Unnamed schools: *New York Age*, 20 November 1886 names Harvard College as a place where professors take "pleasure and delight in saying unkind things about the colored race."

42. Exams: Brown University Catalogue 1886–1887: 6. Cruise: *Providence Journal*, 11 June 1887. Savannah-bound: "J. W. Gilbert" appears as a passenger on steamer *Gate City*, departing Boston on June 9 (*Boston Post*, 10 June 1887) and arriving in Savannah on June 13 (*Savannah Morning News*, 14 June 1887); the latter paper's listing of "J. W. Gilbert (col)" makes the identification fairly certain. John Hope: Torrence 1948: 81–82, Davis 1998: 46–47. Resort: John Hope worked in Newport during summer 1891 and 1892 (Davis 1998: 56). Social scene: *New York Freeman*, 30 July 1887, 27 August 1887. Left Meeting Street: *New Haven Daily Morning Journal and Courier*, 07 June 1887, *Washington Bee*, 30 July 1887.

43. J. T. Jenifer (1835–1919): Northrop et al. 1896: 35–36, *The Crisis* 4.2, June 1912: 69, Wright Jr. 1916: 129–130, Ronnick 2005a: 125, 348 n. 3, Dilbeck 2018: 158, 160–162. Arrival in Providence: *New York Freeman*, 11 June 1887. Upshaw at Bethel: *Providence Journal*, 17 March 1888.

44. Senior curriculum: Brown University Catalogue 1887–1888: 36–38, Brown University Annual Report 1888: 21–23. Languages: Torrence Papers 3A/6/16; compare also Paine Institute 1888–1889, 1890–1891, 1894–1895. Paine College Archives PA3951.K38, a copy of C. R. Kennedy's translation

of Demosthenes (Kennedy 1885), probably dates to Gilbert's senior year at Brown. "High praise": Brown University Annual Report 1888: 22.

45. A. S. Packard, Jr. (1839–1905): Brown et al. 1909: 431–432, Bronson 1914: 475. Geology: Brown University Annual Report 1888: 34–35, Torrence Papers 3A/6/16; Fries 2017 shows Gilbert read Darwin for this class. Paine Institute 188–189: 15 and 1894–1895: 7 list a one-semester Geology course; the course is absent from Paine Institute 1890–1891: 21, the year Gilbert was in Greece.

46. Prehistoric archaeology: Brown University Annual Report 1880: 40, 1881: 34, 1884: 29; Brown University Catalogue 1887–1888: 38. Lanciani: *Providence Journal*, 02 March 1887, 07 April 1887, 14 April 1887; *The Brunonian*, 09 April 1887; Dyson 1998: 49–50, Dyson 2006: 104–105. Lyon: *Providence Journal*, 29 November 1887, 09 December 1887, 22 December 1887.

47. Classical archaeology and casts: Brown University Annual Report 1888: 12–14, 24, 1889: 38–39; *The Brunonian* 19 January 1889. Hermes: *Providence Journal*, 21 June 1888, 20 August 1888, *The Brunonian*, 22 December 1888; see Aijootian 1996 for the controversy over assigning this sculpture to Praxiteles. *The Brunonian*, 27 October 1888 gives a list of the casts, which came from Berlin, Munich, Naples, and Rome.

48. Increasingly aware: *The Brunonian*, 04 December 1886, 03 January 1887, 23 April 1887, 03 December 1887, 17 December 1887, 23 January 1888, 14 April 1888; also *Providence Journal*, 29 May 1887. "All the alumni": *Providence Journal*, 20 June 1888.

49. Wiley Lane (1852–1885): Ronnick 2002b; *Cleveland Gazette*, 17 January 1885, 21 February 1885, *The Evening Critic*, 17 February 1885; *New York Freeman*, 14 March 1885, 21 March 1885; *Southwestern Christian Advocate*, 09 April 1885. Lane had been a year behind Milford and Page at Howard (Logan 1967: 37–38, 104). Public memorials: Patton and Hoar 1885; Frederick Douglass spoke briefly at one of these services (Blassingame and McKivigan eds. 1992: 170–171). Upshaw and Lane: *Washington Bee*, 06 January 1883, Roberts 2010. Bethel Literary: *The Critic*, 03 April 1883, *New York Globe*, 05 July 1884.

50. Annie S. Peck: Providence Directory 1887: 425. A series of newspaper advertisements from September to November 1887 (e.g., *Providence Journal*, 01 September 1887) offers "private lessons in preparatory or college studies," including modern Greek and archaeology, by an unnamed university graduate who "has spent two years in study and travel in Europe." Identical "private lessons" wording appears in a second series of ads from September to October 1888 (the earliest is *Providence Journal*, 04 September 1888), this time giving Peck's name.

51. Forty-three: Brown University Catalogue 1887–1888: 14–15, 24, including four "select course" students. Scarlet fever: *Providence Journal*, 09 November 1887. "Our Band is few": *Liber Brunensis* 1888: 116. Several times: *Liber*

Brunensis 1888: 100, 114, 115, 116. Shakespearean quip: *Liber Brunensis* 1888: 116 ("Now Falstaff sweats to death," quoting *Henry IV, Part I*, scene 2).

52. Senior class photo: Class Album of Robert R. Taft, 1888. Brown University Archives. Since Taft's album contains both versions of the photo, he is unlikely to have demanded a Gilbert-less photo. Indeed, his album includes a labeled space for Gilbert's individual portrait, although the portrait itself is missing. Probably the missing portrait was the same image as Figure 2.5.

53. Centennial: *Evening Star* (DC), 30 April 1887. Newport: *Providence Journal*, 07 November 1887, 10 November 1887; *Newport Mercury*, 12 November 1887. Providence: *New York Age,* 12 November 1887; *Providence Journal*, 14 November 1887, 19 November 1887, 21 November 1887. Five hundred: *New York Age*, 19 November 1887. Large crowd: *New York Age*, 26 November 1887. W. H. Bonaparte: Engs 1979: 152–153.

54. Allen Chapel: Providence Directory 1886: 107, Bayles 1891: 491. Charity drive: *New York Age*, 26 November 1887, 10 December 1887. "Feature of the evening": *New York Age*, 03 December 1887.

55. Well-known: *New York Age*, 09 June 1888. Filled in: *New York Age*, 19 May 1888. Indianapolis: *New York Age*, 11 June 1887.

56. Controversy: Graham 1954: 113–116, Calhoun 1961: 15–17, Clary 1965: 81–83, 133–142, Clary 1971: 30–31. C. H. Carson: *Albany Democrat* (OR), 08 August 1884, *Atlanta Constitution*, 09 December 1887, Rubin 1959: I.187–188, Slater Fund 1887: 29, *Daily World* (Opelousas, LA), 21 August 1968 (omitting his time at Paine). "True, efficient men": *Wesleyan Christian Advocate*, 09 November 1887. Represent the school: *Augusta Chronicle*, 16 December 1887. By his own admission: *Wesleyan Christian Advocate*, 21 December 1887.

57. Letter: *Wesleyan Christian Advocate*, 21 December 1887; Carson, along with MECS minister W. C. Dunlap, had just represented Paine at an MECS conference in Sandersville, Georgia (*Augusta Chronicle*, 16 December 1887).

58. Wide readership: *The Independent*, 26 January 1888; Mott 1938: 65–71. "The most disgusting": *Southwestern Christian Advocate*, 12 January 1888. "Take care of itself": *The Christian Index*, 28 January 1888. "Disgraced": *Southwestern Christian Advocate*, 08 March 1888. Nothing more: *Southwestern Christian Advocate*, 29 March 1888. Pressed Holsey: *Southwestern Christian Advocate*, 07 June 1888.

59. Walker to Candler, 20 February 1888, Paine Presidents File 53/9.

60. Original plan: Graham 1954: 116. "I went so far": Graham 1954: 114. Holsey and Wright tussled over Wright's coverage of the affair in the *Augusta Sentinel*, which Wright edited (*Christian Index*, 10 March 1888). Northern visitors: *New York Freeman*, 02 April 1887.

61. Already suggested: Brown University Annual Report 1889: 27.

62. May 4, 1888: Paine College 50/1/89, Clary 1965: 133–136, Bauman 1981: 44. Spring semester: Brown University Catalogue 1887–1888: 6.

63. Met in Augusta: Paine College 50/1/97–99; *Augusta Chronicle*, 07 June 1888, *Southwestern Christian Advocate*, 12 July 1888, Clary 1965: 136–142. "Utmost confidence": *Wesleyan Christian Advocate*, 20 June 1888. "Almost unbelievable": Peters 1937.

64. Commencement: Brown University Catalogue 1887–1888: 5–6; *Providence Journal*, 15 June 1888, 16 June 1888, 20 June 1888, 21 June 1888, *The Brunonian*, 20 June 1888. Graduating class: Brown University Catalogue 1888–1889: 62–63 (thirty-nine bachelor's degrees conferred in 1888, including one to an 1868 alumnus and another to a postgraduate student). Some reports (*Wesleyan Christian Advocate*, 20 June 1888, *Southwestern Christian Advocate*, 23 January 1890) place Gilbert fourth or twelfth in his class, but he does not appear in the class honors list (Brown University 1888–1889: 60–62). Into perspective: Du Bois 1903: 105, Du Bois and Dill eds. 1910: 45–50.

65. Commencement dinner: *Providence Journal*, 21 June 1888.

66. John Hope and Room 45: Torrence 1948: 97–98 with more detail in Torrence papers 3A/6/9–10; Davis 1998: 50–54, 62. Trimble: Titcomb 2001: 97. Okada: Brown University 1936: 375. Stewart: Brown University Catalogue 1894–1895: 218. Tobias: Brown University Catalogue 1894–1895: 223. Thomas Hope: Brown University Catalogue 1896–1897: 239, 1899–1900: 173. Other African Americans: E.g., Edwin Miles Pertilla (Brown University Catalogue 1899–1900: 182), Francis Elliott Young (Brown University Catalogue 1900–1901: 191, 1902–1903: 195), and John Brown Watson (Brown University Catalogue 1902–1903: 200, Brown University 1936: 492).

67. "Among the graduates": *New York Age*, 30 June 1888.

Chapter 3

1. Flood: *Augusta Chronicle*, 11 September 1888, 13 September 1888. Jones and Dutcher 1890: 189–190, Augusta Bicentennial 1935: 32–35, Cashin 1980: 170–172, Tilson 2002: 13–32. Floods and fire: Tilson 2002. *Augusta Sentinel* (later the *Weekly Sentinel*): Floyd 1902: 47, Wan 2015: 9.

2. Unscathed: *Augusta Chronicle*, 22 September 1888 says Woodlawn was not flooded. Fourth year: Paine Institute 1888–1889: 22. Gained the trust: E.g., *Christian Index*, 17 March 1888. M. Z. Hankinson (1856–1933): *Augusta Chronicle*, 30 September 1919, 15 January 1928, 01 January 1934; De Bardeleben 1920: 245, Tobias 1953: 180–181, Graham 1955: 141 (giving her last name as Hankerson). Hankinson appears as Mary Z. Luther in Wesleyan Female College catalogues for 1867–1868, 1868–1869, and 1869–1870, but not in later alumnae lists.

3. Dryscoll: Paine Institute 1888–1889: 5. R. L. Campbell (1845–1920): Paine Institute 1888–1889: 5, *Augusta Chronicle*, 08 August and 10 August 1920, Clary 1965: 61–63. "All in my power": De Bardeleben 1920: 425–426. "Negro students": Gray 1948: 23. "Valiant men": *Augusta Chronicle*, 15 August 1920.

Campbell's son Robert Walton Campbell later taught music and foreign languages at Paine.

4. Fretted: *Southwestern Christian Advocate*, 31 May 1888. Lewis Goodrich: Rubin 1959: II.8-9. S. A. Goodrich (1857–1934): *Augusta Chronicle*, 08 June 1888. Susan and George had no children of their own, but adopted the Baillie (Bailey) cousins: Jim, Sally, and Mattie. More aware: *Augusta Chronicle*, 25 July 1888.

5. "Day-dawn": *Christian Index*, 11 August 1888. Strained: *Wesleyan Christian Advocate*, 22 August 1888, Rubin 1959: II.29. Salary: Slater Fund 1889: 34; after the MECS began paying Gilbert's salary in 1890, Walker supplemented it with CME funds (Paine 50/1/111–117). Lane Institute: E.g., *Christian Index* 29 October 1887, 11 August 1888. "Destined": *Christian Index*, 01 December 1888. "Bright and cheerful": *Christian Index*, 15 December 1888.

6. No sciences: Clary 1965: 161–162. Modeled: Brown University Catalogue 1886–1887: 31–35, Paine Institute 1888–1889: 13–15, Torrence Papers 3A/6/16.

7. John Hope: Appendix 2. G. C. Taylor (1862–?): Paine Institute 1890–1891: 6–7, Wright 1916: 221, Phillips 1925: 132, 165–166. R. A. Carter (1867–1954): Phillips 1925: 567–568, [no author] 1954: 158–160; Carter was "ever rock and oak" to Carter G. Woodson, founder of the Association for the Study of Negro Life and History. Oration: Carter 1893.

8. W. C. Thomas: Paine Institute 1888–1889: 10, Paine Institute 1890–1891: 10. Largest class yet: Paine Institute 1890–1891: 7–8. "Most prosperous year": Paine 50/1/107 (05 June 1889).

9. "Reading Greek": Brown University Annual Report 1889: 27. Does not appear: Brown University Catalogue 1888–1889: 13. Immediately: Brown University Annual Report 1891: 33. Rosters: Brown University Catalogue 1889–1890: 101, *Liber Brunensis* 1890: 60.

10. Regulations: Brown University Catalogue 1887–1888: 82–83. Addresses: Brown University Catalogue 1889–1890: 101; also Brown University Catalogue 1890–1891: 122–123 (only 2 of 5 PhD students and 6 of 21 MA students living in Providence).

11. Graduate programs: Brown University Annual Report 1883: 9–10; Bronson 1914: 407–408. "Thorough course": Brown University Annual Report 1887: 8; Brown University Catalogue 1887–1888: 54–55. First two MAs and PhDs: Brown University Annual Report 1888: 3–4, 1889: 9, 1895: 79.

12. Johnson family: Johnson 1982: 16–17, Cashin 1995: 36, Rowland 2006a: 9. Pleasant family: Augusta Directory 1865: 42, 1882: 333; US Federal Census, Richmond County, Augusta, Ward 1, 04 June 1870: 16, Freedman's Savings Bank, Augusta, no. 6209 (Sarah E. Pleasant, 13 August 1873). On the two families, see also *Augusta Chronicle*, 12 March 1867, US Federal Census, Richmond County, Augusta, Ward 1, 04 June 1870: 16–17, Walker 1998: 55, 366–367. Born about 1864: Appendix 1. Eldest sister: Baptist Home Missions 1883: 565 (Miss Sarah E. Pleasant, age sixteen, teaching at Augusta Institute from February to April 1870).

13. Disease: Cedar Grove Cemetery B173 (Isabella, dysentery, buried 20 June 1871), B292 (Robert, lung hemorrhage, buried 14 July 1874), B350 (Margaret, consumption, buried 26 September 1876), B438 (Robert H., consumption, buried 28 December 1879). W. S. Dixson (1855–1931): *Augusta Chronicle*, 22 March 1882 and 23 August 1931, *The State* (Columbia, SC), 24 August 1931. Postmaster: https://about.usps.com/who-we-are/postal-history/african-american-postmasters-19thc-2010.pdf, accessed 14 November 2016.

14. Nashville: Fisk University 1881–1882: 12 (Class D, Normal); 1884–1885: 20 (Class C, Common English); 1885–1886: 19, 25 (Class B, Common English); 1886–1887: 19 (Class B, Common English, apparently repeating a grade); Osceola Pleasant is absent from the 1883–1884 catalogue and no known copy of the 1882–1883 catalogue survives. I am unable to consult the 1880–1881 catalogue that survives in Mississippi Department of Archives and History, Alfred H. Stone Collection, vol. 53, no. 6. Since Fisk's Normal Department in the early 1880s began with Class E, presumably she is in Class E in 1880–1881.

15. Gainesville: *The Fisk Herald,* December 1886: 9, Webb 1887: 414. Union Academy: Laurie 1986. M. J. Maddox: *Morning News* (Savannah), 17 August 1889; *Sioux City Journal*, 11 November 1890; Walker 1892: 34. Maddox's sister Ruth D. Maddox graduated from Paine Institute in 1887 and joined her brother in Gainesville (*Spelman Messenger* June 1886: 4 and January 1888: 2, Paine Institute 1888–1889: 6). Millett: *American Missionary* February 1888: 145 (donation from "little children in Miss Osceola Pleasant's Sch.") First Ward: *Sixteenth Annual Report of the Board of Education of Richmond County* 1888: 6, Augusta Directory 1889: 38, 326, Rowland and Rowland 2009: 155.

16. "Expects to be married": *The Brunonian*, 22 December 1888. How the *Brunonian* got "Franklin College" is unknown; I am unable to identify any school by this name in Tennessee. Annual meeting: *Columbus Enquirer-Sun*, 01 May 1889, *Columbus Daily Enquirer*, 03 May 1889. First child: Appendix 1. "Gentle partner": Crogman 1898: 483.

17. "Why should": *New York Times*, 26 February 1882. AIA and ASCSA: Seymour 1902, Lord 1947, Sheftel 1979, Dyson 1998: 53–60, Turner 1999: 277–296, Will 2002, Winterer 2002a: 170–174, Winterer 2002b.

18. "Honorable rivalry": AIA First Annual Report of the Executive Committee, 1879–1880: 25. National venture: Turner 1999: 279–280. Consortium: Lord 1947: 20.

19. Frederick Barnard: Lord 1947: 8–10, Turner 1999: 293.

20. Skillfully promoted: Goodwin 1884: 8–11, Lord 1947: 33–40.

21. Assessed: Goodwin 1884: 6–7. Facilities: ASCSA 1889a: 7–8, Lord 1947: 20–30.

22. Tarbell: Seymour to Norton, multiple letters, AIA 3/3, 3/4. Waldstein: multiple letters, AIA 3/3, 3/4, 3/6, Turner 1999: 320–321, 328–329; Lord 1947: 32–33, 50–52.

23. Students: Lord 1947: 13–14. Far away: Faunce et al. 1907: 39. Cholera: ASCSA 1885: 14, Lord 1947: 40. Bandits and dogs: Lord 1947: 39. Walter Miller: *Springfield Daily Republic*, 05 September 1886, Lord 1947: 278–294.

24. Ardent: Seymour 1907: 38–41. At least five: Annual Report of the President 1890: 23–24, 34; Brown University Graduate Record Book: 65 lists Arthur Warren Smith as a graduate student in 1890, on the same page as John Wesley Gilbert, but Smith never completed his degree.

25. Proposed students: ASCSA 309/1 Memo Book: 55–56 (24 June 1889). Harkness may have first mentioned Gilbert at the 24 May 1889 Managing Committee (ASCSA 309/1 Copy Book: 86), where Seymour "reported the names of three or four students already applying for next year."

26. "I never expected": Walker 1901: 476.

27. Orris: ASCSA 1889b: 19–20, *Princeton Alumni Weekly*, 06 January 1906. "Living language": Rose 1895: 484. "Our finances": Seymour to Norton, 01 January 1889, AIA 3/4. "Shabby trick": Goodwin to Norton, 08 May 1890, ASCSA 301/2, Folder 2; cf. Lord 1947: 52–54.

28. Students: Orris to Waldstein, 26 November 1889, IOC 205926 (R. D. Taylor ill and W. I. Hunt living out). At odds: Seymour to Waldstein, 28 January 1890; Norton to Waldstein, 11 February 1890; Seymour to Waldstein, 25 March 1890, all IOC 205926. "Not apparent": Brooks 1891: 48. Trickled in: ASCSA 1890: 19–20. "Even now": Goodwin to John Williams White, 14 April 1890 (quoted in ASCSA 309/1 Copy Book: 64); similar sentiments in Goodwin to Norton, 08 May 1890, ASCSA 301/2, Folder 2.

29. 1889–1890: The catalogue for this year does not survive, but details can be reconstructed from Paine Institute 1888–1889, 1890–1891, and 1894–1895. Ola Gilbert probably completed the Normal program, as her previous work at Fisk did not include the languages necessary for the Higher Normal course. Mathematics and surveying: Paine Institute 1888–1889: 15, 1890–1891: 20, 1894–1895: 6.

30. Barnwell massacre: *Augusta Chronicle*, 29 December 1889, Finnegan 2013: 196–198, Murphy 2018: 58–61. Headlines: E.g., *Cleveland Plaindealer*, 03 January 1890, *Huntsville Gazette*, 04 January 1890, *New York Age*, 04 January 1890. "Cruel, cowardly, brutal": *Augusta Chronicle*, 03 January 1890. "Good people": quoted in *Atlanta Constitution*, 05 January 1890.

31. "Preparing to leave": *Southwestern Christian Advocate*, 23 January 1890. Albert lists "Prof. J. W. Gilbert, graduate of Brown University" among Paine's faculty, but mistakenly names Charles Dryscoll (spelling his name "Dryshall") as the scholar headed to Greece. Alma Gilbert: Appendix 1.

32. Rufus Richardson: ASCSA 309/1 Memo Book: 61, Copy Book: 90 (15 November 1889). "Genial gentleman": Seymour to Waldstein, 18 November 1889, IOC 205926. "We have reason": Seymour to Waldstein, 06 January 1890, IOC 205926.

33. "All the preparation": Waldstein to Seymour, 23 January 1889 (quoted in ASCSA 309/1 Memo Book: 49). Three students: ASCSA 309/1 Memo Book: 62 (undated, but written sometime between 25 March and 12 May 1890). Met in Boston: ASCSA 309/1 Memo Book: 63–64, Copy Book: 98–99; these records note "the two young ladies may be received if their recommendations are found to be good."

34. Gildersleeve: Lupher and Vandiver 2011: 345, ASCSA 309/1 Memo Book: 67, Lord 1947: 11. White to Norton, 04 January 1886, AIA 3/2 notes Gildersleeve would "delight to do nothing" regarding the School. Virginia (contributing member 1882–1884) and Missouri (1887–1890): Lord 1947: 12–13. Wiley Lane: *Cleveland Gazette*, 17 January 1885, Patton and Hoar 1885. Annie Peck: Kimberley 2017: 66–69.

35. Possibilities: White to Scarborough, 08 February 1886; Scarborough to White, 08 March 1886; White to Scarborough, 16 March 1886, all in William Sanders Scarborough Papers, Box 8, Folder 1881–1889, Wilberforce University.

36. Picked up the story: *Freeman* (Indianapolis), 22 March 1890, *Cleveland Gazette*, 22 March 1890. At least thrice: *Freeman*, 05 April 1890, 24 May 1890, 02 August 1890; as far as I can determine, the paper did not repeat any other item during this period. Similar announcements: E.g., *Huntsville Gazette,* 19 April 1890 (mislocating the School in France); on the *Gazette*'s circulation and influence, see Robinson 2013. Most visible: *New York Age*, 17 May 1890 (*Huntsville Gazette*, 24 May 1890, is a copy of this notice, with the ASCSA correctly located). The *Age* and *Huntsville Gazette* both cite the *Norfolk Standard*, but no copies of the latter newspaper seem to survive. In some notices "treat" appears as "feat." Reprinted: *Southwestern Christian Advocate*, 04 September 1890.

37. Fellowships: First Annual Report of the Committee on the ASCSA 1882: 53. "Will continue": Brown University Annual Report 1890: 24.

38. Annie Peck: See Chapter 3. Reading list: Brown University Graduate Record Book: 65 (21 October 1890). The Plato and Demosthenes assignments clearly follow Harkness's recent work with on-campus students (Brown University Annual Report 1889: 26–27). Charles Dennis: Brown University Annual Report 1890: 24. Beyond philology: Turner 1997: 139. Schliemann: ASCSA 1889a: 36, ASCSA 1889b: 10, ASCSA 1890: 34.

39. Commencement: *Augusta Chronicle*, 03 June 1890, *Christian Index*, 05 July 1890, *Southwestern Christian Advocate*, 17 July 1890. Five of eight: Paine Institute 1890–1891: 8. Ware High School: *Augusta Chronicle*, 24 June 1890. R. R. Wright, Jr.: Wright 1965: 30.

40. Leave and salary: Paine Trustees Minutes 50/1/112-113 (04 June 1890). Cottin: Paine Institute 1890–1891: 5, *Christian Index*, 04 October 1890. Five hundred dollars: Brown University Annual Report 1890: 16. To Athens: ASCSA 1889: 53, the most recent report Gilbert could have read, gives a range of forty to one-hundred-twenty-five dollars for the Atlantic crossing, plus sixty-five to

one-hundred dollars onward to Athens; room and board estimates range from
five and a half to fourteen dollars per week, or about two hundred dollars for
the eight months of the ASCSA school year. Stepbrother: *Augusta Chronicle*,
04 July 1890. Letter of credit: Baedeker 1889: xxvii, Perkins 1979.

41. Application: NARA M1372-359-0061 (no. 20676); on the form, see Hunt
    1898: 64–65. State Department: Hunt 1898: 169. Guidance: ASCSA 1889: 53.
    In Greece: Baedeker 1889: xxvii–xxviii. Between 1887 and 1891, only three
    of sixteen regular ASCSA students did not apply for passports, and one of the
    three was a Greek citizen. Required: *FRUS* 1891: 310. Mary Eliza Church
    (later Mary Church Terrell) went to Europe in 1888 without a passport, but
    got one as soon as she reached Berlin in 1889 (NARA M1384-32-1157).

42. Withheld: Pryor 2016: 103–125. Slaves: E.g., NARA M1372-37-150. Denied
    a passport: Douglass 1892: 393–394.

43. Racial markers: Robertson 2010: 64–77. Later applications: M1372-585-
    0517 (1901), M1490-146-0929 (1911).

44. Day or two: Compare the passports in Robertson 2010: 34–35 with the cor-
    responding applications. Lewis Frederick Eisig (M1372-262-0637) applied
    in New York on 22 March 1884; his passport was issued in Washington on
    24 March. Julius L. Partz (M1372-448-0437) applied in Philadelphia on 17
    June 1895; his passport was issued 18 June 1895. Two and four days: see the
    1889–1891 applications from Augusta in NARA M1372-325-0664 to 0666,
    M1372-334-0330, M1372-352-0099, M1372-366-0244, M1372-369-26266.
    Back to Augusta: *Augusta Chronicle*, 12 February 1890 and 26 February
    1890. "European museums": ASCSA 1893: 23; see also Goodwin 1884: 12,
    ASCSA 1895: 15.

45. Notary: Passport regulations (Hunt 1898: 55, 210–211) required a notary
    to affix his official seal. Dixson did not have a seal, so, in accordance with
    regulations, Barnwell County court clerk William Gilmore Simms penned a
    statement on the back of the application validating Dixson's notary status.
    Simms was the eponymous son of antebellum Southern writer William Gilmore
    Simms; see *The State* (Columbia, SC), 16 October 1912.

46. Expects to finish": The *Barnwell People* was published on Thursdays in 1890,
    so this report originally appeared on 11 September 1890, but that issue of the
    paper has perished. A successor paper, the *Barnwell People-Sentinel*, reprinted
    the story on 26 May 1977; that issue, too, has been lost. A partial photo-
    copy of the 1977 reprint survives in Paine College Archives, Box 87. Given
    the *People*'s limited circulation, the *New York Freeman*, 20 September 1890
    reports that Gilbert "left last week for Athens, Greece to study modern Greek"
    (reprinted verbatim in Leavenworth, Kansas *Daily Advocate*, 27 September
    1890) likely derives from another source.

47. Ninety thousand: Dupont et al. 2008: 13–14, 18, Dupont et al. 2012: 146–
    148. Mary Church: Terrell 1940. Elites: Matthews 1890, Gatewood 1988: 8,
    Gatewood 1990: 207–208.

48. Mega-preacher: Talmage 1890: 156. D. P. Seaton: *Daily Gazette* (Cincinnati), 08 September 1877, *Baltimore Sun*, 28 April 1878, *Daily Star* (Cincinnati), 18 November 1878, Seaton 1895. Returned in 1889: Walters 1917: 70–81. Two black Americans: In 1827, James Williams of Baltimore was wounded fighting for Greek independence (Miller 1828: 160). In 1853, David Dorr of New Orleans accompanied his master to Athens while enslaved (Dorr 1858: 134–142, Schueller 1999, Kramer 2014). Frederick Douglass: For more on his visit to Athens, see Blight 2018: 673–674, Chapter 5 and also Lee (forthcoming b).

49. Express train: Walker 1892: 31–32 describes leaving Augusta at 10:15 AM on Thursday, 15 April 1891 and reaching Jersey City at 4:00 PM the next day; also National Railway Publications Company 1890: 556–569. September 30: Richardson to Waldstein, 11 October 1890, IOC 205926; ASCSA 1891: 31. Letters: *Indianapolis Freeman*, 22 November 1890, *New York Age*, 24 January 1891. Most prominent: *Indianapolis Freeman*, 31 May 1890 and 18 June 1890, Floyd 1902: 43–48. R. R. Wright, Sr. was the *Sentinel*'s editor earlier in 1890 (*New York Age*, 12 April 1890). *Georgia Baptist*: Pegues 1892: 536–539, Donaldson 2001: 142–143.

50. Summer travel: *Brooklyn Daily Eagle*, 13 September 1890. Plentiful: Steamship schedules (e.g., *Brooklyn Daily Eagle*, 09 September 1890) advertised tickets for vessels departing the next day; *New York Times*, 11 September 1890 records six ships departing with a total of some three hundred first-class passengers, about half the number that had just come in on a single liner. Fares and tickets: Dupont et al. 2008: 24, Dupont et al. 2012: 158–159, Dupont et al. 2016. Parliament: Appleton 1891: I.141, Cassell 1890: 142. September 20–21: Logically, this is the only possibility. Gilbert could not have gone from London via Paris to Athens in two days, so September 27–28 are out. So, too, are September 13–14, because he could not have reached London from Barnwell in seven days; that also fixes the date of his departure from Barnwell as September 6. Seven steamships: *Philadelphia Inquirer*, 05 September 1890, *Wall Street Journal*, 08 September 1890, *Brooklyn Daily Eagle*, 09 September 1890, *London Daily News*, 19 September 1890, 20 September 1890 and 22 September 1890. Four of the five Liverpool-bound ships (*Nevada*, *City of Chicago*, *Gallia*, *Germanic*, *Etruria*) made first landfall at Queenstown (today Cobh) in Ireland; *Etruria* skipped Queenstown because of a strong gale.

51. On *Nevada* and the other ships see Frye 1896, Gould 1891, Smith 1947. *Etruria*: Cunard 1886: 21–24, Fox 2003: 291–295; *Etruria* sailed with just 134 of 550 first-class and 68 of 160 second-class berths occupied (*Leeds Mercury*, 15 September 1890). Forced to travel: Douglass 1892: 290–291, 318–319. Friend to black travelers: *Cleveland Plaindealer*, 30 October 1891, Walters 1917: 57–58. "On a Cunarder": Green 1929: 333; similarly Matthews 1890: 293–294. Fellow passengers: *New York Times*, 11 September 1890, gives partial passenger lists for *City of Chicago*, *Gallia*, and *Germania*. "Your average Southerner": *New York Age*, 06 September 1890.

52. "To a colored person": Chicago *Inter Ocean*, 09 April 1894. "I immediately forgot": Green 1929: 224. Liverpool to London: Cassell 1890: xiv–xv, 36–40, Appleton 1891: I.129–132. Walker 1892: 138 reports reaching Liverpool from London in less than five hours.

53. Quickest and cheapest: ASCSA 1889: 49. The sights: Cassell 1890: 136–145, Appleton 1891: I.139–141. Sunday, September 21: *Pall Mall Gazette*, 20 September 1890. C. H. Spurgeon: Kruppa 1982: 226–228, Larsen 2011: 247–276. Pastor's College: Magee 1873: 97–98. High on the list: Matthews 1890: 288–289, Walker 1892: 14–15. Frederick Douglass: Douglass Diary, 05 June 1887; Douglass to Spurgeon, 06 July 1887 (Spurgeon 1900: 176).

54. Four days: Baedeker 1889: xi (99 hours), Joanne 1890: 9–12. To Paris: Cassell 1890: 159–160, Appleton 1891: I.262–263. Rail route: Reeve 1891: 6. Midnight steamer: Sandys 1887: 145, Baedeker 1889: xxb, 3–7, Joanne 1890: xix. Travelers also went from Paris to Trieste, then via Corfu to Patras, but this route was about twenty hours longer than the route via Patras and thus seems less likely; in addition, the Trieste steamer went on to Piraeus, the port of Athens, leaving little reason for a traveler from Trieste to disembark at Patras. Annie Peck took the Trieste route in 1885 and did not recommend it (Peck 1893: 493). Virgil: Classically educated travelers often made this connection, e.g., Matthiesen et al. 1993: IV.173 (George Gissing, 20 December 1889), Reeve 1891: 14–15. Corfu: Baedeker 1889: 5–7, *Springfield Republican*, 12 April 1890.

55. "Seat of the nomarch": Baedeker 1889: 30; a typesetter for the *Georgia Baptist* or *New York Age*, unfamiliar with the Greek vocabulary, turned "nomarch" into "monarch" in the newspaper text. Patras: *Morning Journal and Courier* (New Haven, CT), 16 October 1889, *Evening Star* (Washington, DC), 19 April 1890; on US Orientalism, see Schueller 1998. Cigars: Baedeker 1889: xxviii, Joanne 1890: xxxiii.

56. Atrocious: Reeve 1891: 18–20. Hôtel de Patras: Baedeker 1889: 29, Joanne 1890: 213, Reeve 1891: 386–387; *Morning Journal and Courier*, 06 May 1892, praises the hotel's breakfast.

57. Train east: Baedeker 1889: 31, 143–145, Joanne 1890: 14–16, 27–31. Midday: Trains left Patras daily at 7:40 and 11:40 AM, arriving in Athens at 4:25 and 7:00 PM (Joanne 1890: xxxi). Gilbert mentions traveling all day and arriving at Athens around sunset, which in the last days of September occurs between 7:10 and 7:15 PM. He either took the 7:40 AM train and stopped or was delayed en route, or took the 11:40 AM and arrived on time. That he had time for a morning meal in Patras may suggest the latter. Just opened: *Railway Review*, 25 May 1889.

58. Patras to Corinth: Baedeker 1889: 31–32, 233–236, Joanne 1890: 14–16. Natural beauty: For contemporary travelers' accounts, see *Aberdeen Daily News* (SD), 16 November 1889, *Springfield Republican*, 12 April 1890, *Evening Star* (DC), 19 April 1890, *Baltimore Sun*, 27 May 1890, Doane

1896: 4, Mattheisen et al. 1993: IV.158, Reeve 1891: 384–385, Sachtleben Diary 1891: 2–3, Talmage 1895: 34, Walker 1892: 124–126.

59. Olive trees: Only a few grew in Georgia in the 1880s (*Macon Telegraph*, 23 July 1887, Krewer 2016). "Stamping energetically": Hubbell 1890: 171–172; see also *Weekly Graphic* (Kirksville, MO), 02 January 1891 (October 1890 traveler).

60. Currants: Amandry 1992: 112, Campbell 2004, Gallant 2015: 234–235, 255–259, Petmezas 2000. Political players: Amandry 1992: 95–96, Scott 2014: 264–267. Spindles: Jones and Dutcher 1890: 420, Manatt 1895: 141–142; Augusta's Sibley Mill alone had some 40,000 in 1890, compared to 37,000 in all of Greece in 1893.

61. Broadened: Joanne 1890: 14–15, Baedeker 1889: 233–234. Corinth: Baedeker 1889: 228–230. Time to visit: Joanne 1890: xxxi shows a three-hour window between trains in which Gilbert could have disembarked at New Corinth for a rapid visit to ancient Corinth, then returned to catch the last train for Athens. American traveler T. B. Willson reports doing just that in mid-October 1890 (*Muskegon Daily Chronicle*, 08 November 1890).

62. Corinth canal: Baedeker 1889: 232, *The Guardian*, 12 December 1890, Matthiesen et al. 1993: IV.158 (George Gissing, 17 December 1889), *The Nation*, 02 July 1891 (Horace White, 02 June 1891), Meriwether 1892: 318–319, Palmer 1896: 48.

63. Saronic Gulf to Aegalion: *Springfield Republican*, 12 April 1890, *Baltimore Sun*, 27 May 1890, Pickard MS: 1–4, Meriwether 1892: 313. Cliffside: Tricha 2001: 89.

64. Gilbert is not embellishing. Jabez Brooks, in a letter Gilbert could not have seen (*Ariel*, 21 April 1890), describes his own first view of Athens from the train in strikingly similar terms.

Chapter 4

1. First spouse: ASCSA 1891: 10. Harris and Potter: ASCSA 1891: 10, 34; Charles Waldstein calls Pickard's family "several women" (ASCSA 1891: 20). "Keep my letters": Caroline Gerrish to Harriet Kimball, undated fragment ca. 08 November 1890; Gerrish mentions a recent St. Michael's Day, celebrated on November 8 (Gregorian) in Greece (Panhellenic Calendar 1890: 15).

2. Herbert de Cou and John E. Dinsmore, listed in ASCSA 309/1 Memo Book: 62–64, Copy Book: 98–99, did not show up; nor did the "two young ladies" from Smith and the Harvard Annex.

3. Carleton Lewis Brownson (1866–1948): Barber 1899, Hill 1909: 98–99; Yale University Obituary Record 1950: 14. Illness: *Yale Daily News*, 27 February 1884, 25 March 1884. "Enthusiastic and docile": Seymour to Waldstein, 05 February 1892, IOC 205928. Traveled: personal communication, Dr. William

Brownson, Jr., 2016; *Yale Daily News*, 14 October 1889. Yale students: *Yale Daily News*, 21 January 1891, Seymour 1902: 35–36, 57–69. Left the United States: Brownson applied for his passport (M1372-353-0474) on 13 June 1890; it was sent to New Canaan the next day. He may have attended Yale's class day exercises in late June, where he was awarded the Soldiers' Memorial Fellowship for his travel (*Yale Daily News*, 27 June 1890). A blur: Brownson 1927, so vivid in its recollections of other aspects of Athens in 1890–1891, says nothing of his journey to Greece.

4. Andrew Fossum (1860–1943): Biographical File, St. Olaf College Archives; Andrew Fossum Papers, Luther College Archives, LCA/RG15; Biographical File, Concordia College Archives. Luther College: Norlie et al. 1922. Johns Hopkins: *College Chips* (Decorah, IA), 26 January 1884, NAHA P0541/1/1; other materials are in the file of his son Paul R. Fossum (JHU Special Collections 17/3). Half-dozen: Norlie 1925: 292–293.

5. Drisler School: *New York Times*, 15 October 1887. Drisler and Merriam: NAHA P0541/1/1, P0541/1/5; AIA 3/11/67. Together: ASCSA 309/1 Memo Book: 55–56 (24 June 1889). Consul: Allison to Fossum, 01 April 1889, NAHA P0541/1/3. Hill School: John Meigs to Fossum, 23 August 1889, NAHA P0541/1/3. "The dream": Josephine Chester to Fossum, 16 December 1890, NAHA P0541/1/5.

6. Berlin: NARA M1834-33-0782 (passport application dated 12 July 1890), NAHA P0541/1/1 (passport). Dresden: Ernest Sihler to Fossum, 16 November 1890 (NAHA P0541/1/5); during the summer, St. Olaf College unsuccessfully tried to contact him about a job offer (Bjork 1949). Around 1937: Fossum's account is undated except for "December 7, 1937" written at the top of a page about halfway through (Fossum Journal: 23). Early days: Fossum Journal: 1–6. Fossum calls the caretaker "Kostis"; his full name appears in ASCSA 1892: 33.

7. "Bummed around": Fossum Journal: 6. Research institution: Geiger 2015: 324–331. Fluent Greek: Pickard MS: 31.

8. John Pickard (1858–1937): Brown et al. 1909: 51, Moore 1918: 252, 265–266, Dartmouth College 1940: 248, Dartmouth College Biographical File, University of Missouri Faculty File. Public school: *New England Journal of Education*, 20 February 1875. Amos Hadley: *Independent Statesman* (Concord), 01 July 1880, Dartmouth 1940: 151. Sophomore: Dartmouth College Catalogue 1880–1881: 14.

9. Brothers: Maxwell 1916: 140 (Henry Pickard), Dartmouth College 1940: 866 (Daniel Pickard); J. H. Wright: Perrin 1909, Reinhold 1994; William Sanders Scarborough met Wright at Dartmouth in 1884 and the two became good friends (Ronnick 2005a: 82–83). Lucy Wright Mitchell: https://www.brown.edu/Research/Breaking_Ground/results.php?d=1&first=Lucy%20Wright&last=Mitchell, accessed 14 September 2020. Contribute: Lord 1947: 7, 10, 12. New professor: Lord 1913: 430–431, 441.

10. Vermont: *Vermont Tribune* (Ludlow), 20 July 1883. Portsmouth: *Vermont Watchman and State Journal* (Montpelier), 05 August 1885; *The Dartmouth* (Hanover, NH), 18 September 1885, New Hampshire Public Schools 1886: 121, 244–245, Sammons and Cunningham 2004: 200. English literature: *Dartmouth Literary Monthly* 2.6, March 1888: 291; New Hampshire Public Schools 1886: 288 and 1889: 337–338; *New Hampshire Patriot and State Gazette*, 01 November 1888. Became active: *Boston Daily Advertiser*, 25 March 1887, *Providence Journal*, 13 July 1888, *Boston Journal*, 22 January 1889 and 06 February 1889. Close ties: *Burlington Free Press*, 13 June 1889. Master's degree: Dartmouth College 1940: viii.

11. David Kimball: [no author] 1887: 51, Morrison and Sharples 1897: 685–686. George Gerrish: *Boston Journal*, 03 September 1866, Morrison and Sharples 1897: 974. Moved in: US Census, Portsmouth, NH, 30 July 1870: 54; US Census 1880, Portsmouth, NH, 10 June 1880: 23. Harriet Kimball: Clarke 1902: 93–94, Lyons 2006; Kimball was friends with poet John Greenleaf Whittier. John and Jeanie: A letter describing the sudden 1887 death of Jeanie's brother Arthur (Portsmouth MS121/2/9) does not mention Pickard, suggesting he and Jeanie had not yet met. "Brilliant": *Boston Post*, 16 July 1889, *Boston Globe*, 16 July 1889. Two years: *New Hampshire Patriot and State Gazette* (Concord), 06 June 1889, *Boston Journal*, 13 June 1889, *Dartmouth Literary Monthly,* September 1889: 39.

12. Unclear: Pickard does not appear in ASCSA records, nor does Dartmouth show up as a potential contributor of students; news reports of Pickard's departure do not mention Greece. Leipzig: John Pickard to Edith Harris, 03 November 1889, Jeanie Pickard to Edith Harris, 04 February 1890, Werner 2013b: 137; on Americans at Leipzig, see Werner 2013a. Overbeck: Miller 1896, Cain 2014. Walter Miller: Lord 1947: 41–44, Seelinger 1994. Carl Buck: Lane 1955, Werner 2013b: 26. Two other Americans at Leipzig, John Roe and William Hammond, visited the School in summer 1889 (ASCSA 1890: 33, Werner 2013b: 76, 147). The news: ASCSA 309/1 Memo Book: 61, Copy Book: 90 (15 November 1889 vote to offer Richardson the directorship), *Boston Weekly Globe*, 15 March 1890 (March 7 public announcement at Dartmouth).

13. Berlin: Jeanie Pickard to Edith Harris, 16 April 1890, University of Berlin 1890: 105. Carl Buck went to Berlin at the same time (University of Berlin 1890: 145). Curtius: Chambers 1990, Baltrusch 2014. Richardson in Berlin: *Boston Weekly Globe*, 15 March 1890, *The Independent*, 15 May 1890, Richardson 1890a, Richardson 1891a. Greek vases: Caroline Gerrish to Harriet Kimball, 16 September 1890. Got advice: Merriam to Fossum, 03 November 1890 and 20 April 1891, NAHA P0541/1/7.

14. Arrived in Berlin: Edith Harris to Mary Harris, 15 June 1890, Caroline Gerrish to Harriet Kimball, 22 June 1890. Emma Potter: *Boston Post*, 16 July 1889, Jeanie Pickard to Edith Harris, 16 April 1890, [no author] 1901: 882–884.

F. D. Kalopothakes: University of Berlin 1890: 78, Edith Harris to Robert Harris, 07 July 1890, Caroline Gerrish to Harriet Kimball, 26 September 1890, Edith Harris to Lucy Harris, 28 September 1890. It may have been Frank who advised Caroline and Edith to buy winter clothes in Berlin (Caroline Gerrish to Mary Harris, 02 July 1890).

15. Dresden to Athens: Caroline Gerrish to Harriet Kimball, 21 July 1890, 21 August 1890, 16 September 1890, Edith Harris to Lucy Harris, 28 September 1890, Edith Harris to Richard Harris, 28 September 1890. "Mecca": Caroline Gerrish to Harriet Kimball, 26 September 1890.

16. Rufus Richardson (1845–1914): *The Independent* 23 March 1914, Bates 1914: 384, Wheeler 1914: 26, *Obituary Record* 1915: 599–600, Dartmouth College Biographical File. On his parents, see *Massachusetts Ploughman and New England Journal of Agriculture*, 22 February 1851, Vinton 1876: 145, Cutter 1908: 1735. Enlisted: Richardson 1889b. Respected him: *New Haven Register* 09 June 1882. "Gifted": *Dartmouth Alumni Magazine*, April 1914: 220. Aeschines: Richardson 1889a. Richardson also wrote about the Civil War; his study of Andersonville prison (Richardson 1880) is still cited today.

17. Bowen family: Bowen 1930. *Independent*: Mott 1938: 367–379, Filler 1954, Voskuil 1989: 73–74; Caroline Gerrish to Harriett Kimball, 09 February 1891 notes Richardson's articles were "accepted and published quickly" thanks to his father-in-law.

18. Corfu: Richardson 1890b. Reached Athens: Richardson to Waldstein, 11 October 1890, IOC 205926 writes "I have now been here twelve days," meaning September 29 or 30, depending whether or not Richardson counted the day he wrote. The regular Saturday night steamer from Corfu (Baedeker 1889: xxb, Joanne 1890: xix–xxiii) could have brought the Richardsons to Corinth by the morning of September 29, with a train connection to Athens by evening. Governess: Richardson to Waldstein, 05 November 1890, IOC 205926. Ethel Moore: *Brooklyn Daily Eagle*, 04 January 1890, Bowen 1930. Caroline Gerrish and Edith Harris refer to her as Mrs. Richardson's "friend Miss Moore."

19. "Four students": Richardson to Waldstein, 11 October 1890, IOC 205926.

20. Construction: *Springfield Republican*, 30 April 1890. Italians: William Ware to Waldstein, 08 October 1890, IOC 209526.

21. "Unrivalled": ASCSA 1887: 34; cf. Lord 1947: 26–27. Water: ASCSA 1890: 11. "Awful": Edith Harris to Mary Harris, 29 December 1890. "Bare hillside": ASCSA 309/1 Copy Book: 12 (21 November 1890).

22. Showcase: ASCSA 1887: 34–37, Lord 1947: 25–31. Balcony: Richardson to Waldstein, 26 May 1891, IOC 205927. Greek staff: Richardson to Waldstein, 20 August 1890, 15 October 1890, 23 November 1890, IOC 205926; Richardson to Waldstein, 26 May 1891, IOC 205927 (Katrina); Waldstein 1892: 420 (Nikolaki). ASCSA 309/1 (W. C. Poland accounts 1892: 9) mentions

Stamatina, perhaps Costi's wife, who sometimes worked at the School. Correspondence: ASCSA 309/1 Copy Book: 60 (25 March 1890); Seymour to Norton, 02 August 1890, Ware to Norton, 24 August 1890, both AIA 3/7, 3/8; Richardson to Waldstein, 20 August 1890, 15 October 1890, both IOC 205926, Richardson to Waldstein, 05 November 1890, 23 November 1890, both IOC 205927; Waldstein Diary, 17 December 1890.

23. Next door: BSA 1891: 4–5.

24. "Ample sleeping": Richardson to Waldstein, 15 October 1890, IOC 205926. "Prof. Merriam": Fossum Journal: 6.

25. "Met prejudice": Walker 1901: 476–477, reprinted verbatim by Goddard and MacDonell ca. 1919: 139–140; Fridy ca. 1925: 1–2 invents additional detail.

26. "Enjoys his position": *Christian Index*, 06 December 1890. "Colored young man": *The Independent*, 08 January 1891, reprinted verbatim in the influential Minneapolis-based African American paper *The Appeal*, 24 January 1891.

27. Personal reminiscences: Brownson Diary (1927), Fossum Journal (ca. 1937). All-white: JBHE Foundation 1999. Gildersleeve's views: Lupher and Vandiver 2011. "Three more": Fossum Journal: 6.

28. "Four regular students": Richardson 1891b: 183–184. Richardson and others list the students alphabetically in ASCSA 1891: 10, 19, 31. Rejected: Drisler 1863.

29. "White or black": Ronnick 2005a: 266–267. Committee: APA Proceedings 1885: xxx. Dartmouth: APA Proceedings 1884: xiv, xliii–xliv; Ronnick 2005a: 82–83.

30. "Boston ladies": Walker 1901: 477. Baptist congregation: *Providence Journal*, 28 September 1890, *Fort Wayne* (IN) *Sentinel*, 25 October 1890, Shaw 1937: 120–133, Davis 2015.

31. View: Baedeker 1889: 101–102, Joanne 1890: 152–153, Peck 1893: 495–497.

32. Glowed: George Gissing, 29 November 1889 (Matthiesen et al. 1993: IV.147), Bourchier 1890: 880, Holyoke 1893: 550. Piraeus: McDowall 1891, George Gissing, 14 December 1889 (Matthiesen et al. 1993: IV.164).

33. Dizzying changes: Travlos 1972, Bastéa 2000: 181–204. Population: Joanne 1891: xxxvi–xxxvii. Immigrants: *The Adelbert* (Cleveland), May 1890 (Bernadotte Perrin letter, 29 March 1890). For descriptions of Athens in 1890–1891, see *Springfield Republican*, 12 April 1890, 22 April 1890, 30 April 1890; *Ariel* (Minneapolis), 16 April 1890; *Washington Observer* (PA), 12 June 1890, Hubbell 1890, Shaw 1890, Groome 1891, Reeve 1891, Davis 1893. Marble: *Ariel* (Minneapolis), 10 January 1891. "Verdure": Caroline Gerrish to Harriet Kimball, 26 September 1890, Edith Harris to Robert Harris, 02 November 1890, Hubbell 1890: 173, Peck 1893: 483, Miller 1894: 304. "Thoroughly modern": Shaw-Lefevre 1891: 293–294. "Can this be Athens?": Houghton 1890: 840. "In every way": Baedeker 1889: xxii.

34. Tourism: Dritsas 2006, Dritsas 2009. Thirty million: Ikkos and Koutsos 2019. Just 300: Manatt to State Department, 27 November 1889, NARA T362, Reel

5. "Least betoured": Bickford-Smith 1893: 311, Chatziioanou 2009. "If an American": *Daily Inter Ocean*, 31 August 1890; also Manatt to Jesse Macy, 02 April 1890, Iowa Ms 17/1/24.

35. "Nomad Americans": *The Age* (New York), 12 October 1889. "Do not see": Walker 1892: 46; Atlanta minister Henry Hugh Proctor, visiting Greece in 1911, reported "my color was an attraction, instead of a detraction" (Proctor 1925: 145–146). Reputation: *Daily Inter Ocean*, 31 August 1890. Expatriates: *The Age*, 08 November 1890, records a Charles Garnet of New York moving to Athens to manage a hotel there. Smallwood: Drew 2010, Drew 2011; on the timing of his visit, see *Boston Globe*, 16 November 1890 (tour in 1889), Detroit *Plaindealer*, 04 November 1892 (in Athens "last spring"). "Native black Greek": *Plaindealer*, 04 November 1892; black soldiers served in the Greek army during the 1830s (Stephens 1839: 15), and, in 1890, the island of Crete, which was not yet part of the Greek state, had a significant African population (Ferguson 2010).

36. Meals: ASCSA 1889: 42–44, 53, ASCSA 309/1 Memo Book: 60 (25 March 1890); Seymour to Waldstein, 25 March 1890, IOC 205926. Scarcely believe: ASCSA 309/1 Memo Book: 64 ("The Gardners keep a boarding house!"). Lunches and dinners: Baedeker 1889: xxiv–xxvi, 33, Joanne 1890: xxxv–xxxvi. A regular: NAHA P0541/1/6 preserves one of Fossum's monthly food bills at the Grand Hotel (Baedeker 1889: 33). "Turkish coffee": Caroline Gerrish to Harriet Kimball, 11 October 1890. Little shops: Peck 1893: 500–501. "A preparation": Caroline Gerrish to Harriet Kimball, 21 December 1890; Gerrish also gushes "And the honey . . . oh, the honey!"

37. Wiley Lane: *New York Freeman*, 14 March 1885. Jabez Brooks: *Ariel*, 06 December 1890.

38. *Katharévousa* and *demotikí*: Horrocks 2014. Reading and speaking: *Brooklyn Daily Eagle*, 02 September 1883, Matthiesen et al. eds. 1993: IV.148–149, *Daily Nebraska State Journal*, 10 March 1890, *The Adelbert* (Cleveland), May 1890, *Springfield Republican*, 31 May 1890, Holyoke 1893: 515, Peck 1893: 503–505, Miller 1894: 304, Buckley 1895: 30, Barrows 1898: 230–231. Pronunciation: *The Adelbert* (Cleveland), May 1890 (B. Perrin letter dated 29 March 1890), *Ariel* (Minneapolis, MN), 10 January 1891, *Boston Daily Advertiser*, 23 April 1891. Biblical Greek: E.g., *Providence Journal*, 13 February 1886, *Ariel* (Minneapolis, MN), 10 December 1890. "If John C. Calhoun": [no author] 1902: 459–460.

39. M. D. Kalopothakes (1825–1911): Caroline Gerrish to Harriet Kimball, 16 November 1890, "Letter from Mr. John Pickard relating to Rev. M. D. Kalopothakes (Copy)" in Portsmouth MS078, Brooks 1911, Moore 1914, Shaw 1937: 135–156, Tsevas 2009, Tsevas 2018. Jonas King: Repousis 2009, Repousis 2013: 71–91. "To the cause": Brooks 1911: 816. To the United States: *Alexandria Gazette* (VA), 01 May 1857, *Vermont Chronicle*, 21 July 1857.

40. Martha Blackler (1830/31–1871): *New York Observer*, 01 February 1872, Leveson Gower 1900: 155–156; Martha had three other children who died in infancy. Margaret Kyle (1831–1904): *St. Johnsbury Caledonian* (VT), 30 April 1875, *Staunton Spectator* (VA), 13 March 1877, Byington 1890: 41, 59. Maria Kalopothakes: Tsevas 2012.

41. St. Paul: *Presbyterian of the South*, 20 September 1911. "Luther of Greece": Moore 1914: 21. Michael Anagnos: *Boston Globe*, 23 June 1889. "Gospel preached": Wharton 1892: 46. "This house": C. Gerrish to H. Kimball, 11 October 1890 (with a long discussion of Anagnos, Keller, and Sullivan).

42. Close links: Goodwin 1884: 4, ASCSA 1889: 36, Lord 1947: 35, 277, 284; Αστήρ της Ανατολής, 21 May 1883, 09 July 1883, 17 November 1884, 09 March 1885, 06 April 1885. *The Star of the East*, still published today, is the oldest periodical in Greece, although lack of funds forced Kalopothakes to suspend publication from 1885 to 1893. Daphne: ASCSA 1893: 24, 1895: 6, 1896: 6.

43. "A colored man": C. Gerrish to H. Kimball, 19 October 1890. Confined: Caroline Gerrish to Harriet Kimball, 11 October 1890, 02 November 1890, Caroline Gerrish to Sarah Kittredge, 24 November 1890.

44. Touch of home: *The Hesperian* (Omaha, NE), 15 March 1890, *Washington Observer* (PA), 12 June 1890, *Christian Advocate*, 16 October 1890, Holyoke 1893: 512. Hymns: E. Harris to L. Harris, 12 October 1890, Barrows 1898: 227. Bouey: see Chapter 2. Lambuth: *Christian Index*, 14 March 1891. Mission Society: *Christian Index*, 11 April 1891.

45. Irving James or James Irving Manatt (1845–1915): Allinson 1915. Although Manatt's obituary and tombstone name him James Irving, he appears as Irving James in official documents, news reports, and official publications until about 1895. "Unusual acquaintance": Manatt to Jesse Macy, 16 December 1888, Iowa Ms 17/1/24. Snowden: *Philadelphia Inquirer*, 02 July 1889, *Boston Post*, 22 July 1889. Consulship: Manatt dispatch, 01 October 1889, NARA T362, Reel 5.

46. Ranked so low: Repousis 2013: 119, 121. Mansion: Sachtleben Diary, 08 January 1891. Hotel room: Snowden to Secretary of State, 25 October 1889 and 05 November 1889, NARA T159, Reel 10.

47. Tourists: *The News* (Newport, PA), 07 February 1890, *Washington Observer* (PA), 12 June 1890, *Omaha Daily Bee*, 20 April 1891. Mining and metallurgy: Manatt 1891c. Essays: E.g., Manatt 1890a, 1890b, 1891d, and numerous items in the *Omaha Daily Bee*. Booster: *Springfield Republican*, 30 April 1890, 31 May 1890, Allinson 1915: 371; see also ASCSA 1890: 34. "Just the place": C. Gerrish to H. Kimball, 08 March 1891.

48. Joined by his wife: Manatt to Macy, 05 September 1890, Iowa Ms 17/1/24; C. Gerrish to H. Kimball, 08 March 1891, Edith Harris to Mary Harris, 22 March 1891. In letters, Manatt calls his youngest child Demeter; Harris

reports she was nicknamed "Snip," as she had not yet been formally named. "Consular location": Manatt to State, 01 September 1890, NARA T362, Reel 5, no. 32. Managed affairs: Manatt to State, 03 June 1891, NARA T362, Reel 5, no. 42. Turned heads: Sachtleben Diary, 05 February 1891; C. Gerrish to H. Kimball, 08 March 1891. "Artemis": Manatt to Macy, 05 September 1890, Iowa Ms 17/1/24, Manatt 1893: 806. Wrote about: *Omaha Daily Bee*, 21 July 1892, 06 November 1892, 25 December 1892.

49. King George: Reeve 1890: 377, Deschamps 1892: 57–65, Gallant 2015: 146–147. "Without a scandal": Manatt to Macy, 02 April 1890, Iowa Ms 17/1/24. Popular and visible: C. Gerrish to H. Kimball, 11 October 1890, Edith Harris to Mary Harris, 11 November 1890. Gave the American School: Lord 1947: 21–27. American visitors: E.g., *Augusta Chronicle*, 05 September 1889, *Christian Advocate*, 16 October 1890, Palmer 1896: 80–81. "Rustic Americans": *Pittsburg [sic] Dispatch*, 01 September 1889.

50. Tricoupis and Deliyannis: Gallant 2015: 144–149, 171–184, Repousis 2013: 121–127.

51. Development: Tricha 2001. Debt and taxes: Gallant 2015: 182–183; see also Manatt to Macy, 02 April 1890, Iowa Ms 17/1/24, Lynch 1893: 463. Tobacco shops: Meriwether 1892: 313. "People are groaning": Caroline Gerrish to Harriet Kimball, 27 October 1890.

52. Election: Caroline Gerrish to Harriet Kimball, 27 October 1890, Shaw-Lefevre 1891: 297, Deschamps 1892: 82–94. Into the night: *Pall Mall Gazette*, 17 November 1890. "Liveliness": Manatt to Macy, 12 December 1890, Iowa Ms 17/1/24.

Chapter 5

1. "At the American School": *The Brunonian*, 11 October 1890; this notice probably derives from a letter Gilbert sent to Brown. Studying abroad: *Providence Journal*, 29 October 1890. W. C. Poland: Brown University Catalogue 1890–1891: 34, 40; Brown University Annual Report 1891: 34–35. Paine Institute 1890–1891: 5 proudly notes Gilbert is "in Athens, Greece prosecuting his studies."

2. Frederic Allen: Allen to George Peck, 05 July 1885, Peck Collection 2/8/5; W. J. Stillman to C. E. Norton, 17 July 1887, AIA 3/2; ASCSA 1887: 8–11, Lord 1947: 43. "Only supplementary": ASCSA 1887: 30. Early students: Ten of the School's first enrolled forty-two students, Andrew Fossum among them, came to Athens with PhDs (list in Seymour 1902: 57–69).

3. "Quickening influences": White to Scarborough, 08 February 1886, Scarborough Papers 8/1881–1889. "This contact": Seymour 1888b: 374.

4. Merriam: ASCSA 1889a: 28–30, 40–43, 56–61. Dörpfeld: Vogeikoff-Brogan 2019.

5. "No stone unturned": Richardson 1891b: 182, 184.

6. Sunny and pleasant: Edith Harris to Robert Harris, 02 November 1890. Out early: Richardson to Waldstein, 11 October 1890, IOC 205926. Pausanias: Beard 2000, Beard 2001, Pretzler 2007. Reading aloud: ASCSA 309/1, Folder 1: 81–83 (Frank Tarbell, 25 October 1888). Pausaniacs: D. S. MacColl quoted in Beard 2000: 96; Ribeyrol 2017: 212–215. Harrison and Verrall 1890: 397 write "the Pausaniac mind"; was MacColl riffing on that phrase? MacColl mentions "Schuchardt (is it?)" but he may have been thinking of Schubart's Greek text. Bindings: ASCSA 1891: 32. The ASCSA library holds both the three-volume first edition of Pausanias (Schubart and Walz 1838–1839) and a subsequent two-volume edition (Schubart 1881–1883); these may well be the very volumes Gilbert and his fellows carried.

7. Refuting: Gurlitt 1890, Reinach 1890: 226. Frazer: Ackerman 1987: 111–113, Henderson 2001: 212–215. *Mythology and Monuments*: Arlen 1990: 19–79, Beard 2000, Beard 2001, Robinson 2002: 100–103, Gloyn 2016: 154–157. Reviewers: List in Arlen 1990: 33. "Incomparably": Gardner 1890: 125. Both sides: E.g., *The Guardian*, 22 April 1890, *New York Times*, 25 May 1890. Famous: Beard 2001: 237.

8. Reading list: ASCSA 1890: 47; by 1893 students were told to bring copies of the book with them to Athens (ASCSA 1893: 60). "Where's Jane?": Edith Harris to Robert Harris, 02 November 1890; also Caroline Gerrish to Harriet Kimball, 08 March 1891. Edith also mentions reading Harrison 1885. Proofs: Harrison and Verrall 1890: xiv, 21, 207; cf. Gardner 1890: 126.

9. Still buried: Camp 2001 provides an overview of the archaeology of Athens. Northwest entry: Harrison and Verrall 1890: 6–13, Joanne 1890: 80–87; Caroline Gerrish to Harriet Kimball, 02 November 1890. Fenced: Gardner 1890: 211. Resumed work: Παλιγγενεσία (Athens), 09/21 August 1890, Halbherr 1891: 12–13, Reinach 1892: 81–82. "An old Greek skull": *Springfield Republican*, 27 August 1890; *Daily Chronicle* (Muskegon, MI), 08 November 1890 describes a visit to the site with Manatt in October 1890.

10. Theseum or Hephaesteum: Baedeker 1889: 81–82, Joanne 1890: 87–90. "Solemn and grand": Douglass Diary, 19 March 1887; Blight 2018: 673–674. Learned otherwise: Harrison and Verrall 1890: 112–123; Caroline Gerrish to Harriet Kimball, 08 March 1891.

11. Medical College: Sanborn 1884: Map 14, Savitt and Floyd 1996, Barnes 1997. Gilbert probably also knew about the macabre underside of the Medical College; his grade school classmates included Charlie Harris (Walker 1998: 224), whose father Grandison Harris robbed graves to supply the College with cadavers (Sharpe 1997).

12. Agora excavations: Mauzy 2006. Vrysaki: Dumont 2020: 9–10. Competing theories: Murray 1884: 257, Joanne 1890: 90–94. Lay south: Harrison and Verrall 1890: 5 (plan), 16–17, 39–43; for other conjectural plans see Hitzig and Blümner 1896. The Americans likely did not have access to Wachsmuth 1890, which appeared late in the year. Rail line: Gardner 1891: 386–387, Reinach 1891: 191, Tricha 2001: 82–83, 91.

13. "Giants" and Attalos: Harrison and Verrall 1890: 16–21; three photographs in Sachtleben UCLA 1841, all taken 28 January 1891, show the Stoa as Gilbert would have seen it. "Dragons": Dumont 2020: 29. A few years later, the Stoa of the Giants was restored to make it more attractive to visitors (Mallouchou-Tufano 1998: 65–66); today the remains are identified as a late Roman complex overlying the Odeion of Agrippa (Camp 2001: 217–218, 232).

14. Bazaar: *ΠΑΕ (1885)* 1886: 13–25. Stoa of Hadrian and Tower of Winds: Harrison and Verrall 1890: 195–203. Roman Agora: Halbherr 1891: 13–14, Dickenson 2015.

15. "Don't care much": Edith Harris to Robert Harris, 02 November 1890. "The boys": G. Aitchison letter in *The Builder* (London), 22 November 1890.

16. Every inch: Hurwit 1999: 299. Paint and gilding: G. Aitchison letter in *The Builder*, 22 November 1890.

17. Looked different: The March 1891 photographs by American traveler William Sachtleben (available online by searching "UCLA Collection 1841") show the Acropolis as Gilbert saw it. Balanos: Mallouchou-Tufano 1994: 76–82, Mallouchou-Tufano 1998: 69–75. Museum: Papalexandrou 2016. Little time: Richardson to Waldstein, 11 October 1890, IOC 205926.

18. "Not as well prepared": C. Gerrish to H. Kimball, 21 December 1890. Papers: See Chapter 6.

19. "One feature": ASCSA 1891: 31. "Fond of hikes": Fossum Journal: 6. Shoes: Fossum Journal: 8–9.

20. Salamis: Richardson 1891a: 184. "Invaluable": Richardson 1903: 111. Most likely they used the first English edition of Baedeker 1889, a close translation of the German second edition (Baedeker 1888); the 1883 original was mostly the work of the German Archaeological Institute's H. G. Lolling (Chambers 1993, Chambers 1996). Paper: Goodwin 1885.

21. Route: Curtius and Kaupert eds. 1881–1903, Baedeker 1889: 108–110; Joanne 1890: 160–162.

22. "Spent a day": Fossum Journal: 6. Rallying cry: Aesch. *Pers.* 402–405 (transl. Herbert Weir Smith, professor at the ASCSA in 1899–1900). Second trip: ASCSA 1891: 31.

23. Last week: Richardson to Waldstein, 27 October 1890, IOC 205926 was probably written just before the group left; Richardson to Waldstein, 05 November 1890, IOC 205927 was written several days after the trip. Summer's end: Edith Harris to Mary Harris, 24 October 1890, Caroline Gerrish to Harriet Kimball, 27 October 1890. Three-day: Richardson 1891a: 184, ASCSA 1891: 31. Northeast Attica: see Goette 2001 for the region today. Expensive and inconvenient: Baedeker 1889: 119–121, Meriwether 1892: 309; Frederick Douglass (Douglass Diary, 19 March 1887) was told he could "almost see" Marathon from Lycabettus. Bandits: Gallant 2015: 151–152. Two groups: ASCSA 1889a: 30, 41–42. Lawyer: Manatt to Macy, 05 September 1890, Iowa Ms 17/ 1/24, Manatt 1891d. Footsteps: ASCSA 1889a, Milchhöfer 1889, Frazer 1898.

24. Train: Baedeker 1889: 115–116, Joanne 1890: xxix, 169–170; Tricha 2001: 80 (photo of Kephissia station). Rural Attica: Groome 1891: 252, Meriwether 1892: 317. Kephissia to Icaria: ASCSA 1889a: 56–57, Nouchaki 1890: 54, Fossum Journal: 6–7, Frazer 1898: II.462. Fossum writes of "a visit to Marathon 26 miles by the road," which might suggest the group hiked all the way from the School, but Richardson most likely followed Merriam's directions to take the train (ASCSA 1889a: 56). Two hours: ASCSA 1889a: 56–60, Joanne 1890: 175–176.

25. Elections: *St. Louis Post-Dispatch*, 05 October 1890, *Pall Mall Gazette*, 28 October 1890, 11 November 1890, Tricha 2016: 467–469. Caroline Gerrish to Harriet Kimball, 27 October 1890, records election details and Pickard's polling station visit; part of her letter was later published (Gerrish 1891). Gerrish notes "Mr. K. and all good citizens regret [Tricoupis's] defeat." Voting procedures: Tricha 2016: 135–145; Pickard did not reference the parallels with fourth-century jury voting (*Ath. Pol.* 68–69) because in October 1890 that text was not yet published. Walkover and "clean sweep": Manatt to Macy, 12 December 1890, Iowa Ms17/1/24.

26. Delphi: Amandry 1992, Sheftel 2002, Repousis 2013: 122–124, Vogeikoff-Brogan 2014. Gloomy report: Richardson to Waldstein, 27 October 1890. "Shattered": Waldstein Diary, 29 October 1890. I barely scratch the surface of the Delphi saga; a mass of material awaits researchers in the AIA, ASCSA, IOC, State Department, and other archives.

27. "Little chance": Caroline Gerrish to Harriet Kimball, 02 November 1890. "If not for": Pickard Manuscript: 25.

28. Icaria: ASCSA 1889a: 47–80, Buck 1889a, 1889b, Frazer 1898: II.461–463, Biers and Boyd 1982, Scullion 2015, Wilson 2015. Although the deme's ancient name is Ikarion, in 1890 the Americans knew it as Icaria; the modern place name is Dionyso.

29. Poetic: ASCSA 1889a: 59–61. "Woodland beauty": *Springfield Republican*, 14 May 1890. Fires: *Pall Mall Gazette*, 23 August 1890, *New York Times*, 25 August 1890.

30. Rapedosa (Rapendosa) and Argaliki (Agrileiki): Buck 1889a: 160–161; I use the toponyms Gilbert would have employed. "The very spot": Brownson 1927: 35–36. "We followed": Fossum Journal: 6–7. "The mountains": *Don Juan*, Canto III; Richardson 1907: 119 (Position 31) shows the view.

31. Black Phalanx: Wilson 1882, Wilson 1887, Strauss 2005, Varon 2018. "Greatest historian": Franklin 1998: 236. "Two regiments": Williams 1883: II.310; cf. Williams 1888: 145–147.

32. Helped shape: *National Leader* (Alexandria, VA), 22 December 1888, Johnson 1890: 106, *Detroit Plaindealer*, 07 August 1891, *Indianapolis Freeman*, 29 August 1896, *Broad Ax* (Salt Lake City, UT), 09 July 1898. Freed slaves: Paus. 1.32.3,7.15.7; Hunt 2002: 42–52, Krentz 2010: 129–130, Rhodes 2013: 12–13.

33. "The wines": *Boston Daily Advertiser*, 30 January 1891.

34. *Sorós*: Baedeker 1889: 119–122, Joanne 1890: 174–179, *Springfield Republican*, 07 May 1890, Frazer 1898: II.433–434, van der Veer 1982, Fromherz 2011; Richardson 1901: 167 and Richardson 1907: 123 (Position 32) show photographs of the mound as Gilbert might have seen it. "The theory": Manatt 1891d. Excavated again: Staïs 1890: 129, Staïs et al. 1890: 66, Gardner 1891: 390; see also Fossum Journal: 7. Seemed to confirm: Fromherz 2011: 388–391 casts doubt on the identification. "Original shape": Halbherr 1891: 12. "Soros" wine: *Springfield Republican*, 07 May 1890.

35. Met Schliemann: Caroline Gerrish to Harriett Kimball, 02 January 1891. "Great blow": Richardson 1907: 123–125; also Richardson 1901: 171–172.

36. Estate: Fossum Journal: 7, Richardson 1907: 120, Brownson 1927: 36, Vanderpool 1970, Daskalakis 2015. Later American School groups also stayed at the estate (ΛSCSA 1892: 39), as did others with a letter of introduction (Joanne 1890: 182, Bickford-Smith 1893: 293–294).

37. "So you are Americans?": Manatt 1894a: 642. "Le nom brillant": Joanne 1890: 182; also Bickford-Smith 1893: 20–21. *Tropaion*: Vanderpool 1966.

38. "Sixty stades": Paus. 1.33.2–8. New finds: Εφημερίς, 09/21 September 1890, *Pall Mall Gazette*, 11 October 1890, Frothingham 1890c: 565–568, Gardner 1891: 391–392, Halbherr 1891: 14, Frazer 1898: II.453–458. "I suppose": Richardson to Waldstein, 05 November 1890, IOC 205927.

39. "It may sound": Richardson 1891a: 184. For the beach, see Goette 2001: 249.

40. Headed northwest: ASCSA 1891: 31 does not mention the Amphiareion, but Fossum Journal: 7 does. Steamer: BSA 1887: 12, ASCSA 1889a: 28–29. Exact route: For some possibilities, see Murray 1884: II.378, Milchhöfer 1887, 1888a, 1888b, 1889, Frazer 1898: II.465. Still slogging: In the last week of October 1890, the sun rose about 6:35 AM and set about 4:50 PM, giving the group about ten and a half hours of daylight. If the Americans left Beï in the predawn twilight, 6:00 AM or earlier (compare Pickard MS: 31), took three hours to cover the seven miles to Rhamnus, and spent two hours at Rhamnus, they would have about six daylight hours for the fifteen to twenty miles to Kalamos. Almost as fast: Pickard MS: 35; cf. Murray 1884: II.378 (six hours on horseback from Rhamnus to Kalamos).

41. Aleko Kiousis: Baedeker 1889: 176. Kalamos: Nouchaki 1890: 58. "On the floor": Caroline Gerrish to Lucy Kimball, 19 April 1891. "From Marathon": Fossum Journal: 7.

42. Amphiareion: Merriam 1888: 54–56, ASCSA 1889a: 28–29, Baedeker 1889: 176, Joanne 1891: 2–3, Frazer 1898 II.466–473, Goette 2001: 249–255. Theater: Fossum Journal: 7.

43. Markopolou and Aphidna: Fossum Journal: 7. Kapandriti: Baedeker 1889: 176, Nouchaki 1890: 58, Joanne 1891: 1. Main route: Fachard and Pirisino 2015. Aphidna: Finlay 1838, Milchhöfer 1889: 60, Frazer 1898 II.162–163, McCredie 1966: 81–83, Goette 2001: 145. The Markopoulo-Kapandriti-Aphidna route appears on the map of Finlay 1838, reprinted in

ASCSA 1889a; Richardson and the students may have had the ASCSA reprint of this map with them.

44. Excavations: Forsén 2010, Hielte 2018. Many years: Richardson never seems to have returned to Aphidna, and the School's Annual Reports up to 1924 do not mention the site. It is possible Gilbert and his fellows picked up some of the sherds from Aphidna now in the ASCSA Antiquities Collection (A-008).

45. Last stop: Fossum Journal: 7 writes Richardson "wanted Aphidna and Decelea." Mistakenly: Aeschylus was actually from the deme of Eleusis, although Dekeleia was in the same civic tribe (Hippothontis). Tatoï and Decelea: Murray 1884: II.382–383, Baedeker 1889: 115–117, Joanne 1890: 186, Frazer 1898: II.229, Goette 2001: 269–270. Bicycling: ASCSA 1895: 23, Richardson 1903: 50.

46. Last train: Joanne 1890: xxix. Sixty-five miles: Seventeen miles on day 1, twenty-three to twenty-eight miles on day 2, and twenty-five to thirty-four miles on day 3, for a range of sixty-five to seventy-nine miles; Murray 1884: I.92 gives an itinerary for a very similar three-day trip—on horseback!

47. Central Greece: Lee (forthcoming a).

48. Baby: John and Ola's son John Jr. was born 30 April 1891; see Appendix 1.

49. Splashed: Caroline Gerrish to Harriett Kimball, 16 November 1890. Cold and wet: Caroline Gerrish to Harriet Kimball, 16 November 1890, Edith Harris to Robert Harris, 23 November 1890, Edith Harris to Lucy Harris, 28 November 1890. Phyle: Fossum Journal: 16. Winter quarters: Richardson 1891b: 184, Fossum Journal: 17. Class sessions: ASCSA 1891: 32–33.

50. Celebration: Caroline Gerrish to Sarah Kittredge, 24 November 1890; on Thanksgiving in this period, see Siskind 1992, Pleck 1999, and on African American celebrations Du Bois 1899: 196. "The dinner": Edith Harris to Robert Harris, 28 November 1890; also Edith Harris to Lucy Harris, 28 November 1890.

51. "Less than a mulatto": Caroline Gerrish to Harriet Kimball, 21 December 1890. "Quite pleasant": Edith Harris to Lucy Harris, 28 November 1890.

52. "Georgian in Greece": see Chapter 4.

53. To join him: Among those readers was C. T. Walker, who would briefly visit Athens in April 1891 (Walker 1892: 121–124).

54. "The ages": Gilbert's phrasing echoes Baedeker 1889: 55–77. "Sit with Shakespeare": Du Bois 1903: 109. Keenly interested: Colclough 1925: 28.

55. Christian past: A third-hand report (*Indianapolis Freeman*, 22 November 1890) of an earlier letter Gilbert sent home similarly notes "he has visited Corinth where the Apostle Paul labored. Stood on Mars Hill, where the Apostle preached." Most important: Harrison and Verrall 1890: 554–555, silent about the hill's Christian past, is an exception to the general trend. Generally accepted: Baedeker 1889: 54–55, Joanne 1890: 76–77. Late in 1891, German archaeologist Ernst Curtius would argue that Paul had not actually stood on the Areopagus hill but rather had been brought before the *archon basileus*

(King Archon), the Athenian magistrate who led the Areopagus council, at his office in the Royal Stoa. Curtius did not know where the Royal Stoa was (only in 1970 did the American School unearth its remains, almost beneath the tracks of the Athens-Piraeus electric railway), but his views gained wide circulation, stoking a debate that continues today. See also Curtius and Milchhöfer 1891: 262, Curtius 1893, Manatt 1891b, Findlay 1894/95, Gardner 1902: 504–505, Manatt 1902. "Not a few": Richardson 1901: 166.

56. "Patron saint": Callahan 2006: 30. Touchstone: Callahan 2006: 30–40, 115–116, Martin 1991: 216, Powery and Sadler 2016: 92–94, 140–142, Smith 2007, Smith 2017: 202–203.

57. "On Mars Hill": Dorr 1858: 137–138. Civil rights: Douglass 1892: 669. "Stood for the first time": Frederick Douglass Diary, 24 March 1887; the next page begins with his arrival in Naples on 28 March. "Intense gratification": Douglass 1892: 713. Lee forthcoming b examines the visits of Dorr and Douglass to Greece in more detail.

58. Helped ground: Colclough 1925: 29–33. "Footsteps of St. Paul": *Baltimore Sun*, 16 November 1907, *Alexandria Gazette* (VA), 16 November 1907.

59. Commonplace: E.g., Hurst 1887: 226, Hubbell 1890: 175–177, Whittle 1890: 237, Groome 1891: 239–241, Buckley 1895: 521–522, Doane 1896: 5, Lincoln 1894: 138–139, Palmer 1896: 59–60; Edith Harris to Robert Harris, 28 September 1890. Most famous: Hood 2017: 188, Reynolds 1980: 494–495. Talmage in Athens: *New York Times*, 23 November 1889, *New York Herald*, 24 November 1889, *Brooklyn Daily Eagle*, 29 December 1889, *Omaha World-Herald*, 29 December 1889; Manatt to State Department, 17 December 1889, NARA T362, Reel 5, Talmage 1890: 41–52, Talmage 1892: 555–559, Talmage 1895: 33–39. Klopsch: Curtis 2018: 115–117. Read about: *Augusta Chronicle*, 25 December 1889, 5 January 1890 (reprinting Klopsch's letters from Athens).

60. Areopagus block: *Washington Star* (DC), 19 April 1890, *Brooklyn Daily Eagle* 26 April 1891, Talmage 1892: 38. The block, embedded below the other three stones, is visible at the lower right of a photograph taken before the Tabernacle burned down in 1894 (www.brooklynvisualheritage.org/home/sites/default/files/images/S10_21_US_Brooklyn_Brooklyn_Churches_Synagogues019(1).jpg, accessed 28 January 2017). "Hewn out": *Omaha Daily Bee*, 23 February 1891. Cave of the Furies: Harrison and Verrall 1890: 554–555 identify it with the cleft on the east side of the Areopagus; Manatt's wording suggests the block was cut from somewhere under the northern edge.

Chapter 6

1. Scarborough: see Ronnick 2006 for his collected essays, papers, and articles. At home: Ronnick 2005a: 109–110. Screeds: *The Independent*, 04 December 1890. The *Independent* had invited southern white politicians to state their

objections to the 1890 Federal Elections Bill, or Lodge Bill, that was intended to protect the African American franchise in the South. "Kind of education": The congressman was George T. Barnes, Georgia Tenth District (he lost his 1890 re-election bid). The Richardsons received *The Independent* in Athens and others in the American School group read it regularly (Caroline Gerrish to Harriet Kimball, 01 March 1891), so most likely Gilbert saw this issue.

2. "Even while I write": Scarborough 1891: 219, reprinted with notes in Ronnick 2006: 376–379. Although this essay was not published until July 1891, the words "in March" suggest Scarborough was writing in January or perhaps early February; a letter from Greece might have taken three or four weeks to reach Ohio. "I am trying": Ronnick 2005a: 84. Scarborough dates this quotation to 1892, but his autobiography often misdates events and most likely he refers to Gilbert's 1891 letter. No letter from Gilbert survives in Scarborough's papers.

3. Advanced degree: Fikes 2002, Ronnick 2004, JBHE Foundation 2009, Ronnick 2020.

4. Charles Waldstein (1856–1927; Walston after 1918): CW/X/1/Misc.103/31, Singer 1906: 458–459, Reinach 1927, Dyson 1998: 56–58. Olympics: Anthony 1997. Lapith: Waldstein 1882. Reputation: Waldstein 1885, Wilson and Fiske 1889: 322–323, Beard 1993. Iris: *New York Times*, 13 January 1889, ASCSA 1889b: 10–11, 25. "Crowning event": Waldstein 1889: 1, Waldstein 1890a: 630–632.

5. Directorship: Fitzwilliam Syndicate to Waldstein, 05 November 1889, IOC 205296; Beard 1993: 14–15. Henry Waldstein: *New York Tribune*, 15 June 1890, *American Israelite* (Cincinnati), 19 June 1890. Too late: New York, Passenger and Crew Lists, 1820–1897, NARA M237, Roll 550 (21 June 1890).

6. Dragged on: New York, Wills and Probate Records, 1659–1999, vol. 439: 479–481 (03 November 1890). Frances Johnston: Named as "F. J.," she can be identified from context in Waldstein Diary, 16–17 September 1890, 22 September 1890. Made the rounds: Waldstein Diary, 08–20 August 1890. Harvard: Waldstein Diary, 20 September 1890, ASCSA 309/1 Memo Book: 65 (20 September 1890), Norton to Waldstein, 23 September 1890, IOC 205926. Taking ship: Waldstein Diary, 30 September–01 October 1890. Valet: Waldstein Diary, 06 December 1890; Fossum Journal: 17. I have been unable to find Lyon's full name. "Much better": Waldstein Diary, 16 December 1890.

7. Connections: Ware to Norton, 01 May 1890, AIA 3/7, 3/8. "The whole Acropolis": Seymour to Norton, 22 January 1889, AIA 3/4. "Impetuous": Norton, 05 May 1890, ASCSA 301/1, Folder 3; compare ASCSA 309/1, Memo Book: 64 (Goodwin to Norton, 14 April 1890). "Frankenstein": ASCSA 301/1, Folder 2.

8. Vases: ASCSA 1891: 33, BSA 1891: 10. Gardner: Gill 2011: 32–38. Dörpfeld: *AA* 1890: 3.110, *AM* 1891: 149–152, Vogeikoff-Brogan 2019. Barely saw: Waldstein Diary, 16–24 December 1890 records a single library lecture on 22 December.

9. "New life": Fossum Journal: 17. "Society man" and Pickard's worries: Caroline Gerrish to Harriet Kimball, 21 December 1890. Subordinate: Richardson to Waldstein, 05 November 1890, IOC 205927. Worked well: Waldstein to Norton, 26 December 1890, ASCSA 301/1, Folder 2. "Immense": Waldstein Diary, 16 December 1890. George and Mary Bakhmetieff: *Evening Star* (Washington, DC), 01 March 1890, Goodwin to Norton, 07 April 1890, AIA 3/8; George Bakhmetieff was the last Czarist ambassador (1911–1917) to the United States, and Mary Beale Bakhmetieff was a daughter of Edward Beale, creator of California's immense Tejon Ranch. Waldstein's diary records about two dozen luncheons or dinners at "the Bakhs" during January–March.

10. "Eminent persons": Benson 1930: 122 (recounting events in the 1880s). Modern Greek: Turner 1999: 321; Waldstein Diary, 30 October 1890, 11 November 1890 mentions modern Greek lessons.

11. "Unbusinesslike": Waldstein Diary, 16 December 1890. Racial slur: Waldstein Diary, 03 March 1891; see Chapter 7. Unequally: Waldstein Diary, 25 December (Fossum), 26 December (Brownson), 29 December (Pickard).

12. Christmas Eve: Waldstein Diary, 24 December 1890, IOC 205974; ASCSA 1891: 21. "An enjoyable evening": Fossum Journal: 17; Waldstein records going to the British School after dinner but Fossum's account does not mention him, so he may have arrived after the students left.

13. Sunny and mild: Edith Harris to Mary Harris, 05 January 1891. Christmas again: Fossum Journal: 18, Sachtleben Diary, 06 January 1891.

14. Day after Christmas: BSA 1891: 9–11. Schliemann: Traill 1995: 293–297.

15. Reached Athens: Νέα Εφημερίς, 15/27 December 1890, Waldstein Diary, 27 December 1890. Mourning: Νέα Εφημερίς, 17/29 December 1890. Organizing: Snowden to Blaine, 28 December 1890, NARA T159, Reel 10, Waldstein Diary, 30–31 December 1890. Will: Νέα Εφημερίς, 19/31 December 1890. Duplicate: Manatt to State, 24 January 1891, NARA T362, Reel 6. Fraudulently: Traill 1982, Traill 1995: 60. Open meeting: Waldstein Diary, 27 December 1890–04 January 1891.

16. Schliemann's funeral: Νέα Εφημερίς, 24 December 1890/04 January 1891, Παλιγγενεσία, 24 December 1890/05 January 1891; Waldstein Diary, 04 January 1891; Snowden to Blaine, 06 January 1891, NARA T159, Reel 10; ΑΔ 1890 (November–December Julian): 166–171; BSA 1891: 17. "Perfection": Brownson 1891b. All Athens: Manatt 1891a, Sachtleben Diary, 07 January 1891.

17. Open meeting: Νέα Εφημερίς, 25 December 1890/06 January 1891, 27 December 1890/08 January 1891; Brownson 1891a, Caroline Gerrish to Harriet Kimball, 11 January 1891; Waldstein Diary, 05–06 January 1891; CW/4/4/3 (eulogy and Lycosoura), *The Independent*, 05 February 1891, ASCSA 1891: 21–22. Headlines: E.g., *New York World*, 10 February 1891.

18. Hunting: Waldstein Diary, 07–12 January 1891; Rodd 1922: 235–237. Waldstein's official report (ASCSA 1891: 22–23) camouflages this outing

as an archaeological exploration of the site of Oiniadae in Acarnania. Whitelaw Reid: Waldstein Diary, 16–22 January 1891, ASCSA 1891: 20, Cortissoz 1921: 153–155. Eretria: Waldstein Diary, 16 January 1891, Fossum Journal: 17; Waldstein 1891a: 846 dates his interest in Eretria to summer 1890. Relatives: Caroline Gerrish to Miss Mathes, 02 January 1891, Caroline Gerrish to Harriett Kimball, 13 January 1891, Caroline Gerrish to Sarah Kittredge, 20 January 1891. Crowds: Edith Harris to Robert Harris, 09 February 1891. "Work of the universe" and "not many facts": Caroline Gerrish to Harriett Kimball, 21 February 1891. "Music itself": Caroline Gerrish to Harriett Kimball, 14 February 1891. Disorganized and repetitive: Caroline Gerrish to Harriett Kimball, 11 January 1891.

19. *Giri*: Waldstein Diary, 13 January 1891, 24 January 1891, 07 February 1891. "Crazy on Dörpfeld": Caroline Gerrish to Harriet Kimball, 14 February 1891; Pickard 1893: 57. So clearly: Edith Harris to Mary Harris, 11 January 1891; see also Vogeikoff-Brogan 2019: 256. Humor: Caroline Gerrish to Harriet Kimball, 24 January 1891. Go on forever: Edith Harris to Mary Harris, 11 January 1891, Richardson 1891b: 185.

20. Penrose and Waldstein on Acropolis: Caroline Gerrish to Harriet Kimball, 24–26 January 1891, Waldstein Diary, 26 January 1891, ASCSA 1891: 10, BSA 1891: 17. Sellers: Beard 2000: 68, Dyson 2004, Gill 2011: 115–121.

21. Museums: Gardner 1890: 212, Sturgis 1890: 538, Gardner 1891: 396–397, Shaw-Lefevre 1891: 294, Gazi 1994, Bastéa 2000: 168–172, Papalexandrou 2016. Ancient history: Paine College 1913–1914: 34. Artifacts: mentioned in Martin 1924. German: Paine Institute 1888–1889: 15, Paine Institute 1894–1895: 7, Paine College 1917–1918: 7. Paine College Archives, Box 147, preserves Gilbert's 1900 gradebook, showing more than twenty students enrolled in German.

22. Rainy: Caroline Gerrish to Sarah Kittredge, 20 January 1891. Other activities: Caroline Gerrish to Harriet Kimball, 13 January, 24 January, 01 February 1891; Edith Harris to Lucy Harris, 08 February 1891.

23. Birthday: Caroline Gerrish to Harriet Kimball, 13 January 1891; Waldstein Diary, 19 January 1891.

24. "Must present": ASCSA 1890: 42. Gave papers: ASCSA 1891: 21–23. Handwritten: The School had a Remington typewriter (Edith Harris to Robert Harris, 09 February 1891), but the publication committee complained students submitted handwritten texts (Ludlow to Waldstein, 15 January 1892, IOC 205927). Library: Martin 1924: 106. Title: Waldstein Diary, 12 February 1891, ASCSA 1891: 21, 31. In 1894, Gilbert gave the title as "The Demes of Attica" on a slip he returned to Brown's alumni association (John Wesley Gilbert biographical file, Brown University Archives).

25. Cleisthenes: Hdt. 5.69; for the state of knowledge in the 1880s, see, e.g., Grote 1880: IV.127–143, Abbott 1888: 476–481.

26. Fragments: Chambers 1967 (the Berlin papyrus includes *Ath. Pol.* 21.4–22.4, which begins with Kleisthenes and the demes).

27. Topographical side: Whitehead 1986: xviii–xxv, Wagstaff 2001, Greco 2014b: 1530–1540. Brother-in-law: Kastromenos 1886. One more: In January 1891, the deme of Pallene was identified at the village of Koropi (Brückner 1891), just west of today's international airport.

28. Into demes: ASCSA 1887: 11–16, 31; ASCSA 1889a: 26–27, 47–53; ASCSA 1889b: 14. Erchia: Young 1891.

29. Uncertain: Milchhöfer 1887a: 42; some place names considered demes in the 1880s have since been shown not to be demes at all. Oral report: ASCSA 1887: 14, ASCSA 1889a: 31.

30. Many years: The copy of Sauppe 1846 now in the ASCSA's Gennadius Library came in 1926 from the collection of statesman Joannes Gennadius. Frank Tarbell, Annual Director in 1888–1889, had no access to the book (Tarbell 1889: 135); Tarbell also reports (ASCSA 309/1 Copy Book: 80–81, 25 October 1888) that the School had no copy of Haussoullier 1884, an important book on the civic life of demes. Unaware: Richardson 1889a does not cite Sauppe. The same book: Pickard 1893: 57.

31. Kynosarges: Billot 1992, Greco 2011: 503–509.

32. Kynosarges and Alopekê: Leake 1821: 149–150, Leake 1829: 129, Leake 1841: II.41; the Asomaton monastery is better known today as Moni Petraki. Wide acceptance: E.g., Curtius and Kaupert 1878: 15, Curtius and Kaupert 1881, ASCSA 1887: 34, Baedeker 1889: 117, Joanne 1890: 97, 101–102. Further south: Dyer 1873: 105–106, 285–287, Harrison and Verrall 1890: 216–217.

33. Short cut: Edith Harris to Mary Harris, 29 December 1890.

34. Reiterates: Pickard 1893: 56–57; cf. Greco 2011: 423–426. Across the Ilissus: Ath. Mitt. 1895: 507, Marquand 1895: 528–529. Unavailable: E.g., Skias 1894. British excavations in 1895–1896 seemingly confirmed Dörpfeld's relocation of Kynosarges, although debate continues (Greco 2011: 503–509).

35. Demes and Dionysus: Baedeker 1889: 35–36. Instruments: Pickard 1893: 78–79. Admitted: ASCSA 1889b: 34. Took up: Waldstein Diary, 20 January 1891, 14 February 1891, Brownson 1893: 29, Fossum Journal: 17.

36. Avalanche: London Standard, 30 January 1891. Froze to death: Evening Star (DC), 03 February 1891. Bad news: Waldstein Diary, 20–31 January 1891, Νέα Εφημερίς, 15/27 January 1891. Set off: Waldstein Diary, 01 February 1891.

37. Cold and damp: Sachtleben Diary, 08 January–05 February 1891; Caroline Gerrish to Sarah Kittredge, 20 January 1891; Edith Harris to Lucy Harris, 08 February 1891. Furnace: Poland to Waldstein, 16 November 1891, IOC 205929, ASCSA 1893: 34.

38. Sachtleben and Allen: Allen 1896, Herlihy 2010. To visit: Sachtleben Diary, 05 February 1891.

39. Sachtleben's visit: Sachtleben Diary, 05 February 1891; ASCSA 1891: 23.

40. Cycling: Richardson 1899a, Richardson 1907.

41. Got back: Waldstein Diary, 06–15 February 1891; the doctor was Andreas Anagnostakis, rector of the University of Athens (Wayenborgh 2002: 25–26).

Dust: Caroline Gerrish to Harriett Kimball, 14 February 1891. "Read his paper": Waldstein Diary, 12 February 1891. Newspapers: *New York Times*, 15 March 1891, *Plaindealer* (Detroit), 20 March 1891, *Pittsburgh Daily Post*, 23 March 1891.

42. Greek papers: E.g., Εφημερίς, 23 January/04 February 1891. Foreign newspapers: Baedeker 1889: 33–34. "Almost unprecedented": *London Times*, 19 January 1891. Added enormously: See, e.g., Oman 1892. Edition: Kenyon 1891. Made its way: The first Greek edition (Agathonikos 1891), which was based on Kenyon, appeared at the very end of February (Νέα Εφημερίς, 25 February/09 March 1891); the first copy of Kenyon reached the United States in early March (*Brooklyn Daily Eagle*, 12 March 1891).

43. Cites it: Pickard 1893: 55, 77–78, 80. Sent off: Pickard to Waldstein, 30 April 1891, IOC 205927. Pickard was in the Peloponnesus with Dörpfeld from 09 April to 22 April and may have read the text only after that trip. Left Athens: Caroline Gerrish to Harriet Kimball, 04 April 1891.

44. "Gilbert &c.": Waldstein Diary, 14 February 1891. Commend: Brown University 1890–1891: 33.

Chapter 7

1. Archives: Vogeikoff-Brogan (forthcoming). Prints: ASCSA ExcRec 008, Prints 001–005, 007; Kavvadias to Waldstein, 14 May 1891, IOC 205927; Fossum to Waldstein, 31 July 1891, IOC 205927; Fossum 1898: 188–189. Prints 001, 004, and 005 are from James William Gordon Oswald's visit on 18 March 1891. Gordon Oswald, of Scotstoun near Glasgow, spent winter 1890–1891 in Athens with his wife Eugénie; he was a generous supporter of the British School and of Rev. Kalopothakes (Smith and Mitchell 1878, Caroline Gerrish to Harriet Kimball, 24–26 January 1891, BSA 1891: 31, Greek Evangelical Union 1898: 6, 13). The other three prints (002, 003, 007) are from Dörpfeld's visit on 05 May 1891; the original glass plates are in the archives of the German Archaeological Institute in Athens. Film sheets: ASCSA ExcRec 008, FN001–019; Harding 2008: 249–250. Glass plates: ASCSA ExcRec 008, N0021–0024, N0026–28, N0030; Coe 1978: 31–50, personal communication, Prof. John Hannavy. Overboard: Richardson 1891c: 6. Third glass plate: ASCSA Archaeological Photographic Collection Y0066.

2. Eretria: Reber et al. 2004: 651–655, Ducrey 2004, Kaltsas et al. 2010. In Gilbert's day: Baedeker 1889: 202.

3. Reborn: Pajor 2006, Pajor 2010. Village: Nouchaki 1890: 41, 233–234. Mosquitoes remain a problem even today (personal communication, Kyriaki Katsarelia).

4. Cemeteries: Gex 1993: 13–16. Guards: Εφημερίς, 16/28 July 1885. Tsountas: Νέα Εφημερίς, 9/21 September 1885, Ducrey 2004: 64, Voutsaki 2017. Private individuals: Hatzidimitriou 2012: 218–219. Further work: *AΔ*

1889: 74–79, 98–101, 115–117, 202–203, Gardner 1890: 212, BSA 1891: 15, Sellers 1892–1893.

5. Wanted *lekythoi*: Waldstein Diary, 29 January 1891, 16 February 1891, ASCSA 1891: 23, Waldstein 1892a: 702–703. Artemis Amarysia: Fachard et al. 2017, Reber et al. 2019. Dispute: Dörpfeld et al. 1891. Refounded: Strabo 10.1.10.

6. Contogianni: Waldstein Diary, 16 January 1891; ASCSA 1891: 24 (spelled Condoyanni). Several men named Κοντογιάννης appear in Nea Psara's municipal records (Νικολάος in *MA* 1862: 11; Δημήτριος in *Πρωτ.* 550, 20 September/02 October 1890); Waldstein's Contogianni had a house in Nea Psara (Waldstein Diary, 03 February 1891), but wintered in Chalkis (Waldstein Diary, 08 March 1891). "Great trouble": Waldstein Diary, 23 January 1891. Permit: *AΔ* 1891: 4; Waldstein 1891a: 846 claims he received a permit in summer 1890, but *AΔ* does not record it. Two days later: Waldstein Diary, 25 January 1891; Fossum 1891a: 253, Waldstein 1891b: 846, Waldstein 1892b: 414 cover up Fossum's early departure; cf. ASCSA 1897: 95. Steamer: Fossum Journal: 18, with no mention of the "great trouble."

7. Leonardos: Waldstein Diary, 02 February 1891, Petrakos 2007: 21–23. Leonardos was a representative of the Archaeological Society of Athens, a private group that often stood in for the government's overstretched Archaeological Service. Joined Fossum: Waldstein Diary, 03 February 1891. Made friends: Fossum Journal: 18–19. Belissarios: Fossum Journal: 18, Waldstein 1892b: 415; Nea Psara's records have a Νικολάος Βελισσάριος born in 1852 and another in 1853, both on Syros (*MA* 1852: 4, 1853: 51). Demarch: *Πρωτ.* 261, 14/26 May 1890. At odds: Waldstein Diary, 03 February 1891, dramatized in Waldstein 1892b: 416–417.

8. Workmen and excavations: Fossum Journal: 22, Waldstein Diary, 04 February 1891. Barba Spiro: Gilbert 1891b, Pickard 1891a, Waldstein 1892b: 414; he does not appear in Nea Psara's municipal records, but these record births only from 1845 onward, and the term Barba (μπάρμπας) usually indicates an older man. In tow: Waldstein Diary, 06 February 1891 does not mention them, but the expense list in his diary includes the items "Fare Lyon, Barbaspiro & self Peiraeus [*sic*]" and "Barbaspiro wages."

9. Nikolaki: Waldstein Diary, 07 February 1891, Waldstein 1892b: 420. Supplies: Waldstein Diary, 09 February 1891 and expenses list; Waldstein ordered supplies from the dragoman Sigala, on whom see MacMillan and Co. 1904: 93. Snow: Edith Harris to Lucy Harris, 16 February 1891, Edith Harris to Lucy Harris, 22 February 1891. Roof: Waldstein Diary, 16 February 1891. Finally left: Waldstein Diary, 18–23 February 1891, Richardson 1891c, Waldstein 1892b: 417–418; Lyon was left behind in Athens.

10. Left Athens: Caroline Gerrish to Harriet Kimball, 21 February 1891. Illness: Caroline Gerrish to Harriet Kimball, 14 February 1891. Assigned them: Waldstein Diary, 30 January 1891. Fossum: ASCSA 1891: 23–24. Rhamnus: BSA 1891: 19. Overland: Pickard 1891: 372 mentions the steamer

route and two overland routes to Skala Oropou without specifying which route he and Gilbert took.

11. First glance: ASCSA ExcRec 008, No021 and No023; Pickard 1891b: 375, Richardson 1891f: 246, Gennadius 1897: 440. Lovely day: Waldstein Diary, 26 February 1891.

12. House and kitchen: Waldstein Diary, 23 February 1891, Waldstein 1892b: 420, 423. "Great squeeze": Waldstein Diary, 26 February 1891. Gilbert and Pickard's original survey map (ASCSA ExcRec 008) labels the "dormitory" and "salle à manger"; the published map (Pickard 1891b: Plate XIX) omits them. The "salle à manger" was on modern Philosophou Menedemou St., between Apostoli and Archaiou Theatrou, while the "dormitory" was on the other side of block facing Aristogeitonos Philoxenous Street; maps in Pajor 2006: I.161, II.24–25.

13. First look: Richardson was out walking on February 27 (Richardson 1891g: 251); it would be natural for him to show Gilbert and Pickard around. Unheated: Fossum Journal 18–19, Waldstein Diary, 23 February 1891. Original plan: Pickard 1891b: 375; Pajor 2006: I.123–126.

14. Museum: *Boston Herald*, 26 April 1891, Richardson 1891g: 248–249, Pajor 2006: I.106. Telegraph: Nouchaki 1890: 233–234. Updates: *Εφημερίς*, 20 February/04 March 1891; *Νέα Εφημερίς*, 21 February/05 March 1891, 25 February/09 March 1891; *Παλιγγενεσία*, 23 February/07 March 1891. European press: E.g., *Pall Mall Gazette*, 10 March 1891. Garbled: *Νέα Εφημερίς*, 21 February/05 March 1891 and *Εστία*, 24 February/08 March 1891 report the French excavating at Eretria; *Νέα Εφημερίς*, 28 February/11 March 1891 makes it the Germans. Mail: Gilbert 1891b, undated but with the byline "Euboea, Greece," must have been put in the mail before the American School group left on March 20. Gilbert may also have sent a letter from Nea Psara to Paine Institute (mentioned in *Indianapolis Freeman*, 09 May 1891, with no summary of contents). Several letters Waldstein sent from Eretria between February 4 and 6 had by February 22 made it no further than the Chalkis post office (Waldstein Diary, 22 February 1891; Waldstein 1892b: 419). From Athens: Pickard 1891a is datelined "Athens, April 7th, 1891"; Pickard likely mailed this essay before his April 9 departure for the Peloponnesus with Dörpfeld. Pickard probably also wrote an unsigned *Boston Herald*, 26 April 1891 article about Eretria, also datelined Athens, April 7, which displays clear textual parallels with Pickard 1891a.

15. At the theater: Waldstein Diary, 24–27 February 1891, Fossum 1891a, Fossum 1891b, Brownson 1891c. "Really exciting": Gilbert 1891b. Dramatic flourish: The marble finger and sculpted head fragment were found several days before Gilbert and Pickard arrived (Waldstein Diary, 24 February 1891; ASCSA ExcRec 008 No02 shows the head). The inscription is Richardson 1891g: 253 (no. 33); Brownson 1891c: 275 mentions fragments of marble priests' chairs.

16. Opening graves: Waldstein Diary, 27 February 1891. "The pick": Waldstein 1892b: 414. Both quote: Gilbert 1891b, Pickard 1891a; on the sand, see also Waldstein 1891b: 847. Morakis: Waldstein Diary, 27 February 1891; Waldstein 1892b: 420, Richardson to Waldstein, 11 May 1891, IOC 205927; no trace of Morakis appears in Nea Psara's municipal records.

17. "These people": Waldstein 1892a: 703, 707. "Morally and intellectually": Waldstein 1892b: 414. Waldstein's prejudice was not confined to workmen. Of Kavvadias he writes, "I fear even he is a slippery Greek. These people's idea of honour & honesty is after all mentally different from our own" (Waldstein Diary, 15 February 1891).

18. Private deal: Waldstein Diary, 25 February 1891, Waldstein 1892b: 423, Richardson 1891g: 247; cf. Ziebarth 1915: 71. Under the cover: Πρωτ. 622, 08/20 November 1890; 77, 24 February/08 March 1892; cf. ΠΑΕ (1892) 1894: 62 for Belissarios's late 1891 work with Christos Tsountas. Owner's permission: Waldstein 1892a: 703–704. Foundations: Waldstein Diary, 24–25 February 1891; Waldstein 1892b: 422. Reimbursement: Pickard 1891a. "Mausoleum": Waldstein Diary, 04 March 1891, Pickard 1891a, Pickard 1891b: 372.

19. Inscribed stele: Richardson 1891g: 251–253, IG XII.9 290; the stone was apparently still there in 1908 (Ziebarth 1915: v), but could not be found in the 1930s (Peek 1942: 27).

20. Told Waldstein: "Piccard [sic] and Gilbert to work plan of walls &c." (Waldstein Diary, 27 February 1891) is Waldstein's last mention of the pair for the next three weeks. Began working: Pickard 1891b: 372–375. Chairephanes: Richardson 1891f: 245. "Worthy of mention": Hdt. 6.106.3; Herodotus has the Athenian messenger Philippides (Phidippides) speak these words. Pickard 1891b: 389 translates "no mean city."

21. Pnyx: ASCSA 1886: 14–15, Crow and Clarke 1888; on Clarke, see also Allen 2002. H. S. Washington: ASCSA 1889b: 9, Belkin and Gidwitz 2020. Surveying equipment: The early ASCSA excavation reports (Cushing 1888, Earle 1889, McMurtry 1889, Miller 1888, Rolfe 1890a, Rolfe 1890b, Waldstein et al. 1890; see also Lord 1947: 296–297) show no sign of transit or theodolite, with one exception: Buck 1889a: 165 thanks Washington for taking elevations at Ikaria in 1888. Washington was wealthy enough to fund his own excavations (ASCSA 1889b: 25–26), and it is a good guess that he could afford a theodolite. Plataea: ASCSA 1889b: 34, ASCSA 1890: 22, Waldstein 1890b, Washington 1890a, Washington 1890b, Hunt 1890; cf. Grundy 1894: 53–59. Reached Athens: Pickard 1891b: Plate XIX follows Washington's example in several respects, such as using identifying letters for towers, but the original Eretria survey map does not contain these letters. Spoil heaps: Poland to Waldstein, 14 January 1892, IOC 205928.

22. Photographs: ASCSA ExcRec 008, Prints 001–002; Fossum 1898: 188–189. The day these shots were taken, Pickard was measuring the theater cavea (Brownson

1891c: 269). Theodolite: Stanley 1890: 202–271, Turner 1983: 248–261; personal communication, Dr. Sara Schechner. Took charge: Pickard 1891b: 371. Chain and tape: Stanley 1890: 444–460. Metric chains of the day came in twenty- and twenty-five-meter lengths; I infer Pickard and Gilbert had the twenty-meter length because the scale on their hand-drawn survey map has a base increment of twenty meters. Poland to Waldstein, 18 January 1892, IOC 205928 mentions "the School measuring tape and chain," probably the same items used in 1891. Measurements: Pickard 1891b: 372, 380, 384–385, 388–389. The original survey map (but not the published map) marks the spot where the 116-meter elevation was taken; cf. Reber et al. 2004: 654 (123 meters), Fachard 2004: 100 (120 meters). There was no benchmark for Gilbert and Pickard to reference.

23. Dartmouth: Dartmouth College 1880–1881: 22, Forman 2009: 17. "Industrial education": Graham 1954: 122–124, Johnson 1970: 205–210; on surveying, see also *Fisk Herald*, May 1886: 1–2.

24. First day: ASCSA ExcRec 008-N0024 shows snow on the mountains but dry ground, indicating it was taken before the heavy snow and rain that began late on February 28 and continued for several days (Waldstein Diary, 28 February–03 March 1891). In addition, Gilbert and Pickard appear relatively clean and fresh, suggesting they had recently arrived; cf. the scruffiness of Pickard and Brownson in ASCSA ExcRec 008-FN003, 013, 016, 018. Round towers: Pickard 1891b: 374–375, Fachard 2004: 102, 107, Plate 14.2. Chaining: Stanley 1890: 451–452. Jokes: Fossum Journal: 9. Destruction: Pickard 1891b: 386; one massive acropolis tower, visible in 1891, was entirely gone in 1894 (ASCSA ExcRec 008-Eretria notebook 1894: 5).

25. Second photograph: ASCSA ExcRec 008-N0027. In this image, Gilbert wears a bowler or derby, Pickard what appears to be a deerstalker hat; in their photo by the towers, Gilbert is bare-headed while Pickard wears a bowler or derby. Did Pickard have two hats, or were the men sharing headgear? The guard's rifle butt can just be seen at the photo's right edge. Resumed digging: Waldstein Diary, 28 February 1891, Waldstein 1891a: 23. Waldstein 1891b: 847–848, Waldstein 1892b: 422–423. Treasures: Ἑστία 10/22 March 1891, ΑΔ 1891: 100–103.

26. Two days straight: Waldstein Diary, 01–02 March 1891; Pickard 1891a remembers "three or four days." Last time: Edith Harris to Lucy Harris, 01 March 1891. Six inches: Waldstein Diary 01 March 1891; Waldstein 1892b: 423 claims a foot and a half of snow fell by the evening of March 2. Discussing: Waldstein Diary, 01 March 1891; Baumeister 1864 (based on an 1854 trip), Lolling 1885 (the best candidate for what Waldstein calls "Lolling's paper"); the American Schoolers apparently did not know about Dürrbach 1890.

27. "Quite desperate": Waldstein Diary, 03 March 1891; dramatized in Waldstein 1892b: 423–424. "sighing for a change": Pickard 1891a. "Crazy foreigners": Waldstein 1892b: 424.

28. "Comical": Waldstein 1892b: 424. "Lent a hand": Pickard 1891. Empty grave: Waldstein Diary, 03 March 1891. In this diary entry, Waldstein writes: "We all worked like niggers"; he later used the racist term at least once in a publication (Walston 1924: 242 n. 53). After much deliberation I have chosen to relegate this sentence to a footnote. Waldstein's private racist comment to his diary must be placed against his public acknowledgment of Gilbert's thesis research and his acceptance of Gilbert as part of the group at Eretria. By keeping this sentence in a footnote, I hope to maintain the focus on John Gilbert's experiences and archaeological contributions at Eretria, rather than on Waldstein's inner thoughts.

29. Work continued: Waldstein Diary, 04–06 March 1891, Παλιγγενεσία, 23 February/07 March 1891, Νέα Εφημερίς, 25 February/09 March 1891; Waldstein 1891b: 848–849, Waldstein 1892b: 424–425. Stele: Richardson 1891g: 246–447, IG XII.9 565. "Praying for": Waldstein Diary, 06 March 1891.

30. Popular accounts: Waldstein's diary and official reports (ASCSA 1891: 25–28, Waldstein 1891a) offer the most reliable record of the "mausoleum" excavations; Waldstein 1891b describes the six graves but omits chronological details; Waldstein 1892b manipulates the sequence of events and adds details for dramatic effect. The original dig notebook was apparently lost (Richardson to Waldstein, 11 May 1891, IOC 205927). Mixed up: Pickard 1891a. "Imagine if you can": Gilbert 1891b.

31. "Luckiest days": Waldstein Diary, 04–06 March 1891. Left for Athens: Waldstein Diary, 07 March 1891. "No less important": Gilbert 1891b. Gilbert's contributions: Pickard 1891b: 371–372; this list notably omits Fossum.

32. Enough time: Pickard 1891b: 376–379, 388–389 gives no chronological markers, but this area must have taken several days to survey. Wind and waves: Pickard 1891b: 31. Harbors: Mauro 2019: 69. Aerial photographs (Pajor 2010: 109–111) show how this area has changed since the 1890s.

33. Round tower: Pickard 1891b: 378, Georgiades 1913, Fachard 2004: 102; also Blandin 2007: 61. Remains of this tower, built into a beachside terrace, are still visible today. Base point: Pickard 1891b: 388, following Lolling 1885: 352–354 on Strabo 9.2.6 (New Eretria forty stades from Oropos and sixty stades from Delphinion) and Thuc. 8.95 (Oropos sixty stades from Eretria). Lighthouse: Pickard 1891b: 78–379. West Gate: Fachard 2004: 97–99.

34. Tortoise: Pickard 1891b: Plate XIV; as Pickard does not even mention Fossum in his publication and Richardson left in early March, Brownson and Gilbert are the most likely photographers. Menedemus: Knoepfler 1991: 185, Van Dijk 1997: 184–186, 344–345.

35. Acropolis: Gilbert 1891b, Pickard 1891b: 379–385. "Our good fortune": Pickard 1891b: 389. "Best remains": Gilbert 1891b.

36. Four phases: Pickard 1891b: 386; Pickard's comparanda (Asea, Lepreon,
Mantinea, Midea, Mycenae, Tiryns) reflect his April 1891 trip with Dörpfeld
to the Peloponnesus. "This work": Gilbert 1891b. Dörpfeld: Richardson to
Waldstein, 11 May 1891, IOC 205927.

37. Test of time: for current knowledge, see Fachard 2004, Fachard 2007, Reber
et al. 2008: 148–149, Reber et al. 2015: 135–136. Misunderstood: E.g.,
Pickard 1891b: 381 reconstructs a northwest wall extension, now identified as
an entry ramp (Fachard 2004: 102). No access: E.g., the 1814 plan of Eretria
by C. R. Cockerell, published in 1831 (Knoepfler 1969, Pajor 2010: 49).

38. From the summit: Pickard 1891b: 389.

39. "When we remember": Gilbert 1891b. Incompatible: Plato, *Phaedrus* 276c.
Elated: Caroline Gerrish to Harriet Kimball, 15 March 1891 (reporting a communication from Pickard at Eretria, probably carried by Richardson).

40. Telegraphed: Homolle 1891a: 450–451 cites Ἐφημερίς, 23 February/7 March
1891; I am unable to obtain the original Ἐφημερίς article. Chalcis: Waldstein
1891: 845 claims someone else sent this telegram. "Tomb of Aristotle": Ἐφημερίς,
27 February/11 March 1891 already expresses skepticism and asks Waldstein
for more information; Νέα Ἐφημερίς, 28 February/12 March 1891 mentions the
telegram (and the German School). Abuzz: Ἐφημερίς 24 February/08 March, 25
February/09 March 1891. "Resurrecting": Manatt to Macy, 12 March 1891,
Iowa Ms17/1/24; Manatt sent Frederick Sanborn a similar letter (*Boston Daily
Advertiser*, 30 March 1891).

41. "Must stop": Waldstein Diary, 11 March 1891. Cautioning: Waldstein Diary,
12–13 March 1891, Ἐφημερίς 01/13 March 1891. Letter to New York: *The
Nation*, 02 April 1891 (Waldstein letter dated 12 March 1891), reprinted in
The Academy (London), 18 April 1891 and thence in *Classical Review,* May
1891: 236. Global news: Palmer 2019: 49–50. Mentions: Reuter's March
9 telegram (*London Daily News*, 10 March 1891) was repeated dozens of
times across the United States, reaching as far as Utah and California by
March 11 (*Ogden Standard,* 10 March 1891, *San Francisco Bulletin*, 11
March 1891); follow-up telegrams from Athens between March 11 and 13
received similar treatment. *Boston Daily Advertiser*, 14 March 1891(written
by Frederick Sanborn) shows how quickly debate arose over the identification
of "Aristotle's tomb."

42. "I congratulate you": Waldstein Diary, 11 March 1891. Royal family: Queen's
chamberlain [name illegible] to Waldstein, 14 March 1891, IOC 205927. One
hundred words: Waldstein Diary, 13 March 1891. Cost: Baedeker 1889: xxviii
(1.57–2.375 drachmas or 23–35 cents per word to the United States, not
counting double fees for twenty-four-hour delivery; currency conversion
from historicalstatistics.org, accessed 16 August 2020. Salary: Paine 50/1/112
(1890–1891 Financial Exhibit).

43. Head splitting: Waldstein Diary, 13 March 1891. Preliminary report: *The Guardian* (London), 17 March 1891, *The Independent*, 02 April 1891. Theater: Waldstein to Fossum, 13 March 1891, NAHA P0541/ 1/5. Nafplio: Waldstein Diary, 20 March 1891 (Richardsons return). Skittered: Waldstein Diary, 17-20 March 1891. Cash: ASCSA 1891: 25; cf. Merriam to Fossum, 20 April 1891, NAHA P0541/1/7, faulting Waldstein for not knowing the School had excavation funds to spend.

44. Longer campaigns: Lord 1947: 77, 80, 84. Copyist's error: Fachard et al. 2017: 169; the copyist made an easy slip: in Greek alphabetic numerals, seven is transcribed ζ and sixty by the very similar ξ. Identified: Fachard et al. 2017: 178.

45. Photograph: ASCSA ExcRec 008, Print 001. Late evening: Edith Harris to Lucy Harris, 22 March 1891. "On purpose": BSA 1891: 19. Leuctra and Syros: Martin 1924. No later: Gilbert left Athens on March 27 for a Peloponnesus trip with Pickard's family (Caroline Gerrish to Harriet Kimball, 04 April 1891).

46. The same day: *The Independent*, 19 March 1891; some newspapers published parts of the cable before *The Independent*, e.g., *Morning Call* (San Francisco), 18 March 1891. Waldstein or a surrogate would later anonymously criticize *The Independent* for its "scare-heads" (*New York Tribune*, 31 December 1893); note also *Daily Alta California* (San Francisco), 26 April 1891, reprinting a *New York Tribune* Waldstein puff piece. "Miss Aristotle": *Daily Picayune* (New Orleans), 28 March 1891. Months afterward: *The Morning Press* (Santa Barbara), 12 September 1891. "We are glad": *Christian Index*, 28 March 1891; the words in square brackets are restored because the bottom of the article is damaged in the only available microfilm copy of the *Christian Index*.

47. Regulations: ASCSA 1891: 42. Busy: Waldstein Diary, 20 March-01 April 1891. "Tooth-pick": Waldstein Diary, 26 March 1891. Constantinople (Istanbul): Waldstein Diary, 21 March and 31 March 1891; Richardson 1891f: 240 mentions seeing the Serpent Column. Also along on this trip were Mrs. Richardson's siblings Edward Bowen and Grace Bowen. Brownson: Waldstein Diary, 31 March 1891, Caroline Gerrish to Harriet Kimball, 04 April 1891. Argos and Sparta: Waldstein Diary, 01-10 April 1891. Pickard and family: Caroline Gerrish to Harriet Kimball, 09 February 1891, Edith Harris to Mary Harris, 15 March and 22 March 1891. "Peloponnesreise": Caroline Gerrish to Harriet Kimball, 26 April 1891, *AA* 1891: 2.91-92, ASCSA 1891: 32. Brownson raced from traveling with Waldstein to join Dörpfeld (Waldstein Diary, 10 April 1891). Though he welcomed women to his Athens lectures, Dörpfeld discouraged women from joining this trip because of its rough travel conditions (Vogeikoff-Brogan 2019: 257-258).

48. Meeting: Waldstein Diary, 27 March 1891; cf. ASCSA 1891: 23. CW/4/4/3 contains an undated set of lecture notes on "Aristotle's grave" and Eretria, perhaps for this meeting. Peloponnesus trip: Walker 1901: 476-477 claims

Gilbert needed fifty more dollars to complete his work at the American School, adding he earned the money as a tour guide for "some Boston ladies . . . who wanted to go through the Peloponnesus." According to Walker, the "local director in Athens" chose Gilbert because he knew modern Greek so well. The "Boston ladies" can only be Pickard's family and the "local director" must be Pickard; it would be unsurprising if Pickard helped Gilbert financially. At noon: Caroline to Harriet, 04 April 1891.

49. Dimitsas: *Παλιγγενεσία*, 05/17 April 1891. Greek report: Waldstein 1891a. Declared: Waldstein Diary, 20–21 Apri, 1891; *Pall Mall Gazette*, 21 April 1891; *Νέα Εφημερίς*, 17/29 April 1891; *Παλιγγενεσία*, 17/29 April 1891, *Daily Evening Bulletin* (San Francisco), 04 May 1891. Reprints: E.g., *Knoxville Journal* (Tennessee), 08 December 1891. Dictated: Waldstein Diary, 24–25 April 1891. Come-hither: Waldstein 1891b: 850.

50. Leaned into: ASCSA 1891: 27–28 (dated 09 May 1891). Dörpfeld: Richardson to Waldstein, 11 May 1891, IOC 205927; cf. Waldstein to Fossum, 24 June 1891, NAHA P0541/1/7. "Incomprehensible": Kavvadias to Waldstein, 14 May 1891, IOC 205927 ("ein unbegreifliches Missglücken"). Eminent people: E.g., Henry Sidgwick to Waldstein, 02 May 1891 and George Wyndham to Waldstein, 12 May 1891, both IOC 205927. Lecture: Frederick Bramwell to Waldstein, 16 May 1891, IOC 205927 (mentioning fee of twelve pounds sterling, about sixty dollars in 1891); lecture notes in CW/4/4/3. Critics: *The Guardian* (London), 27 August 1891, Homolle 1891b: 668, Homolle 1892: 278. Pitching: Waldstein to Century Magazine, 05 May 1891, Century Company Records, Series I, Manuscripts and Archives Division, NY Public Library. Merriam to Waldstein, 03 July 1891, IOC 205927. "For the present": Waldstein 1892b: 426. "Juvenile audience": *Journal of the Royal Society of the Arts*, 01 January 1909; *London Times*, 07 January 1909. Stagira: Sismanidis 2016.

51. Reduced: ASCSA 1891: 24, Waldstein 1891a: 24, Waldstein 1891b: 849, Waldstein 1892b: 423. Excerpted: Frothingham 1891: 139–142. "Undigested": Frothingham 1891: 143; the anonymous letter-writer was almost certainly Columbia's Augustus Merriam for the same information appears in the July 1891 letter Merriam sent Waldstein.

52. Good terms: Reinach 1927: 392. "Je n'ai jamais cessé de le placer dans la troisième catégorie des archéologues," writes Reinach; "il ne suffit pas d'être un homme aimable et de se pâmer devant l'*Hermès* [i.e., of Praxiteles] pour appartenir aux deux premières." Distinction: *Boston Daily Advertiser*, 11 August 1897; *Missionary Voice* 1930. Responding: John Wesley Gilbert biographical file, Brown University Archives.

53. Reducing: Du Bois and Dill 1910: 7.

54. Inscription reading [Συνα]γωγὴ Ἑβρ[αίων]: Richardson 1899b, Powell 1903: 60–61; the stone is on display today in the Corinth archaeological

museum. Bitner 2015: 91–99 discusses its dating and interpretation by modern scholars. "He reasoned": Acts 18:4 KJV.

Chapter 8

1. "Made famous": Martin 1924: 106; also Richardson 1919: 123. Steamer tour: Baedeker 1889: 3–4, 135–142, Joanne 1891: 425–464.
2. Whirlwind: Caroline Gerrish to Harriet Kimball, 13 April 1891 describes the trip in detail. Only the first page of Edith's account (Edith Harris to Mary Harris, 05 April 1891) survives. Steamer: The weekly departure from Patras to Brindisi was Wednesdays at 10 PM (Baedeker 1889: xxb).
3. Berlin: ASCSA 1891: 32, Culp 1902: 193; Martin 1924: 106 says Gilbert followed Dörpfeld to Berlin, but Dörpfeld was in the Peloponnesus in April. Kletzing and Crogman 1898: 483 do not mention Berlin. *Slavonia*: *Hamburger Passagierlisten* 373–377 I, VIII.A.1-071-351 (Microfilm K-1743), Staatsarchiv Hamburg; Boas 1893: 11–12, Kludas and Bischoff 1979: 45. Departure: *Boston Post*, 14 April 1891, *New York Herald*, 14 April 1891. Arrival: NARA M255-49-168 (Baltimore, Passenger Lists, 1820–1964), *Der Deutsche Correspondent*, 28 April 1891, *Baltimore Sun*, 29 April 1891. Son's birth: see Appendix 1.
4. Waldstein: Lord 1947: 54–57, 76–80, 86–89.
5. Richardson: *The Independent*, 23 March 1914, *Dartmouth Alumni Magazine* 6.6, April 1914: 220–221, Yale Obituary Record 1915: 599–600, Lord 1947: 79. "Generous and lovable": ASCSA 1914: 26.
6. "Absolute certainty": ASCSA 1891: 35. Years to come: Fossum 1898: 189, ASCSA 1902: 19.
7. Fossum's career: Andrew Fossum Biographical Files, St. Olaf College Archives and Concordia College Archives; letters in NAHA P0541/1/5. Hampered: Larson 1927. Articles: Fossum 1898, 1905, 1926. Greek restaurant: Biographical File, Concordia College Archives. Bible verse: ὡς τὸ φῶς ἔχετε, πιστεύετε ("While ye have light, believe": John 12:36, KJV).
8. Traveled together: Brownson to Waldstein, 11 May 1891, IOC 205927; Brownson to Waldstein, 21 October 1891, IOC 205928. Edith went home: Caroline Gerrish to Edith Harris, 04 September 1891. Roland Goodbody, the researcher with whom I first worked on the Athenaeum materials, lives just two doors down from the Austin Street house. According to Goodbody, his landlady Nancy Beck purchased the Austin Street house in the late 1950s; she found the Harris and Gerrish letters and donated them to the Portsmouth Athenaeum.
9. Sailed back: NARA T843-3-0785 (arrival in Boston, 27 August 1892). Brownson's career: *New York Times*, 27 November 1948, ASCSA 1949: 16, Yale Obituary Record 1950: 14. Revisited Greece: Brownson 1927.
10. Pickard at Missouri: Weller 1999, DiSalvo 2013, University of Missouri Faculty File.

11. Did not know: John Wesley Gilbert Biographical File, Brown University (1894 alumni response naming "Mr. Pickard, of Dartmouth College"). Williams College: APA *Proceedings* 1894: i–ii, Ronnick 2005a: 134. Close friend: Ronnick 2005a: 82–83, 161. Urging him: Ronnick 2005a: 146; Scarborough misdates this conversation to the 1896 Brown meeting, which Fowler did not attend. Teachers' Association: Ronnick 2005a: 122, *Morning News* (Savannah, GA), 14 June 1893, Wright 1894: 47. No list of the 300–500 participants exists, but Gilbert was a regular at this gathering (e.g., *Savannah Tribune*, 18 February 1893), and Scarborough had been invited to speak by his Atlanta University classmate R. R. Wright, Sr., who of course knew Gilbert. Muddled: Scarborough dates this meeting to Philadelphia in December 1900, but the phrase "just returned from Greece" (Ronnick 2005a: 161) could hardly describe Gilbert in 1900. Scarborough also writes of Gilbert's "early death," but Gilbert died just three years before Scarborough; possibly he confused Gilbert with Wiley Lane.

12. Brown University: APA *Proceedings* 1896: i–iv; Ronnick 2005a: 146. Moore: Ronnick 2004: 100, Ronnick 2005a: 84, DBCS s.v. Gregory: Ronnick 2004: 94. First elected in 1881, Gregory let his membership lapse by 1886; he lapsed again by 1898 (APA *Proceedings* 1881: 15, 1886: xlv, 1898: lxxxi). Bulkley: Fikes 2002: 121, DBCS s.v. Elected to APA: APA *Proceedings* 1897: iii, *Atlanta Constitution*, 08 August 1897 (native Georgians), *Boston Daily Advertiser*, 11 August 1897 (reprinting an August 10 article from an unnamed Augusta paper, perhaps *The Georgia Baptist*); see also *National Reflector* (Wichita, KS), 04 September 1897, *Indianapolis Freeman*, 11 December 1897, Kletzing and Crogman 1898: 484. Also worth noting here is that Atlanta's William Crogman was elected to the APA in 1898. For more information on these African American scholars, see Ronnick 2018.

13. Personal invitations: *Augusta Chronicle*, 04 March 1898, with full text of White's letter to Gilbert, dated 16 February 1898; Scarborough quotes an identical closing sentence from his invitation (Ronnick 2005a: 153). Managing Committee: *Colored American* (Washington, DC), 30 July 1898 describes Scarborough as "a member of the board" of the School. "Knows no color": Scarborough 1904: 312.

14. Local societies: Heuck and Hebert 2002, O'Brien 2002. Cleveland: AIA Appendix to Annual Reports 1897–1898: 36, Ronnick 2005a: 153; Scarborough appears on Cleveland's roster through 1907, but his membership lapsed in 1908, and he was invited to rejoin in 1909 (Ronnick 2005a: 206, 376 n. 377). Baltimore: AIA Appendix to Annual Reports 1897–1898: 23–24. Bulkley remained an AIA member after moving to Brooklyn in 1900, but disappears thereafter. General meeting: Sheftel 1979: 10; this event is now called the Annual Meeting.

NOTES TO PAGES 210–213

15. New York: APA *Proceedings* 1899: i–ii, vii, xxxiii. Philadelphia: AIA 1901, APA *Proceedings* 1901: iii–xlv, Ronnick 2005a: 160–161. None of the groups that met in Philadelphia seems to have published an attendance list.

16. Visited: *Christian Recorder*, 03 January 1901, mentioning "William Howard of Maryland" accompanying Gilbert; I am unable to identify Mr. Howard. "Enthusiastic students": *Washington Bee*, 12 January 1901.

17. London: Crawford et al. 1901: xxv–xxvi, 42. Tuskegee: *The Tuskegee Student*, 28 April 1906, Ronnick 2005a: 196.

18. Hayes in Augusta: *Augusta Chronicle*, 07 November 1891, Williams 1922: V.33.

19. Industrial College: *Savannah Morning News*, 12 April 1891, Wright 1894: 38, Ronnick 2011: 365, Elmore 2014. C. T. Walker: *Augusta Chronicle*, 23 December 1890. Applied: *Atlanta Constitution*, 23 June 1891. Greek and Latin: Haynes 1952: 71–72, 92; Wright, Jr. 1965: 34–36; cf. Wright 1894: 55.

20. Lincoln Institute: *Indianapolis Freeman*, 20 June 1891, Curtis 1962. Job offer and controversy: *The Appeal* (Minneapolis), 23 July 1892; *Indianapolis Freeman*, 30 July 1892. Attractive: Tobias 1953: 181. New recruits: Missouri Public Schools 1893: 174, Missouri Public Schools 1894: 206.

21. "Not one instance": Gilbert to Susan Walker, 26 May 1911, reprinted in Peters 1937. "Very difficult": Paine 50/1/119. More than doubled: Paine 50/1/121–122. "A great help": Paine 50/1/137. Gilbert's pay: Graham 1954: 117.

22. Three more children: US Census, 123rd Militia District, Richmond County, Georgia, Supervisor District 10, Enumeration District 46, 18 June 1900: 12. Panic: White 2017: 771–773. Did not suffer: Augusta Bicentennial 1935: 36. Home: The 1900 census records Gilbert as a Magnolia Street homeowner. Called 13th Street until 1898, Magnolia became Forest in 1912; a back alley paralleling Forest is still called Magnolia Lane. Gilbert appears in city directories at 1616 13th Street from 1892 to 1898, then at 1620 (renumbered 1421 in 1908) Magnolia from 1899 to 1912, and intermittently from 1913 to 1921 at 1415 or 1433 Forest. 1616 13th and 1620 (1421) Magnolia may well be the same location. My thanks are due to Erick Montgomery for his expert analysis of Gilbert's addresses.

23. Enrollment: Paine Institute 1890–1891: 17, Paine 50/1/146 (1899–1900), Clark 1933: 28; Clary 1965: 152–153, relying on documents lost in the 1968 fire, gives yearly figures consistently higher than those of G. W. Walker's surviving annual reports. Cross-checking with the three surviving pre-1900 catalogues shows that while Walker did not count theological students, Clary added them into his enrollment count for some (but not all) years. Carter: See Chapter 4. Jones and Tyus: Paine 50/1/127. Haygood Seminary: Phillips 1925: 592–593.

24. Fire risk: *New Orleans Christian Advocate*, 11 March 1897. Haygood Hall: Clary 1965: 102–106, Montgomery and Speno 2010; Walker reports the building was still unfinished and unheated in June 1901 (Paine 50/1/

150). Clock: *Augusta Chronicle*, 14 October 1956; but note the illustration in Phillips 1925: 159.

25. New name: Paine 50/1/150–154, Clary 1971; APA 1903: cxxv, ASCSA 1907: 149.

26. "Noblest profession": Gilbert 1902b: 408. Lectures: *Savannah Tribune*, 05 May 1892. "Greek scholar": *Cleveland Gazette*, 27 August 1892, *Savannah Tribune*, 08 November 1902. Speaker: E.g., *Savannah Tribune*, 18 February 1893, *The State* (Columbia, SC), 05 December, 1895, *Augusta Chronicle*, 10 December 1897, 31 December 1902, *Atlanta Constitution*, 20 June 1897, 10 July 1898, 05 February 1899, 30 August 1900, *Evening Star* (Washington, DC), 03 November 1900. Militia: *Savannah Tribune*, 18 February 1893. Republican party: *Augusta Chronicle*, 25 January 1898, 04 February 1900. CME delegate: *Memphis Commercial-Sun*, 06 May 1894, *Huntsville Gazette* (AL), 12 May 1894, *St. Louis Globe-Democrat*, 13 May 1894.

27. "His very soul": *Christian Index*, 06 December 1923. Ministry: Gammon Seminary 1897: 35. Possibly Gilbert took a sabbatical to study away from Augusta, as several Paine colleagues later did (Johnson 1970: 319), but the details are uncertain as Walker's annual 1897–1898 and 1898–1899 annual reports do not survive. He is listed as a "middle class" (second-year) student, and Gammon's second-year curriculum included a Hebrew elective using William Rainey Harper's textbook; this probably explains the statement in Martin 1924 that Gilbert "studied under the late famous Dr. Harper." Ordained: Richardson 1919: 123 dates this to 1895; Holsey 1898: 3 calls him "Rev. Prof." in March 1898; the earliest newspaper reference I find to "Rev. J. W. Gilbert" is *Augusta Chronicle*, 06 November 1898. "Independence of thought": *Atlanta Constitution*, 27 March 1898; Butler describes Gilbert as "in the city this week," suggesting he did not spend the entire academic year in Atlanta. Encouraged: Holsey 1898: 3.

28. Training ground: Cashin 1980: 185–186. "Immunes": Cunningham 2020; *Augusta Chronicle*, 14 August, 18 August 1898.

29. Dickson: *San Francisco Examiner*, 23 January 1893 (Gilbert and Dickson new arrivals at Grand Hotel), Paine: 1895: 21, Leslie and Gatewood 1993. Amanda America Dickson: Leslie 1995. Further afield: E.g., *Evening Star* (DC), 03 November 1900; *Augusta Chronicle*, 22 November 1900 shows he returned to Augusta between these two trips.

30. Delegates: *Christian Advocate*, 16 May 1901, *Augusta Chronicle*, 11 August 1901, Crawford et al. 1901: xxvi (giving incorrect initials for delegates J. F. Lane and G. W. Stewart), Phillips 1925: 317–320. Carter, Gilbert, Williams, and possibly Stewart traveled together from Augusta to New York. Passports: NARA M1372, Roll 585, 497–500, 540–542 (13–14 August 1901); I am unable to locate passport applications for Cottrell and Doyle, but the former appears in the *Potsdam*'s departure notice (*New York Tribune*, 17 August 1901). Doyle: *Nashville Christian Advocate*, 01 June 1923. Visiting: Phillips

1932: 169–170; Phillips places this portion of the trip after the conference, but Paine Box 53 includes a postcard Gilbert sent from Waterloo to G. W. Walker, dated 01 September 1901.

31. Attendees: Crawford et al. 1901: xxv–xxvii (three of the fifty-eight listed delegates did not attend). St. Ermin's: *Topeka Daily Capital*, 24 August 1901, *Pittsburgh Press*, 25 August 1901, Ronnick 2005a: 173–175.

32. Shout-out: Crawford et al. 1901: 42, Walters 1917: 250–251. Against lynching: *Cleveland Gazette*, 28 September 1901. Full participants: Crawford et al. 1901: xi. "A Methodist, regardless": Phillips 1932: 168. McKinley: Crawford et al. 1901: xii, xliii-iv, 73, 96–97, Ronnick 2005a: 178–179. "Such a President": Crawford et al. 1901: 144–145. Scarborough: Ronnick 2005a: 148–149, 179. Gilbert may have been part of the huge crowd that greeted McKinley during his brief 1898 stop in Augusta (*Augusta Chronicle*, 22 December 1898).

33. London: Ronnick 2005a: 179–180; Scarborough mentions (Ronnick 2005a: 180) he missed the AME group photo. Bookstores: Paine BX8276.T45 1899, a copy of the third edition of John Telford's *Popular History of Methodism*, bears Gilbert's handwritten inscription, "London, Eng. September. 6, '01." Retired Paine College professor George Clary, Jr. rediscovered this book at Lake Junalaska, North Carolina, in July 1996.

34. W. R. Lambuth (1854–1921): Robert 1999, Sledge 2005: 220–249. New Orleans: Crawford et al. 1901: 548, Walker 1901. Missionaries: Crawford et al. 1901: 243, 541–548. First met: Gilbert 1913: 36 refers to a first meeting "two decades ago."

35. Seasick: Phillips 1932: 170; I have not been able to identify the return ship or itinerary. Scarborough's group crossed about the same time on the Cunard liner *Umbria* and also got seasick (Ronnick 2005a: 185).

36. Apartheid: Cashin 1980: 178–188, Davis 1998: 78–84, 114–116, Donaldson 2001, Eskew 1992, Leslie 2001. Lyons: *Augusta Chronicle*, 18 May 1897, 02 July 1897, 23 March 1898. "Never rode": Weatherford 1910: 173.

37. Atlanta Compromise: Harlan 1974–1975: 3.583–587. "Most opportune": Harlan 1974–1975: 4.23–24. Reactions of Hope and Du Bois: Davis 1998: 78–84. Scarborough: Ronnick 2005a: 322–323.

38. "*Must make our friends*": Harlan 1974–1975: 4.23–24. Another letter: *The Independent*, 30 January 1896. "Narrow and erroneous": Harlan 1974–1975: 4.346. "One of the best": Washington 1899: 581. Cordial terms: E.g., *Augusta Chronicle*, 30 December 1904, *Afro-American Ledger* (Baltimore), 11 August 1906, *The Broad Ax* (Chicago), 26 August 1906.

39. Ware High School: Kousser 1978, Kousser 1980, Cashin 1985: 36–41, Leslie 2001. Very existence: Cashin 1985: 41. Not until 1945: Kousser 1980: 43.

40. Despaired: Davis 1998: 125–127, Donaldson 2001, Leslie 2001. Completed: Kousser 1978: F-14. "We always do": Peters 1937.

41. Essay: Gilbert 1902a. Pilgrim Health: Greene 2013. Supporters: *Alabama Tribune* (Montgomery), 07 May 1948; *Augusta Chronicle*, 06 June 1905 records Gilbert as co-founder of a mutual aid society, perhaps one of the several such societies that joined together as the Pilgrim Company in 1905; see also *Atlanta Constitution,* 22 June 1906.

42. Emancipation Day: *Augusta Chronicle*, 02 January 1904. John Temple Graves: *New York Times*, 12 August 1903, *Cleveland Gazette*, 15 August 1903, *Colored Citizen* (Wichita, KS), 12 September 1903, *Savannah Tribune*, 12 September 1903. Published: Gilbert 1904; I am grateful to Michele Valerie Ronnick for rediscovering and sharing this text. Another copy once existed in Paine's archives because Calhoun 1961: 42-45 quotes from it extensively. An early version of the speech can be seen in quotations from a letter Gilbert sent to Warren Candler in September 1903 after Candler published an essay against lynching (*Atlanta Constitution*, 09 September 1903, 15 September 1903).

43. "We have contributed": Gilbert 1904: 1. "White-hot": Gilbert 1904: 2. Adam: Gilbert 1904: 20. "Eleusinian mystery": Gilbert 1904: 4; see also Gilbert 1904: 10. "Another womanhood": Gilbert 1904: 12.

44. Carefully appeals: Gilbert 1904: 23-24.

45. Colorado: *The Statesman* (Denver), 30 June 1905, *North Carolina Christian Advocate* (Raleigh), 19 July 1905. "Square deal": *Augusta Chronicle*, 02 January 1906, *Montgomery Advertiser*, 05 January 1906. Set the facts straight: *Augusta Chronicle*, 03 January 1906. Back in Macon: Georgia Equal Rights Convention 1906 (Daniel Murray Collection, Library of Congress), *Savannah Tribune*, 24 February and 10 March 1906, Davis 1998: 153-155. Ohio State: *Afro-American Ledger* (Baltimore), 11 August 1906, *The Broad Ax* (Chicago), 26 August 1906.

46. Massacre: Davis 1998: 164-171, Godschalk 2005. John Jr.: Atlanta University Catalogue 1907: 29; the fall 1906 term began October 2, and Davis 1998: 167-68 notes most students were not yet on campus. Atlanta University Catalogue 1908: 29 again lists Gilbert and several 1906-1907 first-year students in the 1907-1908 first-year class, perhaps suggesting that their families had kept them home from Atlanta. W. J. White: *Augusta Chronicle*, 26 September, 29 September 1906. "Good negroes": *Augusta Chronicle*, 02 October 1906. Silas Floyd: *Augusta Chronicle*, 03 November 1907. "Prematurely gray": Miller 1906: 11.

47. MECS funding: Green 2008: xxvii. Lambuth: Paine 50/1/157, 159. Hammond: *Nashville Christian Advocate*, 21 December 1923, Green 2008: xiii, xviii-xxi; Hammond was the first Georgian to attend Drew Theological Seminary, which helps explain why Channing Tobias went there. Women's groups: Paine 149/36. Divinity program: Paine 50/1/159-162, Johnson 1970: 132; the coal baron was John Calvin Martin, on whom see *Morning Journal* (Lancaster, PA), 19 November 1913. Philanthropists: Johnson 1970: 9-10, 44-48, 62-63, 369;

also Davis 1998: 177–178. Cut funding: Johnson 1970: 61–62, 133, Lakey 1996: 449, Green 2008: xxxiii; Paine's 1907–1912 financial reports show sporadic CME support, but nothing like the levels of the early 1900s; cf. the amount recorded for 1898–1907 in Du Bois 1907: 86.

48. Fundraising: *Nashville Tennessean*, 08 September 1907. "Fallen behind": Paine 50/1/164–165. Odyssey: Green 2008: 32. October and December: *Official Record of the Holston Annual Conference* (WV) 1907: 28–29, *Evening News* (Norfolk, VA), 15 October 1907, *Fort Worth Star-Telegram* (TX), 02 November 1907, *Daily Arkansas Gazette* (Little Rock), 09 November 1907, *Batesville Daily Guard* (AR) 12 November 1907, *Baltimore Sun*, 16 November 1907, *Augusta Chronicle*, 23 November 1907, *Atlanta Constitution*, 23 November 1907, *The Charlotte News* (NC), 30 November 1907, *Gaffney Ledger* (SC), 01 December 1907, *Journal of the North Carolina Annual Conference* 1907: 13; *Augusta Chronicle*, 01 October and 11 December 1907 give the termini for these travels, which must have been spread out over at least two trips. The Arkansas and Texas stops were probably part of a single long swing out west. "More proud": *Baltimore Sun*, 16 November 1907.

49. June 1908: Paine 50/1/167–168. Had to sell: Paine 50/1/171–175. Grueling tour: News reports and conference minutes show Gilbert, usually with Hammond, visited Arkansas, Georgia, Kentucky, Maryland, Mississippi, and the Carolinas between September and December 1908; in 1909, he added Florida and Oklahoma; in 1910, he scaled back to Georgia, Tennessee, South Carolina, and Texas, partly because he spent a month as a volunteer census enumerator. Lambuth: *White River Annual Conference* (AR) 1908: 6. Later lore: E.g., *Missionary Voice*, 01 April 1930, Calhoun 1961: 18. "How Gilbert stands it": Green 2008: 32–33.

50. "An instrument": *Daily Arkansas Gazette* (Little Rock), 09 November 1907; Jacobs 2011: 10. Flattered: *Arkansas Gazette* (Little Rock), 05 November 1909. "Flunkey": *The Appeal*, 27 November 1909. "Social equality": *The Horizon*, 01 January 1910. Into print: Gilbert 1911. Unrealistic: Davis 1998: 187–188.

51. YMCA: Davis 1998: 185–187. Board member: *Augusta Chronicle*, 10 June 1912. Volume: Weatherford 1910, Luker 1991: 188, Davis 1998: 187. Invited: *Vanderbilt University Quarterly*, 04 March 1909.

52. Ranking: Du Bois and Dill 1910: 13, 22; Johnson 1970: 135–136, 331–332. Annual report: Paine 50/1/177. Bedridden: *Missionary Voice* 1.7 (July) 1911: 37. Funeral: *Augusta Chronicle*, 18 May, 20 May 1911; Magnolia Cemetery D185. "A score of times": Gilbert to Susan Walker, 26 May 1911, reprinted in Peters 1937. Hammond: *Augusta Chronicle*, 07 June 1911. Goodrich: *Augusta Chronicle*, 02 June, 03 June 1911.

53. David Thomas: US Census, Augusta, Supervisor District 40, Enumeration District 51, 15 June 1900; Augusta Directory 1901: 699, Cedar Grove D103. Sarah Thomas: Cedar Grove E38.

Chapter 9

1. A busy time: *Augusta Chronicle*, 19 August 1956, Calhoun 1961: viii–xi. First missionaries: Earlier treatments include Reeve 1921, Pinson 1925, Cannon 1926, and Sheffey 1939. Both Gilbert and Lambuth intended to write books (Pinson 1925: 227, Calhoun 1961: 47); neither did so before dying, although Lambuth 1915: 142–147 offers some episodes from the journey. Congo diaries: *Paducah Sun-Democrat* (KY), 02 June 1961, Calhoun 1961: x, xv. Calhoun 1961: 70 states that Gilbert's diary began on January 1, 1912, but several of the quotations Calhoun gives (Calhoun 1961: 75–76, 79) mention Luebo, where Lambuth's diary records the two men stopped from December 7–21, 1911; Calhoun's latest Gilbert quotation is from March 14, 1912 (Calhoun 1961: 98–99). The Paine College typescript of Lambuth's 1911–1912 diary (Calhoun Papers 1/23a and 1/23b) runs from October 24, 1911 to May 11, 1912 with several gaps, notably February 13–April 12, 1912; in other sections, entries appear out of chronological order, perhaps suggesting the diary's binding had come loose by the time the copy was typed. Lambuth's diary also includes a day-by-day itinerary for January 22–February 19, 1912 (Lovell 2013: 5–8 reprints this itinerary along with an extremely helpful map). The pandemic has prevented me from investigating archives in Belgium (on which see Legros and Keim 1996, Piret 2015), and I have not delved into the American Presbyterian Congo Mission records and other relevant archival collections that might shed light on Gilbert's Congo experience. Future researchers will undoubtedly find much to add to this chapter.

2. Independence: Vanthemsche 2012: 202–204, Van Reybrouck 2014: 267–276. Gilbert-Lambuth Chapel: *Augusta Chronicle*, 03 October 1965, 12 February 1968. Back north: Calhoun 1961: xv. Disappeared: Typescripts of Lambuth's diaries exist at Paine College and at the United Methodist Study Center in Lake Junalaska, North Carolina. E. C. Calhoun sent the handwritten originals to Lambuth College in Tennessee after completing his book. Lambuth College closed in 2011, and the diaries may have gone to the archives of the Tennessee Conference of the United Methodist Church, but I was unable to confirm their location at the time this book went to press.

3. Dreamed of Africa: Pinson 1925: 129–130, 135–136. Visit to Paine: *Nashville Christian Advocate*, 07 March 1891; *Raleigh Christian Advocate*, 11 March 1891; *Christian Index*, 14 March 1891, 11 April 1891. Stanley, the Congo, and Leopold: Van Reybrouck 2014: 11–12, 34–36, 41–55, Vanthemsche 2012: 17–26. Conversation: Kasongo 1998b: 260 dates this meeting to 1890, but Stanley did not lecture in Nashville until 4 April 1891 (*Nashville Banner*, 06 April 1891); Lambuth must have met Stanley just before or after that lecture. Sheppard and Lapsley: Sheppard 1917, Phipps 2002, Carton 2009, Jacobs 2011, Dworkin 2017. Crossed paths: Hochschild 1998: 153, Phipps 2002: 38; on Conrad in the Congo, see Najder 2007: 138, 144, 161–162.

4. Urged: Lambuth Diary, 10 November 1911, Lambuth 1913b: 288–289. Foreign endeavors: Lakey 1996: 304–305. "Land of our ancestry": Lakey 1996: 573. "Ready to go": Paine Institute 1895: 17. Vanderhorst Society: Lakey and Stephens 1994: 208. "Debt and lack of conviction": Lambuth Diary, 10 November 1911. In the meantime: Pinson 1925: 99–118.

5. London conference: See Chapter 8. Discussions: Jacobs 2011: 15.

6. Zulu students: Paine 50/1/156 (1903–1904), 50/1/176 (1909–1910), *Augusta Chronicle*, 29 May 1910, Colored Methodist Episcopal Church 1922: 25, Paine College Catalogue 1928–1929: 84, McAfee 1945: 68, Lakey 1996: 574–576. Dube: Hughes 2011; several young men connected with Dube studied at Benedict College in Columbia, South Carolina (Hughes 2011: 82), just seventy-five miles northeast of Augusta. Other African students: *Augusta Chronicle*, 29 May 1910 names Anthony Nasito of the Orange Free State and a Mr. Dobson from Liberia. Another student, D. D. Lewis, falsely claimed to be from Africa and was expelled; see *The Jeffersonian* (Atlanta), 05 May 1910.

7. Funding cuts: See Chapter 8. For the broader context of African mission work by African Americans, see Jacobs 2011.

8. J. A. Lester: *Christian Index,* 06 December 1923 (typescript in Calhoun Papers 1/21), Calhoun 1961: 40–41.

9. Board of Missions: *The Tennessean* (Nashville), 29 April 1910, *Nashville Christian Advocate*, 06 May 1910; the partial transcription of a newspaper editorial (*Christian Index*, 06 April 1911) preserved in Calhoun Papers 1/21 suggests that the idea of Gilbert and Lambuth going to Africa together was already public knowledge in early April. Elected bishop: *Nashville Banner*, 06 May 1910; Pinson 1925: 120–123. "No colored man": *Augusta Chronicle*, 15 May 1910. Superintendent: Phillips 1925: 387–388, Lakey 1996: 375–376. CME-MECS cooperation: Calhoun 1961: 48–50.

10. "Locate a site": *Augusta Chronicle*, 29 May 1910. Replacement: Paine 50/1/176. Farewell: *Atlanta Constitution*, 30 July 1910. "My heart leaped": *Nashville Christian Advocate*, 16 September 1910; the Nyatikazis left New York on August 10, then connected through Southampton for South Africa; *UK and Ireland, Outward Passenger Lists, 1890–1960*, 20 August 1910 (departure from Southampton for South Africa). Still anticipated: *Austin Statesman* (TX), 31 October 1910. "We are waiting": *Missionary Voice* 1.3, 1911: 42–43.

11. Fundraising: *Augusta Chronicle*, 15 May 1910, *Christian Index*, 05 October 1911. "As I go": Gilbert to Walker, 26 May 1911, reprinted in Peters 1937; the Bible references are to Hebrews 11:4 and Psalm 126:6. Meager estate: Gilbert 1913: 35. The editors' preface to this article claims Gilbert's mother "bequeathed the proceeds of her cabin home" to him just before he left for Africa, information likely based on a statement by Gilbert himself. In reality, Sarah Thomas sold the small lot she owned in Augusta in 1901 to her son (Richmond County Deed Records, Book 5-X: 395, 121 Broad Street, 01 August 1901). Gilbert's sister-in-law Sarah Seaborough (Ola Pleasant's older sister)

is listed at this address the same year (Augusta City Directory 1901: 685); Sarah Thomas is unlisted in 1901, but she and her husband David Thomas appear at 136 Walker Street in the 1900 census, and David Thomas appears there in 1901 (Augusta City Directory 1901: 699), suggesting the Broad Street property was not Sarah Thomas's home. Donations and Lambuth's support: *Christian Index*, 05 October 1911 (typescript in Calhoun Papers 1/21), *Nashville Christian Advocate*, 16 September 1910, CME General Conference 1914: 88–89.

12. Sheppard's return: *Cleveland Gazette*, 20 May 1911; Phipps 2002: 178–179 places Sheppard in Staunton, Virginia, during 1911. The timing of Gilbert's visit is unclear, but news reports (*Baltimore Afro-American*, 26 August 1911, *Richmond Planet*, 02 September 1911) place him near Staunton in late August–early September; another possibility is that he visited Sheppard at the end of September, en route to New York. "I have opened": *Christian Index*, 05 October 1911 (Calhoun Papers 1/21). Recent history: Van Reybrouck 2014: 79–106, Vanthemsche 2012: 36–44. Lawsuit and aftermath: Phipps 2002: 161–179, Dworkin 2017: 55–61.

13. Tensions: Dworkin 2017: 61–65. "Best prepared": *Christian* Index, 05 October 1911 (Calhoun Papers 1/21; Calhoun 1961: 74–75).

14. Farewell: *Augusta Chronicle*, 02 October 1911, CME General Conference 1914: 89. New York: Calhoun Papers 1/21; NARA M1490–0146–997 (no. 61191, 30 September 1911) shows Gilbert obtained his passport in New York. "As I see it": *Christian Index*, 05 October 1911 (Calhoun Papers 1/21). *Mauretania*: *UK and Ireland, Incoming Passenger Lists, 1878–1960*, National Archives BT 26, Liverpool, 10 October 1911; Phillips 1925: 425–426. Lambuth: *UK and Ireland, Incoming Passenger Lists, 1878–1960*, National Archives BT 26, 07 October 1911 (arriving Southampton from Buenos Aires). London to Antwerp: Lambuth 1913b: 290.

15. Reading: CME General Conference 1914: 89; Morrison called the language Buluba-Lulua, after the Baluba and Lulua people who spoke it. "What a blessing": Calhoun 1961: 72. Baptist missionary: Phillips 1925: 427 (quoting from a letter of Gilbert's). "Reverential spirit": Lambuth Diary, 29 October 1911.

16. Canary Islands: Phillips 1925: 426. Gilbert's letters: *Christian Index*, 31 November 1911 (typescript in Calhoun Papers 1/21). Dakar: Lambuth Diary, 24 October 1911. Conakry and Freetown: Lambuth Diary, 26 October 1911. Arriving: Lambuth Diary, 02 November 1911.

17. Boma: Lambuth Diary, 02 November 1911, Lambuth 1913a: 14, Van Reybrouck 2014: 61–62. "We entered": CME General Conference 1914: 89. US Consul: *Consular Registration Certificates, Compiled 1907–1918, General Records of the Department of State, 1763–2002*, Record Group 59, National Archives, nos. 29394 (Lambuth), 29395 (Gilbert), both 02 November 1911. Pandemic: Van Reybrouck 2014: 94, 106. Lapsley's grave: Lambuth

1915: 186. Rail line: Van Reybrouck 2014: 83–85. Léopoldville: Lambuth Diary, 09 November 1911, reports "Léopoldville. Still waiting for trunks from Matadi"; the entries for the preceding five days are missing.

18. Missed the boat: *The Tennessean* (Nashville), 29 December 1911, Lambuth 1913a: 14. Léopoldville to Dima: Lambuth Diary, 19–27 November 1911, CME General Conference 1914: 89. "Much disturbed": Lambuth Diary, 20 November 1911. French and Tshiluba: Lambuth Diary, 19 November 1911; see also Lambuth Diary, 02, 09, 11, 29 November 1911.

19. Onward from Dima: Lambuth Diary, 19 November–07 December 1911.

20. Lazarus John: Lambuth Diary, 03 December 1911. The Harrises: Lambuth Diary, 04 December 1911; Hochschild 1998: 216–217, 242–243, 273. Doctor: Lambuth Diary, 06 December 1911.

21. Reached Luebo: Lambuth Diary, 07 December 1911. Lambuth 1913b: 290 gives the distance as 900 miles, while Gilbert (CME General Conference 1914: 89) records it as 1,200. Community: Calhoun 1961: 146 (quoting Gilbert's diary entry for 08 January 1912), Lambuth 1913a: 14–15. "Preacher, pastor": Calhoun 1961: 75; see Dworkin 2017: 60–61 on Sheppard and Morrison. Alonzo and Althea Edmiston: CME General Conference 1914: 89 (naming "Rev. and Mrs. Edmiston"), Dworkin 2017: 109–117. Althea Edmiston completed her Bushong grammar in 1913, but it was not published until years later. Tshiluba as lingua franca: Morrison 1906: v–vi. "These Presbyterians": Calhoun 1961: 75 (note the plural).

22. Moses Mudimbi (sometimes spelled Mudimbe) and his wife: *Raleigh Christian Advocate*, 04 April 1912 (reprinting Lambuth letters dated 27, 28, 31 December 1911), Morrison 1913: 284–285, Lambuth 1913b: 291–292. Congolese historian M. O. Kasongo interviewed Mudimbi in 1964 (Kasongo 1998a: 149). Pinson 1925: 146 prints a letter from Mudimbi's wife Malendola to Lambuth. Ngongo Luteta (sometimes spelled Lutete): Lemarchand 1964: 33, Gordon 2014, Gordon 2017. Mudimbi made his escape before Luteta's death in 1893.

23. Iconic: The MECS would later offer frameable prints of this photograph in return for donations to support its Congo mission (e.g., *Raleigh Christian Advocate*, 17 July 1913). Protector: Pinson 1925: 128. "As a brother": Lambuth to Candler, 16 October 1911, quoted in Fish 1970: 209. "On an equality": Lambuth Diary, 13 January 1912.

24. Decided to explore: Lambuth Diary, 14–20 December 1911, Lambuth 1913a: 16, Lambuth 1913b: 290–291, CME General Conference 1914: 89–90. Batetela: On their ethnogenesis, see Turner 1993, De Rezende 2012: 38–41. Morrison hoped: Omasombo Tshonda and Verhaegen 1998: 56–57. Elders and porters: Lambuth Diary, 19 December and 22 December 1911, Gilbert 1913: 35, Lambuth 1913b: 291, Lambuth 1915: 143–145, Kasongo 1998b: 263. Various spellings of the three elders' names appear in the sources (e.g., Lambuth Diary, 02 February 1912 gives the cook's name as Mbwashan; Gilbert 1913: 37 has Difonda rather than Dufanda).

25. "Touched our heart": Lambuth Diary, 22 December 1911; Gilbert's diary (Calhoun 1961: 76) has only fragmentary comments on the volunteers. Mutombo Katshi and Kabengele: Kasongo 1998b: 263, Lovell 2013: 11. Joint Publications Research Service 1968: 113–115 describes a line of chiefs named Mutombo Katshi, the oldest of whom (Mutombo Katshi I) died in 1911; Bedinger 1920: 48, 106 describes the realm of Mutombo Katshi I. The word *katshi* in Tshiluba means "little wooden stick" (personal communication, Cécile Bushidi). Route to Lusambo: Bedinger 1920: 93, 97.

26. Twenty days: Lambuth's itinerary puts them at Lusambo on 10 January 1912, but his diary describes their arrival on 13 January 1912 and departure on 18 January 1912; Gilbert Diary, 11 January 1912 (Calhoun 1961: 87) shows they had not yet reached Lusambo that day. Headed the column: Lambuth Diary, 18 January 1912, Lambuth 1913b: 292. Conversations: Calhoun 1961: 104 suggests Gilbert wrote about Greece in his diary.

27. Kanyoke: Gilbert Diary, 01 January 1912 (Calhoun 1961: 98); see also Lambuth 1915: 49. "They pray": Calhoun 1961: 146; this entry, written at the village of Kalamba, probably dates to 07 January 1912 (Lovell 2013: 6). Leap-frog: Lambuth Diary, 26 December 1911. "Providential": Lambuth to John R. Pepper, 28 December 1911 (published in *Raleigh Christian Advocate*, 04 April 1912 and reprinted in Pinson 1925: 141–142).

28. Mutoto: Bedinger 1920: 93. Pritchard: Lambuth Diary, 05 January 1912, Bedinger 1920: 213. "Kind to us": Calhoun 1961: 59; Declerq 1897 was probably one of the pamphlets. Genuine concern: Calhoun 1961: 60, summarizing entries from Gilbert's diary. Gilbert and Pritchard also shared a knack for entertaining native children with sleight-of-hand tricks (Lambuth Diary, 10 January 1912; Calhoun 1961: 87). Parting ways: Pritchard last appears in Lambuth Diary, 13 January 1912. Photographs: *Thirty-First Annual Report of the Board of Church Extension of the Methodist Episcopal Church South, 1912–1913*: 351, 353.

29. At Lusambo: Lambuth Diary, 13–18 January 1912. Sermon: Gilbert Diary, 14 January 1912 (Calhoun Papers 1/22). Letter: Phillips 1925: 428–429, quoting *Christian Index*, 14 March 1912.

30. Replacements: Lambuth Diary, 18 January 1912. Hospitality: Lambuth Diary, 26 January, 30 January 1912. "Off the native": Lambuth Diary, 12 April 1912. "No genuine interest": Calhoun 1961: 68.

31. Sunday service: Lambuth Diary, 21 January 1912. "All the children": Lambuth Diary, 23 January 1912. "We had to wade": Calhoun 1961: 79. Rotten bridge: Lambuth Diary, 22 January 1912. Ants and mosquitoes: Lambuth Diary, 18–19 January 1912, Gilbert Diary, 18 January 1912 (Calhoun 1961: 100); Calhoun reports Gilbert's capital letters were a half-inch high, with a broken pencil point at the end.

32. "I did what I could": CME General Conference 1914: 90. Vivid scene: Lambuth to J. D. Hammond, 22 January 1912 (Pinson 1925: 144). Dictionary: Stilz 1925: ii. New Testament: Kasongo 1998a: 74–75.

33. Lubefu: Lambuth Diary, 26–30 January 1912; Lambuth Diary, 26 January 1912 seems to describe two suspension bridges, but only one is visible in Figure 9.3.

34. Worried: Lambuth 1915: 145–146. Rejected: Lambuth Diary, 25 January 1912. Lost: Lambuth Diary, 31 January 1912. Capital: Named Muina Senga (Lambuth Diary, 01 February 1912) but usually referred to by the chief's name; Lambuth 1913b: 292 mistakenly calls it Mibangu, the next village after the capital.

35. Wembo Nyama (also spelled Wembo Niama): Lambuth Diary, 01 February 1912, with different details in Lambuth 1913b: 291–292, Lambuth 1915: 146–147. Turner 1992: 395–396, 399 records oral traditions heard from members of the chief's family in 1970. Feared lieutenant: Omasombo Tshonda and Verhaegen 1998: 34–37, De Rezende 2012: 64.

36. Debate: Kasongo 1998a: 13–17; Kasongo interviewed Mudimbi in 1964. Asked Gilbert: Lambuth Diary, 02 February 1912. "One of the finest": CME General Conference 1914: 90.

37. Loop: Lovell 2013: 8 reprints Lambuth's itinerary, but most of Lambuth diary entries from this period are missing. The day and distance counts come from Gilbert's report (CME General Conference 1914: 90).

38. Formal letters: Anet 1913: 227–228 quotes portions of one letter. Brutality and repression: Calhoun 1961: 91–96. "Most correct": Lambuth to J. A. Martin, 19 February 1918 (full text in Pinson 1925: 126–127).

39. "Such a workman": Pinson 1925: 127–128; Pinson does not give the date of this letter, but it was most likely composed after Lambuth and Gilbert returned downriver.

40. Stayed on: Lambuth's last extant diary entry (11 May 1912) from his first trip was written at Nouvelle-Anvers (today Makanza) in the northern Congo. Brazil: *The Tennessean* (Nashville), 04 May 1912. Introduction and outline: Calhoun 1961: 47. Brief accounts: Gilbert 1913, CME General Conference 1914: 88–90. Sailed home: *U.K. and Ireland Outward Passenger Lists, 1890–1960*, National Archives BT 27, 27 April 1912 (departure from Liverpool); *Passenger and Crew Lists of Vessels Arriving at New York, New York, 1897–1957*, NARA T715, arrival 02 May 1912. On edge: *London Observer*, 28 April 1912. Alma: Paine 50/1/184.

Chapter 10

1. "On his return": *Christian Index*, 06 December 1923 (typescript in Calhoun Papers 1/21). "To the Congo": *Augusta Chronicle*, 26 May 1912. Situation at Paine: Paine 50/1/184. Missionary training: Paine 50/1/186. Gilbert spoke: E.g., *Augusta Chronicle*, 10 June 1912, 20 March 1913, *Greenville News* (SC), 03 November 1912, *Daily Ardmoreite* (OK), 18 November 1912, *Nashville Banner*, 12 April 1913, *New York Age*, 14 August 1913,

Montgomery Advertiser (AL), 06 December 1913. Joined him: *Augusta Chronicle*, 06 February 1913, *Nashville Banner*, 27 March 1913. "The highest moment": Calhoun 1961: 148.

2. Announced: *Augusta Chronicle*, 06 February 1913. News reports: E.g., *Nashville Banner*, 27 March 1913. "Chosen to pioneer": *Missionary Voice* 3.5, May 1913: 265, reprinted as late as *North Carolina Christian Advocate*, 10 July 1913. Alma: Augusta Directory 1913: 327. John Jr.: Gilbert's 1911 consular registration certificate (Department of State, Record Group 59, no. 29395) gives his son's place of residence as Nashville. Elated: *Raleigh Christian Advocate*, 30 May 1912. Junalaska: *New Orleans Christian Advocate*, 12 June 1913, Lowry 2010: 23–29.

3. Threatened to leave: Kasongo 1998b: 264–265. Cannon 1926: 232–233 suggests that the Belgians in 1913 were reluctant to grant African American missionaries permission to reside permanently in the Congo. Shuffled off: *Raleigh Christian Advocate*, 19 June 1913. In his place: *Asheville Gazette-News* (NC), 30 June 1913. "At a later date": Lambuth 1913b: 294–295.

4. Floundering: Johnson 1970: 318–323, Green 2008: xxxiii–xxxv. Enrollment: Paine 50/1/190; Clark 1933: 28. Choosing: Paine 50/1/195. W. J. White: *Augusta Chronicle*, 21 April 1913, *Savannah Tribune*, 26 April 1913. Trustees hoped: Paine 50/1/194. Miles Memorial: *New York Age*, 05 June 1913.

5. Rise above: Birmingham News, 14 September 1913. "Not safe any more": Green 2008: 54. Four properties: Richmond County, Georgia, Deed Book 10-E: 22–25 shows the April 1924 distribution of Gilbert's properties among his three surviving children.

6. "Renewed confidence": *Birmingham News*, 03 May 1914. Bishopric: *Augusta Chronicle*, 26 April 1914, *Birmingham News*, 03 May 1914; *Plain Dealer* (Kansas City, KS), 28 March 1958 records oral history about this election. General conference: Phillips 1925: 455–477. Training for Africa: J. D. Hammond report on Paine College, June 1914, Warren A. Candler Papers, Series 2, Box 44, Folder 12, Emory University Archives. "Just as soon": CME General Conference 1914: 90.

7. Conference: Trawick 1914, Beach 1915. Overnight train: The St. Louis CME meeting ran from May 6 to May 20, while the Atlanta conference went from May 14 to May 18. Gilbert gave his Congo report in St. Louis on May 15, then disappears from St. Louis until May; he spoke in Atlanta between May 16 and May 18. "We owe it": Gilbert 1914: 130. Mt. Berkel is Jebel Barkal in present-day Sudan; it sits above ancient Napata, home of the Kushite pharaohs of Egypt (Kendall 2012); Meroe, also in Sudan, flourished from the tenth century BC to the fourth century AD (Welsby 2013). Where Gilbert got his information about these sites is unclear; Williams 1883: I.22 is one possibility. "So-called civilization" and "instead of bread": Gilbert 1914: 133.

8. Did not officially decide: Colored Methodist Episcopal Church 1922: 25, Phillips 1925: 431. Reunited: E.g., *Nashville Christian Advocate*, 31 May

1918, *Nashville Tennessean*, 05 June 1919. Chaplains: *Nashville Christian Advocate*, 14 June 1918. Local people: Lambuth Diary, 12 December 1913. Still asking: *Sheperdstown Register* (VA), 02 December 1920. Channing Tobias: *The Plaindealer* (Detroit), 28 March 1947. Still honored: Calhoun 1961: 121–122, Lovell 2016.

9. Resigned: *Birmingham News*, 30 August 1914, *New York Age*, 08 October 1914. Dean of Ministerial Training: Paine 50/1/196. Curriculum: Paine 50/1/ 199. Enrolment, funding resignations: Paine 50/1/200–206; on Hammond's resignation see Green 2008: xxxiii–xxxiv. Told Candler: J. D. Hammond report on Paine College, June 1914, Warren A. Candler Papers, Series 2, Box 44, Folder 12, Emory University. Re-elected: Paine 50/1/217.

10. Atkins: *Augusta Chronicle*, 29 September 1915; Johnson 1970: 145–147. Sarah Gilbert: Cedar Grove E90 (date of death 13 October 1915), *Augusta Chronicle*, 17 October 1915, *Indianapolis Freeman*, 23 October 1915. Beg money: *Daily Oklahoman* (Oklahoma City), 05 November 1915, *Fort Worth Record* (TX), 07 November 1915, *Muskogee Times-Democrat* (OK), 13 November 1915, *Times-Picayune* (New Orleans), 15 November and 18 November 1915, *Richmond Planet*, 11 December 1915. Paid lectures: E.g., *St. Louis Argus*, 17 December 1915. Renew its support: *Augusta Chronicle*, 06 December 1915. Financial commissioner: Paine 50/1/213.

11. Conferences: E.g., *Augusta Chronicle*, 14 September 1916. Arizona: *Arizona Republic* (Phoenix), 17 October 1916, *Santa Ana Daily Register*, 21 October 1916. Santa Monica: Lakey 1996: 349. "I am writing this letter": Phillips 1932: 214–215 (dated 24 October 1916). Federal Council: *St. Louis Globe-Democrat*, 08 December 1916, *New York Age*, 14 December 1916, *Kansas City Sun* (MO), 16 December 1916, *Cleveland Gazette*, 23 December 1916, *Broad Ax* (Chicago), 06 January 1917, *Wisconsin Weekly Blade* (Madison), 18 January 1917; for Gilbert's work with the Council, see also McFarland 1916: 95–96. Du Bois: *The Crisis* 13.6, April 1917: 299. Bishopric: *Augusta Chronicle*, 18 December 1916.

12. Tried to resign: Paine 50/1/218, *Augusta Chronicle*, 07 January 1917. NAACP: Charter application, 09 February 1917, copy held at Lucy Craft Laney Museum of Black History, Augusta. Last-ditch: *Christian Advocate*, 20 April 1917. Addressed to him: Paine 50/1/222.

13. Fire: Cashin 1980: 218–219. Training ground: Cashin 1980: 221–222. Rallied: E.g., *Augusta Chronicle*, 05 June 1917. "God's War": *Augusta Chronicle*, 23 September 1917. Red Cross: *Augusta Chronicle*, 28 May and 23 December 1917. Registrar: Gilbert 1917: 74. Blue Ridge: *New York Age*, 16 August 1917, Weatherford 1917. Teach French: *Augusta Chronicle*, 15 August 1917. Black officers: Thompson 1917: 67 (Artemus Kendall), 96 (George Witherspoon).

14. "Black men are ready": *The Survey* (NY), 18 August 1917: 443–444. "Lift up our hands": *Muskegon Chronicle*, 17 April 1917. John Jr.'s draft

registration (NARA M1509, Michigan, Muskegon County, Draft Card G, no. 206) mentions four years at Claflin University, but his name does not appear in Claflin's records.

15. Kept up: *Daily Arkansas Gazette* (Little Rock), 22 September 1917, *Houston Post*, 03 November 1917, *Wichita Beacon* (KS), 08 November 1917, *Nashville Christian Advocate*, 23 November 1917, *Augusta Chronicle*, 03 February, 14 June 1918, *Knoxville Sentinel*, 10 April 1918. Betts: Johnson 1970: 128–129, 147–154. De Bardeleben: E.g., *North Carolina Christian Advocate*, 15 November 1917. "The old veteran": *Augusta Chronicle*, 21 April 1918.

16. Chicago: Phillips 1925: 501–512. Sunday School: CME Doctrines and Discipline 1918: 222–228, CME Quadrennial Address 1918: 15–16, Colored Methodist Episcopal Church 1922: 20. "A new thing": *Augusta Chronicle*, 26 May 1918. Alma: *Augusta Chronicle*, 19 August 1917, 14 July, 15 September, 05 December 1918. John Jr.: *Augusta Chronicle*, 23 June 1922 shows him in New York; there is no sign of him in Muskegon after 1917. Juanita: *Augusta Directory* 1917: 346.

17. Legend: John Hope to A. H. Gurney, 15 May 1928, John Wesley Gilbert Biographical File, Brown University; *Missionary Voice* 20.4 April 1930: 40, Pierce 1948: 162, Calhoun 1961: 129–130. Lambuth 1913b: 292 states the two men were "bitten by the tsetse fly constantly" in Africa. Trypanosomiasis: Checchi et al. 2008, Büscher et al. 2017.

18. Influenza: Cashin 1980: 223, Cashin 1985: 57. Accident: *Augusta Chronicle*, 23 February and 09 March 1919. Handwriting: Compare Paine 50/1/231 (30 December 1918) with Paine 50/1/234–235 (27 May 1919). To Nashville: *Nashville Banner*, 15 June 1919. Final appearance: *Nashville Tennessean*, 05 June 1919. "Mentally and physically": Colored Methodist Episcopal Church 1922: 20.

19. Last meeting: Paine 50/1/243–248 (10 March 1920). Lester: Colored Methodist Episcopal Church 1922: 20. Juanita: *Augusta Directory* 1921: 437 lists her occupation as "stenographer," a clear reference to CME Doctrines and Discipline 1918: 225. Broken health: Paine 50/1/2149 (09 March 1921). Mumpower: *Nashville Christian Advocate*, 10 October 1919; Calhoun 1961: 130. Pension: *Nashville Tennessean*, 21 November 1923. Confined to bed: *Augusta Chronicle*, 13 March and 17 July 1921.

20. "He loved [the] Bishop so": Calhoun 1961: 129. Campbell and Holsey: *Augusta Chronicle*, 15 August 1920. Walker: *Augusta Chronicle*, 29 July 1921, *Savannah Tribune*, 04 August 1921. Floyd: *New York Age,* 29 September 1923. John Jr.: Augusta Directory 1921: 437, *Augusta Chronicle*, 21 November 1923. Osceola died: *Augusta Chronicle*, 23 June 1922; Cedar Grove E140 (burial date 21 June 1922) and Georgia State Board of Health, Standard Certificate of Death, no. 15982, filed 20 June 1922, list her cause of death as nephritis. Gilbert's death: *Augusta Chronicle*, 19 November 1923, *Nashville Tennessean*, 19 November 1923. Pneumonia: Georgia State Board of Health, Standard

Certificate of Death, no. 33222, filed 22 November 1923; Cedar Grove E149 (burial date 19 November 1923) lists heart disease.

Conclusion:

1. Obituary: *Nashville Banner*, 09 December 1923. J. A. Martin (ca. 1876–1934): Paine Institute 1894–1895: 23, Caldwell 1920: 294–295, *Plaindealer* (Kansas City, KS), 14 December 1934, Yenser 1942: 359. Biography: Martin calls it a "monograph"; this text had been lost by 1933, when John Hope wrote Paine to request biographical information about Gilbert (correspondence in John Hope Records 134/3). The material Paine sent in response was written after 1925, because it quotes Colclough 1925: 78. Hope had a copy of Paine's material typed and sent to a Brown classmate of Gilbert's, Arthur E. Watson; this copy survives in the Brown archives. E. C. Calhoun rediscovered Martin's 1918 text and quoted portions of it (Calhoun 1961: 17–18), before it was destroyed in the 1968 fire at Paine.
2. Not the only one: See especially J. A. Lester in *Christian Index*, 06 December 1923. Expanded version: *Nashville Christian Advocate,* 25 January 1924; the *Advocate* had earlier (30 November 1923) published a brief death notice using erroneous information from MECS minister J. W. Perry (*Nashville Tennessean*, 21 November 1923). Most influential: Mott 1938: II.68, III.71. Reprinted: *The Crisis* 28.1, May 1934: 26. Hagiography: Colclough 1925; Colclough's letterhead from the 1940s (e.g., Colclough to McCray, 05 April 1943, John Henry McCray Papers, Box 1, Folder 2, University of South Carolina) lists a second book, *Life and Work of John W. Gilbert,* of which I can find no trace. Many others: E.g., [no author] 1930, Gray 1933, Brown 1941; another group of Gilbert profiles (e.g., Goddard and McDowell ca. 1919, Fridy ca. 1925) descends from Walker 1901. Researching: *Brown Alumni Monthly* 35.3, October 1934: 72.
3. John Jr.: *Jersey Journal* (Jersey City, NJ), 08 September 1931, *New York Age,* 19 September 1931. Juanita: *Augusta Chronicle,* 09 November 1924, 01 October 1971. Alma: *Augusta Chronicle,* 27 December 1925, 30 September 1928, 15 September 1929; *New York Age,* 27 July 1929. Eldridge Sims (some sources give his name as Eledreg or Eldrege, and his last name sometimes appears as Simms): *New York Amsterdam News* (Jersey City, NJ), 29 January 1930; *New York, New York, U.S., Extracted Marriage Index, 1866–1937*, no. 2595 (11 January 1930). Sims (who died in 1967) and Alma are buried together at The Evergreens Cemetery, Brooklyn, New York (information from cemetery staff). Unmarked: Federal Writers Project 1938: 116.
4. "All but tragic": Calhoun 1974: 1004. More documents: This possibility is not fanciful, as Natalia Vogeikoff-Brogan's rediscovery of a third photograph of Gilbert demonstrates. In 2009, a contractor cleaning out an abandoned house in Chicago found a cache of documents belonging to Richard Theodore

Greener (1844–1922), the first African American graduate of Harvard College and later dean of Howard University's law school.

5. Hammond: *Nashville Christian Advocate*, 21 December 1923. Tomlin: *Augusta Chronicle*, 28 September 1919, 02 July 1921, Johnson 1970: 160–161. Funeral: *Augusta Chronicle*, 21 November and 23 November 1923; cf. Pierce 1948: 162. The funeral was conducted by Trinity CME pastor I. H. Jones, only recently arrived in Augusta (*Augusta Chronicle*, 09 September 1919). J. A. Martin: E.g., *Augusta Chronicle*, 08 January, 28 January, 27 March 1928.

6. "Our friend and brother": *Christian Index*, 06 December 1923.

7. At that table: Millender 2012: 5. Memorial Chapel: *Augusta Chronicle*, 12 February 1968, 12 December 1982, 18 March 2010.

8. Markers and monuments: See www.historicaugusta.com. Trinity CME: *Augusta Chronicle*, 23 June 2018; during my visits to Augusta, I was able to see Mother Trinity in both her old and new locations.

9. "Negro missionary": E.g., *Tuskegee News* (AL), 12 May 1932, *Ruston Daily Leader* (LA), 09 September 1935, *San Saba News and Star* (TX), 05 September 1935, *Charlotte News* (NC), 06 February 1937, *Blanchard News* (OK), 20 May 1937, *Alexander City Outlook* (AL), 10 February 1938. Gilbert Center: *Asheville Citizen-Times*, 03 August 1941, Lowry 2010: 71–73. In the north: *Daily Times-Press* (Streator, IL), 14 July 1944, *Daily News* (Huntingdon, PA), 11 February 1948, *Canton Independent-Sentinel* (PA), 01 July 1948. Materials: Gray 1933, Gray 1948; see also the clipping from an article by I. C. Brown in Paine 53. Negro History Week: *Indianapolis Recorder*, 27 December 1951, *Los Angeles Sentinel*, 07 February 1952, *Union Springs Herald* (AL), 14 February 1952, *Jet*, 11 July 1963, *New Pittsburgh Courier*, 10 July 1965.

10. Out of touch: *Brown Alumni Monthly*, January 1917: 162. Renewed interest: John Hope to A. H. Gurney, 15 May 1928 (John Wesley Gilbert biographical file, Brown University Archives), John Hope Records 134/3. Advanced degree: Mitchell 1993. "The first": Flewellen and Dunnavant 2012.

11. "In that order": Calhoun 1974: 1005. Certainly recognized: Calhoun 1961: 104.

BIBLIOGRAPHY

I. Archival Materials

The abbreviations shown below in boldface are used in the endnotes. Archival materials not listed here are cited in full in the endnotes.

Archives. American School of Classical Studies at Athens. Athens, Greece.
Correspondence. **ASCSA 301/1**
Administrative Records. **ASCSA 309/1**
Eretria Excavation Records. **ASCSA ExcRec 008**
Archives. Archaeological Institute of America. Presidential Papers, President Norton Era Papers. Boston, Massachusetts. **AIA box/folder**
Charles C. Benson. *Ancient Days in Augusta*. Charles C. Benson Diaries, 1898–1953. MS 81–18. Reese Library Special Collections. Augusta University. Augusta, GA. **Benson 1953**
Carleton L. Brownson. European Tour Diary, 1927. W01-1258.8. William C. Brownson, Jr. (1928–) Papers, 1958–[ongoing]. Joint Archives of Holland, Hope College. Holland, MI. **Brownson 1927**
Archives. Brown University. Providence, Rhode Island.
Frederick Douglass Diary (Tour of Europe and Africa), September 15, 1886–June 14, 1888. Frederick Douglass Papers, Library of Congress Manuscript Collection. **Douglass Diary**
Δήμος Ερέτριας/Municipality of Eretria (Nea Psara). Eretria, Greece.
Μητρῷον Ἀρρένων τῆς Κοινότητος Νέων Ψαρῶν τῆς Ἐπαρχίας Χαλκίδος τοῦ Νομοῦ Εὐβοίας. Περιλαμβάνον τους γεννηθέντας κατὰ τὰ ἔτη 1845–1923. **MA**
Πρωτόκολλον τοῦ Δήμου Νέων Ψαρῶν (01 January 1890–16 May 1891, 15 May 1891–1892). **Πρωτ.**

Andrew Fossum Papers, P0541. Norwegian-American Historical Association. Northfield, MN. Correspondence. **NAHA P0541/box/folder**
Journal [ca. 1937]. **Fossum Journal**
Gerrish Kimball Collection, MS121, Correspondence, Caroline Gerrish to Harriet Kimball. Portsmouth Athenaeum. Portsmouth, NH. **Correspondent names, letter date**
Harris Family Papers, MS078. Series I. Correspondence, Box 1, Folders 5–11 (September 1890–April 1891). Portsmouth Athenaeum. Portsmouth, NH. **Correspondent names, letter date**
John Hope Records, Box 134, Folder 3 (John Wesley Gilbert). Archives Research Center. Robert W. Woodruff Library at Atlanta University Center. Atlanta, GA. **John Hope Records 134/3**
Jesse Macy Papers, State Historical Society of Iowa. Iowa City Collection. MS 17, Correspondence, 1862–1925. Box 1, Folder 24 (1888–1896). Iowa City, IA. **Iowa Ms 17/1/24**
National Archives and Records Service, General Services Administration. Washington, DC.
  Despatches from United States Ministers to Greece, 1868–1906. **NARA T159**
  Despatches from United States Consuls in Athens, 1837–1906.sss **NARA T362**
Archives. Paine College. Augusta, GA.
Trustees Minutes. **Paine 50/1/page number**
  E. Clayton Calhoun Personal Papers. **Calhoun Papers box/folder**
  Other items. **Paine box/folder**
The Annie Smith Peck Collection, Brooklyn College Archives & Special Collections, Brooklyn College Library. **Peck Collection series/box/folder**
John Pickard. "That First Trip in Central Greece." Manuscript in the family collection of Mrs. Katherine Tenthoff, great-grandaughter of John Pickard. **Pickard MS**
William Lewis Sachtleben papers (Collection 1841), Athens travel diary. Library Special Collections, Charles E. Young Research Library, UCLA. Los Angeles, CA. **Sachtleben Diary**
William Sanders Scarborough Papers. Box 8, Correspondence, Various Persons to WSS, Folder 1881–1889. Wilberforce University. Wilberforce, OH. **Scarborough Papers**
Ridgely Torrence Papers, C0172, Subseries 1A: Biography—The Story of John Hope. Manuscripts Division, Department of Special Collections, Princeton University Library. **Torrence Papers box/folder/page.**

Papers of Charles Waldstein. International Olympic Committee Historical Archives. Lausanne, Switzerland. [letters, 1889–1891; journal, 1889–1891]. IOC file number

The Papers of Sir Charles Walston. King's College Archive Centre. Cambridge, UK.
    Drafts of fictional work, notes on sociology and Greek art. CW/4/4/3
    Biographical file. CW/X/1/Misc. 103/31

II. Annual Catalogues, Directories, and Reports

Annual reports or proceedings of the American School of Classical Studies at Athens (ASCSA), the American Philological Association (APA), the Archaeological Institute of America (AIA), the British School at Athens (BSA), and Brown University are cited by year of publication. Two ASCSA reports include material from multiple years: ASCSA 1887 (1885–1886, part of 1886–1887), ASCSA 1889a (part of 1886–1887, 1887–1888); ASCSA 1889b covers only 1888–1889. Annual school catalogues are cited by the school year (e.g., Brown University 1886–1887 and Paine Institute 1894–1895), regardless of when in that year they were published. Historical and alumni catalogues of schools are listed in Section IV. City directories are cited by year of publication.

III. Newspapers and Periodicals

Newspaper articles are cited by date. Short articles or notices in periodicals are cited by date and page number. Longer or more significant periodical articles (e.g., those written by Gilbert and his fellow American Schoolers from Greece in 1890–1891) have full entries in Section IV. Greek newspapers and periodicals that used Julian dating (12 days behind the Gregorian calendar) are cited with Gregorian equivalents (e.g., *Νέα Εφημερίς*, 25 December 1890/06 January 1891).

IV. Books, Articles, Essays, and Other Works

[no author]. 1887. *Leading Manufacturers and Merchants of New Hampshire*. New York, Chicago, and Philadelphia.

[no author]. 1901. *Biographical Sketches of Representative Citizens of the Commonwealth of Massachusetts*. Boston.

[no author]. 1902. "Report of Fraternal Delegates." *African Methodist Episcopal Church Review* 19.1: 432–462.

[no author]. 1930. "Let Me Tell You a Good Story." *The Missionary Voice* 20.4: 40 (184).

[no author]. 1954. "Randall Albert Carter." *Journal of Negro History* 39.2: 158–160.

[no author]. 2002. "School Pioneer Is Profiled." *Ákoue* 47: 15.

Abbott, E. 1888. *A History of Greece. From the Earliest Times to the Ionian Revolt.* New York.

Abernethy, A. 1907. *A History of Iowa Baptist Schools.* Osage, IA.

Ackerman, R. 1987. *J. G. Frazer: His Life and Work.* Cambridge, UK.

Adams, M. W. 1918. *General Catalogue of Atlanta University, 1867–1918.* Atlanta.

Agathonikos, A./Αγαθόνικος, A. 1891. *Αριστοτέλους Αθηναίων Πολιτεία.* Athens.

Agbe-Davies, A. 2002. "Black Scholars, Black Pasts." *SAA Archaeological Record* 2.4: 24–28.

Agbe-Davies, A. 2003. "Conversations: Archaeology and the Black Experience." *Archaeology* 56.1: n.p.

Aijootian, A. 1996. "Praxiteles," in *Personal Styles in Greek Sculpture*, ed. O. Palagia and J. J. Pollitt, 91–129. Cambridge, UK.

Allen, S. H. 2002. "'Americans in the East': Francis Henry Bacon, Joseph Thacher Clarke, and the AIA at Assos," in *Excavating Our Past: Perspectives on the History of the Archaeological Institute of America*, ed. S. H. Allen, 63–92. Boston.

Allen, S. H., and K. M. Hebert. 2002. "Current Local Societies of the Archaeological Institute of American in Order of Their Charters of Foundation," in *Excavating Our Past: Perspectives on the History of the Archaeological Institute of America*, ed. S. H. Allen, 217–220. Boston.

Allen, Jr., T. 1896. "The Invasion of the Bicycle: Athens." *Outing* 28.3: 173–180, 28.4: 310–312.

Allinson, F. 1915. "In Memoriam: James Irving Manatt: [Born February 17, 1845; Died February 13, 1915]." *The Classical Journal* 10.8: 370–373.

Alvord, J. W. 1867. *Third Semi-Annual Report on Schools for Freedmen, January 1, 1867.* Washington, DC.

Alvord, J. W. 1870. *Letters from the South, Relating to the Condition of Freedmen, Addressed to Major General O.O. Howard.* Washington, DC.

Amandry, P. 1992. "Fouilles de Delphes et raisins de Corinthe: histoire d'une négociation," in *La redécouverte de Delphes*, ed. O. Picard and E. Pentazos, 77–128. Paris.

Anderson, J. D. 1988. *The Education of Blacks in the South, 1860–1935.* Chapel Hill and London.

Anet, H. 1913. *En eclaireur: Voyage d'Étude au Congo Belge*. Brussels.

Anthony, D. 1997. "The Remarkable Waldstein." *Journal of Olympic History* 5.1: 18–19.

Antrobus, A. M. 1915. *History of Des Moines County Iowa and Its People, Volume I*. Chicago.

Appleton. 1891. *Appleton's European Guide for English-Speaking Travellers, Twenty-Eighth Edition*. New York and London.

Arlen, S. 1990. *The Cambridge Ritualists: An Annotated Bibliography of the Works by and About Jane Ellen Harrison, Gilbert Murray, Francis M. Cornford, and Arthur Bernard Cook*. London.

Augusta Bicentennial Pageant Commission. 1935. *Augusta Bicentennial, 1735–1935. May 12th–18th. Pageant Book*. Augusta.

Baedeker, K. 1888. *Griechenland. Handbuch für Reisende von Karl Baedeker*. Leipzig.

Baedeker, K. 1889. *Greece. Handbook for Travellers*. Leipsic and London.

Baltrusch, E. 2014. "Curtius, Ernst," in *Brill's New Pauly. History of Classical Scholarship: A Biographical Dictionary*, ed. P. Kuhlmann and H. Schneider, 130–131. Leiden and Boston.

Baptist Home Missions. 1883. *Baptist Home Missions in North America*. New York.

Barber, A. E. 1899. "William Greene Brownson, M. A., M. D., Noroton," in *Proceedings of the Connecticut Medical Society*, ed. H. P. Stearns, C. S. Rodman, and N. E. Wordin, 362–364. Bridgeport.

Barnes, M. R. 1997. "Architectural, Archaeological, and Historical Investigation of the Old Medical College of Georgia Building," in *Bones in the Basement: Postmortem Racism in Nineteenth-Century Medical Training*, ed. R. L. Blakely and J. M. Harrington, 28–47. Washington, DC.

Barrows, I. C. 1913. *A Sunny Life: The Biography of Samuel June Barrows*. Boston.

Barrows, S. J. 1898. *The Isles and Shrines of Greece*. Boston.

Bartlett, I. H. 1954. *From Slave to Citizen: The Story of the Negro in Rhode Island*. Providence.

Bastéa, E. 2000. *The Creation of Modern Athens: Planning the Myth*. Cambridge and New York.

Bates, W. 1914. "Archaeological News." *American Journal of Archaeology* 18.3: 381–423.

Bauman, M. K. 1981. *Warren Akin Candler: The Conservative as Idealist*. Metuchen, NJ, and London.

Baumeister, A. 1864. *Topographische Skizze der Insel Euboia*. Lübeck.

Bayles, R. M. 1891. *History of Providence County, Rhode Island, Volume I*. New York.

Beach, H. A. 1915. "The Negro Christian Student Conference, May 14–18, 1914." *International Review of Mission* 4.2: 275–282.

Beard, M. 1993. "Casts and Cast-Offs: The Origins of the Museum of Classical Archaeology." *Proceedings of the Cambridge Philological Society* 39: 1–29.

Beard, M. 2000. *The Invention of Jane Harrison*. Cambridge, MA.

Beard, M. 2001. "'Pausanias in Petticoats,' or *The Blue Jane*," in *Pausanias: Travel and Memory in Roman Greece*, ed. S. Alcock, J. Cherry, and J. Elsner, 224–239. Oxford, UK.

Becker, T. H. 1999. "Daniel B. Williams, 1861–1895." *The Classical Outlook* 76.3: 94–95.

Bedinger, R. D. 1920. *Triumphs of the Gospel in the Belgian Congo*. Richmond and Texarkana.

Belkin, H. E., and T. Gidwitz. 2020. "The Contributions and Influence of Two Americans, Henry S. Washington and Frank A. Perret, to the Study of Italian Volcanism with Emphasis on Volcanoes in the Naples Area," in *Vesuvius, Campi Flegrei, and Campanian Volcanism*, ed. B. De Vivo, H. E. Belkin, and G. Rolandi, 9–32. Amsterdam.

Benson, E. F. 1930. *As We Were: A Victorian Peep-Show*. London, New York, and Toronto.

Bickford-Smith, R. A. H. 1893. *Greece Under King George*. London.

Biers, W. R., and T. D. Boyd. 1982. "Ikarion in Attica: 1888–1981." *Hesperia* 51.1: 1–18.

Billot, M.-F. 1992. "Le Cynosarges, Antiochos et les tanneurs. Questions de topographie." *Bulletin de correspondance hellénique* 116.1: 119–156.

Bitner, B. J. 2015. *Paul's Political Strategy in 1 Corinthians 1–4: Constitution and Covenant (Society for New Testament Studies Monograph Series 163)*. New York.

Bjork, K. 1949. "Thorstein Veblen and St. Olaf's College: A Group of Letters by Thorbjørn N. Mohn [1890]." *Norwegian-American Studies and Records* 15: 122–130.

Blandin, B. 2007. *Eretria XVII. Fouilles et recherches. Les pratiques funéraires d'époque géometrique à Érétrie, Volume I – Texte*. Renens.

Blassingame, J. W., and J. R. McKivigan (eds.). 1992. *The Frederick Douglass Papers. Series One: Speeches, Debates and Interviews. Volume 5: 1881–1895*. New Haven.

Blight, D. W. 2018. *Frederick Douglass: Prophet of Freedom*. New York.

Boas, E. 1893. *The European Travelers' Memorandum Book. Issued by the Hamburg-American Packet Co.* New York and Chicago.

Boegehold, A. 1963. "Toward a Study of Athenian Voting Procedure." *Hesperia* 32: 366–374.

Bonitz, H. 1880. *The Origin of the Homeric Poems* [transl. L. R. Packard]. New York.

Bowen, H. C. 1930. *The History of Woodstock, Connecticut. Genealogies of Woodstock Families, Volume II.* Norwood, MA.

Brawley, B. 1917. *History of Morehouse College. Written on the Authority of the Board of Trustees.* Atlanta.

Breaux, E. E., and T. D. Perry. 1969. "Inman E. Page: Outstanding Educator." *Negro History Bulletin* 32.5: 8–12.

Bronson, W. C. 1914. *The History of Brown University, 1764–1914.* Boston.

Brooks, J. W. 1891. "A Few Things About Athens." *Ariel* 14.4: 47–49.

Brooks, J. W. 1911. "Dr. Kalopothakes and the Modern Greeks." *The Missionary Review of the World* 24.11: 815–820.

Brown, P. B., R. P. Henry, H. L. Koopman, and C. S. Brigham. 1909. *Memories of Brown. Traditions and Recollections Gathered from Many Sources.* Providence.

Brown, R. K. 2006. "Post-Civil War Violence in Augusta, Georgia." *Georgia Historical Quarterly* 90.2: 196–213.

Brown, R. K. 2017. "A Martyr to Duty: The Life and Tragic Death of Thomas L. Cottin, African American Educator and Soldier." *Augusta Richmond County History* 48.1: 19–31.

Brown, W. G., J. Pickard, and M. K. Organ. 1909. *Phi Beta Kappa. Catalogue of the Alpha of Missouri. 1901–1909.* Columbia, MO.

Brown University. 1936. *Historical Catalogue of Brown University, 1736–1934.* Providence, RI.

Brownson, C. 1891a. "The Opening of the American School at Athens." *The Independent* 43.2202: 8.

Brownson, C. 1891b. "The Burial of Schliemann." *New York Evangelist* 62.15: 2.

Brownson, C. 1891c. "Excavations by the School at Eretria, 1891. V. The Theatre at Eretria. Orchestra and Cavea." *AJAHFA* 7.3: 266–280.

Brownson, C. 1893. "The Relation of the Archaic Pediment Reliefs from the Acropolis to Vase-Painting." *AJAHFA* 8.1: 28–41.

Brownson, C. 1897. *A Smaller History of Greece.* New York.

Bourchier, J. D. 1890. "A Glance at Contemporary Greece." *The Fortnightly Review* n.s. 47: 864–880.

Buck, C. 1889a. "Discoveries in the Attic Deme of Ikaria, 1888. IV. Chronological Report of Excavations. V. Topography of the Ikarian District. VI. Architectural Remains." *AJAHFA* 5.2: 154–181.

Buck, C. 1889b. "Discoveries in the Attic Deme of Ikaria, 1888. VII. Inscriptions from Ikaria. No. 8–17." *AJAHFA* 5.3: 304–319.

Buckley, J. M. 1895. *Travels in Three Continents*. New York and Cincinnati.

Burke, W. L. 2017. *All for Civil Rights: African American Lawyers in South Carolina, 1868–1968*. Athens, GA.

Burr, V. I. (ed.). 1990. *The Secret Eye: The Journal of Ella Gertrude Clanton Thomas, 1848–1889*. Chapel Hill and London.

Büscher, P., G. Cecchi, V. Jamonneau, and G. Priotto. 2017. "Human African Trypanosomiasis." *The Lancet* 390.10110: 2397–2409.

Butchart, R. E. 2010. *Schooling the Freed People: Teaching, Learning, and the Struggle for Black Freedom, 1861–1876*. Chapel Hill.

Byington, E. H. 1890. "Historical Address," in *Addresses and Letters for the Centennial of the Congregational Church, Hinesburgh, Vermont, 1789–1890*, 12–61. Burlington, VT.

Cable, G. W. 1888. *The Negro Question*. Washington, DC.

Cain, H.-U. 2014. "Overbeck, Johannes," in *Brill's New Pauly. History of Classical Scholarship: A Biographical Dictionary*, ed. P. Kuhlmann and H. Schneider, 459–460. Leiden and Boston.

Caldwell, A. B. 1917. *History of the American Negro and His Institutions, Georgia Edition. Original Edition, Illustrated*. Atlanta.

Caldwell, A. B. 1919. *History of the American Negro, South Carolina Edition*. Atlanta.

Caldwell, A. B. 1920. *History of the American Negro, Georgia Edition. Volume II*. Atlanta.

Caldwell, L. 2015. "Pure in Heart, Brave in Spirit: the Life of Silas X. Floyd." *Augusta Magazine*, 01 February 2015. https://augustamagazine.com/2015/02/01/pure-in-heart-brave-in-spirit-the-life-of-silas-x-floyd/. 10 September 2017.

Calhoun, E. C. 1961. *Of Men Who Ventured Much and Far: The Congo Quest of Dr. Gilbert and Bishop Lambuth*. Atlanta.

Calhoun, E. C. 1974. "Gilbert, John Wesley (1865–1923)," in *Encyclopedia of World Methodism, Volume I*, ed. N. Harmon, 1004–1005. Nashville.

Callahan, A. D. 2006. *The Talking Book: African Americans and the Bible*. New Haven and London.

Callaway, M. 1884. *Every Seventh Soul*. Atlanta.

Camp, J. M. 2001. *The Archaeology of Athens*. New Haven and London.

Campbell, C. 2004. *Phylloxera: How Wine Was Saved for the World*. London.

Canady, A. 2009. "The Limits to Improving Race Relations in the South: The YMCA Blue Ridge Assembly in Black Mountain, North Carolina, 1906–1930." *The North Carolina Historical Review* 86.4: 404–436.

Cannon, J. 1926. *History of Southern Methodist Missions.* Nashville.

Carter, E. R. 1894. *The Black Side. A Partial History of the Business, Religious, and Educational Side of the Negro in Atlanta, Ga.* Atlanta.

Carter, R. A. 1893. *Address Before the Paine Institute Literary and Debating Society.* Augusta.

Carton, B. 2009. "From Hampton '[i]nto the Heart of Africa': How Faith in God and Folklore Turned Congo Missionary William Sheppard into a Pioneering Ethnologist." *History in Africa* 36: 53–86.

Cashin, E. J. 1978. *An Informal History of Augusta.* Augusta.

Cashin, E. J. 1980. *The Story of Augusta.* Augusta.

Cashin, E. J. 1985. *The Quest: A History of Public Education in Richmond County, Georgia.* Augusta.

Cashin, E. J. 1995. *Old Springfield: Race and Religion in Augusta, Georgia.* Augusta.

Cassell. 1890. *Cassell's Complete Pocket-Guide to Europe.* London.

Chace, E. B. 1891. *Anti-Slavery Reminiscences.* Central Falls, RI.

Chambers, M. 1993. "A Tour Through Greek Guidebooks," in *Alpha to Omega. Studies in Honor of George John Szemler on His Sixty-Fifth Birthday*, ed. W. Cherf, 7–22. Chicago.

Chambers, M. 1990. "Ernst Curtius," in *Classical Scholarship: A Biographical Encyclopedia*, ed. W. W. Briggs and W. M. Calder III, 37–42. New York and London.

Chambers, M. 1996. "Guidebooks to Greece," in *Encyclopedia of the History of Classical Archaeology*, ed. N. de Grummond, 548–550. Westport, CT.

Chang, D. 2010. *Citizens of a Christian Nation: Evangelical Missions and the Problem of Race in the Nineteenth Century.* Philadelphia.

Chatziioanou, M. C. 2009. "Like a Rolling Stone, R. A. H. Bickford-Smith (1859–1916) from Britain to Greece," in *Scholars, Travels, Archives: Greek History and Culture Through the British School at Athens*, ed. M. Llewellyn Smith, P. M. Kitromilides, and E. Calligas, 39–48. Athens.

Checchi, F., J. A. N. Filipe, M. P. Barrett, and D. Chandramohan. 2008. "The Natural Progression of Gambiense Sleeping Sickness: What Is the Evidence?" *PLOS Neglected Tropical Diseases* 2.12: e303.

Cheshire, P. 2018. *William Gilbert and Esoteric Romanticism: A Contextual Study and Annotated Edition of "The Hurricane."* Liverpool.

Chi Psi Fraternity. 1902. *The Sixth Decennial Catalogue of the Chi Psi Fraternity*. Auburn, NY.

Clark, E. T. 1933. *The Unique Adventure (Paine College)*. Augusta, GA.

Clark, K. 2003. "Making History: African American Commemorative Celebrations in Augusta, Georgia, 1865–1913," in *Monuments to the Lost Cause: Women, Art, and the Landscapes of Southern Memory*, ed. C. Mills and P. H. Simpson, 46–63. Knoxville.

Clark, W. A. 1909. *A Lost Arcadia or The Story of My Old Community*. Augusta.

Clarke, G. K. 1902. *The Descendants of Nathaniel Clarke and His Wife Elizabeth Somerby of Newbury, Massachusetts. A History of Ten Generations, 1642–1902*. Boston.

Clary, Jr., G. E. 1965. *The Founding of Paine College: A Unique Venture in Inter-Racial Cooperation in the New South (1882–1903)*. PhD Dissertation, University of Georgia.

Clary, Jr., G. E. 1971. "Southern Methodism's 'Unique Adventure' in Race Relations: Paine College, 1882–1903." *Methodist History* 9.1: 22–33.

Clary, Jr. G. E. 1974. "The Story of the Founding of Paine College, Augusta, Georgia." *Historical Highlights* 4: 26–31.

Clary, Jr. G. E. 1975. "The Story of the Founding of Paine College, Augusta, Georgia: Part II." *Historical Highlights* 5: 5–12.

Cobb, T. 1851. *A Digest of the Statute Laws of the State of Georgia*. Athens, GA.

Coe, B. 1978. *Cameras: From Daguerreotype to Instant Picture*. New York.

Colclough, J. 1925. *The Spirit of John Wesley Gilbert*. Nashville.

Cody, C. A. 1982. "Naming, Kinship, and Estate Dispersal: Notes on Slave Family Life on a South Carolina Plantation, 1786 to 1833." *William and Mary Quarterly* 39.1: 192–211.

Cody, C. A. 1987. "There Was No 'Absalom' on the Ball Plantations: Slave-Naming Practices in the South Carolina Low Country, 1720–1865." *American Historical Review* 92.3: 563–596.

Colored Methodist Episcopal Church. 1922. *Quadrennial Address of the Bishops of the Colored Methodist Episcopal Church to the Fourteenth Session of the General Conference*. Chicago.

Corey, C. H. 1895. *A History of the Richmond Theological Seminary, with Reminiscences of Thirty Years' Work Among the Colored People of the South*. Richmond.

Cornell, N. 2000. *The 1864 Census for Re-Organizing the Georgia Militia*. Baltimore.

Cortissoz, R. 1921. *The Life of Whitelaw Reid. Volume II: Politics-Diplomacy*. New York.

Crawford, H., A. Crombie, S. J. Herben, and H. B. Kendall (eds.). 1901. *Proceedings of the Third Œcumenical Methodist Conference held in City Road Chapel, London, September 1901*. New York and Cincinnati.

Crogman, W. H. 1885. "Negro Education: Its Helps and Hindrances." *Eighteenth Annual Report of the Freedmen's Aid Society of the Methodist Episcopal Church*, 37–48. Cincinnati.

Crogman, W. H. 1896. *Talks for the Times*. Atlanta.

Cromwell, J. W. 1896. *History of the Bethel Literary and Historical Association*. Washington, DC.

Crow, J. M., and J. T. Clarke. 1888. "The Athenian Pnyx." *Papers of the American School of Classical Studies at Athens* 4: 207–260.

Crummell, A. 1898. "The Attitude of the American Mind toward the Negro Intellect." *The American Negro Academy Occasional Papers* 3: 8–19.

Cunard. 1886. *History of the Cunard Steamship Company*. London.

Cunningham, R. D. 2020. "The Black 'Immune' Regiments in the Spanish-American War." *Army Historical Foundation*, [undated]. https://armyhistory.org/the-black-immune-regiments-in-the-spanish-american-war/. 06 October 2020.

Curtis, H. 2018. *Holy Humanitarians: American Evangelicals and Global Aid*. Cambridge, MA.

Curtis, L. S. 1962. "The Negro Publicly-Supported College in Missouri." *Journal of Negro Education* 31.3: 251–259.

Curtius, E. 1893. "Paulus in Athen." *Sitzungsberichte der Königlich Preussischen Akademie der Wissenschaften zu Berlin. Philosophisch-historische Klasse* 43.2: 925–938.

Curtius, E., and A. Milchhöfer. 1891. *Die Stadtgeschichte von Athen, mit einer Übersicht de Schriftequellen zur Topographie von Athen*. Berlin.

Curtius, E., and J. A. Kaupert. 1878. *Atlas von Athen*. Berlin.

Cushing, W. L. 1888. "The Theatre of Thoricus, Supplementary Report." *Papers of the American School of Classical Studies at Athens (1885–1886)* 4: 23–34.

Cutter, W. R. 1908. *Historical Homes and Places and Genealogical and Personal Memoirs Relating to the Families of Middlesex County, Massachusetts. Volume IV*. New York.

Daggett, L. H. 1879. *Historical Sketches of Womans' Missionary Societies in American and England*. Boston.

Dartmouth College. 1940. *Dartmouth College and Associated Schools General Catalogue, 1769–1940*. Hanover, NH.

Daskalakis, V./Δασκαλάκης, B. 2015. *Οινοποιείο Σκουζέ στο Μαραθώνα Αττικής: πρόταση αποκατάστασης και επανάχρησης*. Athens.

Davis, J. 2015. "Archives from the Trash: The Multidimensional Annie Smith Peck: Mountaineer, Suffragette, Classicist." *From the Archivist's Notebook*, 01 May 2015. https://nataliavogeikoff.com/2015/05/01/archives-from-the-trash-the-multidimensional-annie-smith-peck-mountaineer-suffragette-classicist/. 18 September 2019.

Davis, L. 1998. *A Clashing of the Soul: John Hope and the Dilemma of African American Leadership and Black Higher Education in the Early Twentieth Century*. Atlanta.

Davis, R. H. 1893. *The Rulers of the Mediterranean*. New York.

de Bardeleben, M. 1920. "Beginnings in a Stable." *The Epworth Era* 26.10: 423–427.

de Bardeleben, M. 1921. "The Story of a Great Choice," in *When God Walks the Road and Other Missionary Stories*, ed. S. E. Haskin, 30–32. Nashville.

Declerq, P. 1897. *Grammaire de la langue des Bene Lulua*. Brussels.

de Grummond, N. (ed.). 1996. *Encyclopedia of the History of Classical Archaeology*. Westport, CT.

Dempsey, E. L. 1940. *Atticus Green Haygood*. Nashville.

de Rezende, I. M. 2012. *Visuality and Colonialism in the Congo: From the "Arab War" to Patrice Lumumba, 1880s to 1961*. PhD dissertation, University of Michigan.

Deschamps, G. 1892. *La Grèce d'aujourd'hui*. Paris.

Develin, B., and M. Kilmer. 1997. "What Kleisthenes Did." *Historia* 46.1: 3–18.

Dilbeck, D. H. 2018. *Frederick Douglass: America's Prophet*. Chapel Hill.

DiSalvo, L. 2013. "Situating Classical Archaeology in the Midwest: The Early History of the University of Missouri's Plaster Cast Collection." *MVSE: Annual of the Museum of Art and Archaeology, University of Missouri* 47: 25–57.

Donaldson, B. 2001. "Standing on a Volcano: The Leadership of William Jefferson White," in *Paternalism in a Southern City: Race, Religion, and Gender in Augusta, Georgia*, ed. E. Cashin and G. Eskew, 135–176. Athens, GA and London.

Donaldson, B. 2002. *New Negroes in a New South: Race, Power, and Ideology in Georgia, 1890–1925*. PhD Dissertation, Emory University.

Doane, W. C. 1896. "A Visit to Athens." *Harper's New Monthly Magazine* 93.553 (June): 3–14.

D'Ooge, M. L. 1893a. "The American School at Athens: First Article." *The Chautauquan* 16.4: 387.

D'Ooge, M. L. 1893b. "The American School at Athens: Second Article." *The Chautauquan* 16.5: 515.

Dörpfeld, W., E. Gardner, and W. Loring. 1891. "The Theatre at Megalopolis." *Classical Review* 5.6: 284–285.

Dorr, D. F. 1858. *A Colored Man Round the World*. Cleveland.

Douglass, F. 1892. *Life and Times of Frederick Douglass* [new revised ed.]. Boston.

Drew, M. E. C. 2010. *Divine Will, Restless Heart: The Life and Works of Dr. John Jefferson Smallwood, 1863–1912*. Bloomington.

Drew, M. E. C. 2011. *One Common Country for One Common People: Selected Writings and Speeches of Dr. John Jefferson Smallwood*. Bloomington.

Drisler, H. 1863. *"Bible View of Slavery, by John H. Hopkins, D. D., Bishop of the Diocese of Vermont," Examined*. New York.

Dritsas, M. 2006. "From Travellers' Accounts to Travel Books and Guide Books: The Formation of a Greek Tourism Market in the 19th Century." *Tourismos* 1.1: 27–52.

Dritsas, M. 2009. "Tourism and Business During the Twentieth Century in Greece: Continuity and Change," in *Europe at the Seaside: The Economic History of Mass Tourism in the Mediterranean*, ed. L. Segreto, C. Manera, and M. Pohl, 49–71. New York and Oxford.

Drower, M. S. 1985. *Flinders Petrie: A Life in Archaeology*. London.

Du Bois, W. E. B. 1899. *The Philadelphia Negro: A Social Study*. Philadelphia.

Du Bois, W. E. B. 1903. *The Souls of Black Folk. Essays and Sketches*. Chicago.

Du Bois, W. E. B. (ed.). 1907. *Economic Co-Operation Among Negro Americans*. Atlanta.

Du Bois, W. E. B., and A. G. Dill (eds.). 1910. *The College-Bred Negro American*. Atlanta.

Ducrey, P. 2004. *Eretria: A Guide to the Ancient City*. Athens.

Dumont, S. 2020. *Vrysaki: A Neighborhood Lost in Search of the Athenian Agora*. Princeton.

Duncan, W. B. 1901. *Twentieth Century Sketches of the South Carolina Conference, M. E. Church, South*. Columbia, SC.

Dupont, B., A. Gandhi, and T. J. Weiss. 2008. "The American Invasion of Europe: The Long Term Rise in Overseas Travel, 1820–2000." *National Bureau of Economic Research*, working paper 13977.

Dupont, B., A. Gandhi, and T. J. Weiss. 2012. "The Long-Term Rise in Overseas Travel by Americans, 1820–2000." *Economic History Review* 65.1: 144–167.

Dupont, B., D. Keeling, and T. Weiss. 2016. "First Cabin Fares from New York to the British Isles, 1826–1914." *National Bureau of Economic Research*, working paper 22426.

Dürrbach, F. 1890. *De Oropo et Amphiari Sacro*. Paris.

Dworkin, I. 2017. *Congo Love Song: African American Culture and the Crisis of the Colonial State*. Chapel Hill.

Dyson, S. L. 1998. *Ancient Marbles to American Shores: Classical Archaeology in the United States*. Philadelphia.

Dyson, S. L. 2004. *Eugénie Sellers Strong: Portrait of An Archaeologist*. London.

Dyson, S. L. 2006. *In Pursuit of Ancient Pasts: A History of Classical Archaeology in the Nineteenth and Twentieth Centuries*. New Haven and London.

Dyson, S. L. 2014. *The Last Amateur: The Life of William J. Stillman*. Albany.

Earle, M. E. 1889. "Excavations by the American School at the Theatre of Sikyon. II. Supplementary Report of the Excavations." *AJAHFA* 5.3: 286–292.

Ellison, C., et al. 2003. *Cedar Grove Cemetery*. Augusta.

Elmore, C. J. 2014. "Savannah State University." *New Georgia Encyclopedia*. 29 July 2014. https://www.georgiaencyclopedia.org/articles/education/savannah-state-university. 01 October 2020.

Engs, R. F. 1979. *Freedom's First Generation: Black Hampton, Virginia, 1861–1890*. New York.

Eskew, G. T. 1992. "Black Elitism and the Failure of Paternalism in Postbellum Georgia: The Case of Bishop Lucius Henry Holsey." *Journal of Southern History* 58.4: 637–666.

Eskew, G. T. 2001. "Paternalism Among Augusta's Methodists: Black, White, and Colored," in *Paternalism in a Southern City: Race, Religion, and Gender in Augusta, Georgia*, ed. E. Cashin and G. Eskew, 85–109. Athens, GA and London.

Etienne, R. 1996. "L'École française d'Athènes, 1846–1996." *Bulletin de correspondance hellénique* 120.1: 3–22.

Ewell, J. L. 1891. "A Glimpse at Schliemann's Discoveries in Hellas." *The New England Magazine* n. s. 4.5: 634–646.

Fachard, S. 2004. "L'enceinte urbaine d'Érétrie: un état de la question." *Antike Kunst* 47: 91–109.

Fachard, S. 2007. "Les fortifications de l'acropole: sondage dans le secteur de la tour nord." *Antike Kunst* 50: 129–134.

Fachard, S. 2012. *La défense du territoire: étude de la "chôra" érétrienne et de ses fortifications*. Athens.

Fachard, S., D. Knoepfler, K. Reber, A. Karapschalidou, T. Krapf, T. Theurillat, and P. Kalamara. 2017. "Recent Research at the Sanctuary of Artemis Amarysia in Amarynthos (Euboea)." *Archaeological Reports* 63: 167–180.

Fachard, S., and D. Pirisino. 2015. "Routes out of Attica," in *Autopsy in Athens: Recent Archaeological Research on Athens and Attica*, ed. M. M. Miles, 139–153. Oxford and Philadelphia.

Faunce, W. H. P, T. D. Seymour, and W. G. Everett. 1907. *Memorial Addresses in Honor of Professor Albert Harkness in Sayles Hall, Brown University, October the Thirty-First, MDCCCVII. With Addresses by President W. H. P. Faunce, Professor Thomas D. Seymour and Professor Walter G. Everett*. Providence.

Federal Writers' Project in Georgia, Augusta Unit. 1938. *Augusta*. Augusta.

Ferguson, M. 2010. "Enslaved and Emancipated Africans on Crete," in *Race and Slavery in the Middle East: Histories of Trans-Saharan Africans in Nineteenth-Century Egypt, Sudan, and the Ottoman Mediterranean*, ed. T. Walz and K. M. Cuno, 171–195. Cairo.

Fikes Jr., R. 2002. "African-American Scholars of Greco-Roman Culture." *Journal of Blacks in Higher Education* 35: 120–124.

Filler, L. 1954. "Liberalism, Anti-Slavery, and the Founders of *The Independent*." *The New England Quarterly* 27.3: 291–306.

Findlay, A. F. 1894/95. "St. Paul and the Areopagus." *Annual of the British School at Athens* 1: 78–89.

Finlay, G. 1838. *Remarks on the Topography of the Oropia and Diacria*. Athens.

Finnegan, T. 2013. *A Deed So Accursed: Lynching in Mississippi and South Carolina, 1881–1940*. Charlottesville.

Fish, J. O. 1970. "Southern Methodism and Accommodation of the Negro, 1902–1915." *Journal of Negro History* 55.3: 200–214.

Fleming, W. L. 1927. *The Freedman's Bank: A Chapter in the Economic History of the Negro Race*. Chapel Hill and London.

Flewellen, A., and J. Dunnavant. 2012. "Society of Black Archaeologists." *African Diaspora Archaeology Network Newsletter*, Spring: n. p.

Floyd, S. X. 1892. *A Sketch of Charles T. Walker, D. D., Pastor of Tabernacle Baptist Church, Augusta, GA*. Augusta.

Floyd, S. X. 1902. *Life of Charles T. Walker, D. D. ("The Black Spurgeon")*. Nashville.

Foner, E. 1988. *Reconstruction: America's Unfinished Revolution, 1863–1877*. New York.

Forman, Mrs. G. W. 1913. "The Los Angeles Annual Conference of the Woman's Missionary Society." *The Missionary Voice* 3.4: 252–253.

Forman, M. 2009. "Invisible Hands of Science." *Dartmouth Engineer Magazine* 5.1: 16–21.

Forsén, J. 2010. "Aphidna in Attica – revisited," in *Mesohelladika. La Grèce continentale au Bronze Moyen*, ed. A. Philippa-Touchais et al. (*Bulletin de correspondance hellénique* suppl. 52), 223–234. Paris and Athens.

Fossum, A. 1891a. "Excavations by the School at Eretria, 1891. III. Excavations in the Theatre of Eretria." *AJAHFA* 7.3: 253–257.

Fossum, A. 1891b. "Excavations by the School at Eretria, 1891. IV. The Stage-Building of the Theatre of Eretria." *AJAHFA* 7.3: 257–266.

Fossum, A. 1898. "The Eiskyklema in the Eretrian Theatre." *AJAHFA* 2.3/4: 187–194.

Fossum, A. 1905. "The Theater at Sikyon." *AJAHFA* 9.3: 263–276.

Fossum, A. 1918. *The Norse Discovery of America*. Minneapolis.

Fossum, A. 1926. "Harmony in the Theatre at Epidauros." *American Journal of Archaeology* 30.1: 70–75.

Fox, S. 2003. *Transatlantic: Samuel Cunard, Isambard Brunel, and the Great Atlantic Steamships*. New York.

Franklin, J. H. 1998. *George Washington Williams: A Biography* [reprint]. Durham, NC.

Franklin, M. 1997. "Why Are There So Few Black American Archaeologists?" *Antiquity* 71: 799–801.

Frazer, J. G. 1898. *Pausanias's Description of Greece. Vol. II: Commentary on Book I*. London.

Freedman, D. 1999. "African-American Schooling in the South Prior to 1861." *Journal of Negro History* 84.1: 1.47.

Frey, S., and B. Wood. 2000. *Come Shouting to Zion: African American Protestantism in the American South and British Caribbean to 1830*. Chapel Hill.

Fridy, A. [ca. 1925]. *Meeting Life's Challenge: Story of John Wesley Gilbert*. Nashville. [Courtesy of the Methodist Library, Drew University].

Friedemann, P. 1996. "À propos du nouveau plan archéologique d'Érétrie." *Antike Kunst* 39.2: 102–106.

Fries, A. 2017. "John Wesley Gilbert Book List." Unpublished typescript, Brown University.

Fromherz, P. 2011. "The Battlefield of Marathon: The Tropaion, Herodotos, and E. Curtius." *Historia* 60.4: 383–412.

Frothingham Jr., A. 1890a. "Archaeological News." *AJAHFA* 6.1/2: 154–260.

Frothingham Jr., A. 1890b. "Archaeological News." *AJAHFA* 6.3: 321–402.

Frothingham Jr., A. 1890c. "Archaeological News." *AJAHFA* 6.4: 504–595.

Frothingham Jr., A. 1891. "Archaeological News." *AJAHFA* 7.1/2: 81–197.

Frothingham Jr., A., and A. Marsh. 1885. "Archaeological News." *AJAHFA* 1.4: 420–462.

Frye, H. 1896. *The History of North Atlantic Steam Navigation*. London.

Fuks, A. 1951. "Κολωνος μίσθιος: Labour Exchange in Classical Athens." *Eranos* 49: 171–173.

Gallant, T. W. 2015. *The Edinburgh History of the Greeks, 1768 to 1913: The Long Nineteenth Century*. Edinburgh.

Gannon, B. 2011. *The Won Cause: Black and White Comradeship in the Grand Army of the Republic*. Chapel Hill.

Gardner, E. A. 1888. "Review of *Griechenland*. 2nd edition. Baedeker, Leipzig. 1888. *Grèce I; Athènes et ses environs*. Guides Joanne. Paris. 1888." *Journal of Hellenic Studies* 9: 391–394.

Gardner, E. A. 1890. "Archaeology in Greece, 1889–90." *Journal of Hellenic Studies* 11: 210–217.

Gardner, E. A. 1891. "Archaeology in Greece, 1890–91." *Journal of Hellenic Studies* 12: 385–397.

Gardner, E. A. 1902. *Ancient Athens*. London.

Garvey, J. 1998. *Spirit of the Centuries: A History of St. John United Methodist Church, 1798–1998*, Franklin, TN.

Gatewood, W. E. 1988. "Aristocrats of Color South and North: The Black Elite, 1880–1920." *Journal of Southern History* 54.1: 3–20.

Gatewood, W. E. 1990. *Aristocrats of Color South and North: The Black Elite, 1880–1920*. Bloomington.

Gazi, A. 1994. "Archaeological Museums and Displays in Greece 1829–1909: A First Approach." *Museological Review* 1.1: 50–69.

Geiger, R. L. 2015. *The History of American Higher Education: Learning and Culture from the Founding to World War II*. Princeton.

Gennadius, J. 1897. "American Excavations in Greece: Plataia and Eretria." *The Forum* 23: 432–447.

Genovese, E. D. 1974. *Roll Jordan, Roll: The World the Slaves Made*. New York.

Giorgiades, A./Γεωργιάδης, A. 1907. *Les ports de la Grèce dans l'antiquité qui subsistent encore aujourd'hui*. Athens.

Giorgiades, A./Γεωργιάδης, A. 1913. "Εἰς τὴν ἄνω Ερετρικὴν επιγραφὴν." *AE* ser. 3: 214–215.

Gerrish, C. K. 1891. "Election Day in Greece." *The Youth's Companion* 64.18 (30 April): 257.

Gex, K. 1993. *Eretria IX: Rotfigurige und weissgrundige Keramik.* Lausanne.

Gibson, C., and K. Jung. 2005. *Historical Census Statistics on Population Totals by Race, 1790 to 1990, and by Hispanic Origin, 1970 to 1990, for Large Cities and Other Urban Places in the United States.* Washington, DC.

Gibson, J., and Crogman W. 1901. *The Colored American, From Slavery to Honorable Citizenship.* Atlanta.

Gilbert, J. W. 1887. "Did Bacon Write the Plays Known as Shakespeare's?" *The Paine Institute Herald* 1.3 (May): 1.

Gilbert, J. W. 1891a. "A Georgian in Greece." *The New York Age* 18 (24 January): 4.

Gilbert, J. W. 1891b. "The Excavations at Eretria." *The Independent* 43.2213 (30 April): 19 (643).

Gilbert, J. W. 1902a. "How Can the Negroes Be Induced to Rally More to Negro Enterprises and to Their Professional Men?," in *Twentieth Century Negro Literature or a Cyclopedia of Thought on the Vital Topics Relating to the American Negro by One Hundred of America's Greatest Negroes*, ed. D. Culp, 190–193. Toronto, Naperville, and Atlanta.

Gilbert, J. W. 1902b. "The Necessity for High Moral Character in the Teacher," in *The United Negro: His Problems and His Progress*, ed. I. Penn and J. Bowen, 406–409. Atlanta.

Gilbert, J. W. 1904. *"The Problem of the Races:" A Reply to Hon. John Temple Graves.* Augusta.

Gilbert, J. W. 1911. "A Voice from the Negro Race." *Methodist Quarterly Review* 60.2: 717–730, 774–775.

Gilbert, J. W. 1913. "Pioneering in Africa." *The Missionary Voice* 3.1: 35–37.

Gilbert, J. W. 1914. "The Southern Negro's Debt and Responsibility to Africa," in *The New Voice in Race Adjustments, Addresses and Reports Presented at the Negro Christian Student Conference, May 14–18, 1914*, ed. A. Trawick, 129–133. New York.

Gilbert, J. W. 1915. "City Housing of Negroes in Relation to Health," in *The New Chivalry: Health*, ed. J. McCulloch, 405–412. Nashville.

Gill, D. W. 2011. *Sifting the Soil of Greece: The Early Years of the British School at Athens (1886–1919).* London.

Givens, D. R. 2008. "The Role of Biography in Writing the History of Archaeology," in *Histories of Archaeology: A Reader in the History of Archaeology*, ed. T. Murray and C. Evans, 177–193. Oxford and New York.

Gloyn. L. 2016. "This Is Not a Chapter About Jane Harrison: Teaching Classics at Newnham College, 1882–1922," in *Women Classical Scholars: Unsealing the Fountain from the Renaissance to Jacqueline de Romilly*, ed. R. Wyles and E. Hall, 153–175. Oxford and New York.

Goddard, O. E., and MacDonell, R. W. [ca. 1919]. *Making America Safe: A Study of the Home Missions of the Methodist Episcopal Church, South*. Nashville.

Godshalk, D. F. 2005. *Veiled Visions: The 1906 Atlanta Race Riot and the Reshaping of American Race Relations*. Chapel Hill.

Goette, H. R. 2001. *Athens, Attica and the Megarid: An Archaeological Guide*. London.

Goodwin, W. W. 1884. *Report of the Director of the American School of Classical Studies at Athens for the Year 1882–'83*. Washington, DC.

Goodwin, W. W. 1885. "The Battle of Salamis." *Papers of the American School of Classical Studies at Athens* 1: 237–262.

Gordon, D. M. 2014. "Interpreting Documentary Sources on the Early History of the Congo Free State: The Case of Ngongo Luteta's Rise and Fall." *History in Africa* 41: 5–33.

Gordon, D. M. 2017. "Precursors to Red Rubber: Violence in the Congo Free State, 1885–1895." *Past and Present* 236: 133–168.

Gould, J. H. 1891. "Ocean Passenger Travel." *Scribner's Magazine* 9.4: 399–418.

Graham, W. L. 1954. *Patterns of Intergroup Relations in the Cooperative Establishment, Control, and Administration of Paine College (Georgia) by Southern Negro and White People: A Study of Intergroup Process*. PhD Dissertation, New York University.

Gravely, W. B. 2005. "Christian Methodist Episcopal Church," in *Religion in the South* [second ed.], ed. S. S. Hill and C. H. Lippy, 189–191. Macon.

Gray, E. C. W. 1933. "Let Me Tell You a Good Story." *World Outlook* 23: 33.

Gray, E. C. W. 1948. "Paine College: An Essay in Brotherhood," in *That Thy Way May Be Known Upon Earth. Programs for Women's Societies of Christian Service, Wesleyan Service Guilds. January-August, 1948*, ed. unknown, 23–32, 125. New York [Records of the Women's Division of the General Board of Global Ministries, 2599–6–2: 3. GCAH Archives, Madison, NJ].

Greco, E. 2011. *Topografia di Atene. Sviluppo urbano e monumenti dalle origini al III secolo d. C., Tomo 2: Colline sud-occidentali, Valle dell'Ilisso*. Athens and Paestum.

Greco, E. 2014a. *Topografia di Atene. Sviluppo urbano e monumenti dalle origini al III secolo d. C., Tomo 3* e Tomo 3**: Quartieri a nord e a nord-est dell'Acropoli e Agora del Ceramico*. Athens and Paestum.

Greco, E. 2014b. *Topografia di Atene. Sviluppo urbano e monumenti dalle origini al III secolo d. C., Tomo 4: Ceramico, Dipylon e Accademia*. Athens and Paestum.

Greek Evangelical Union. 1898. *Sixteenth Annual Report of the Greek Evangelical Union (formerly "Alliance")*. Bristol, UK.

Green, E. C. (ed.). 2008. *In Black and White: An Interpretation of the South, by Lily Hardy Hammond*. Athens, GA and London.

Green, J. P. 1929. *Fact Stranger than Fiction*. Cleveland.

Greene, J. D. 2013. "Pilgrim Health and Life Insurance Company." *New Georgia Encyclopedia*. 05 March 2013. https://www.georgiaencyclopedia. org/articles/business-economy/pilgrim-health-and-life-insurance-company. 16 October 2020.

Greenwood, E. 2009. "Review Essay: Re-rooting the Classical Tradition: New Directions in Black Classicism." *Classical Receptions Journal* 1.1: 87–103.

Groome, P. L. 1891. *Rambles of a Southerner in Three Continents*. Greensboro, NC.

Grundy, G. B. 1894. *The Topography of the Battle of Plataea*. London.

Gurlitt, W. 1890. *Über Pausanias*. Graz.

Gutman, H. G. 1976. *The Black Family in Slavery and Freedom, 1750–1925*. New York.

Halbherr, F. 1891. "A Review of Greek Archaeology During 1890." *The Antiquary* 23: 11–15.

Haley, S. 1989. "Classics and Minorities," in *Classics: A Discipline and Profession in Crisis?*, eds. P. Culham and L. Edmonds, 333–338. New York.

Haley, S. 1993. "Black Feminist Thought and Classics: Re-membering, Re-claiming, Re-empowering," in *Feminist Theory and the Classics*, N. S. Rabinowitz and A. Richlin eds., 23–38. New York.

Hall, S. 2009. *A Faithful Account of the Race: African American Historical Writing in Nineteenth-Century America*. Chapel Hill.

Hamilton, F. M. 1887. *A Plain Account of the Colored Methodist Episcopal Church in America. Being an Outline of Her History and Polity; Also, Her Prospective Work*. Nashville.

Hammond, L. 1914. *In Black and White: An Interpretation of Southern Life*. New York and Chicago.

Harding, C. 2008. "Camera Design 5: Portable Hand Cameras (1880–1900)," in *Encyclopedia of Nineteenth-Century Photography*, ed. J. Hannavy, 249–251. New York.

Harlan, L. R. (ed.). 1974–1975. *The Booker T. Washington Papers, Volume 3 and Volume 4*. Urbana.

Harris, A. W., and F. M. Thomas (eds.). 1918. *Joint Commission on Unification of the Methodist Episcopal Church and the Methodist Episcopal Church, South. Volume I. Proceedings at Baltimore, Md., December 28, 1916–January 2, 1917, and at Traverse City, Mich., June 27–30, 1917.* New York and Nashville.

Harrison, J. 1885. *Introductory Studies in Greek Art*. London.

Harrison, J. 1888. "Archaeology in Greece, 1887–1888." *Journal of Hellenic Studies* 9: 118–133.

Harrison, J., and Verrall, M. 1890. *Mythology and Monuments of Ancient Athens, Being a Translation of a Portion of the 'Attica" of Pausanias, with Introductory Essay and Archaeological Commentary by Jane E. Harrison*. London and New York.

Hatzidimitriou, A./Χατζηδημητρίου, A. 2012. "Οδοιπορικό στη διασπορά των ευβοϊκών αρχαιοτήτων," in *«Ξενιτεμένες» ελληνικές αρχαιότητες. Αφετηρίες και διαδρομές*, ed. S. Mathaiou and A. Hatzidimitriou, 215–243. Athens.

Haussoullier, B. 1884. *La vie municipale en Attique. Essai sur l'organisation des dèmes au quatrième siècle*. Paris.

Hawley, M. F., and J. Speth. 2016. "A Note on African Americans in Early Wisconsin Archaeology." *The Wisconsin Archaeologist* 97.1: 47–52.

Haynes, E. R. 1952. *The Black Boy of Atlanta*. Boston.

Herlihy, D. 2010. *The Lost Cyclist: The Epic Tale of an American Adventurer and His Mysterious Disappearance*. New York.

Hill, E. 1984. *Shakespeare in Sable: A History of Black Shakespearean Actors*. Amherst.

Hill, G. E. 1909. *Vicennial Record of the Class of 1887 in Yale College*. Bridgeport, CT.

Hitzig, H., and H. Blümner. 1896. *Pausaniae Graeciae Descriptio. Voluminis Prioris Pars Prior. Liber Primus: Attica*. Berlin.

Hochschild, A. 1998. *King Leopold's Ghost*. New York.

Holsey, L. H. 1898. *Autobiography, Sermons, Addresses, and Essays of Bishop L. H. Holsey, D. D.* Atlanta.

Holyoke, M. B. 1892. *Golden Memories of Old World Lands; Or, What I Saw in Europe, Egypt, Palestine and Greece*. Chicago.

Homolle, T. 1891a. "Nouvelles et correspondance [19 June 1891]." *Bulletin de correspondance hellénique* 15: 441–458.

Homolle, T. 1891b. "Nouvelles et correspondance (1)." *Bulletin de correspondance hellénique* 15: 641–699.

Homolle, T. 1892. "Rapport de M. Homolle, Directeure de l'École Française d'Athènes (séance du 3 Juillet 1891)" *Académie des inscriptions et belles-lettres. Comptes rendus des séances de l'année 1891* (series 4) 19: 275–292.

Hood, C. 2017. *In Pursuit of Privilege: A History of New York City's Upper Class and the Making of a Metropolis*. New York.

Hornblower, S. 1991. *A Commentary on Thucydides. Volume I: Books I–III*. Oxford.

Horrocks, G. 2014. *Greek: A History of the Language and Its Speakers* [second ed.]. Malden, MA.

Houghton, G. 1890. "Strolls about Modern Athens. Two Parts. I.: Approaches and First Glimpses." *Christian Union* 42.25: 840.

Howard University. 1896. *Alumni Catalogue of Howard University, with List of Incorporators, Trustees, and other Employees, 1867–1896*. Washington, DC.

Hubbell, N. 1890. *My Journey to Jerusalem*. New York.

Hughes, H. 2011. *First President: A Life of John L. Dube, Founding President of the ANC*. Auckland Park, South Africa.

Hunt, G. 1898. *The American Passport*. Washington, DC.

Hunt, W. 1890. "Discoveries at Plataia in 1890. IV. Notes on the Battlefield of Plataia." *AJAHFA* 6.4: 463–475.

Hunt, P. 2002. *Slaves, Warfare, and Ideology in the Greek Historians*. Cambridge and New York.

Hurst, J. F. 1887. "Mars Hill and the Oldest Athens." *The Chautauquan* 7.4: 226–288.

Hurwit, J. M. 1999. *The Athenian Acropolis*. Cambridge and New York.

Husman, J. 2013. "June 21, 1879: The Cameo of William Edward White: Cleveland at Providence," in *Inventing Baseball: The 100 Greatest Games of the 19th Century*, ed. B. Felber, 116–117. Phoenix.

Ikkos, I., and S. Koutsos. 2019. *The Contribution of Tourism to the Greek Economy in 2018*. Athens.

Jacobs, S. 2011. "African Missions and the African American Christian Churches," in *Encyclopedia of African American Religions*, ed. L. G. Murphy, J. G. Melton, G. L. Ward, 10–23. London and New York.

JBHE Foundation, Inc. 1999. "The Racial Record of Johns Hopkins University." *Journal of Blacks in Higher Education* 25: 42–43.

JBHE Foundation, Inc. 2009. "JBHE Chronology of Major Landmarks in the Progress of African Americans in Higher Education." *Journal of Blacks in Higher Education* 64: 97–111.

Joanne, P. 1890. *Grèce. I: Athènes et ses environs.* Paris.

Joanne, P. 1891. *Grèce. II: Grèce continentale et îles.* Paris.

Johnson, A. C. 1970. *The Growth of Paine College: A Successful Interracial Venture, 1903–1946.* PhD Dissertation, University of Georgia.

Johnson, E. A. 1890. *A School History of the Negro Race in America from 1619 to 1890.* Raleigh.

Johnson, W. B. 1982. "Free Blacks in Antebellum Augusta, Georgia: A Demographic and Economic Profile." *Richmond County History* 14: 10–21.

Joiner, S., and G. Smith. 2004. *Augusta, Georgia (Black America Series).* Mt. Pleasant, SC.

Joint Publications Research Service, US Department of Commerce. 1968. *Translations on Africa, No. 723.* Washington, DC.

Jones, C. C., and S. Dutcher. 1890. *Memorial History of Augusta, Georgia.* Syracuse, NY.

Jones, E. A. 1967. *A Candle in the Dark: A History of Morehouse College.* Valley Forge, PA.

Jones, F. V. 1962. *The Education of Negroes in Richmond County, Georgia, 1860–1960.* MA Thesis, Atlanta University.

Jones, J. 1980. *Soldiers of Light and Love: Northern Teachers and Georgia Blacks, 1865–1873.* Chapel Hill.

Kasongo, M. O. 1998a. *History of the Methodist Church in the Central Congo.* New York.

Kasongo, M. O. 1998b. "A Spirit of Cooperation in Mission: Professor John Wesley Gilbert and Bishop Walter Russell Lambuth." *Methodist History* 36.4: 260–265.

Kastromenos, P. G. 1886. *Die Demen von Attika.* Leipzig.

Ken, S. 1972. "The Chinese Community of Augusta, Georgia from 1873–1971." *Richmond County History* 4.1: 51–60.

Kendall, T. 2013. "Napata," in *The Encyclopedia of Ancient History*, ed. R. S. Bagnall et al., 4691–4694. Oxford and New York.

Kennedy, C. R. 1885. *The Orations of Demosthenes. On the Crown and on the Embassy, Volume II.* New York.

Kennedy, M. D. 2005. "Crogman, William H(enry), 1841–1931," in *Africana: The Encyclopedia of the African and African American Experience*, ed. K. A. Appiah and H. L. Gates, Jr., 265–266. Oxford, UK.

Kenyon, F. G. 1891. *ΑΘΗΝΑΙΩΝ ΠΟΛΙΤΕΙΑ: Aristotle on the Constitution of Athens*. London.

Kimberley, Hannah. 2017. *A Woman's Place Is at the Top: A Biography of Annie Smith Peck, Queen of the Climbers*. New York.

Kletzing, H., and W. Crogman. 1898. *Progress of a Race*. Atlanta.

Kludas, A., and H. Bischoff. 1979. *Die Schiffe der Hamburg-Amerika Linie, Bd. 1: 1847–1906*. Herford, UK.

Knoepfler, D. 1969. "ΟΦΡΥΟΕΣΣΑ ΠΟΛΙΣ: Note sur l'acropole d'Érétrie." *Antike Kunst* 12.2: 83–87.

Knoepfler, D. 1991. *La Vie de Ménédème d'Érétrie de Diogène Laërce*. Basel.

Knox, T. W. 1888. *The Pocket Guide for Europe* [new ed.]. New York and London.

Kornweibel, Jr., T. 2010. *Railroads in the African American Experience: A Photographic Journey*. Baltimore.

Kousser, M. J. 1978. *Separate but Not Equal: The Supreme Court's First Decision on Discrimination in Schools*. California Institute of Technology Social Science Working Paper 204. Pasadena.

Kousser, M. J. 1980. "Separate but *not* Equal: The Supreme Court's First Decision on Racial Discrimination in Schools." *The Journal of Southern History* 1: 17–44.

Kramer, L. S. 2014. "David Dorr's Journey Toward Selfhood in Europe," in *Biography and the Black Atlantic*, ed. L. A. Lindsay and J. W. Sweet, 149–171. Philadelphia.

Krentz, P. 2010. *The Battle of Marathon*. Princeton.

Krewer, G. 2016. "Historical Perspective on Olives in Georgia." [undated]. *Georgia Olive Growers Association*. https://georgiaolivegrowers. com/documents/Historical_Perspective_of_Olives_in_Georgia.pdf. 24 February 2017.

Kruppa, P. S. 1982. *Charles Haddon Spurgeon: A Preacher's Progress*. New York.

Lakey, O. H. 1996. *The History of the CME Church (Revised)*. Memphis.

Lakey, O. H., and B. B. Stephens. 1994. *God in My Mama's House: The Women's Movement in the CME Church*. Memphis.

Lamb, D. S. 1900. *Howard University Medical Department, Washington, D.C. A Historical, Biographical and Statistical Souvenir*. Washington, DC.

Lambuth, W. R. 1913a. "The Call of Africa." *The Missionary Voice* 3.1: 13–16.

Lambuth, W. R. 1913b. "In the Heart of the Congo," in *The Junalaska Conference: A Report of the Second General Missionary Conference of the Methodist Episcopal Church, South*, ed. G. B. Winton, 288–295. Nashville.

Lambuth, W. R. 1915. *Winning the World for Christ. A Study in Dynamics.* New York, Chicago, Toronto, London, and Edinburgh.

Lane, G. S. 1955. "Carl Darling Buck." *Language* 31.2: 181–189.

Larrabee, S. A. 1957. *Hellas Observed: The American Experience of Greece, 1775–1865.* New York.

Larsen, T. 2011. *A People of One Book: The Bible and the Victorians.* Oxford and New York.

Larson, L. M. 1927. "The Norwegian Pioneer in the Field of American Scholarship." *Publications of the Norwegian-American Historical Association (Studies and Records)* 2: 62–77.

Laurie, M. D. 1986. "The Union Academy: A Freedmen's Bureau School in Gainesville, Florida." *The Florida Historical Quarterly* 65.2: 163–174.

Leake, W. M. 1835. *Travels in Northern Greece, Volume II.* London.

Lee, J. M. III. 1997. *Augusta in Vintage Postcards.* Charleston, SC.

Lee, J. W. I. (forthcoming a). "That First Trip to Central Greece: The ASCSA Expedition to Thermopylae and Back, November 1890."

Lee, J. W. I. (forthcoming b). "African American Travelers Encounter Greece, ca. 1850–1900."

Legros, H., and C. A. Keim. 1996. "Guide to African Archives in Belgium." *History in Africa* 23: 401–409.

Leland, L. 1890. *Traveling Alone. A Woman's Journey Around the World.* New York.

Leslie, K. A. 1995. *Woman of Color, Daughter of Privilege: Amanda America Dickson, 1849–1893.* Athens, GA.

Leslie, K. A. 2001. "No Middle Ground: Elite African Americans in Augusta and the Coming of Jim Crow," in *Paternalism in a Southern City: Race, Religion, and Gender in Augusta, Georgia*, ed. E. Cashin and G. Eskew, 110–134. Athens, GA and London.

Leslie, K. A., and W. B. Gatewood, Jr. 1993. "'This Father of Mine . . . a Sort of Mystery:' Jean Toomer's Georgia Heritage." *Georgia Historical Quarterly* 77.4: 789–809.

Leveson Gower, A. F. G. 1900. "Monumental Inscriptions to British Subjects Buried in the Various Cemeteries in Athens, Greece," in *Miscellanea Genealogica et Heraldica (Volume III, Third Series)*, ed. J. J. Howard, 149–157. London.

Lincoln, W. E. 1894. *In Memoriam. John Larkin Lincoln, 1817–1891.* Boston and New York.

Link, W. A. 2013. *Atlanta: Cradle of the New South: Race and Remembering in the Civil War's Aftermath*. Chapel Hill.

Litwack, L. F. 1979. *Been in the Storm So Long: The Aftermath of Slavery*. New York.

Logan, R. W. 1969. *Howard University: The First Hundred Years, 1867–1967*. New York.

Lolling, H. G. 1885. "Das Delphinion bei Oropos und der Demos Psaphis." *Athenische Mitteilungen* 10: 350–358.

Lord, J. K. 1913. *A History of Dartmouth College, 1815–1909*. Concord, NH.

Lord, L. 1947. *A History of the American School of Classical Studies at Athens, 1882–1942. An Intercollegiate Project*. Cambridge, MA.

Lord & Thomas. 1894–5. *Lord & Thomas' Pocket Directory for 1894–5*. Chicago.

Lovell, W. E. 2013. *100th Anniversary of the Methodist Church in Central Congo, 1912–2013*. Nashville.

Lovell, W. E. 2016. "Reflections of Life as a Child of Missionaries in the Belgian Congo." United Methodist News Service, 05 February 2016. https://www.umnews.org/en/news/reflections-of-life-as-a-child-of-missionaries-in-the-belgian-congo. 04 August 2021.

Lowry, Bill. 2010. *The Antechamber of Heaven: A History of the Lake Junalaska Assembly*. Franklin, TN.

Luker, R. E. 1991. *The Social Gospel in Black and White: American Racial Reform, 1885–1912*. Chapel Hill and London.

Lupher, D., and E. Vandiver. 2011. "Yankee She-Men and Octoroon Electra: Basil Lanneau Gildersleeve on Slavery, Race, and Abolition," in *Ancient Slavery and Abolition: From Hobbes to Hollywood*, ed. R. Alston, E. Hall, and J. McConnell, 320–351. Oxford and New York.

Lyons, S. 2006. "Harriet McEwen Kimball (1834–1917). Poet." *The New Hampshire Gazette* 250: 24.

Macan, R. 1891. "ΑΘΗΝΑΙΩΝ ΠΟΛΙΤΕΙΑ." *Journal of Hellenic Studies* 12: 17–40.

MacFarland, C. S. (ed.). 1916. *The Churches of the Federal Council. Their History, Organization and Distinctive Characteristics and a Statement of the Development of the Federal Council*. New York, Chicago, Toronto, London, Edinburgh.

MacMillan and Co., Ltd. 1904. *Guide to the Eastern Mediterranean*. London and New York.

Magee, J. H. 1873. *The Night of Affliction and the Morning of Recovery: An Autobiography*. Cincinnati.

Mairs, R. 2016. *From Khartoum to Jerusalem: The Dragoman Solomon Negima and His Clients (1885–1933)*. London.

Malamud, M. 2016. *African Americans and the Classics: Antiquity, Abolition and Activism*. London and New York.

Malaval, A., and S. Reinach. 1892. "Chronique d'Orient (No. XXV)." *Revue Archéologique* (series 3) 19: 395–435.

Mallouchou-Tufano, F. 1994. "The History of Interventions on the Acropolis," in *Acropolis Restoration: The CCAM Interventions*, ed. R. Economakis, 68–85. London.

Mallouchou-Tufano, F. / Μαλλούχου-Tufano, Φ. 1998. *Η αναστήλωση των αρχαίων μνημείων στη νεώτερη Ελλάδα (1834–1939)*. Athens.

Manatt, I. J. 1890a. "Rural Attica: Glimpses of Harvest and Vintage." *The Independent* 42.2173 (24 July): 6.

Manatt, I. J. 1890b. "Rural Attica." *The Independent* 42.2174 (31 July): 3–4.

Manatt, I. J. 1891a. "The Last Days of Doctor Schliemann." *The Independent* 43.2202 (12 February): 5–6 (221–222).

Manatt, I. J. 1891b. "The Setting of St. Paul's Apology." *The Old and New Testament Student* 12.6: 327–338.

Manatt, I. J. 1891c. "Greek Mining and Metallurgy." *Monthly Consular and Trade Reports* 35.124–127: 20–36.

Manatt, I. J. 1891d. "Rural Attica: A Decoration Day at Marathon." *The Independent* 43.2230 (27 August): 4.

Manatt, I. J. 1893. "Some Reminiscences of Dr. Schliemann." *Atlantic Monthly* 71.4: 803–808.

Manatt, I. J. 1894a. "Behind Hymettus. In Two Parts. Part One." *The Atlantic Monthly* 73.439: 636–644.

Manatt, I. J. 1894b. "Behind Hymettus. In Two Parts. Part Two." *The Atlantic Monthly* 73.440: 763–770.

Manatt, J. I. 1895a. "Cotton Industry in Greece [January 5, 1893]," in *Report of the Committee on Agriculture and Forestry on Condition of Cotton Growers in the United States, the Present Prices of Cotton, and the Remedy; and on Cotton Consumption and Production, Volume II*, 141–142. Washington, DC.

Manatt, J. I. 1895b. "The Living Greek: A Glance at His Politics and Progress." *Review of Reviews* 11: 398–412.

Manatt, J. I. 1902. "With St. Paul at Athens." *The Independent* 54.2809: 2356–2360.

Mann, H. W. 1965. *Atticus Greene Haygood, Methodist Bishop, Editor, and Educator*. Athens, GA.

Marquand, A. 1895. "Archaeological News." *AJAHFA* 10.4: 507–586.

Martin, C. J. 1991. "The *Haustafeln* (Household Codes) in African American Bible Interpretation: 'Free Slaves' and 'Subordinate Women,'" in *Stony the Road We Trod: African American Biblical Interpretation*, ed. C. H. Felder, 206–231. Minneapolis.

Martin, H. 2004. *"New York Age,"* in *Encyclopedia of the Harlem Renaissance, K-Y*, ed. C. D. Wintz and P. Finkelman, 901–902. New York.

Martin, J. A. 1924. "John Wesley Gilbert." *Nashville Christian Advocate* 85.4: 106–107.

Massachusetts Reformatory, Inmates of. 1918. "A Dollar a Week and What It Did." *Our Paper* (14 December): 536.

Mather, F. L. 1915. *Who's Who of the Colored Race. A General Biographical Dictionary of Men and Women of African Descent. Volume One*. Chicago.

Mathews, W. B. 1889. "The Negro Intellect." *The North American Review* 392: 91–109.

Mattheisen, P. F, A. C. Young, and P. Coustillas (eds.). 1993. *The Collected Letters of George Gissing. Volume IV, 1889–1891*. Athens, OH.

Matthews, W. E. 1890. "A Summer Vacation in Europe." *AME Church Review* 6.3: 292–306.

Mauzy, C. A. 2006. *Agora Excavations 1931–2006: A Pictorial History. With Contributions by John McK. Camp II*. Princeton.

Maxwell, J. L., P. A. Stovall, and T. R. Gibson. 1878. *Hand Book of Augusta*. Augusta, GA.

Maxwell, W. J. 1916. *General Alumni Catalogue of the Long Island College Hospital*. New York.

McAfee, S. 1945. "Pathfinder: John Wesley Gilbert," in *History of the Woman's Missionary Society in the Colored Methodist Episcopal Church, Comprising Its Founders, Organizations, Pathfinders, Subsequent Developments and Present Status*, ed. S. McAfee, 65–70. Phenix City, AL. [revised ed.; originally published 1934 under name "Mrs. L. D. McAfee."]

McCluskey, A. T. 2006. "Manly Husbands and Womanly Wives:' The Leadership of Educator Lucy Craft Laney," in *Post-Bellum, Pre-Harlem: African American Literature and Culture, 1877–1919*, ed. B. McCaskill and C. Gebhard, 74–88. New York.

McCluskey, A. T. 2014. "Building Character and Culture: Lucy Craft Laney and the Haines School Community," in *African American Women Educators: A Critical Examination of their Pedagogies, Educational Ideas, and Activism from the Nineteenth to Mid-Twentieth Century*, ed. K. A. Johnson, A. Pitre, and K. L. Johnson, 55–71. New York.

McCredie, J. 1966. *Fortified Military Camps in Attica*. Princeton.

McDowall, A. C. 1891. "Commerce and Industries of Piraeus." *Consular Reports on Commerce, Manufactures, Etc.* 35.126: 345–348.

McHenry, E. 2002. *Forgotten Readers: Recovering the Lost History of African American Literary Societies.* Durham, NC.

McMurtry, W. J. 1889. "Excavations by the American School at the Theatre of Sikyon. I. General Report of the Excavations." *AJAHFA* 5.3: 267–286.

McPherson, B., and J. Klein. 1995. *Measure by Measure: A History of New England Conservatory from 1867.* Boston.

Meriwether, L. 1892. *Afloat and Ashore on the Mediterranean.* New York.

Messick, D. P., J. W. Joseph, and N. P. Adams. 2001. *Tilling the Earth: Georgia's Historic Agricultural Heritage: A Context,* Atlanta.

Milchhöfer, A. 1887a. "Über Standpunkt und Methode der attischen Demenforschung." *Sitzungsberichte der Königlich Preußischen Akademie der Wissenschaften zu Berlin, Erster Halbband* 4: 41–56.

Milchhöfer, A. 1887b. "Vorläufiger Bericht über Forschungen in Attika." *Sitzungsberichte der Königlich Preußischen Akademie der Wissenschaften zu Berlin, Zweiter Halbband* 2: 1095–1097.

Milchhöfer, A. 1888a. "Attische Studien I." *Deutsche Rundschau* 54: 409–418.

Milchhöfer, A. 1888b. "Attische Studien II." *Deutsche Rundschau* 55: 204–217.

Milchhöfer, A. 1889. *Karten von Attika: Erläuternder Text, Heft III–VI.* Berlin.

Millender, M. 2012. "We All Have a Stake in Paine College's Success." *Metro Spirit* (Augusta) 23.24: 5.

Miller, J. P. 1828. *The Condition of Greece in 1827 and 1828.* New York.

Miller, K. 1906. *An Appeal to Reason. An Open Letter to John Temple Graves.* Washington, DC.

Miller, W. 1888. "The Theatre of Thoricus, Preliminary Report." *Papers of the American School of Classical Studies at Athens (1885–1886)* 4: 1–21.

Miller, W. 1894. "Impressions of Greece." *The Westminster Review* 142: 304–314.

Miller, W. 1896. "Overbeck." *AJAHFA* 11.3: 361–370.

Mills, F. V. 2017. "Methodist Church: Overview." *New Georgia Encyclopedia.* 26 July 2017. https://www.georgiaencyclopedia.org/articles/arts-culture/methodist-church-overview. 25 November 2017.

Mills, Q. T. 2013. *Cutting Along the Color Line: Black Barbers and Barber Shops in America.* Philadelphia.

Missouri Public Schools. 1893. *Forty-Third Report of the Public Schools of the State of Missouri, for the School Year Ending June 30, 1892.* Jefferson City.

Missouri Public Schools. 1894. *Forty-Fourth Report of the Public Schools of the State of Missouri, for the School Year Ending June 30, 1893.* Jefferson City.

Mitchell, M. 1993. "African Americans." *Encyclopedia Brunoniana,* [undated]. https://www.brown.edu/Administration/News_Bureau/ Databases/Encyclopedia/search.php?serial=A0080. 30 August 2016.

Montgomery, E., and Speno, L. 2010. "Paine College Historic District." Historic Preservation Division, Department of Natural Resources, Atlanta, GA.

Moore, H. 1918. *The Descendants of Ensign John Moor of Canterbury, N. H. Born 1696–Died 1786.* Rutland, VT.

Moore, T. V. 1914. "The Gospel in Greece, and Kalopothakes Its Modern Apostle." *Record of Christian Work* 33.1: 18–23, 33.2: 87–90, 33.3: 151–155.

Morgan, C. 2016. "The Foundation and Early Development of the British School at Athens," in *British-Greek Relations: Aspects of their Recent History,* ed. A. Karapanou, 13–28. Athens.

Morgan, R. C. 1911. *Glimpses of Four Continents.* London.

Morrison, L. A., and S. P. Sharples. 1897. *History of the Kimball Family in America, From 1634 to 1897, and of Its Ancestors the Kemballs or Kemboldes of England.* Boston.

Morrison, W. M. 1906. *Grammar and Dictionary of the Buluba-Lulua Language as Spoken in the Upper Kasai and Congo Basin.* New York.

Mott, F. 1938. *A History of American Magazines, 1850–1865.* Cambridge, MA.

Mount Holyoke. 1889. *General Catalogue of Officers and Students of Mount Holyoke Seminary, South Hadley, Mass. 1837–1887. With an Appendix, 1887–1889.* Springfield, MA.

Murphy, M. B. 2018. *Jim Crow Capital: Women and Black Freedom Struggles in Washington, D.C., 1920–1945.* Chapel Hill.

Murray, P. M., and C. N. Runnels. 2007. "Harold North Fowler and the Beginnings of American Study Tours in Greece." *Hesperia* 76: 597–626.

Najder, Z. 2007. *Joseph Conrad: A Life* [second ed.]. Rochester, NY.

National Railway Publications Company. 1890. *Travelers' Official Guide of the Railway and Steam Navigation Lines in the United States and Canada.* New York.

New Hampshire Public Schools. 1886. *Annual Report of the Superintendent of Public Instruction, being the Fortieth Annual Report upon the Public Schools of New Hampshire.* Manchester.

New Hampshire Public Schools. 1889. *Annual Report of the Superintendent of Public Instruction, Being the Forty-Third Annual Report upon the Public Schools of New Hampshire*. Manchester.

Norlie, O. M. 1925. *History of the Norwegian People in America*. Minneapolis.

Norlie, O. M., O. A. Tingelstad, and K. T. Jacobsen. 1922. *Luther College Through Sixty Years, 1861–1921*. Minneapolis.

Northrop, H. D., J. R. Gay, and I. G. Penn. 1896. *The College of Life or Practical Self-Educator. A Manual of Self-Improvement for the Colored Race*. Washington, DC.

Nouchaki, I. / Νουχακη, I. 1890. *Νέος Χωρογραφικος Πίναξ*. Athens.

O'Brien, W. 2002. "Inclusive List of AIA Local Societies with Name Changes and Dates of Foundation and Dissolution," in *Excavating Our Past: Perspectives on the History of the Archaeological Institute of America*, ed. S. H. Allen, 221–226. Boston.

Oman, C. W. C. 1892. "Some Notes on the ΠΟΛΙΤΕΙΑ ΤΩΝ ΑΘΗΝΑΙΩΝ." *Transactions of the Royal Historical Society* 6: 125–143.

Omasombo Tshonda, J., and B. Verhaegen. 1998. *Patrice Lumumba: Jeunesse et apprentissage politique, 1925–1956*. Tervuren and Paris.

Osthaus, C. R. 1976. *Freedmen, Philanthropy, and Fraud: A History of the Freedman's Savings Bank*. Urbana, Chicago, and London.

Owen, C. H. 1998. *The Sacred Flame of Love: Methodism and Society in Nineteenth-Century Georgia*. Athens, GA.

Pajor, F. 2006. *Eretria XV. Ausgrabungen und Forschungen. Eretria-Nea Psara: Eine Klassizistische Stadtanlage über der Antiken Polis (Band I – Text; Band II – Bildinventar und Tafeln)*. Renens.

Pajor, F. 2010. *Ερέτρια-Νέα Ψαρά. Το χρονικό μιας πολιτείας*. Athens.

Palmer, L. A. 1896. *Grecian Days*. New York, Chicago, and Toronto.

Palmer, M. B. 2019. *International News Agencies: A History*. London.

Panhellenic Calendar. 1890. *Πανελλήνιον Ημερολόγιον του έτους 1890*. Athens.

Papalexandrou, N. 2016. "The Old Acropolis Museum, Athens, Greece: An Overdue Necrology." *Journal of Modern Greek Studies* 34.1: 1–22.

Patton, J. O. 1978. "The Black Community of Augusta and the Struggle for Ware High School, 1880–1899," in *New Perspectives on Black Educational History*, ed. V. P. Franklin and J. D. Anderson, 45–59. Boston.

Patton, W. W., and G. F. Hoar. 1885. *Obituary Addresses on the Occasion of the Funeral of Professor Wiley Lane*. Washington, DC.

Peek, W. 1942. "Ge theos in griechischen und römischen Grabschriften." *Zeitschrift für Kirchengeschichte* 61: 27–32.

Pegues, A. 1892. *Our Baptist Ministers and Schools*. Springfield, MA.

Perkins, E. J. 1979. "Tourists and Bankers: Travelers' Credits and the Rise of American Tourism, 1840–1900." *Business and Economic History* (2nd series) 8: 16–28.

Perrin, B. 1909. "John Henry Wright, 1852–1909." *Classical Philology* 4.2: 199.

Peters, E. C. 1937. *Dr. George Williams Walker, Founder of Paine College.* Augusta, GA. [courtesy of the Methodist Library, Drew University].

Peters, E. C. 1945. "John Wesley Gilbert: A Pioneer," in *History of the Woman's Missionary Society in the Colored Methodist Episcopal Church, Comprising Its Founders, Organizations, Pathfinders, Subsequent Developments and Present Status*, ed. S. McAfee, 257–260. Phenix City, AL.

Petmezas, S. D. 2000. "Export-dependent Agriculture, Revenue Crisis and Agrarian Productivity Involution: The Greek Case (1860s-1930s)." *Histoire & Mesure* 15.3–4: 321–337.

Petrakos, V. Ch. 2007. "The Stages of Greek Archaeology," in *Great Moments in Greek Archaeology*, ed. P. Valavanes and A. Delevorrias, 16–35. Los Angeles.

Phillips, C. H. 1925. *The History of the Colored Methodist Episcopal Church in America: Comprising Its Organization, Subsequent Development and Present Status* [third ed.]. Jackson, TN.

Phillips, C. H. 1932. *From the Farm to the Bishopric: An Autobiography.* Nashville.

Phillips Exeter Academy. 1903. *General Catalogue of the Officers and Students of the Phillips Exeter Academy.* Exeter, NH.

Phipps, W. E. 2002. *William Sheppard: Congo's African American Livingston.* Louisville, KY.

Pickard, J. 1891a. "The Tombs at Eretria." *The Independent* 43.2212 (23 April): 21 (605).

Pickard, J. 1891b. "Excavations by the School at Eretria in 1891. VI. A Topographical Study of Eretria." *AJAHFA* 7.4: 371–389.

Pickard, J. 1893. "Dionysus ἐν Λίμναις." *AJAHFA* 8.1: 56–82.

Pickard-Cambridge, A. 1968. *The Dramatic Festivals of Athens* [second ed., revised by John Gould and D. M. Lewis]. Oxford.

Pierce, A. 1948. *Giant Against the Sky: The Life of Bishop Warren Akin Candler.* New York.

Pinson, W. 1925. *Walter Russell Lambuth: Prophet and Pioneer.* Nashville.

Piret, Bérengère. 2015. "Reviving the Remains of Colonization: The Belgian Colonial Archives in Brussels." *History in Africa* 42: 419–431.

Pleck, E. 1999. "The Making of the Domestic Occasion: The History of Thanksgiving in the United States." *Journal of Social History* 32.4: 773–789.

Plugge, D. E. 1938. *History of Greek Play Production in American Colleges and Universities from 1881 to 1936.* New York.

Powell, B. 1903. "Greek Inscriptions from Corinth." *American Journal of Archaeology* 7.1: 26–71.

Powery, E. B., and R. S. Sadler. 2016. *The Genesis of Liberation: Biblical Interpretation in the Antebellum Narratives of the Enslaved.* Louisville, KY.

Pretzler, M. 2007. *Pausanias: Travel Writing in Ancient Greece.* London.

Pride, A. S., and C. C. Wilson. 1997. *A History of the Black Press.* Washington, DC.

Proctor, H. H. 1925. *Between Black and White: Autobiographical Sketches.* Boston and Chicago.

Pryor, E. S. 2016. *Colored Travelers: Mobility and the Fight for Citizenship before the Civil War.* Chapel Hill.

Range, W. 1951. *The Rise and Progress of Negro Colleges in Georgia, 1865–1949.* Athens, GA.

Reber, K., M. H. Hansen, and P. Ducrey. 2004. "Euboia," in *An Inventory of Archaic and Classical Poleis,* ed. M. H. Hansen and T. H. Nielsen, 643–663. Oxford and New York.

Reber, K. et al. 2008. "Les activités de l'École Suisse d'archéologie en Grèce 2007." *Antike Kunst* 51: 146–179.

Reber, K. et al. 2015. "Bericht über die Aktivitäten der Schweizerischen Archäologischen Schule in Griechenland 2014." *Antike Kunst* 58: 129–151.

Reber, K. et al. 2019. "Το ιερό το Αμαρυσίας Αρτέμιδος στην Εύβοια." *Θέματα Αρχαιολογίας* 3.2: 206–215.

Reed, W. P. 1889. *History of Atlanta, Georgia.* Syracuse.

Reeder, G. L. 1999/2000. "The History of Blacks at Yale University." *Journal of Blacks in Higher Education* 26: 125–126.

Reeve, C. M. 1891. *How We Went and What We Saw. A Flying Trip Through Egypt, Syria, and the Aegean Islands.* New York and London.

Reeve, T. E. 1921. *In Wembo-Nyama's Land. A Story of the Thrilling Experiences in Establishing the Methodist Mission Among the Atetela.* Nashville, Dallas, and Richmond.

Reinach, S. 1890. "Chronique d'Orient (n. XXIII)." *Revue Archéologique* (ser. 3) 16: 225–273.

Reinach, S. 1892. "Chronique d'Orient (n. XXIV)." *Revue Archéologique* (ser. 3) 19: 65–155.

Reinach, S. 1927. "Sir C. Walston (Waldstein)." *Revue Archéologique* (ser. 5) 25: 392.

Reinach, T. 1891. "Bulletin archéologique." *Revue des Études Grecques* 14.4: 189–193.

Reinhold, M. 1994. "Wright, John Henry," in *Biographical Dictionary of North American Classicists*, ed. W. W. Briggs, Jr., 729–730. Westport, CT.

Repousis, A. 2009. "The Devil's Apostle": Jonas King's Trial against the Greek Hierarchy in 1852 and the Pressure to Extend U.S. Protection for American Missionaries Overseas." *Diplomatic History* 33.5: 807–837.

Repousis, A. 2013. *Greek-American Relations from Monroe to Truman.* Kent, OH.

Reynolds, D. 1980. "From Doctrine to Narrative: The Rise of Pulpit Storytelling in America." *American Quarterly* 32.5: 479–498.

Rhode Island Black Heritage Society. 1984. *Creative Survival: The Providence Black Community in the 19th Century.* Providence.

Rhodes, P. J. 1993. *A Commentary on the Aristotelian Athenaion Politeia.* Oxford, UK.

Rhodes, P. J. 2013. "The Battle of Marathon and Modern Scholarship," in *Marathon: 2,500 Years*, ed. C. Carey and M. Edwards, 3–21. London.

Ribeyrol, C. 2017. "Hellenic Utopias: Pater in the Footsteps of Pausanias," in *Pater the Classicist: Classical Scholarship, Reception, and Aestheticism*, ed. C. Martindale, S. Evangelista, and E. Prettejohn, 201–218. Oxford and New York.

Richardson, C. 1919. *The National Cyclopedia of the Colored Race.* Montgomery, AL.

Richardson, R. B. 1880. "Andersonville." *The New Englander* 39.6: 729–773.

Richardson, R. B. 1889a. *Aeschines, Against Ctesiphon (On the Crown).* Boston and London.

Richardson, R. B. 1889b. "Washington in September, 1862." *The Dartmouth Literary Monthly* 4.2: 43–46.

Richardson, R. B. 1890a. "A Science Theater." *The Independent* 42.2178: 13.

Richardson, R. B. 1890b. "Corfu." *The Independent* 42.2189: 6.

Richardson, R. B. 1890c. "The Sanctuary of Greece." *The Independent* 42.2194: 8.

Richardson, R. B. 1891a. "Life from a Berlin Point of View." *Andover Review* 15.85: 94–100.

Richardson, R. B. 1891b. "The American School at Athens." *The Dartmouth Literary Monthly* 5.5: 183–185.

Richardson, R. B. 1891c. "A Journey from Athens to Eretria." *The Independent* 43.2210: 6–7 (522–523).

Richardson, R. B. 1891d. "Sparta." *The Independent* 43.2219: 10.

Richardson, R. B. 1891e. "Off the Beaten Track in Greece." *The Independent* 43.2224: 1.

Richardson, R. B. 1891f. "Excavations by the School at Eretria, 1891. I. Eretria: Historical Sketch." *AJAHFA* 7.3: 236–246.

Richardson, R. B. 1891g. "Excavations by the School at Eretria, 1891. II. Inscriptions Discovered at Eretria, 1891." *AJAHFA* 7.3: 246–253.

Richardson, R. B. 1894. "An Excavation Campaign in Eretria." *The Independent* 46.237x (14 June): 4.

Richardson, R. B. 1899a. "The Bicycle in Greece." *The Nation* 68.1759 (16 March): 198–199.

Richardson, R. B. 1899b. "American Discoveries at Corinth, Including a Relic of St. Paul." *The Century Magazine* 57 (n. s. 35): 852–859.

Richardson, R. B. 1901. "Attica, Boeotia, and Corinth." *The Chautauquan* 33: 164–179.

Richardson, R. B. 1903. *Vacation Days in Greece*. New York.

Richardson, R. B. 1906. "Schools of Classical Studies in Athens and Rome." *The Chautauquan* 43.1: 11–29.

Richardson, R. B. 1907. *Greece Through the Stereoscope*. New York and London.

Richter, C. 2015. "Exceptional Perspectives: National Identity in U.S. Women's Travel Accounts of Greece, 1840–1913," in, *Politics, Identity, and Mobility in Travel Writing*, ed. M. A. Cabañas, J. Dubino, V. Salles-Reese, and G. Totten, 69–82. New York and London.

Robert, D. L. 1999. "Walter Russell Lambuth," in *Biographical Dictionary of Christian Missions*, ed. G. H. Anderson, 382. Grand Rapids, MI, and Cambridge, UK.

Robert, H. M. 1876. *Robert's Rules of Order. Pocket Manual of Rules of Order for Deliberative Assemblies, Revised*. Chicago.

Robert, J. T. 1878. *Historical Sketch of the Augusta Institute for the Education of Freedman Preachers and Teachers*. Augusta.

Robert, J. T. 1879. "Atlanta Seminary, Atlanta, Ga." *BHMM* 1.15: 235.

Robert, J. T. 1880. "Atlanta Seminary, Atlanta, Ga." *BHMM* 2.8: 159–160.

Robert, J. T. 1882a. "The Atlanta Baptist Seminary." *BHMM* 4.8: 215–216.

Robert, J. T. 1882b. "Bible Instruction in Freedmen Schools: In the Atlanta Baptist Seminary." *BHMM* 4.8: 218–219.

Robert, M. A. 1878. *Our Immediate Need of an Educated Colored Ministry*. Augusta.

Roberts, K. 2010. "The Bethel Literary and Historical Society." *Poetry Quarterly* 11.2: n. p.

Robertson, C. 2010. *The Passport in America: History of a Document.* Oxford and New York.

Robinson, A. 2002. *The Life and Work of Jane Ellen Harrison.* Oxford, UK.

Robinson, E. G. 1883. "Race and Religion on the American Continent." *BHMM* 5.3 (March): 49–53.

Robinson, B. 2011. *Histories of Peirene: A Corinthian Fountain in Three Millennia.* Princeton.

Robinson, S. R. 2013. "Rethinking Black Urban Politics in the 1880s: The Case of William Gaston in Post-Reconstruction Alabama." *Alabama Review* 66.1: 3–29.

Rodd, J. R. 1922. *Social and Diplomatic Memories, 1884–1893.* London.

Roessel, D. 2002. *In Byron's Shadow: Modern Greece in the English and American Imagination.* Oxford, UK.

Rolfe, J. C. 1890a. "Discoveries at Anthedon in 1889." *AJAHFA* 6.1/2: 96–107.

Rolfe, J. C. 1890b. "Discoveries at Thisbe in 1889: I. Report on Excavations." *AJAHFA* 6.1/2: 112–113.

Ronnick, M. V. 1997. "After Martin Bernal and Mary Lefkowitz: Research Opportunities in Classica Africana." *Negro History Bulletin* 60.2: 5–10.

Ronnick, M. V. 2000. "William Henry Crogman." *Classical Outlook* 77: 67–68.

Ronnick, M. V. 2001. "John Wesley Gilbert." *Classical Outlook* 78: 113–114.

Ronnick, M. V. 2002a. "The African American Classicist William Sanders Scarborough (1852–1926) and the Early Days of CAMWS." *Classical Journal* 97.3: 263–266.

Ronnick, M. V. 2002b. "Wiley Lane (1852–1885): The First African American Professor of Greek at Howard University." *Classical Outlook* 79: 108–109.

Ronnick, M. V. 2004a. "Twelve Black Classicists." *Arion* (third series) 11.3: 85–102.

Ronnick, M. V. 2004b. "Early African-American Scholars in the Classics: A Photographic Essay." *Journal of Blacks in Higher Education* 43: 101–105.

Ronnick, M. V. (ed.). 2005a. *The Autobiography of William Sanders Scarborough: An American Journey from Slavery to Scholarship.* Detroit.

Ronnick, M. V. 2005b. "Classicism, Black, in the United States," in *Africana: The Encyclopedia of the African and African American Experience,* ed. K. A. Appiah and H. L. Gates, Jr., 120–123. Oxford.

Ronnick, M. V. (ed.). 2006. *The Works of William Sanders Scarborough: Black Classicist and Race Leader*. Oxford and New York.

Ronnick, M. V. 2011. "Black Classicism: 'Tell Them We Are Rising." *Classical Journal* 106: 359–370.

Ronnick, M. V. 2016. "Classical Education and the Advancement of African American Women in the Nineteenth and Twentieth Centuries," in *Women Classical Scholars: Unsealing the Fountain from the Renaissance to Jacqueline de Romilly*, ed. R. Wyles and E. Hall, 176–193. Oxford and New York.

Ronnick, M. V. 2018. *Twelve African American Members of the Society for Classical Studies: The First Five Decades (1875–1925)*. New York.

Ronnick, M. V. 2019. "A Look at Herbert P. J. Marshall and *Do Somethin' Addy Man! Or The Black Alcestis*," in *Classics & Communism in Theatre: Graeco-Roman Antiquity on the Communist Stage*, eds. E. Olechowska and D. Movrin, 45–59, 308–319. Warsaw and Ljubljana.

Ronnick, M. V. 2020. "John Wesley Edward Bowen." DBCS. [undated]. https://dbcs.rutgers.edu/all-scholars/8564-bowen-john-wesley-edward. 07 July 2020.

Rose, A. 1895. "Living Greek, the International Language for Physicians." *The Post-Graduate: A Monthly Journal of Medicine and Surgery* 10.12: 482–485.

Ross, L. 1846. *Die Demen von Attika und ihre Vertheilung unter den Phylen*. Halle.

Rowe, G. C. 1890. *Our Heroes. Patriotic Poems on Men, Women and Sayings of The Negro Race*. Charleston, SC.

Rowell, G. P. 1894. *American Newspaper Directory*. New York.

Rowland, A. R. 2006a. *Color: Black or Mulatto in Richmond County. Free Persons of Color Listed in the 1850 and 1860 Federal Census Records*. Augusta.

Rowland, A. R. 2006b. *Hephzibah, Georgia (aka Brothersville) in Richmond County, Georgia. Citizens Listed in U.S. Census Records for 1870, 1880, 1900, 1910, 1920 and 1930*. Augusta.

Rowland, A. R. 2006c. *Slave Owners in the City of Augusta and Richmond County, Georgia from U.S. Census for 1850 and 1860*. Augusta.

Rowland, A. R., and J. T. Rowland. 2009. *Teachers, Principals, Presidents, Librarians and Other Administrators in Augusta and Richmond County, Georgia. 1783–1960*. Augusta.

Rubin, Jr., L. D. 1959. *Teach the Freeman: The Correspondence of Rutherford B. Hayes and the Slater Fund for Negro Education. Volume I, 1881–1887. Volume II, 1888–1893*. Baton Rouge.

Rucker, W. C., and S. K. Jubilee. 2007. "From Black Nadir to Brown v. Board: Education and Empowerment in Black Georgian Communities: 1865 to 1954." *Negro Educational Review* 58.3–4: 151–168.

Sammons, M. J., and V. Cunningham. 2004. *Black Portsmouth: Three Centuries of African-American Heritage*. Durham, NH.

Sanborn, F. B. 1912. "Memories of Ancient and Modern Greece." *The Granite Monthly* 44.8 (n. s. 7.8): 241–248.

Sanborn Map Company. 1890. *Sanborn Fire Insurance Map from Augusta, Richmond County, Georgia*. New York.

Sanborn Map Company. 1904. *Sanborn Fire Insurance Map from Augusta, Richmond County, Georgia*. New York.

Sandys, J. 1887. *An Easter Vacation in Greece, with Lists of Books on Greek Travel and Topography and Time-Tables of Greek Steamers and Railways*. London.

Saunders, R. F. Jr., and G. A. Rogers. 2004. "Joseph Thomas Robert and the Wages of Conscience." *Georgia Historical Quarterly* 88.1: 1–24.

Sauppe, H. 1846. *De demis urbanis Athenarum*. Weimar.

Savitt, T., and A. Floyd. 1996. *National Register of Historic Places Registration Form: Old Medical College/Medical College of Georgia*. Washington, DC.

Scarborough, W. S. 1891. "The Negro Question from the Negro Point of View." *Arena* 4.20: 219–222.

Scarborough, W. S. 1904. "The Negro and the Louisiana Purchase Exposition." *Voice of the Negro* 1: 312.

Schliepake, C. 2016. "'Black Classicism:' The African American Reception of the Classical Tradition in the Writings of Reginald Shepherd." *Amerikastudien/American Studies* 61.1: 53–68.

Schubart, J. H. C. 1881–1883. *Pausaniae Descriptio Graeciae* [2 vols.]. Leipzig.

Schubart, J. H. C., and C. Walz. 1838–1839. *Pausaniae Descriptio Graeciae* [3 vols.]. Leipzig and London.

Schubart, J. H. C. 1889. *Pausaniae Descriptio Graeciae*. Leipzig.

Schueller, M. J. 1998. *U.S. Orientalisms: Race, Nation, and Gender in Literature, 1790–1890*. Ann Arbor.

Schueller, M. J. 1999. *David Dorr: A Colored Man Round the World*. Ann Arbor.

Schwarz, H. 1956. *Samuel Gridley Howe: Social Reformer, 1801–1876*. Cambridge, MA.

Scott, M. 2014. *Delphi: A History of the Center of the Ancient World.* Princeton.

Scullion, S. 2015. "Tragedy and Religion: The Problem of Origins," in *A Companion to Greek Tragedy,* ed. J. Gregory, 23–37. Oxford, UK.

Sears, L. 1891. *An Address in Memory of Timothy Whiting Bancroft.* Providence.

Seaton, D. P. 1895. *The Land of Promise; Or, the Bible Land and Its Revelation.* Philadelphia.

Seelinger, R. A. 1994. "Miller, Walter," in *Biographical Dictionary of North American Classicists,* ed. W. W. Briggs, Jr., 415–417. Westport, CT.

Sellers, E. 1892–93. "Three Attic Lekythoi from Etretria." *Journal of Hellenic Studies* 13: 1–12.

Seymour, T. D. 1888a. "Life and Travel in Modern Greece." *Scribners* 4.1: 46–63.

Seymour, T. D. 1888b. "The Modern Greeks." *Scribners* 4.3: 366–376.

Seymour, T. D. 1896. "The American School of Classical Studies at Athens." *American University Magazine* 4.3–4: 171–175 and 4.5: 291–296.

Seymour, T. D. 1902. *Bulletin of the School of Classical Studies at Athens V: The First Twenty Years of the American School of Classical Studies at Athens.* Norwood, MA.

Sharpe, T. F. 1997. "Grandison Harris: The Medical College of Georgia's Resurrection Man," in *Bones in the Basement: Postmortem Racism in Nineteenth-Century Medical Training,* ed. R. L. Blakely and J. M. Harrington, 206–226. Washington, DC.

Shaw, A. 1890. "The Greeks of To-Day." *The Chautauquan* 11.3: 303–307.

Shaw, G. D. 2006. "Landscapes of Labor: Race, Religion, and Rhode Island in the Painting of Edward Mitchell Bannister," in *Post-Bellum, Pre-Harlem: African American Literature and Culture, 1877–1919,* ed. B. McCaskill and C. Gebhard, 59–73. New York and London.

Shaw, P. E. 1937. *American Contacts with the Eastern Churches, 1820–1870.* Chicago.

Shaw-Lefevre, G. 1891. "Athens Revisited." *The Contemporary Review* 59: 290–305.

Sheffey, Mrs. C. P. M. 1939. *Congo Tides.* Nashville.

Sheftel, P. 1979. "The Archaeological Institute of America, 1879–1979: A Centennial Review." *American Journal of Archaeology* 83.1: 3–17.

Sheftel, P. 2002. "'Sending out of Expeditions': The Contest for Delphi," in *Excavating Our Past: Perspectives on the History of the Archaeological Institute of America,* ed. S. H. Allen, 105–114. Boston.

Sheppard, W. H. 1917. *Presbyterian Pioneers in Congo.* Richmond, VA.

Sherman, J. R. 1992. *African-American Poetry of the Nineteenth Century: An Anthology.* Urbana and Chicago.

Skias, A./Σκιάς, Α. 1894. *Συμβολαί εις την Αθηναϊκήν τοπογραφίαν.* Αθήναι/ Athens.

Simmons, W. J. 1887. *Men of Mark: Eminent, Progressive and Rising.* Cleveland.

Singer, I., ed. 1906. *The Jewish Encylopedia. Volume XII: Talmud-Zweifel.* New York and London.

Siskind, J. 1992. "The Invention of Thanksgiving: A Ritual of American Nationality." *Critique of Anthropology* 12.2: 167–191.

Sismanidis, K. / Σισμανίδης, Κ. 2016. *Ο τάφος του Αριστοτέλη στα αρχαία Στάγειρα: Η ανασκαφική αποκάλυψη.* Thessaloniki.

Slater, N. 2013. *Euripides: Alcestis.* London and New York.

Slater, R. 1994. "The Blacks Who First Entered the World of White Higher Education." *Journal of Blacks in Higher Education* 4: 47–56.

Slater Fund. 1887. *Proceedings of the Trustees of the John F. Slater Fund for the Education of Freedmen.* Hampton, VA.

Slater Fund. 1889. *Proceedings of the Trustees of the John F. Slater Fund for the Education of Freemen, 1889.* Baltimore.

Sledge, R. W. 2005. *"Five Dollars and Myself": The History of Mission of the Methodist Episcopal Church South, 1845–1939.* New York.

Smith, A. 2007. "Paul and African American Bible Interpretation," in *True to Our Native Land: An African American New Testament Commentary,* ed. B. K. Blount et al., 31–42. Minneapolis.

Smith, A. 2017. "The Bible in African American Culture," in *The Oxford Handbook of the Bible in America,* ed. P. C. Gutjahr, 195–215. Oxford and New York.

Smith, E. W. 1947. *Trans-Atlantic Passenger Ships Past and Present.* Boston.

Smith, G., and G. Clary, Jr. 1980. "John Wesley Gilbert: Black Educator, Missionary Explorer." *Historical Highlights* 10.1: 47–48.

Smith, J. F. 1991. *Slavery and Rice Culture in Low Country Georgia, 1750–1860.* Nashville.

Smith, J. G., and J. O. Mitchell. 1878. *Old Country Houses of the Old Glasgow Gentry.* Glasgow.

Smith, J. H. 1992. "African Americans and Plantation Missions." *Historical Highlights* 22.2: 21–29.

Smith, J. L. 2009. "The Ties that Bind: Educated African-American Women in Post-Emancipation Atlanta," in *Georgia in Black and White: Explorations in Race Relations of a Southern State, 1865–1950,* ed. J. C. Inscoe, 95–105. Athens, GA.

Smith Jr., J. C. 1999. *Emancipation: The Making of the Black Lawyer, 1844–1944*. Philadelphia.

Smith, T. 1964. "Thomas Coke and the West Indies." *Methodist History* 3.1: 1–12.

Somerville, R. R. 2004. *An Ex-Colored Church: Social Activism in the CME Church, 1870–1970*. Macon, GA.

Spragin, O. 2009. *The History of the Christian Methodist Episcopal Church (1870–2009): Faithful to the Vision*. Lima, OH.

Spurgeon, C. H. 1900. *C. H. Spurgeon's Autobiography, Compiled from His Diary, Letters, and Records. Vol. IV. 1878–1892*. London.

Staïs, V. et al. 1890. "Ἀνασκαφαὶ ἐν Ἀττικῇ." *ΑΔ* 6 (Julian April): 65–67.

Staïs, V. 1890. "Ὁ τύμβος τῶν Μαραθωνομάχων." *ΑΔ* 6 (Julian August): 123–132.

Stanley, W. 1890. *Surveying and Levelling Instruments*. London and New York.

Stanton, T. 1890. "The American School at Athens." *The Independent* 42.2164 (22 May): 7–8.

Stephens, J. L. 1839. *Incidents of Travel in Greece, Turkey, Russia, and Poland*. Edinburgh.

Stewart, R. 1975. *A Heritage Discovered: Blacks in Rhode Island*. Providence.

Stilz, E. B. 1925. *Otetela and English Dictionary*. Wembo Nyama.

Stockbridge, J. C. 1882. "Brown University. An Educator of Educators." *Journal of Education* 16.3: 53.

Strauss, B. 2005. "The Black Phalanx: African-Americans and the Classics after the Civil War." *Arion* series 3, 12.3: 39–63.

Strawn, A. W. 1984. *The Ancestors and Descendants of John White and Sarah Elizabeth Green, With Allied Lines*. Salisbury, NC.

Stroszeck, J. 2004. "Greek Trophy Monuments," in *Myth and Symbol II: Symbolic Phenomena in Ancient Greek Culture*, ed. S. des Bouvrie, 303–321. Athens.

Sturgis, R. 1890. "Recent Discoveries of Painted Greek Sculpture." *Harper's New Monthly Magazine* 81.484: 538–549.

Talmage, T. D. W. 1890. *Twenty-Five Sermons on the Holy Land*. New York.

Talmage, T. D. W. 1892. *Trumpet-Blasts or Mountain-Top Views of Life*. Chicago.

Talmage, T. D. W. 1895. *From Manger to Throne. Embracing a New Life of Jesus the Christ and a History of Palestine and Its People*. New York.

Tarbell, F. 1889. "The Decrees of the Demotionidai: A Study of the Attic Phratry." *AJAHFA* 5.2: 135–153.

Terrell, M. C. 1940. *A Colored Woman in a White World*. Washington, DC.

Terrell, L. P., and M. S. C. Terrell. 1977. *Blacks in Augusta: A Chronology, 1741–1977*. Augusta.

Thompson, J. L. 1917. *History and Views of Colored Officers Training Camp: For 1917 at Fort Des Moines, Iowa*. Des Moines.

Tilson, M. A. 2002. *Augusta: Surviving Disaster*. Charleston, SC.

Titcomb, C. 2001. "The Earliest Black Members of Phi Beta Kappa." *Journal of Blacks in Higher Education* 33: 92–101.

Tobias, C. 1953. "[no title]," in *Thirteen Americans: Their Spiritual Autobiographies*, ed. L. Finkelstein, 177–199. New York and London.

Tolley, K. 2016. "Slavery," in *Miseducation: A History of Ignorance-Making in America and Abroad*, ed. A. J. Angulo, 13–33. Baltimore.

Torrence, R. 1948. *The Story of John Hope*. New York.

Towns, G. A. 1934. "William Henry Crogman." *Journal of Negro History* 19.2: 213–217.

Trafton, S. 2004. *Egypt Land: Race and Nineteenth-Century American Egyptomania*. Durham and London.

Traill, D. 1982. "Schliemann's American Citizenship and Divorce." *Classical Journal* 77.4: 336–342.

Traill, D. 1991–92. "Schliemann's Trips 1841–1867 and a Detailed Record of His Movements 1868–1890." *Boreas* 14/15: 207–214.

Traill, D. 1995. *Schliemann of Troy: Treasure and Deceit*. New York.

Traill, J. S. 1986. *Demos and Trittys: Epigraphical and Topographical Studies in the Organization of Attica*. Toronto.

Travlos, J. 1971. *Pictorial Dictionary of Ancient Athens*. New York.

Travlos, J. 1972. *Athènes au fil du temps*. Boulogne.

Tricha, L./Τρίχα, Λ. 2001. *Ο Χαρίλαος Τρικούπης και τα Δημόσια Έργα/Charilaos Tricoupis et les travaux publics*. Athens.

Tricha, L./Τρίχα, Λ. 2016. *Χαρίλαος Τρικούπης. Ο πολιτικός του 'Τις πταίει;' και του 'Δυστυχώς επτωχεύσαμεν.'* Athens.

Tsevas, J./Τσέβας, Ι. 2009. "Ο Μιχαήλ Δ. Καλοποθάκης και οι σχέσεις του με τις αμερικανικές ιεραποστολές: πραγματολογικές και κριτικές παρατηρήσεις." *Τα Ιστορικά* 50: 215–221.

Tsevas, J./Τσέβας, Ι. 2012. "Ο βίος και η εξαίρετη πολιτεία της Μαρίας Καλοποθάκη." *Εθνικός Κήρυξ* 51: 4–12.

Tsevas, J./Τσέβας, Ι. 2018. "Εἰσαγωγή στήν ἱστορία τῆς Ἑλληνικῆς Εὐαγγελικῆς Ἐκκλησίας," in *Ὁ Λούθηρος καί ἡ Μεταρρύθμιση. Ἱστορία, θεολογία, πολιτική*, ed. Σταύρος Ζουμπουλάκης, 257–275. Athens.

Tuckerman, C. K. 1891. "Personal Recollections of Schliemann." *The New England Magazine* n. s. 4.2: 179–183.

Turner, F. 1997. "The Homeric Question," in *A New Companion to Homer*, ed. I. Morris and B. Powell, 123–145. Leiden.

Turner, G. L'E. 1983. *Nineteenth-Century Surveying Instruments*. Berkeley and Los Angeles.

Turner, T. 1992. "Memory, Myth and Ethnicity: A Review of Recent Literature and Some Cases from Zaire." *History in Africa* 19: 387–400.

Turner, T. 1993. "'Batetela', 'Baluba', 'Basonge': Ethnogenesis in Zaire." *Cahier d'Études Africaines* 33: 132: 587–612.

Turner, J. 1999. *The Liberal Education of Charles Eliot Norton*. Baltimore and London.

University of Berlin. 1890. *Amtliches Verzeichniß des Personal und der Studierenden der königlich Friedrich-Wilhelms-Universität zu Berlin auf das Sommerhalbjahr vom 16. April bis 15. August 1890*. Berlin.

Valenti, C. 2006. *L'École française d'Athènes*. Paris.

Vanderpool, E. 1966. "A Monument to the Battle of Marathon." *Hesperia* 35.2: 93–106.

Vanderpool, E. 1970. "Some Attic Inscriptions." *Hesperia* 39: 40–46.

van der Veer, J. A. G. 1982. "The Battle of Marathon: A Topographical Survey." *Mnemosyne* (series 4) 35.3/4: 290–321.

Van Dijk, G. J. 1997. *ΑΙΝΟΙ, ΛΟΓΟΙ, ΜΥΘΟΙ: Fables in Archaic, Classical and Hellenistic Greek Literature*. Leiden.

Van Reybrouck, D. 2014. *Congo: The Epic History of a People*. New York.

Vanthemsche, G. 2012. *Belgium and the Congo, 1885–1980*. New York.

Varon, E. 2018. "Veteran, Author, Activist: Joseph T. Wilson of Norfolk and Black Leadership in the Civil War Era," in *Reconstruction and the Arc of Racial (In)Justice*, ed. J. M. Hayter and G. R. Goethals, 84–98. Cheltenham, UK, and Northampton, MA.

Vaughn, W. P. 1964. "Partners in Segregation: Barnas Sears and the Peabody Fund." *Civil War History* 10.3: 260–274.

Vickers, J. A. 1999. "Gilbert, Nathaniel (c. 1721-1774)," in *Biographical Dictionary of Christian Missions*, ed. G. H. Anderson, 241–242. Grand Rapids and Cambridge, UK.

Vinton, J. A. 1876. *The Richardson Memorial, Comprising a Full History and Genealogy of the Three Brothers, Ezekiel, Samuel, and Thomas Richardson*. Portland, ME.

Visvardi, E. 2016. "Alcestis," in *A Companion to Euripides*, ed. L. K. McClure, 61–79. Chichester.

Vogeikoff-Brogan, N. 2014. "The American Dream to Excavate Delphi or How the Oracle Vexed the Americans (1879–1891)." *From the Archivist's Notebook*, 02 October 2014. https://nataliavogeikoff.com/2014/10/02/

the-american-dream-to-excavate-delphi-or-how-the-oracle-vexed-the-americans-1879-1891/. 23 August 2016.

Vogeikoff-Brogan, N. 2019. "On the Trail of the "German Model": The American School of Classical Studies at Athens and the German Archaeological Institute (DAI), 1881–1918," in *Die Abteilung Athen des Deutschen Archäologischen Instituts und die Aktivitäten Deutscher Archäologen in Griechenland 1874–1933*, ed. K. Sporn and A. Kankeleit, 253–267. Berlin.

Vogeikoff-Brogan, N. (forthcoming). "Doubling Down: The Story of the ASCSA Archives."

Voskuil, D. 1989. "Reaching Out: Mainline Protestantism and the Media," in *Between the Times: The Travail of the Protestant Establishment, 1900–1960*, ed. W. Hutchison, 72–92. Cambridge.

Voutsaki, S. 2017. "The Hellenization of Greek Prehistory: The Work of Christos Tsountas," in *Ancient Monuments and Modern Identities: A History of Archaeology in 19th–20th Century Greece*, ed. S. Voutsaki and P. Cartledge, 130–147. London.

Wachsmuth, K. 1890. *Die Stadt Athen im Alterthum (Vol. II)*. Leipzig.

Wagstaff, J. M. 2001. "Pausanias and the Topographers: the Case of Colonel Leake," in *Pausanias: Travel and Memory in Roman Greece*, ed. S. Alcock, J. Cherry, and J. Elsner, 190–206. Oxford, UK.

Waldstein, C. 1882. "Notice of a Lapith-Head in the Louvre, from the Metopes of the Parthenon." *Journal of Hellenic Studies* 3: 228–233.

Waldstein, C. 1885. *Essays on the Art of Pheidias*. Cambridge and New York.

Waldstein, C. 1889. "The Newly Discovered Head of Iris from the Frieze of the Parthenon." *AJAHFA* 5.8: 1–8.

Waldstein, C. 1890a. "The Restored Head of Iris in the Parthenon Frieze." *Harper's New Monthly Magazine* 80.478: 629–636.

Waldstein, C. 1890b. "Discoveries at Plataia in 1890. I. General Report on the Excavations." *AJAHFA* 6.4: 445–448.

Waldstein, C. 1891a. "Ἀνασκαφαὶ ἐν Ἐρετρίᾳ." *ΑΔ* 7.2: 21–24.

Waldstein, C. 1891b. "Is it Aristotle's Tomb?" *The Nineteenth Century* 29.171: 845–850.

Waldstein, C. 1891c. "Excavations by the School at Eretria, 1891. Introductory Note." *AJAHFA* 7.3: 233–235.

Waldstein, C. 1892a. "How to Excavate in Greece." *The New Review* 6.37: 695–707.

Waldstein, C. 1892b. "The Finding of the Tomb of Aristotle." *The Century Illustrated Monthly Magazine* 44 (n. s. 22): 414–426.

Waldstein, C., F. B. Tarbell, and J. C. Rolfe. 1889. "Report on Excavations at Plataea in 1889." *AJAHFA* 5.4: 39–42.

Walker, A. O. 1998. *Registers of Signatures of Depositors in the Augusta, Georgia, Branch of the Freedman's Savings and Trust Company. Volume I: November 1870–June 1872.* Augusta.

Walker, C. T. 1892. *A Colored Man Abroad: What He Saw and Heard in the Holy Land and Europe.* Augusta.

Walker, G. W. 1884. "The Sonnet." *Quarterly Review of the Methodist Episcopal Church, South* 6.4: 606–618.

Walker, G. W. 1901. "The Development, the Needs, and the Outlook of the Paine Institute," in *Missionary Issues of the Twentieth Century. Papers and Addresses of the General Missionary Conference of the Methodist Episcopal Church, South, Held in New Orleans April 24–30, 1901,* ed. G. W. Caine, 474–480. Nashville.

Walston, C. 1924. "The Establishment of the Classical Type in Greek Art." *Journal of Hellenic Studies* 44.2: 223–253.

Walters, A. 1917. *My Life and Work.* New York, Chicago, and Toronto.

Wan, L. 2015. "Sketch of Early Local Black History." *Urban Pro Weekly* (Augusta) 4.22: 6–9.

Washington, B. T. 1899. "The Case of the Negro." *The Atlantic* 84.505: 577–586.

Washington, H. 1890a. "Discoveries at Plataia in 1890. II. Detailed Report on the Excavations." *AJAHFA* 6.4: 448–452.

Washington, H. 1890b. "Discoveries at Plataia in 1890. III. Description of the Site and Walls of Plataia." *AJAHFA* 6.4: 452–462.

Watson, E., and R. Turnipseed (eds.). 1910. *Minutes of the One Hundred and Twenty-Fifth Session of the South Carolina Annual Conference of the Methodist Episcopal Church, South, Held in Charleston, South Carolina, December 8–13, 1910.* Raleigh.

Wayenborgh, J. P. 2002. *International Biography and Bibliography of Ophthalmologists and Visual Scientists (A-Z).* Amsterdam.

Weatherford, W. 1910. *Negro Life in the South. Present Conditions and Needs.* New York.

Webb, W. S. 1887. *Webb's Jacksonville and Consolidated Directory of Representative Cities in East and South Florida.* Jacksonville and New York.

Welsby, D. 2013. "Meroe," in *The Encyclopedia of Ancient History,* ed. R. S. Bagnall et al., 4453–4455. Oxford and New York.

Weller, A. 1992. "John Pickard, Walter Miller, the College Art Association, and the University of Missouri," in *100 Years of Teaching Art History and Archaeology: University of Missouri-Columbia, 1892–1992*, ed. [not named], 6–37. Columbia, MO.

Werner, A. 2013. *The Transatlantic World of Higher Education: Americans at German Universities, 1776–1914*. New York and Oxford, UK.

West, E. H. 1966. "The Peabody Education Fund and Negro Education, 1867–1880." *History of Education Quarterly* 6.2: 3–21.

Wharton, H. M. 1892. *A Picnic in Palestine*. Baltimore.

Wheeler, J. 1914. "Thirty-third Annual Report of the American School of Classical Studies at Athens, 1913–1914." *Bulletin of the Archaeological Institute of America* 5: 26–30.

White, R. 2017. *The Republic for Which It Stands: The United States during Reconstruction and the Gilded Age, 1865–1896*. Oxford and New York.

Whitehead, D. 1986. *The Demes of Attica, 508/7-ca. 250 B.C.: A Political and Social Study*. Princeton.

Whites, L. 1992. "'Stand by Your Man:' The Ladies' Memorial Association and the Reconstruction of Southern White Manhood," in *Women of the American South*, ed. C. A. Farnham, 133–149. New York.

Whitted, J. A. 1908. *A History of the Negro Baptists of North Carolina*. Raleigh.

Whittle, W. A. 1890. *A Baptist Abroad*. New York.

Wicker, E. 2000. *Banking Panics of the Gilded Age*. Cambridge and New York.

Wickersham, J. P., and J. P. McCaskey (eds.). 1875. "The Truth Not All Told. More Colored Men at Pennsylvania Colleges." *The Pennsylvania School Journal* 24.5: 169–170.

Will, E. L. 2002. "Charles Eliot Norton and the Archaeological Institute of America," in *Excavating Our Past: Perspectives on the History of the Archaeological Institute of America*, ed. S. H. Allen, 49–62. Boston.

Williams, C. R. (ed.). 1922. *The Diary and Letters of Rutherford B. Hayes, Nineteenth President of the United States*. Columbus, OH.

Williams, D. B. 1890. *Freedom and Progress* [fourth ed.]. Petersburg, VA.

Williams, G. W. 1883. *History of the Negro Race in America from 1619 to 1880, Volumes I–II*. New York.

Williams, G. W. 1888. *A History of the Negro Troops in the War of the Rebellion, 1861–1865*. New York.

Williams, S. 1984. "Dr. Morgan Callaway's Genealogy." *Callaway Family Association Journal* 9: 18–22.

Wilson, J. 1882. *Emancipation: Its Course and Progress, from 1481 B. C. to A. D. 1875, With a Review of President Lincoln's Proclamations, the XIII*

Amendment, and the Progress of the Freed People Since Emancipation; with a History of the Emancipation Movement. Hampton, VA.

Wilson, J. 1887. *The Black Phalanx: A History of the Negro Soldiers of the United States in the Wars of 1775–1812, 1861–'65.* Hartford.

Wilson, P. 2015. "The Festival of Dionysos in Ikarion: A New Study of *IG* I³ 254." *Hesperia* 84: 97–147.

Wilson, J. G., and J. Fiske (eds.). 1889. *Appleton's Cyclopaedia of American Biography. Volume VI: Sunderland-Zurita.* New York.

Winterer, C. 2002. "The American School of Classical Studies at Athens: Scholarship and High Culture in the Gilded Age," in *Excavating Our Past: Perspectives on the History of the Archaeological Institute of America*, ed. S. H. Allen, 93–104. Boston.

Winterer, C. 2004. *The Culture of Classicism: Ancient Greece and Rome in American Intellectual Life 1780–1910.* Baltimore.

Wright, R. R. 1894. *A Brief Historical Sketch of Negro Education in Georgia.* Savannah.

Wright Jr., R. R. 1916. *Centennial Encyclopedia of the African Methodist Episcopal Church, Volume I.* Philadelphia.

Wright Jr., R. R. 1965. *87 Years Behind the Black Curtain: An Autobiography.* Philadelphia.

Yale Obituary Record. 1915. *Obituary Record of Graduates of Yale University Deceased during the year ending July 1, 1915, including the record of a few who died previously hitherto unreported.* New Haven.

Yale Obituary Record. 1950. *Yale University Obituary Record of Graduates Deceased During the Year Ending July 1, 1949.* New Haven.

Yale University. 1913. *Quarter-Centenary Record of the Class of 1885, Yale University.* Boston.

Young, C. H. 1891. *Erchia, A Deme of Attica.* New York.

Ziebarth, E. (ed.). 1915. *IG XII.9: Inscriptiones Euboeae Insulae.* Berlin.

INDEX

For the benefit of digital users, indexed terms that span two pages (e.g., 52–53) may, on occasion, appear on only one of those pages.

Figures are indicated by *f* following the page number